ACCA

STUDY TEXT

Paper 3.4

Business Information Management

IN THIS JUNE 2003 EDITION

- Targeted to the syllabus and study guide
- Quizzes and questions to check your understanding
- Clear layout and style designed to save you time
- Plenty of exam-style questions with detailed guidance from BPP
- Chapter Roundups and summaries to help revision

FOR EXAMS IN DECEMBER 2003 AND JUNE 2004

BPP Professional Education
June 2003

First edition 2001
Third edition June 2003

ISBN 0 7517 1159 4 (Previous 0 7517 0240 4)

British Library Cataloguing-in-Publication Data
A catalogue record for this book is available from the British Library

Published by

BPP Professional Education
Aldine House, Aldine Place
London W12 8AW

www.bpp.com

Printed in Great Britain by W M Print
45-47 Frederick Street
Walsall, West Midlands
WS2 9NE

All our rights reserved. No part of this publication may be reproduced, stored in a retrieval system or transmitted, in any form or by any means, electronic, mechanical, photocopying, recording or otherwise, without the prior written permission of BPP Professional Education.

We are grateful to the Association of Chartered Certified Accountants for permission to reproduce past examination questions and questions from the pilot paper. The answers have been prepared by BPP Professional Education.

©
BPP Professional Education
2003

Contents

	Page
THE BPP STUDY TEXT The BPP effective study package	(iv)
HELP YOURSELF STUDY FOR YOUR ACCA EXAMS The right approach - developing your personal study plan - suggested study sequence	(vi)
SYLLABUS	(xi)
STUDY GUIDE	(xvi)
THE EXAM PAPER	(xix)
OXFORD BROOKES BSC (Hons) IN APPLIED ACCOUNTING	(xxi)
OXFORD INSTITUTE OF INTERNATIONAL FINANCE MBA	(xxi)
SYLLABUS MINDMAP	(xxii)

PART A: INFORMATION SYSTEMS AND THE ORGANISATION

1	Organisational information requirements	3
2	The strategic role of information systems	37
3	Knowledge management	69

PART B: BUSINESS SYSTEMS, SYSTEMS ANALYSIS AND BUSINESS CASE DEVELOPMENT

4	Business systems and systems thinking	99
5	Gap analysis and business case development	123

PART C: USING INFORMATION COMPETITIVELY

6	Information systems and competitive position	141
7	The Internet as a strategic business tool	179

PART D: THE IMPACT OF INFORMATION TECHNOLOGY

8	Implementing change	223
9	The impact of IT on work practices	255

EXAM QUESTION BANK	275
EXAM ANSWER BANK	293
INDEX	315

ORDER FORM

REVIEW FORM & FREE PRIZE DRAW

The BPP Study Text

THE BPP STUDY TEXT

Aims of this Study Text

To provide you with the knowledge and understanding, skills and application techniques that you need if you are to be successful in your exams

This Study Text has been written around the **Business Information Management** syllabus.

- It is **comprehensive**. It covers the syllabus content. No more, no less.

- It is written at the **right level**. Each chapter is written with the ACCA's **study guide** in mind.

- It is targeted to the **exam**. We have taken account of the **pilot paper** and **all sittings so far**, questions put to the examiners at ACCA conferences and the assessment methodology.

To allow you to study in the way that best suits your learning style and the time you have available, by following your personal Study Plan (see pages (vii) - (viii))

You may be studying at home on your own until the date of the exam, or you may be attending a full-time course. You may like to (and have time to) read every word, or you may prefer to (or only have time to) skim-read and devote the remainder of your time to question practice. Wherever you fall in the spectrum, you will find the BPP Study Text meets your needs in designing and following your personal Study Plan.

To tie in with the other components of the BPP Effective Study Package to ensure you have the best possible chance of passing the exam (see page (v))

The BPP Effective Study Package

Recommended period of use	Elements of the BPP Effective Study Package
From the outset and throughout	**Learning to learn accountancy** Read this invaluable book as you begin your studies and refer to it as you work through the various elements of the BPP Effective Study Package. It will help you to acquire knowledge, practice and revise efficiently and effectively.
Three to twelve months before the exam	**Study Text and i-Learn** Use the Study Text to acquire knowledge, understanding, skills and the ability to apply techniques. Use BPP's **i-Learn** product to reinforce your learning.
Throughout	**Virtual Campus** Study, practice, revise and take advantage of other useful resources with BPP's fully interactive e-learning site with comprehensive tutor support.
Throughout	**i-Pass** Revise your knowledge and ability to apply techniques. **i-Pass**, our computer-based testing package, provides objective test questions in a variety of formats and is ideal for self-assessment.
One to six months before the exam	**Practice & Revision Kit** Try the numerous examination-format questions, for which there are realistic suggested solutions prepared by BPP's own authors. Then attempt the two mock exams.
From three months before the exam until the last minute	**Passcards** Work through these short, memorable notes which are focused on what is most likely to come up in the exam you will be sitting.
One to six months before the exam	**Success Tapes** These audio tapes cover the vital elements of your syllabus in less than 90 minutes per subject. Each tape also contains exam hints to help you fine tune your strategy.

HELP YOURSELF STUDY FOR YOUR ACCA EXAMS

Exams for professional bodies such as ACCA are very different from those you have taken at college or university. You will be under **greater time pressure before** the exam - as you may be combining your study with work. There are many different ways of learning and so the BPP Study Text offers you a number of different tools to help you through. Here are some hints and tips **based on research and experience.**

The right approach

1 The right attitude

Believe in yourself	Yes, there is a lot to learn. Yes, it is a challenge. But thousands have succeeded before and you can too.
Remember why you're doing it	Studying might seem a grind at times, but you are doing it for a reason: to advance your career.

2 The right focus

Read through the Syllabus and Study guide	These tell you what you are expected to know and are supplemented by exam focus points in the text.
Study the Exam Paper section	The pilot paper is likely to be a reasonable guide of what you should expect in the exam.

3 The right method

The big picture	You need to grasp the detail - but keeping in mind how everything fits into the big picture will help you understand better. • The **Introduction** of each chapter puts the material in context. • The **Syllabus content, Study guide** and **Exam focus points** show you what you need to **grasp**.
In your own words	To absorb the information (and to practise your written communication skills), it helps to **put it into your own words.** • **Take notes.** • Answer the **questions** in each chapter. You will practise your written communication skills, which become increasingly important as you progress through your ACCA exams. • Draw **mind maps**. We have an example for the whole syllabus. • Try 'teaching' to a colleague or friend.

Give yourself cues to jog your memory	The BPP Study Text uses **bold text** to **highlight key points** and **icons** to identify key features, such as **Exam focus points** and **Key terms**.
	• Try **colour coding** with a highlighter pen.
	• Write **key points** on cards.

4 **The right review**

Review, review, review	It is a **fact** that regularly reviewing a topic in summary form can **fix it in your memory**. Because **review** is so important, the BPP Study Text helps you to do so in many ways.
	• **Chapter roundups** summarise the key points in each chapter. Use them to recap each study session.
	• The **Quick quiz** is another review tool to ensure that you have grasped the essentials.
	• Use the **Key terms** highlighted in the index as a quiz.
	• Go through the **Examples** in each chapter a second or third time.

Developing your personal Study Plan

The BPP Learning to Learn Accountancy book emphasises the need to prepare (and use) a study plan. Planning and sticking to the plan are key elements of learning success.

There are four steps you should work through.

Step 1. How do you learn?

First you need to be aware of your style of learning. The BPP Learning to Learn Accountancy book commits a chapter to this **self-discovery**. What types of intelligence do you display when learning? You might be advised to brush up on certain study skills before launching into this Study Text.

> BPP's **Learning to Learn Accountancy** book helps you to identify what intelligences you show more strongly and then details how you can tailor your study process through your preferences. It also includes handy hints on how to develop intelligences you exhibit less strongly, but which might be needed as you study accountancy.

Are you a **theorist** or are you more **practical**? If you would rather get to grips with a theory before trying to apply it in practice, you should follow the study sequence on page (ix). If the reverse is true (you need to know why you are learning theory before you do so), you might be advised to flick through Study Text chapters and look at questions, case studies and examples (Steps 7, 8 and 9 in the **suggested study sequence**) before reading through the detailed theory.

Help Yourself Study for your ACCA Exams

Step 2. How much time do you have?

Work out the time you have available per week, given the following.

- The standard you have set yourself
- The time you need to set aside later for work on the Practice & Revision Kit and Passcards
- The other exam(s) you are sitting
- Very importantly, practical matters such as work, travel, exercise, sleep and social life

Note your time available in box A.   A [Hours]

Step 3. Allocate your time

- Take the time you have available per week for this Study Text shown in box A, multiply it by the number of weeks available and insert the result in box B.   B [ ]
- Divide the figure in Box B by the number of chapters in this text and insert the result in box C.   C [ ]

Remember that this is only a rough guide. Some of the chapters in this book are longer and more complicated than others, and you will find some subjects easier to understand than others.

Step 4. Implement

Set about studying each chapter in the time shown in box C, following the key study steps in the order suggested by your particular learning style.

This is your personal **Study Plan**. You should try and combine it with the study sequence outlined below. You may want to modify the sequence a little (as has been suggested above) to adapt it to your **personal style**.

Help Yourself Study for your ACCA Exams

Suggested study sequence

Tackle the chapters in the order you find them in the Study Text. Taking into account your individual learning style, you could follow this sequence.

Key study steps	Activity
Step 1 **Topic list**	Each numbered topic is a numbered section in the chapter.
Step 2 **Introduction**	This gives you the **big picture** in terms of the **context** of the chapter. The content is referenced to the **Study Guide**, and **Exam Guidance** shows how the topic is likely to be examined. In other words, it sets your **objectives for study.**
Step 3 **Knowledge brought forward boxes**	In these we highlight information and techniques that it is assumed you have 'brought forward' with you from your earlier studies. If there are topics which have changed recently due to legislation for example, these topics are explained in more detail.
Step 4 **Explanations**	Proceed methodically through the chapter, reading each section thoroughly and making sure you understand.
Step 5 **Key terms and Exam focus points**	• **Key terms** can often earn you *easy marks* if you state them clearly and correctly in an appropriate exam answer (and they are indexed at the back of the text). • **Exam focus points** give you a good idea of how we think the examiner intends to examine certain topics.
Step 6 **Note taking**	Take brief notes if you wish, avoiding the temptation to copy out too much.
Step 7 **Examples**	Follow each through to its solution very carefully.
Step 8 **Case examples**	Study each one, and try to add flesh to them from your own experience – they are designed to show how the topics you are studying come alive (and often come unstuck) in the real world.
Step 9 **Questions**	Make a very good attempt at each one.
Step 10 **Answers**	Check yours against ours, and make sure you understand any discrepancies.
Step 11 **Chapter roundup**	Work through it very carefully, to make sure you have grasped the major points it is highlighting.
Step 12 **Quick quiz**	When you are happy that you have covered the chapter, use the **Quick quiz** to check how much you have remembered of the topics covered.
Step 13 **Question(s) in the Question bank**	Either at this point, or later when you are thinking about revising, make a full attempt at the **Question(s)** suggested at the very end of the chapter. You can find these at the end of the Study Text, along with the **Answers** so you can see how you did. We highlight those that are introductory, and those which are of the standard you would expect to find in an exam.

Help Yourself Study for your ACCA Exams

Short of time: *Skim study technique?*

You may find you simply do not have the time available to follow all the key study steps for each chapter, however you adapt them for your particular learning style. If this is the case, follow the **skim study** technique below (the icons in the Study Text will help you to do this).

- Study the chapters in the order you find them in the Study Text.
- For each chapter:
    - Follow the key study steps 1-3, and then skim-read through step 4. Jump to step 11, and then go back to step 5.
    - Follow through steps 7 and 8, and prepare outline answers to questions (steps 9/10).
    - Try the Quick Quiz (step 12), following up any items you can't answer, then do a plan for the Question (step 13), comparing it against our answers.
    - You should probably still follow step 6 (note-taking), although you may decide simply to rely on the BPP Passcards for this.

Moving on...

However you study, when you are ready to embark on the practice and revision phase of the BPP Effective Study Package, you should still refer back to this Study Text, both as a source of **reference** (you should find the list of key terms and the index particularly helpful for this) and as a **refresher** (the Chapter Roundups and Quick Quizzes help you here).

And remember to keep careful hold of this Study Text – you will find it invaluable in your work.

> More advice on Study Skills can be found in the BPP **Learning to Learn Accountancy** book

SYLLABUS

Aim

To ensure that students can exercise judgement and technique in identifying, implementing and managing information systems as part of the strategic management of the organisation.

Objectives

On completion of this paper candidates should be able to:

- Identify the information requirements of different levels of management and understand how information is used to support the objectives of the organisation

- Apply a coherent approach to business analysis including the identification of the current business solution and the gap between that and the required business

- Identify and implement desirable and feasible changes resulting from business analysis

- Prepare a detailed business case to support system changes and use the appropriate tools to support business analysis

- Identify opportunities to use information systems to improve the competitive position of an organisation

- Identify the impact of the development of information systems on the organisation and its environment

Position of the paper in the overall syllabus

The paper assumes the knowledge and understanding of the underpinning principles of Paper 2.1 Information Systems.

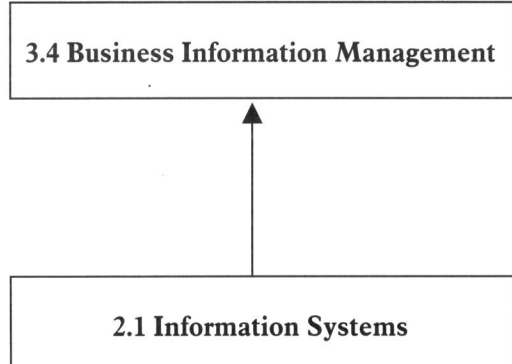

Syllabus

SYLLABUS

1 Organisational information

(a) From a business perspective an information system is an organisational and management solution, based on information technology, to any challenge posed by the environment.

(b) Levels of management and types of information/system required.

(c) The tasks of the manager. The requirements for effective information management.

(d) Types of information system

   (i) Strategic information systems.
   (ii) Management information systems.
   (iii) Transaction processing systems.
   (iv) Automation and support systems.
   (v) Batch processing.

2 Knowledge management and information systems

(a) Data workers and knowledge workers.

   (i) Distribute knowledge: office automation systems.
   (ii) Share knowledge: group collaboration systems.
   (iii) Create knowledge: knowledge work systems.
   (iv) Capture and codify knowledge: artificial intelligence systems.

(b) Database management

   (i) Principles of database management systems.
   (ii) Principles of datamining and data warehousing.

3 IS and the strategic planning process

(a) The organisation and information management.

   (i) The business context.
   (ii) New organisational structures and information.
   (iii) Information and organisational strategy.

(b) PEST analysis.

(c) Strategic information systems.

   (i) Alignment.
   (ii) Using IS to create focus, support linkages and develop information leadership.

(d) Porter's value chain.

4 Business systems, systems thinking as business analysis

(a) Hard systems approach.

    (i) Structured systems life cycle.
    (ii) Deliverables from each stage.

(b) Soft systems approach

    (i) Checkland's soft systems methodology.

(c) Business processing engineering.

    (i) Business processes are analysed, simplified and redesigned. A radical business strategy.

5 Gap analysis and business case development

(a) General framework:

    (i) Where we are W^2R
    (ii) Where we want to be $W^3 2B$
    (iii) Going to get there $(GT)^2$

(b) Business case development

    (i) Reasons, estimating costs and timescales.
    (ii) Estimating benefits.
    (iii) Benefit realisation dependencies.
    (iv) Sensitivity analysis.
    (v) Justification.

(c) Applications portfolio/IT investment decisions:

    (i) Portfolio analysis; risks and benefits. An analysis of the portfolio of potential applications within a firm to determine the risks and benefits and select among alternatives for IS. Scoring model.

    (ii) Determining the best fit with the current system.

6 IS and competitive position

(a) SWOT analysis

    (i) Identify drivers for change.
    (ii) Agree fundamental guiding principles governing design of change.

(b) IS/IT management partnership – internal/outsourcing (in all its forms), facilities management.

(c) Links between business strategy and information systems strategy.

Syllabus

7 Electronic commerce; the Internet as a strategic business tool

(a) Globalisation.

    (i) The virtual company.
    (ii) The internet, intranet and extranet.
    (iii) Security issues.

(b) The Internet.

    (i) The changing world of the net.
    (ii) Good practise requirements, infrastructure required, change of business functions/strategy.
    (iii) The Internet as a system, integration with existing systems.

8 Implementing change

(a) Implementing new systems.

    (i) Strategies for implementation.
    (ii) Managing risk at implementation.

(b) Structuring the information systems function.

    (i) Managing the IT function.
    (ii) Management of change.

(c) Project management.

9 Impact of IT on work practices

(a) Using IT to manage individuals' information requirements.

    (i) Design of critical success factors.
    (ii) Identification of sources of data capture.
    (iii) Measurement of performance.

(b) Impact of IS/IT on employee/employer relations.

    (i) Shorter chain of command, flatter structures.
    (ii) Wider span of control.
    (iii) De-skilling of operatives.
    (iv) Socio-technical design.

Excluded topics

The following topics are specifically excluded from the syllabus.

- Program design, flowcharting, object-oriented design
- Specific hardware platforms

Key areas of the syllabus

The syllabus has four key topic areas:

- Information resource management
- Business analysis
- Information systems and competitive position
- Information systems and the organisation

Paper 3.4

Business Information Management

Study Guide

1 LEVELS OF MANAGEMENT

- Distinguish between strategic, tactical and operational management and their corresponding information requirements.
- Describe the importance of making information accessible.
- Discuss ways of ensuring the reliability and accuracy of information, creating secure information systems and making information available at an appropriate cost.

2 CATEGORIES OF INFORMATION SYSTEMS

- Discuss the six major types of Information Systems: Executive Support Systems (ESS), Management Information Systems (MIS), Decision Support Systems (DSS), Knowledge Work Systems (KWS), Office Automation Systems (OAS) and Transaction Processing Systems (TPS).
- Describe examples of each of the above in terms of an organisation's strategic business position.

3/4 STRATEGIC ROLE OF INFORMATION SYSTEMS

- Explain the strategic role of information systems
- Identify the major management challenges to building and using information systems in organisations.
- Describe the central and crucial role that information systems have within an organisation
- Evaluate Information Systems and the Strategic Planning Process.
- Identify opportunities for use in forecasting, analysing competition, scenario planning, generic strategies/business positioning, improving performance, measuring performance, opportunities for cost reduction, opportunities for service improvement, sales performance, evaluating proposals.

5 ETHICAL ISSUES

- Analyse the relationship among ethical, social and political issues raised by the impact of information systems
- Identify the major moral dimensions of an information society
- Apply an ethical analysis to scenarios
- Discuss the design of organisational policies for ethical conduct

6/7 KNOWLEDGE MANAGEMENT

- Describe the differences between data workers and knowledge workers and the appropriate types of applications used by each, eg
  - Distribute knowledge: Office automation systems
  - Share knowledge: Group collaboration systems
  - Create knowledge: Knowledge work systems
  - Capture and codify knowledge: Artificial intelligence systems

7/8 DATA MANAGEMENT

- Explain the principles of Database Management Systems (DBMS).
- Describe the major characteristics of Integrity, Independence and Integration.
- Discuss the difference between logical and physical data requirements.
- Describe logical models hierarchical and relational.
- Explain the principles of datamining and data warehousing.
- Discuss datamining as the ability to analyse large pools of data to find patterns and rules that can be used by an organisation to guide decision making and predict future behaviour.
- Discuss data warehousing as a database with reporting and query tools, that stores current and historical data extracted from various operational systems and consolidated for management reporting and analysis.

9 ORGANISATIONAL REQUIREMENTS

- Discuss the establishment of organisational information requirements.
- Evaluate linking information systems to the business plan.
- Discuss the requirement to understand the business value of information systems.

10 STRATEGIC ANALYSIS

- Evaluate the importance of Political, Economic, Social and Technological influences on organisations. PEST analysis as a tool for Information systems strategic planning.
- Apply PEST analysis to scenarios.

11 STRATEGIC INFORMATION SYSTEMS

- Discuss the role of Strategic Information Systems as computer systems within an organisation that enable changes to goals, processes, products, services or environmental relationships.
- Discuss the alignment with business strategy. Using IS to create Focus, support Linkages and develop Information Leadership.

12 STRATEGIC IMPACT OF INFORMATION SYSTEMS

- Evaluate Porter's value chain.
- Apply Porter's value chain to scenarios

13 BUSINESS STRATEGY

- Describe the stages in the development of business systems and strategies
- Explain the concept of business automation
- Explain the concept of business rationalisation
- Evaluate and discuss the principles of business process engineering

14 HARD SYSTEMS APPROACH

- Evaluate the structured systems lifecycle emphasising the deliverables from each stage, clarifying the importance of these from a management perspective.

15/16 SOFT SYSTEMS APPROACH

- Evaluate the principles of Checkland's soft systems methodology
- Apply the major tools employed in Checkland's soft systems methodology; Root definitions, CATWOE, conceptual models.

17 BUSINESS ANALYSIS

- Discuss the need for a general framework in the development of a business case:

    Where we are W^2R

    Where we want to be W^32B

    Going to get there $(GT)^2$

- Discuss Business Analysis v Systems Analysis in terms of: A framework for business analysis, exploring and expressing problem situations, understanding what people do – and why they do it, modelling the current situation, introduce the notion of Gap Analysis, modelling the required situation.

18 BUSINESS CASE DEVELOPMENT

- Discuss the major elements of a business case development concentrating on the strategic issues of: Estimating costs and timescales, estimating benefits, benefit realisation dependencies, sensitivity analysis and business justification.

19 GAP ANALYSIS

- Discuss applications portfolio/IT investment decisions.
- Evaluate Portfolio analysis; Risks and benefits. An analysis of the portfolio of potential applications within a firm to determine the risks and benefits and select among alternatives for IS.
- Scoring model.
- Describe determining the best fit with the current system.

20 COMPETITIVE POSITION ANALYSIS

- Evaluate Strengths, Weaknesses, Opportunities and Threats (SWOT analysis) as a technique for identifying opportunities for information systems development.
- Apply SWOT analysis to scenarios.

21 LINKING BUSINESS STRATEGY AND INFORMATION SYSTEMS STRATEGY

- Identify and discuss the links between Business Strategy and Information Systems Strategy using IS/IT as an enabler: Analysis of external (competitive) environment, SWOT output, identify drivers for change, agree guiding principles, infrastructure standards and planning.
- Discuss the potential advantages and disadvantages of IS/IT management partnership – internal/outsourcing (in all its forms), facilities management.
- Evaluate advantages of package solutions versus bespoke solutions.

Study Guide

22 WEB-BASED TECHNOLOGY

- Discuss the business impact of the Internet.
- Identify good practice requirements, infrastructure required, and change of business functions/strategy.
- Understand the Internet as a system.
- Explain how to integrate with existing systems.
- Discuss and describe the uses of an extranet and an intranet.
- Evaluate the problems associated with using web-based technology and the issue of security.

23 ELECTRONIC COMMERCE

- Discuss the impact of Globalisation on business strategy.
- Describe the implications of globalisation in terms of: management and control in a global marketplace, competition in world markets, global work groups, and global delivery systems.
- Describe Virtual Supply Chain (VSC).
- Discuss Electronic Marketing.

24 SUCCESS AND FAILURE

- Identify major problem areas when implementing information systems.
- Apply organisational impact analysis.
- Identify criteria needed to assess whether a system is successful.
- Describe the principal causes of information system failure and how to overcome them.
- Discuss problems of implementation: people-oriented theory, system oriented theory, and interaction theory.
- Describe the relationship between the implementation process and the system outcome.

25 MANAGING CHANGE

- Discuss the appropriate strategies to manage the implementation process.
- Discuss formal planning control framework and tools.
- Evaluate impact of alternative system building techniques and tools.
- Explain how to manage risk.
- Understand the importance of having a process to manage change in an organisation.

26 INDIVIDUALS INFORMATION REQUIREMENTS

- Discuss the use of IT to manage individuals' information requirements.
- Identify how information systems can support the tasks of the manager.
- Describe the design of Critical Success Factors.
- Identify sources of data.
- Identify key performance indicators and how to measure performance.

27 EMPLOYEE/ EMPLOYER RELATIONS

- Discuss the impact of IS/IT on employee/ employer relations in terms of: Shorter chain of command, flatter organisational structures, wider span of control, de-skilling of operatives
- Describe the concept of Socio-Technical design in respect to employee/employer relations.
- Discuss the organisational development issues resulting from the need to develop and implement information systems.

THE EXAM PAPER

The examination is a **three hour written paper** in **two sections**.

		Number of Marks
Section A:	3 compulsory scenario-based questions (no single question will exceed 25 marks)	60
Section B:	Choice of 2 from 3 questions (20 marks each)	40
		100

Section A is based on a short scenario. This section will have three compulsory questions from across the syllabus which relate to the scenario. Each question will be worth between 10 to 25 marks giving a total of 60 marks for this section.

Section B contains three independent questions drawn from across the syllabus. Each question is worth 20 marks. The candidate must answer two questions giving a total of 40 marks for this section.

Additional information

The examination will assume the use of the following specific modelling and analysis tools and techniques.

- PEST analysis
- Conceptual models
- CATWOE
- Checkland's soft systems methodology
- Information systems and competitive position

- SWOT analysis
- Rich pictures
- Porter's value chain

Subsequent information

An article entitled 'How to Pass Paper 3.4' appeared in the November 2002 *Student Accountant*. The article stated that students should also be familiar with 'such models and theories' as:

- Nolan's 'Stage Hypothesis'
- Earl's 'System's Audit Grid'
- Zuboff's 'Automate, Informate, Transformate'
- McFarlan's 'Applications Portfolio' and Peppard's adaptation
- The 'Three Stage' change process and 'Unfreeze, Change, Re-freeze'

- Parson's 'Six IS Strategies'
- Earl's 'Three Leg' analysis

Analysis of past papers

The analysis below shows the topics which were examined in all sittings of the current syllabus so far and in the Pilot Paper.

June 2003

Section A scenario – Department store chain (answer all questions in section A) — Marks

1	Aligning information systems strategy with business strategy	20
2	Commitment, co-ordination and communication in systems development	20
3	Gap analysis, applications portfolio and structured methodologies	20

Section B (answer two questions from section B)

4	Domestic exporter, multinational, franchiser and transnational	20
5	Business Process Re-engineering, virtual supply chain	20
6	Appraising information systems projects	20

The exam paper

December 2002

		Marks
Section A scenario – Life assurance corporation (answer all questions in section A)		
1	SWOT analysis and business strategy	20
2	Sourcing of a new system	20
3	Three legs of IS strategy – business led, top-down and infrastructure led	20
Section B (answer two questions from section B)		
4	Soft Systems Methodology	20
5	Minimising system failure risks; technical infrastructure; social and ethical issues	20
6	Automate, informate and transformate (automation, rationalisation and re-engineering).	20

June 2002

		Marks
Section A scenario – Business strategy/IS strategy review (answer all questions in section A)		
1	Intranet characteristics, benefits and impact	20
2	Technology and globalisation; PEST and e-commerce	20
3	Nolan's Six Stage Growth Model	20
Section B (answer two questions from section B)		
4	Information systems and knowledge management	20
5	Hard and soft methodologies	20
6	Generic strategies for information systems	20

December 2001

		Marks
Section A scenario – Mail order book company (answer all questions in section A)		
1	SWOT analysis and development of an IS strategy	20
2	Porter's value chain and e-commerce	20
3	Business strategy and information strategy development and changes	20
Section B (answer two questions from section B)		
4	Datawarehousing and the Data Base Management Systems Approach; Datamining	20
5	Moral dimensions of the information age	20
6	Virtual companies; Web-based information v paper-based information	20

Pilot paper

		Marks
Section A scenario – Electrical goods retail chain (answer all questions in section A)		
1	Use of web-based technologies (Internet, intranet, extranet)	25
2	Integrating IT/IS development with business strategy; Business process terms – automation, rationalisation and re-engineering	20
3	Reasons for information systems failure	15
Section B (answer two questions from section B)		
4	Checkland's Soft System Methodology	20
5	Porter's value chain and IS/IT strategy	20
6	Purpose-written software versus ready-made package (strategic issues)	20

Oxford Brookes

OXFORD BROOKES BSc (Hons) IN APPLIED ACCOUNTING

The standard required of candidates completing Part 2 is that required in the final year of a UK degree. Students completing Parts 1 and 2 will have satisfied the examination requirement for an honours degree in Applied Accounting, awarded by Oxford Brookes University.

To achieve the degree, you must also submit two pieces of work based on a **Research and Analysis Project.**

- A 5,000 word **Report** on your chosen topic, which demonstrates that you have acquired the necessary research, analytical and IT skills.
- A 1,500 word **Key Skills Statement**, indicating how you have developed your interpersonal and communication skills.

BPP was selected by the ACCA and Oxford Brookes University to produce the official text *Success in your Research and Analysis Project* to support students in this task. The book pays particular attention to key skills not covered in the professional examinations.

> THE OXFORD BROOKES PROJECT TEXT CAN BE ORDERED USING THE FORM AT THE END OF THIS STUDY TEXT.

OXFORD INSTITUTE OF INTERNATIONAL FINANCE MBA

The Oxford Institute of International Finance (OXIIF), a joint venture between the ACCA and Oxford Brookes University, offers an MBA for finance professionals.

For this MBA, credits are awarded for your ACCA studies, and entry to the MBA course is available to those who have completed their ACCA professional stage studies. The MBA was launched in 2002 and has attracted participants from all over the world.

The qualification features an introductory module (*Markets, Management and Strategy*). Other modules include *Global Business Strategy, Managing Self Development,* and *Organisational Change & Transformation.*

Research Methods are also taught, as they underpin the **research dissertation.**

The MBA programme is delivered through the use of targeted paper study materials, developed by BPP, and taught over the Internet by OXIIF personnel using BPP's virtual campus software.

For further information, please see the Oxford Institute's website: www.oxfordinstitute.org

Syllabus mindmap

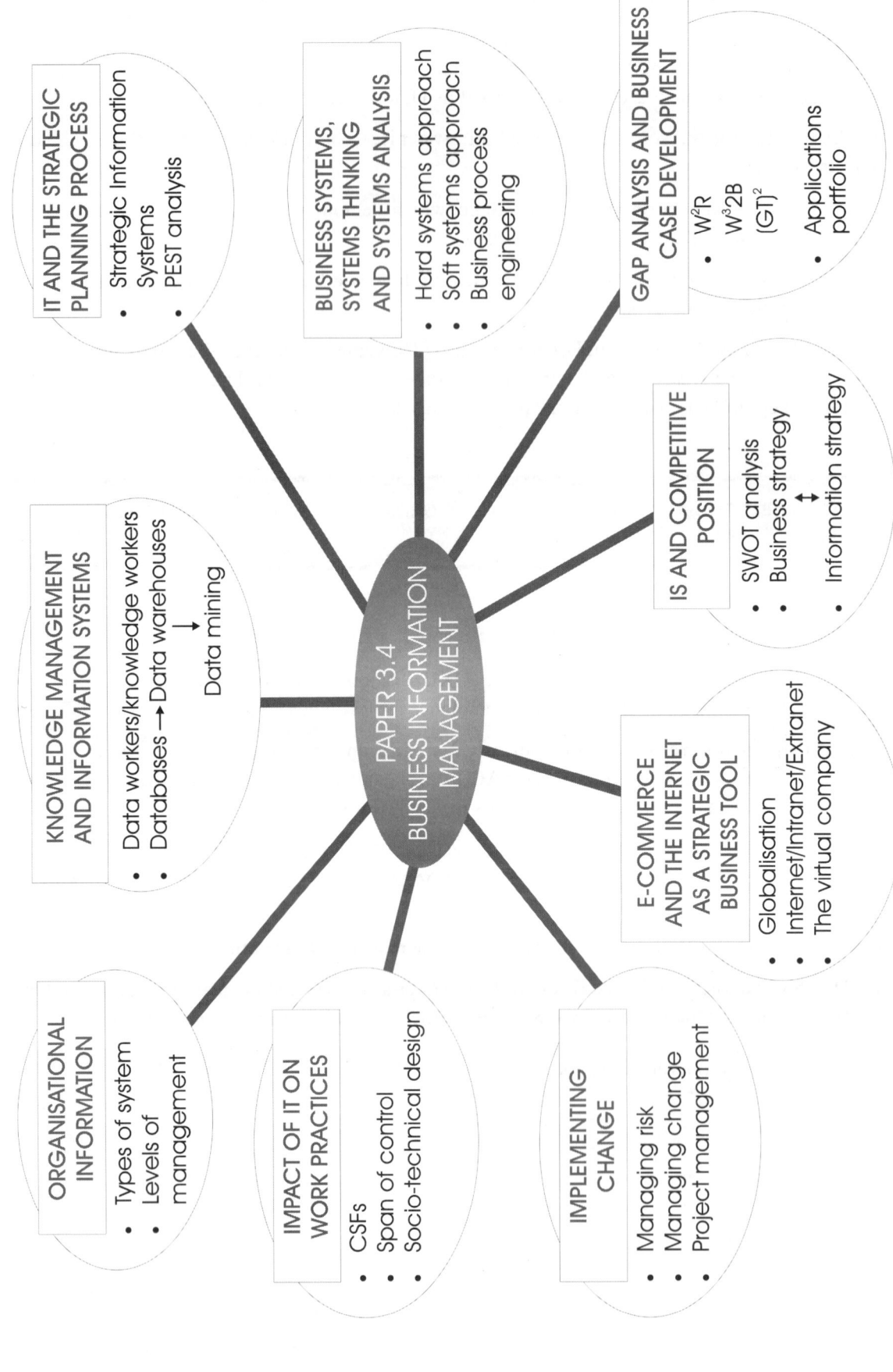

Part A
Information systems and the organisation

Chapter 1

ORGANISATIONAL INFORMATION REQUIREMENTS

Topic list	Syllabus reference
1 Information requirements	1(a), 1(b), 3(a)
2 The value of information	1(b), 1(c)
3 Information management	1(c)
4 Types of information system	1(d)
5 Information system security	1(b)

Introduction

Welcome to Paper 3.4 Business Information Management. As with all level three papers, the examination for this paper will require you to **apply knowledge,** rather than simply testing your ability to recall information. So, when working through this Study Text, consider how the material could be applied or adapted for use in a range of business situations.

We start with the **information requirements** of the modern organisation.

Study guide

1 – Levels of management

- Distinguish between strategic, tactical and operational management and their corresponding information requirements
- Describe the importance of making information accessible *(Also see Chapter 2)*
- Discuss ways of ensuring the reliability and accuracy of information, creating secure information systems and making information available at an appropriate cost

2 – Categories of information systems

- Discuss the six major types of Information Systems: Executive Support Systems (ESS), Management Information Systems (MIS), Decision Support Systems (DSS), Knowledge Work Systems (KWS), Office Automation Systems (OAS), Transaction Processing Systems (TPS)
- Describe examples of each of the six major types of Information Systems (ESS, MIS, DSS, KWS, OAS, TPS) in terms of an organisation's strategic business position *(Also see Chapter 2)*

9 – Organisational requirements

- Discuss the establishment of organisational information requirements
- Discuss the requirement to understand the business value of information systems *(Also see Chapter 2)*

Part A: Information systems and the organisation

> **Exam guide**
> The short scenario that will appear in Section A of the examination provides the examiner with an ideal opportunity to test your understanding of the importance of an organisation utilising suitable systems to meet information requirements.

1 INFORMATION REQUIREMENTS

> **KEY TERMS**
>
> **Data** is the raw material for data processing. Data consists of numbers, letters and symbols and relates to facts, events, and transactions.
>
> **Information** is data that has been processed in such a way as to be meaningful to the person who receives it.
>
> The syllabus defines an **information system** as 'an organisational and management solution, based on information technology, to any challenge posed by the environment'.

1.1 All organisations require information for a range of **purposes**. These can be categorised as follows.

- Information for **planning**
- Information for **controlling**
- Information for **recording transactions**
- Information for **performance measurement**
- Information for **decision making**

Planning

1.2 Planning requires a knowledge of the available resources, possible time-scales and the likely outcome under alternative scenarios. Information is required that helps **decision making**, and how to implement decisions taken.

Controlling

1.3 Once a plan is implemented, its actual performance must be controlled. Information is required to assess **whether it is proceeding as planned** or whether there is some unexpected deviation from plan. It may consequently be necessary to take some form of corrective action.

Recording transactions

1.4 Information about **each transaction or event** is required. Reasons include:

(a) Documentation of transactions can be used as **evidence** in a case of dispute.

(b) There may be a **legal requirement** to record transactions, for example for accounting and audit purposes.

(c) **Operational information** can be built up, allowing control action to be taken.

Performance measurement

1.5 Just as individual operations need to be controlled, so overall performance must be measured. **Comparisons against budget or plan** are able to be made. This may involve the collection of information on, for example, costs, revenues, volumes, time-scale and profitability.

Decision making

1.6 Strategic planning, management control and operational control may be seen as a hierarchy of planning and control decisions. (This is sometimes called the Anthony hierarchy, after the writer Robert Anthony.)

Strategic information

1.7 **Strategic information** is used to **plan** the **objectives** of the organisation, and to **assess** whether the objectives are being met in practice. Such information includes overall profitability, the profitability of different segments of the business, future market prospects, the availability and cost of raising new funds, total cash needs, total manning levels and capital equipment needs.

1.8 Strategic information is:

- Derived from both **internal and external** sources
- **Summarised** at a high level
- Relevant to the **long term**
- Concerned with the **whole organisation**
- Often prepared on an '**ad hoc**' basis
- Both **quantitative and qualitative**
- **Uncertain**, as the future cannot be accurately predicted

Tactical information

1.9 Tactical information is used to decide **how the resources of the business should be employed**, and to **monitor** how they are being and have been employed. Such information includes productivity measurements (output per hour) budgetary control or variance analysis reports, and cash flow forecasts, staffing levels and profit results within a particular department of the organisation, labour turnover statistics within a department and short-term purchasing requirements.

Part A: Information systems and the organisation

1.10 Tactical information is:

- Primarily generated internally (but may have a limited external component)
- **Summarised at a lower level**
- Relevant to the **short and medium term**
- Concerned with **activities or departments**
- Prepared **routinely and regularly**
- Based on **quantitative** measures

Operational information

1.11 Operational information is used to ensure that **specific operational tasks** are planned and carried out as intended.

1.12 In the payroll office, for example, operational information relating to day-rate labour will include the hours worked each week by each employee, the rate of pay per hour, details of deductions, and for the purpose of wages analysis, details of the time each employee spent on individual jobs during the week. In this example, the information is required weekly, but more urgent operational information, such as the amount of raw materials being input to a production process, may be required daily, hourly, or in the case of automated production, second by second.

1.13 Operational information is:

- Derived from **internal** sources
- **Detailed**, being the processing of raw data
- Relevant to the **immediate term**
- **Task-specific**
- Prepared very **frequently**
- Largely **quantitative**

1.14 It may help to clarify the above to consider it in terms of how well **structured** the problem situation is. Examples of unstructured and structured decisions at the different levels of management are given below.

	Example of a structured decision	Example of a semi-structured decision	Example of an unstructured decision
Operational level	Devising stock control procedures	Selecting a new supplier	Employing a supervisor
Tactical level	Selecting products to discount	Budget calculation and allocation	Expanding into a new design
Strategic level	Major investment decisions	Entering a new market; producing a new product line	Restructuring the organisation

The qualities of good information

1.15 'Good' information is information that adds to the understanding of a situation. The qualities of good information are outlined in the following table.

Quality	Example
Accurate	Figures should add up, the degree of rounding should be appropriate, there should be no typos, items should be allocated to the correct category, assumptions should be stated for uncertain information.
Complete	Information should includes everything that it needs to include, for example external data if relevant, or comparative information.
Cost-beneficial	It should not cost more to obtain the information than the benefit derived from having it. Providers or information should be given efficient means of collecting and analysing it. Presentation should be such that users do not waste time working out what it means.
User-targeted	The needs of the user should be borne in mind, for instance senior managers need summaries, junior ones need detail.
Relevant	Information that is not needed for a decision should be omitted, no matter how 'interesting' it may be.
Authoritative	The source of the information should be a reliable one (**not**, for instance, 'Joe Bloggs Predictions Page' on the Internet unless Joe Bloggs is known to be a reliable source for that type of information).
Timely	The information should be available when it is needed.
Easy to use	Information should be clearly presented, not excessively long, and sent using the right medium and communication channel (e-mail, telephone, hard-copy report etc).

> **Exam focus point**
> You will **not be asked simply to produce a list** of the qualities of good information in the exam. Exam questions will expect you to be able to identify **the information problems** that a company is having, and to **suggest solutions**.

Part A: Information systems and the organisation

Improvements to information

1.16 The table on the following page contains suggestions as to how poor information can be improved.

Feature	Example of possible improvements
Accurate	Use computerised systems with automatic input checks rather than manual systems.
	Allow sufficient time for collation and analysis of data if pinpoint accuracy is crucial.
	Incorporate elements of probability within projections so that the required response to different future scenarios can be assessed.
Complete	Include past data as a reference point for future projections.
	Include any planned developments, such as new products.
	Information about future demand would be more useful than information about past demand.
	Include external data.
Cost-beneficial	Always bear in mind whether the benefit of having the information is greater than the cost of obtaining it.
User-targeted	Information should be summarised and presented together with relevant ratios or percentages.
Relevant	The purpose of the report should be defined. It may be trying to fulfil too many purposes at once. Perhaps several shorter reports would be more effective.
	Information should include exception reporting, where only those items that are worthy of note - and the control actions taken by more junior managers to deal with them - are reported.
Authoritative	Use reliable sources and experienced personnel.
	If some figures are derived from other figures the method of derivation should be explained.
Timely	Information collection and analysis by production managers needs to be speeded up considerably, probably by the introduction of better information systems
Easy-to-use	Graphical presentation, allowing trends to be quickly assimilated and relevant action decided upon.
	Alternative methods of presentation should be considered, such as graphs or charts, to make it easier to review the information at a glance. Numerical information is sometimes best summarised in narrative form or vice versa.
	A 'house style' for reports should be devised and adhered to by all. This would cover such matters as number of decimal places to use, table headings and labels, paragraph numbering and so on.

Information requirements in different sectors

1.17 The following table provides examples of the typical information requirements of organisations operating in different sectors.

Sector	Information type	Example(s)	General comment
Manufacturing	Strategic	Future demand estimates New product development plans Competitor analysis	The information requirements of commercial organisations are influenced by the need to make and monitor profit. Information that contributes to the following measures is important: • Changeover times • Number of common parts • Level of product diversity • Product and process quality
	Tactical	Variance analysis Departmental accounts Stock turnover	
	Operational	Production reject rate Materials and labour used Stock levels	
Service	Strategic	Forecast sales growth and market share Profitability, capital structure	Organisations have become more customer and results-oriented over the last decade. As a consequence, the difference between service and other organisation's information requirements has decreased. Businesses have realised that most of their activities can be measured, and many can be measured in similar ways regardless of the business sector.
	Tactical	Resource utilisation such as average staff time charged out, number of customers per hairdresser, number of staff per account Customer satisfaction rating	
	Operational	Staff timesheets Customer waiting time Individual customer feedback	

Part A: Information systems and the organisation

Sector	Information type	Example(s)	General comment
Public	Strategic	Population demographics Expected government policy	Public sector (and non-profit making) organisations often don't have one overriding objective. Their information requirements depend on the objectives chosen. The information provided often requires interpretation (eg student exam results are not affected by the quality of teaching alone). Information may compare actual performance with: • Standards • Targets • Similar activities • Indices • Activities over time as trends
	Tactical	Hospital occupancy rates Average class sizes Percent of reported crimes solved	
	Operational	Staff timesheets Vehicles available Student daily attendance records	
Non-Profit / charities	Strategic	Activities of other charities Government (and in some cases overseas government) policy Public attitudes	Many of the comments regarding Public Sector organisations can be applied to not-for-profit organisations. Information to judge performance usually aims to assess economy, efficiency and effectiveness. A key measure of efficiency for charities is the percentage of revenue that is spent on the publicised cause (eg rather than on advertising or administration).
	Tactical	Percent of revenue spent on admin Average donation 'Customer' satisfaction statistics	
	Operational	Households collected from / approached Banking documentation Donations	

2 THE VALUE OF INFORMATION

Factors that make information a valuable commodity

2.1 Information is now recognised as a valuable resource, and a **key tool in the quest for a competitive advantage.**

2.2 Easy **access** to information, the **quality** of that information and **speedy methods of exchanging** the information have become essential elements of business success.

2.3 Organisations that make **good use of information** in decision making, and which use new technologies to access, process and exchange information are likely to be **best placed to survive** in increasingly competitive world markets.

2.4 Unlike certain commodities the value of **information in general** is **not** based on **scarcity**: indeed the most frequent complaint of many modern managers is that there is **far too much of it** about.

2.5 Moreover, the value of information is **in the eyes of the beholder** to some extent: information about a new type of plastic may be of keen interest and value to a car manufacturer, but of no value whatsoever to a software house.

2.6 The **factors which make information valuable** are as follows.

(a) The **source** of the information

If the information comes from a source that is widely known and respected for quality, thoroughness and accuracy (Reuters, say, or the BBC) it will be more valuable to users than information from an unknown or untested source, because it can be relied upon with confidence.

(b) The **ease of assimilation**

Modern methods of presentation can use not only words and figures but also **colour, graphics, sound and movement**. This makes the receipt of information a richer (and so more valuable) experience, and it means that information can be more easily, and therefore more quickly, understood: again a feature that people will be willing to pay for.

(c) **Accessibility**

If information can be made available in an easily accessible place (such as the **Internet**) users do not have to commit too much time and effort to retrieve it. If just a few sentences of information is required, and they can find these (for instance using an Internet search engine) without having to buy a whole book or newspaper, then they should be willing to pay for this convenience.

The value of obtaining information

2.7 In spite of its value in a general sense, information which is **obtained but not used** has no actual value to the person that obtains it. A decision taken on the basis of information received also has no actual value. It is only the **action taken** as a result of a decision which realises actual value for a company. The cost of collecting information bears no relation to its value. An item of information which leads to an actual increase in profit of £90 is not worth having if it costs £100 to collect.

Part A: Information systems and the organisation

Question 1

The value of information lies in the action taken as a result of receiving it. What questions might you ask in order to make an assessment of the value of information?

Answer

(a) What information is provided?
(b) What is it used for?
(c) Who uses it?
(d) How often is it used?
(e) Does the frequency with which it is used coincide with the frequency of provision?
(f) What is achieved by using it?
(g) What other relevant information is available which could be used instead?

An assessment of the value of information can be derived in this way, and the cost of obtaining it should then be compared against this value. On the basis of this comparison, it can be decided whether certain items of information are worth having. It should be remembered that there may also be intangible benefits which may be harder to quantify.

2.8 Deciding whether it is worthwhile having more information should depend on the **marginal benefits** expected from getting it and the **extra costs** of obtaining it. The benefits of more information should be measured in terms of the difference it would make to management decisions if the information were made available. Since the incremental cost of obtaining extra quantities of information will eventually exceed the marginal benefits derived from them, there will inevitably be **a limit to the economic size of a management information system**.

Assessing cost and value

2.9 The information system is used to produce a wide variety of information. The **cost** of an individual item of information is **not always easy to quantify**. For example, if a manager uses an ESS (Executive Support System) to enquire into the company's database, what is the cost of this enquiry?

(a) The information is **already existent anyway**, as it is used for a number of different purposes. It might be impossible to predict how often it will be used, and hence the economic benefits to be derived from it.

(b) The information system which is used to process these requests has also been purchased. Its **cost is largely fixed**.

2.10 Just as the costs of an item of information are harder to assess than might appear superficially, so too the **benefits are often hard to quantify**. While nobody doubts that information is vital, it is not always easy to construct an economic assessment of the value of information.

(a) A monthly variance analysis will only generate economically consequential decisions if there is some **control failure** leading to variances, and control failures are not easy to predict.

(b) The economic consequences of a decision are **not always easy to predict**.

Traditional methods

2.11 Traditional **investment appraisal methods** can be applied with varying degrees of success to problems of this kind. There principal methods of evaluating a capital project are: the payback method, the accounting rate of return and discounted cashflow methods such as net present value and internal rate of return.

These methods should be familiar from your earlier studies.

Question 2

Draw up a table which identifies, for each of the four methods of evaluating a project (payback, ARR, NPV, IRR), two advantages and two disadvantages.

Answer

Method	Advantages	Disadvantages
Payback	(1) Easy to calculate (2) Favours projects that offer quick returns	(1) Ignores cash flows after payback period (2) Only a crude measure of timing of a project's cash flows.
ARR	(1) Easy to calculate (2) Easy to understand	(1) Doesn't allow for timing of inflows/outflows of cash (2) Subject to accounting conventions.
NPV	(1) Uses relevant cost approach by concentrating on cash flows (2) Represents increase to company's wealth, expressed in present day terms	(1) Not easily understood by laymen. (2) Cost of capital may be difficult to calculate.
IRR	(1) Uses opportunity cost approach (2) Represents breakeven borrowing rate.	(1) Could get several IRRs or no IRRs (2) Ignores scale of project whereas NPV takes this into account.

Question 3

Balanced Approaches Ltd is considering investing in a number of information management projects (all of which will take the same initial amount of capital) and has appraised them as follows.

Project	NPV £'000	Payback Years	IRR %
A	900	5	24
B	500	4	10
C	200	1	19
D	150	3	17
E	100	2	29
F	600	4	31
G	140	3	27

Assuming that the company can only raise enough capital to invest in four of these projects, which four should it undertake?

Answer

The first step is to rank each project, as follows.

Ranking by NPV		Ranking by payback		Ranking by IRR	
1	A	1	C	1	F
2	F	2	E	2	E
3	B	3	D	3	G
4	C	3	G	4	A
5	D	5	B	5	C
6	G	5	F	6	D
7	E	7	A	7	B

Part A: Information systems and the organisation

The data can then be resorted (this is easy with a spreadsheet package, obviously) to show what scores each project achieves under each method and overall.

Ranking by NPV		Ranking by payback		Ranking by IRR		Total score	
1	A	7	A	4	A	12	(1+7+4)
3	B	5	B	7	B	15	etc
4	C	1	C	5	C	10	
5	D	3	D	6	D	14	
7	E	2	E	2	E	11	
2	F	5	F	1	F	8	
6	G	3	G	3	G	12	

Finally we can rearrange the total score column (lowest first because scoring 1 is better than scoring 7), to see which projects did best overall.

Project	Total
F	8
C	10
E	11
A	12
G	12
D	14
B	15

This indicates that projects F, C, and E should definitely be chosen. A decision will have to be made between projects A and G on non-financial grounds.

The benefits of a proposed information system

2.12 The benefits from a proposed information system should be evaluated against the costs. To quantify the benefits several factors need to be considered.

(a) **Savings** generated because the old system will no longer be operated. The savings may include **staff costs** and **other operating costs**.

(b) **Extra savings** or **revenue benefits** because of the **improvements or enhancements** that the new system should bring:

(i) Possibly more **sales revenue** and so additional contribution.

(ii) Better **stock control** (with a new stock control system) and so fewer stock losses from obsolescence and deterioration.

(iii) Savings in **staff time**, resulting perhaps in reduced future staff growth.

2.13 Some benefits might be **intangible**, or impossible to give a money value to. Even if they cannot be quantified, they must be identified and fully explained. It is arguable that the larger proportion of all computerised information systems benefits is intangible.

(a) Greater **customer satisfaction**, arising from a more prompt service (eg because of a computerised sales and delivery service).

(b) Improved **staff morale** from working with a 'better' system.

(c) **Better decision making** is hard to quantify, but may result from a better MIS, DSS or ESS.

1: Organisational information requirements

Case example

Railtrack pays for poor information

Rail regulator Tom Winsor, in his strongest condemnation yet of Railtrack, gave the company until 21 May, effectively telling it: 'Get your act together.'

If Railtrack fails Mr Winsor said he will issue an enforcement notice, a legal procedure which could result in the imposition of heavy and unspecified fines.

Railtrack, which is responsible for the national infrastructure, still has more than 200 speed limits in place as a result of the Hatfield disaster last October in which four died and 34 were injured. That was caused by a broken rail and resulted in chaos as other cracked rails were discovered.

Mr Winsor today put the blame squarely on Railtrack's shoulders. The company, he said, had lacks 'crucial information about its own network'. It had also '**failed to organise and disseminate the information it does have in an accessible, consistent and efficient way**'.

Mr Winsor said that **if**, after Hatfield, **Railtrack had had the information it should have, speed restrictions could have been prevented**'. He said: 'Customer confidence in the railways will revive when Railtrack gets the service back onto a reliable basis. That is the core of my action today.

A Railtrack spokesman said the company was confident that it would have work completed before the deadline. 'We will seek to achieve Mr Winsor's timescale. Most of the work will be done by Easter. There may be one or two areas after that where work will remain, possibly on the longer-distance lines.'

He added: 'We strongly agree with the **development of a national asset register** (which would list the condition and location of equipment owned by the company). 'That is an important step in running a safer and more efficient network and we readily agree to that and we are working hard on it.'

The company, which used to make profits of £1.3 million a day, will announce its **first-ever loss** in two weeks' time.

Adapted from The Evening Standard March 20, 2001

3 INFORMATION MANAGEMENT

3.1 Information must be managed just like any other organisational resource.

> **KEY TERM**
>
> **Information Management (IM) strategy** refers to the basic approach an organisation has to the management of its information systems, including:
>
> - Planning IS/IT developments
> - Organisational environment of IS
> - Control
> - Technology

3.2 Information management entails the following **tasks**.

(a) Identifying current and future **information needs**.

(b) Identifying information **sources**.

(c) **Collecting** the information.

(d) **Storing** the information.

(e) Facilitating existing methods of **using** information and identifying new ways of using it.

Part A: Information systems and the organisation

(f) Ensuring that information is **communicated** to those who need it, and is **not communicated** to those who are not entitled to see it.

3.3 Technology has provided new sources of information, new ways of collecting it, storing it and processing it, and new methods of communicating and sharing it. This in turn has meant that information needs have changed and will continue to change as new technologies become available.

Question 4

Drawing on personal experience (if possible), give examples of the inefficient use of information.

Answer

Some examples are:

(a) Information which is collected but not needed.
(b) Information stored long after it is needed.
(c) Useful information which is inaccessible to potential users.
(d) Information disseminated more widely than is necessary.
(e) Inefficient methods used to collect, analyse, store and retrieve information.
(f) Collection of the same information by more than one group of people.
(g) Duplication of the same information.

3.4 Although computing and telecommunications technology provide fabulous tools for carrying out the information management tasks listed above, they are **not always the best tools**; nor are they always even available.

Users of information

3.5 The information generated by an organisation may be used internally or externally.

3.6 **Internal** users of information include (by status) the following.

- The board (or equivalent)
- Directors with functional responsibilities
- Divisional general managers
- Divisional heads
- Departmental heads
- Section leaders, supervisors
- Employees

Question 5

Information is often required by people **outside** the organisation for making judgements and decisions relating to an organisation. Give four examples of decisions which may be taken by outsiders.

Answer

There are many possible suggestions, including those given below.

(a) The organisation's **bankers** take decisions affecting the amount of money they are prepared to lend.

(b) The **public** might have an interest in information relating to an organisation's products or services.

1: Organisational information requirements

(c) The **media** (press, television etc) use information generated by organisations in news stories, and such information can adversely or favourably affect an organisation's relationship with its environment.

(d) The **government** (for example the Department of Trade and Industry) regularly requires organisational information.

(e) The **Inland Revenue** and **HM Customs and Excise** authorities require information for taxation and VAT assessments.

(f) An organisation's **suppliers** and **customers** take decisions whether or not to trade with the organisation.

3.7 In a small company information systems may be the responsibility of the finance director or the company secretary or simply an office manager. In larger organisations there may be an information director.

3.8 Whatever the case, the manager in charge of information systems needs the following skills.

- General management ability
- An understanding of organisational activities and functions
- Technical expertise in developing and running information systems

3.9 The information systems manager is responsible for ensuring that the organisation's acquisition and use of information technology and computer systems fits the goals and objectives of the organisation as a whole. The **information systems strategy** should tie in with the overall organisation strategy. (We look at this in greater detail in Chapter 2.)

Information infrastructure

3.10 The information systems manager may be responsible for the overall design of an organisation's information systems. This responsibility is likely to be delegated on a day to day basis. Furthermore, the information systems manager should ensure that IT systems activities undertaken by users should firstly satisfy **user demands** and secondly **not be sub-optimal** to the overall system goals and organisational objectives.

3.11 This activity will include overall responsibility for the construction of an **information infrastructure** comprising:

- **Technical** standards
- **Software** standards
- Establishment of **corporate databases**
- Providing an information systems **service function**

Liaison

3.12 **Liaison** between information systems professionals and the **rest of the organisation** is a key role. Such functions include the following.

(a) Provision of **technical assistance**.

(b) Informal discussions with **users as to their needs** before detailed feasibility studies are carried out, which can also include discussions as to the payoffs of a particular IS investment.

(c) Advice on the impact of information systems on **organisational structure, working environment** and so forth.

Part A: Information systems and the organisation

The environment

3.13 Interaction with the environment is important. This is essential for a strategic perspective. An organisation's information systems can affect the way it trades, as there are a growing number of **information systems connections between different organisations** (eg Electronic Data Interchange). The information systems manager will seek to dovetail these types of facility into the organisation's overall commercial strategy.

3.14 Links with external organisations can also be important if the organisation takes over another. **Incompatible information systems** between merged organisations can add significantly to the cost of the merger. Information system **flexibility** is therefore a desirable aim. A suitable approach to public relations is desirable to convince customers and suppliers of the benefits to them of new information systems.

3.15 The information systems manager will gather information relating to the **legal environment of information systems**. This includes handling the impact of data protection legislation, rules governing cross-border dataflows, and ensuring that other areas of legislation are accounted for in information systems development.

Constraints on strategy development

3.16 There are a variety of problems facing senior information systems managers, and their job may require them to implement the organisation's information systems strategy within the framework of certain inevitable constraints.

- Shortage of skilled staff
- Backlogs in application development due to previous time over-runs
- The pressure for **continued expansion**

Two worlds

3.17 To summarise, the information systems manager needs to be able to travel between two worlds: the **organisation as a whole**, its culture, internal politics and strategic objectives, and the specialised world of **information technology**.

(a) The information systems manager, and his or her subordinates, should therefore be able to devise relevant **technical solutions** to identified problems.

(b) The information systems manager must also be a **propagandist**. In many organisations, IT is felt to be the province of junior members of staff, and some of the issues may not be understood at board level. The information systems manager should make IT a 'credible' issue for senior management involvement.

Information sources and capture

3.18 Data and information come from sources both inside and outside an organisation. An organisation's information systems should be designed so as to obtain - or **capture** - all the relevant data and information required.

Internal information

3.19 Capturing data and information from **inside** the organisation involves designing a system for collecting or measuring data and information which sets out procedures for:

- What data and information is collected

1: Organisational information requirements

- How frequently
- By whom
- By what methods
- How data and information is processed, filed and communicated

The accounting records

3.20 The accounting ledgers provide an excellent source of information regarding what has happened in the past. This information may be used as a basis for predicting future events eg budgeting.

3.21 Accounting records can provide more than purely financial information. For example a stock control system includes purchase orders, goods received notes and goods returned notes that can be analysed to provide information regarding the speed of delivery or the quality of supplies.

Other internal sources

3.22 Much information that is not strictly part of the accounting records nevertheless is closely tied in to the accounting system.

   (a) Information about **personnel** will be linked to the **payroll** system. Additional information may be obtained from this source if, say, a project is being costed and it is necessary to ascertain the availability and rate of pay of different levels of staff, or the need for and cost of recruiting staff from outside the organisation.

   (b) Much information will be produced by a **production** department about machine capacity, fuel consumption, movement of people, materials, and work in progress, set up times, maintenance requirements and so on. A large part of the traditional work of cost accounting involves ascribing costs to the **physical information** produced by this source.

   (c) Many **service** businesses, notably accountants and solicitors, need to keep detailed records of the **time spent** on various activities, both to justify fees to clients and to assess the efficiency and profitability of operations.

3.23 **Staff** themselves are one of the primary sources of internal information. Information may be obtained either informally in the course of day-to-day business or through meetings, interviews or questionnaires.

External information

3.24 **Formal** collection of data from outside sources includes the following.

   (a) A company's **tax specialists** will be expected to gather information about changes in tax law and how this will affect the company.

   (b) Obtaining information about any new legislation on health and safety at work, or employment regulations, must be the responsibility of a particular person - for example the company's **legal expert** or **company secretary** - who must then pass on the information to other managers affected by it.

   (c) Research and development (R & D) work often relies on information about other R & D work being done by another company or by government institutions. An **R & D official** might be made responsible for finding out about R & D work in the company.

Part A: Information systems and the organisation

(d) **Marketing managers** need to know about the opinions and buying attitudes of potential customers. To obtain this information, they might carry out market research exercises.

3.25 **Informal** gathering of information from the environment occurs naturally, consciously or unconsciously, as people learn what is going on in the world around them - perhaps from newspapers, television reports, meetings with business associates or the trade press.

3.26 Organisations hold external information such as invoices, letters, advertisements and so on **received from customers and suppliers**. But there are many occasions when an active search outside the organisation is necessary.

> **KEY TERM**
>
> The phrase **environmental scanning** is often used to describe the process of gathering external information, which is available from a wide range of sources.

(a) The government.

(b) Advice or information bureaux.

(c) Consultants.

(d) Newspaper and magazine publishers.

(e) There may be specific reference works which are used in a particular line of work.

(f) Libraries and information services.

(g) Increasingly businesses can use each other's systems as sources of information, for instance via extranets or electronic data interchange (EDI).

(h) **Electronic sources** of information are becoming increasingly important.

   (i) For some time there have been 'viewdata' services such as **Prestel** offering a very large bank of information gathered from organisations such as the Office for National Statistics, newspapers and the British Library. **Topic** offers information on the stock market. Companies like **Reuters** operate primarily in the field of provision of information.

   (ii) The **Internet** is a vast source of information. We cover the Internet in detail in Chapter 7.

Efficient data collection

3.27 To produce meaningful information it is first necessary to capture the underlying data. The method of data collection chosen will depend on the nature of the organisation, cost and efficiency. Some common data collection methods are outlined below.

Document reading methods

3.28 **Document reading methods** save time and money and also **reduce errors.** Some common document reading methods are described below.

MICR

3.29 Magnetic ink character recognition (**MICR**) involves the recognition by a machine of special formatted characters printed in magnetic ink. The characters are read using a specialised reading device. The main advantage of MICR is its speed and accuracy, but MICR documents are expensive to produce. The main commercial application of MICR is in the banking industry – on cheques and deposit slips.

Optical mark reading

3.30 **Optical mark reading** involves the marking of a pre-printed form with a ballpoint pen or typed line or cross in an appropriate box. The card is then read by an OMR device which senses the mark in each box using an electric current and translates it into machine code. Applications in which OMR is used include **National Lottery** entry forms, and answer sheets for multiple choice questions.

Scanners and OCR

3.31 A scanner is device that can **read text or illustrations printed on paper** and translate the information into a **form the computer can use**. A scanner works by digitising an image, the resulting matrix of bits is called a **bit map.**

3.32 To edit text read by an optical scanner, you need **optical character recognition (OCR)** software to translate the image into text. Most optical scanners sold today come with OCR packages. Businesses may use a scanner and OCR to obtain 'digital' versions of documents they have only paper copies of. For good results the copy must be of good quality.

Bar coding and EPOS

3.33 **Bar codes** are groups of marks which, by their spacing and thickness, indicate specific codes or values.

3.34 Large retail stores have Electronic Point of Sale (EPOS) devices, which include bar code readers. This enables the provision of immediate sales and stock level information.

EFTPOS

3.35 Many retailers have now introduced EFTPOS systems (Electronic Funds Transfer at the Point of Sale). An EFTPOS terminal is used with a customers credit card or debit card to pay for goods or services. The customer's credit card account or bank account will be debited automatically. EFTPOS systems combine point of sale systems with electronic funds transfer.

Magnetic stripe cards

3.36 The standard magnetic stripe card contains machine-sensible data on a thin strip of magnetic recording tape stuck to the back of the card. The magnetic card reader converts this information into directly computer-sensible form. The widest application of magnetic stripe cards is as bank credit or service cards.

Part A: Information systems and the organisation

Smart cards

3.37 A smart card is a plastic card in which is embedded **a microprocessor chip**. A smart card would typically contain a **memory** and a **processing capability**. The information held on smart cards can therefore be updated (eg using a PC and a special device).

Touch screens

3.38 A touch screen enables users to make selections by touching areas of the screen with their finger. Sensors, built into the screen surround, detect which area has been touched. These devices are widely used in vending situations, such as the selling of train tickets.

Voice recognition

3.39 Computer software has been developed that can convert speech into computer sensible form via a microphone. Users are required to speak clearly and reasonably slowly.

4 TYPES OF INFORMATION SYSTEM

4.1 A modern organisation requires a **wide range of systems** to hold, process and analyse information. We will now examine the various information systems used to serve organisational information requirements.

4.2 Organisations require different **types of information system** to provide different **levels of information** in a range of **functional areas**. One way of portraying this concept is shown on the following diagram (taken from *Laudon* and *Laudon, Management Information Systems*).

Types of information systems

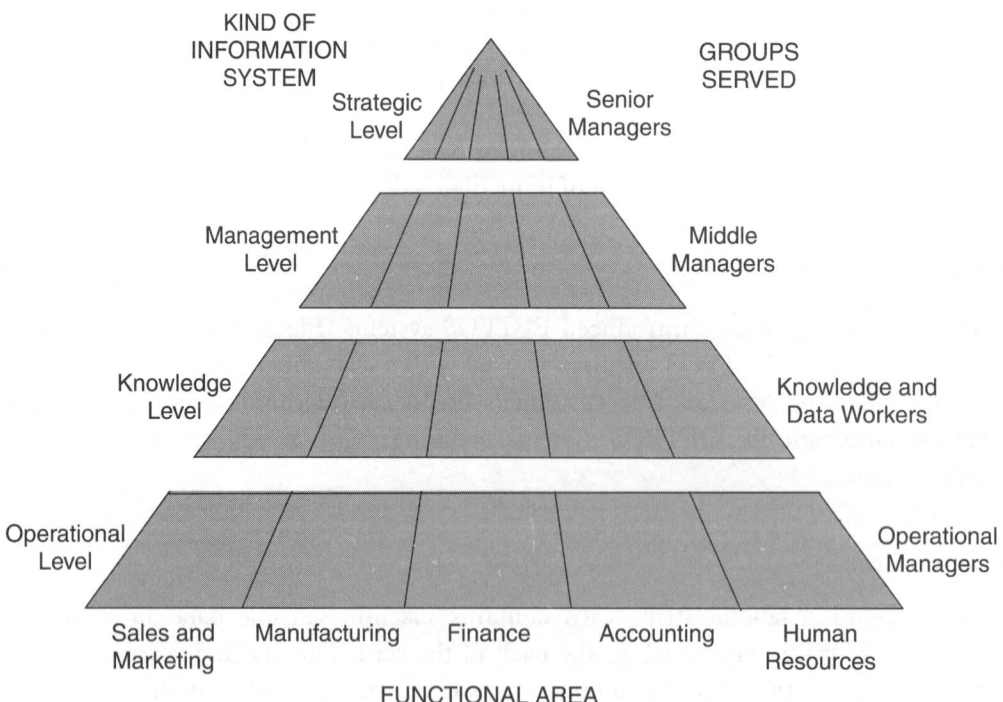

4.3

System level	System purpose
Strategic	To help senior managers with long-term planning. Their main function is to ensure changes in the external environment are matched by the organisation's capabilities.
Management	To help middle managers monitor and control. These systems check if things are working well or not. Some management-level systems support non-routine decision making such as 'what if?' analyses.
Knowledge	To help knowledge and data workers design products, distribute information and perform administrative tasks. These systems help the organisation integrate new and existing knowledge into the business and to reduce the reliance on paper documents.
Operational	To help operational managers track the organisation's day-to-day operational activities. These systems enable routine queries to be answered, and transactions to be processed and tracked.

4.4 There are six **types of information system**:

- Executive Support Systems (ESS)
- Management Information Systems (MIS)
- Decision-Support Systems (DSS)
- Knowledge Work Systems (KWS)
- Office Automation Systems (OAS)
- Transaction Processing Systems (TPS)

Executive Support Systems (ESS)

> **KEY TERM**
>
> An **Executive Support System (ESS)** pools data from internal and external sources and makes information available to senior managers in an easy-to-use form. ESS help senior managers make strategic, unstructured decisions.

4.5 An ESS should provide senior managers with easy access to key **internal and external** information. The system summarises and tracks strategically critical information, possibly drawn from internal MIS and DSS, but also including data from external sources eg competitors, legislation, external databases such as Reuters.

4.6 An ESS is likely to have the following **features**.

- Flexibility
- Quick response time
- Sophisticated data analysis and modelling tools

Part A: Information systems and the organisation

4.7 A model of a typical ESS is shown below.

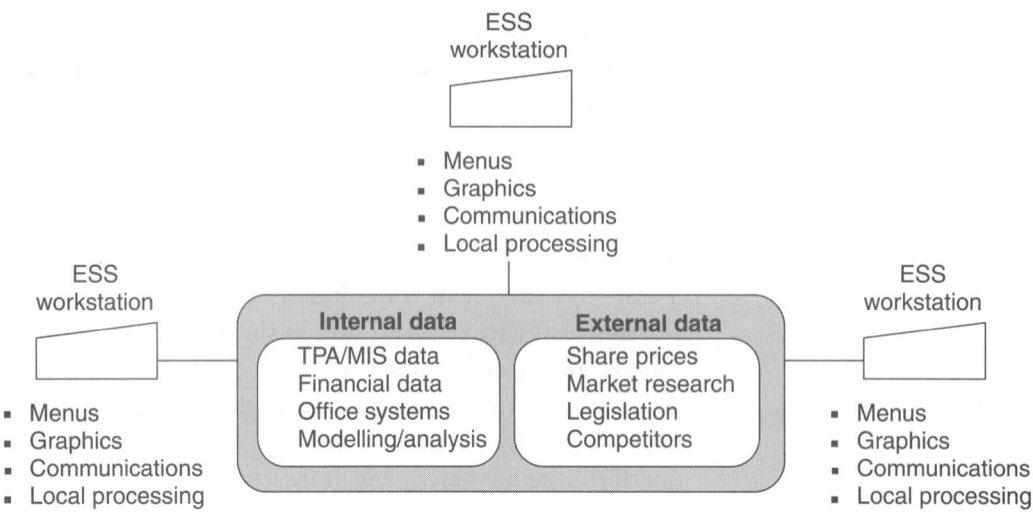

An Executive Support System (ESS)

Management Information Systems (MIS)

KEY TERM

Management Information Systems (MIS) convert data from mainly internal sources into information (eg summary reports, exception reports). This information enables managers to make timely and effective decisions for planning, directing and controlling the activities for which they are responsible.

4.8 An MIS provides regular reports and (usually) on-line access to the organisation's current and historical performance.

4.9 MIS usually transform data from underlying transaction processing systems into summarised files that are used as the basis for management reports.

4.10 MIS have the following characteristics:

- Support **structured** decisions at operational and management control levels
- Designed to report on **existing** operations
- Have little analytical capability
- Relatively **inflexible**
- Have an **internal** focus

Exam Focus Point

Some texts use the term **Management Information System** as an umbrella term for **all information systems** within an organisation. The ACCA study guide follows the classification of information systems given by *Laudon and Laudon*. We have used this narrower definition of a MIS and recommend you do too.

24

Decision Support Systems (DSS)

> **KEY TERM**
>
> **Decision Support Systems (DSS)** combine data and analytical models or data analysis tools to support semi-structured and unstructured decision making.

4.11 DSS are used by management to assist in making decisions on issues which are subject to high levels of uncertainty about the problem, the various **responses** which management could undertake or the likely **impact** of those actions.

4.12 Decision support systems are intended to provide a wide range of alternative information gathering and analytical tools with a major emphasis upon **flexibility** and **user-friendliness**.

4.13 DSS have more analytical power than other systems enabling them to analyse and condense large volumes of data into a form that aids managers make decisions. The objective is to allow the manager to consider a number of **alternatives** and evaluate them under a variety of potential conditions.

Knowledge Work Systems (KWS)

> **KEY TERMS**
>
> **Knowledge Work Systems (KWS)** are information systems that facilitate the creation and integration of new knowledge into an organisation.
>
> **Knowledge Workers** are people whose jobs consist of primarily creating new information and knowledge. They are often members of a profession such as doctors, engineers, lawyers and scientists.

4.14 KWS help knowledge workers create new knowledge and expertise. Examples include:
- Computer Aided Design (CAD)
- Computer Aided Manufacturing (CAM)
- Specialised financial software that analyses trading situations

4.15 We look at KWS in greater detail in Chapter 3.

Office Automation Systems (OAS)

> **KEY TERM**
>
> **Office Automation Systems (OAS)** are computer systems designed to increase the productivity of data and information workers.

4.16 OAS support the major activities performed in a typical office such as document management, facilitating communication and managing data. Examples include:
- Word processing, desktop publishing, and digital filing systems

Part A: Information systems and the organisation

- E-mail, voice mail, videoconferencing, groupware, intranets, schedulers
- Spreadsheets, desktop databases

Transaction Processing Systems (TPS)

KEY TERM

A **Transaction Processing System (TPS)** performs and records routine transactions.

4.17 TPS are used for **routine tasks** in which data items or transactions must be processed so that operations can continue. TPS support most business functions in most types of organisations. The following table shows a range of TPS applications.

	Transaction processing systems				
	Sales/ marketing systems	Manufacturing /production systems	Finance/ accounting systems	Human resources systems	Other types (eg university)
Major functions of system	• Sales management • Market research • Promotion Pricing • New products	• Scheduling • Purchasing Shipping/ receiving • Engineering • Operations	• Budgeting • General ledger • Billing • Management accounting	• Personnel records • Benefits • Salaries • Labour relations • Training	• Admissions • Student academic records • Course records • Graduates
Major application systems	• Sales order information system • Market research system • Pricing system	• Materials resource planning • Purchase order control • Engineering • Quality control	• General ledger • Accounts receivable /payable • Budgeting • Funds management	• Payroll • Employee records • Employee benefits • Career path systems	• Registration • Student record • Curriculum/ class control systems • Benefactor information system

Batch processing and On-line processing

4.18 A TPS will process transactions using either **batch** processing or **on-line** processing.

4.19 Batch processing involves transactions being **grouped** and **stored** before being processed at regular intervals, such as daily, weekly or monthly. Because data is not input as soon as it is received the system will not always be up-to-date.

4.20 The lack of up-to-date information means batch processing is usually not suitable for systems involving customer contact. Batch processing is suitable for internal, regular tasks such as payroll.

4.21 On-line processing involves transactions being input and processed immediately. An airline ticket sales and reservation system is an example.

4.22 The workings of both processing methods are shown in the following diagram.

Batch processing and on-line processing

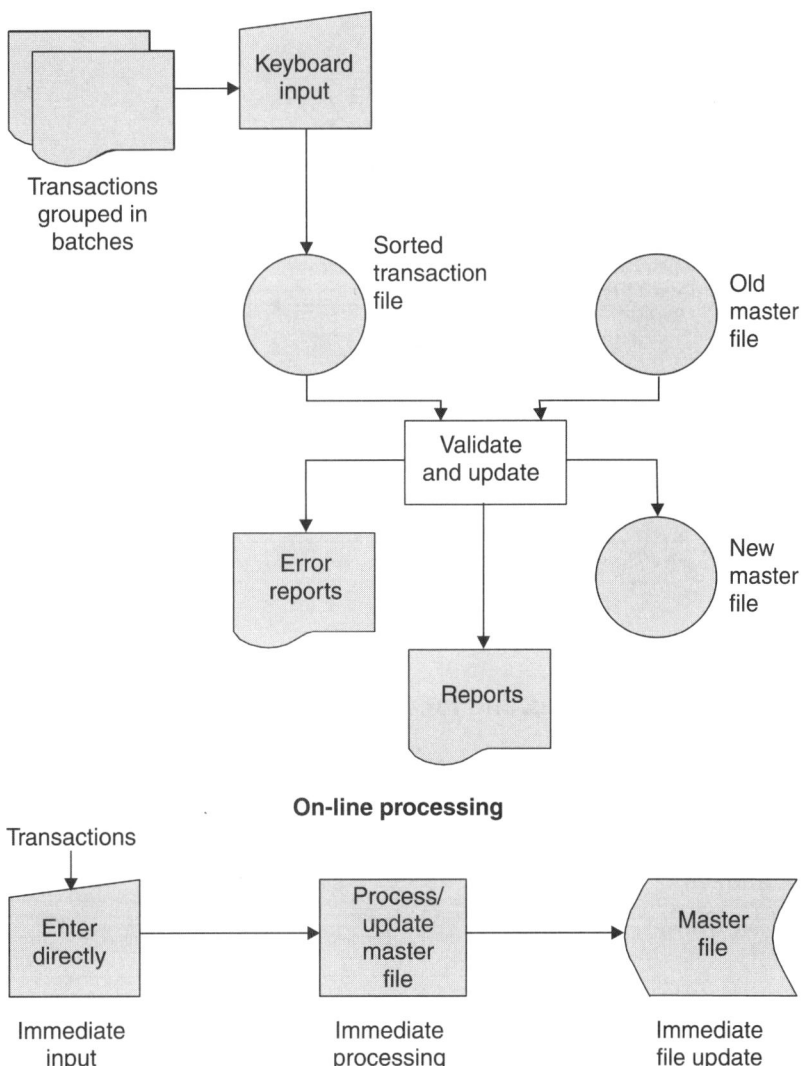

System dependencies and integration

4.23 The six types of system we have identified exchange data with each other. The ease with which data flows from one system to another depends on the extent of **integration** between systems.

4.24 The level of integration will depend on the nature of the organisation and the systems involved. The cost of integrating systems (eg programmer time) should be considered against benefits of integration (quicker availability of information, less time spent inputting information).

Part A: Information systems and the organisation

4.25 Interrelationships between systems are shown in the following diagram from *Loudon and Loudon*.

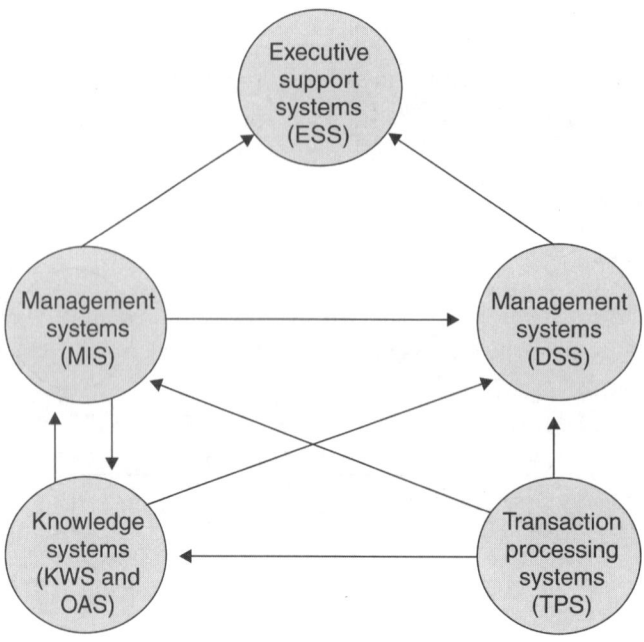

Information systems: levels, types and functions

4.26 Examples of the levels and types of information system we have discussed in this section are shown in the following diagram.

TYPES OF SYSTEMS					
Executive Support Systems (ESS)	**Strategic-Level Systems**				
	5-year sales trend forecasting	5-year operating plan	5-year budget forecasting	Profit planning	Human resource planning
	Management-Level Systems				
Management Information Systems (MIS)	Sales management	Inventory control	Annual budgeting	Capital investment analysis	Relocation analysis
Decision Support Systems (DSS)	Sales region analysis	Production scheduling	Cost analysis	Pricing/profit ability analysis	Contract cost analysis
	Knowledge-Level System				
Knowledge Work Systems (KWS)	Engineering workstations		Graphics workstations		Managerial workstations
Office Automation Systems (OAS)	Word processing		Document imaging		Electronic calendars
	Operational-Level Systems				
		Machine control	Securities trading	Payroll	Compensation
	Order tracking	Plant scheduling		Accounts payable	Training & development
Transaction Processing Systems (TPS)	Order processing	Material movement control	Cash management	Accounts receivable	Employee record keeping
	Sales and Marketing	Manufacturing	Finance	Accounting	Human Resources

5 INFORMATION SYSTEM SECURITY

5.1 We have established that information is a **valuable resource** and a key tool in the quest for a competitive advantage.

5.2 As such, measures need to be taken to ensure data and information entering an organisation's information systems is **reliable** and **accurate**. Once captured by the system, the information must be kept secure and any processing must preserve accuracy.

> **KEY TERM**
>
> **Security** means the protection of data from unauthorised modification, disclosure or destruction, and the protection of the information system from the degradation or non-availability of services.

5.3 The measures an organisation can take to protect information and information systems can be classified into:

- Security controls
- Integrity controls
- Contingency controls

Security controls

5.4 The **risks** to data are:

- Human error
    - Entering incorrect transactions
    - Failing to correct errors
    - Processing the wrong files
- Technical error such as malfunctioning hardware or software
- Natural disasters such as fire, flooding, explosion, impact, lightning
- Deliberate actions such as fraud
- Commercial espionage
- Malicious damage
- Industrial action

5.5 Security can be subdivided into a number of aspects.

(a) **Prevention**. It is in practice impossible to prevent all threats cost-effectively.

(b) **Detection**. Detection techniques are often combined with prevention techniques: a log can be maintained of unauthorised attempts to gain access to a computer system.

(c) **Deterrence**. As an example, computer misuse by personnel can be made grounds for dismissal.

(d) **Recovery procedures**. If the threat occurs, its consequences can be contained.

(e) **Correction procedures**. These ensure the vulnerability is dealt with (for example, by instituting stricter controls).

(f) **Threat avoidance**. This might mean changing the design of the system.

Part A: Information systems and the organisation

Physical security

5.6 A system needs to be protected against **natural and man-made disasters**. Protective measures include the following.

- Site preparation, eg fireproof materials
- Detection equipment, eg smoke detectors
- Extinguishing equipment, eg sprinklers
- Use of uninterruptable power supplies (UPS)

5.7 Physical access controls are designed to prevent intruders getting near to computer equipment and/or storage media.

(a) Personnel, including receptionists and, outside working hours, security guards, can help control human access.

(b) Door locks can be used where frequency of use is low.

(c) This is not practicable if the door is in frequent use.

(d) Locks can be combined with:

    (i) A keypad system, requiring a code to be entered.
    (ii) A card entry system, requiring a card to be 'swiped'.

(e) Intruder alarms.

5.8 Much computer equipment is easily portable and therefore susceptible to theft. Laptops and small printers are designed for portability; even desktops and laser printers can be easily carried by one person. Several protective measures can be taken.

- An equipment log, including booking out procedures
- Postcoding of equipment
- Bolts and/or locks to secure equipment to desks
- Secure storage of disks and CDs

Integrity controls

> **KEY TERMS**
>
> **Data integrity** in the context of security is preserved when data is the same as in source documents and has not been accidentally or intentionally altered, destroyed or disclosed.
>
> **Systems integrity** refers to system operation conforming to the design specification despite attempts (deliberate or accidental) to make it behave incorrectly.

5.9 Data will maintain its **integrity** if it is **complete** and **not corrupted**. This means that:

(a) The original **input** of the data must be controlled in such a way as to ensure that the results are complete and correct.

(b) Any **processing and storage** of data must maintain the completeness and correctness of the data captured.

(c) That reports or other **output** should be set up so that they, too, are complete and correct.

1: Organisational information requirements

5.10 **Input controls** should ensure the **accuracy, completeness and validity** of input.

(a) **Data verification** involves ensuring data entered matches source documents.

(b) **Data validation** involves ensuring that data entered is not incomplete or unreasonable. Various checks can be used, depending on the data type.

   (i) **Check digits**. A digit calculated by the program and added to the code being checked to validate it eg modulus 11 method.

   (ii) **Control totals**. For example, a batch total totalling the entries in the batch.

   (iii) **Hash totals**. A system-generated total used to check the reasonableness of numeric codes entered.

   (iv) **Range checks**. Used to check the value entered against a sensible range, eg balance sheet account number must be between 5,000 and 9,999.

   (v) **Limit checks**. Similar to a range check, but usually based on a upper limit eg must be less than 999,999.99.

5.11 Data may be **valid** (for example in the correct format) but still not match source documents.

5.12 **Processing controls** should ensure the accuracy and completeness of processing. Programs should be subject to development controls and to rigorous testing. Periodic running of test data is also recommended.

5.13 **Output controls** should ensure the accuracy, completeness and security of output. The following measures are possible.

- Investigation and follow-up of error reports and exception reports
- Batch controls to ensure all items processed and returned
- Controls over distribution/copying of output
- Labelling of disks/tapes

5.14 **Back-up controls** aim to maintain system and data integrity. Back-up means to make a copy in anticipation of future failure or corruption. A back-up copy of a file is a duplicate copy kept separately from the main system and only used if the original fails

5.15 Data stored for a long time should be tested periodically to ensure it is still restorable – it may be subject to **damage** from environmental conditions or mishandling.

5.16 In a well-planned data back-up scheme, a copy of backed up data is delivered (preferably daily) to a secure off-site storage facility.

5.17 A tape rotation scheme can provide a restorable history from one day to several years, depending on the needs of the business.

5.18 A well-planned back-up and **archive strategy** should include:

(a) A plan and schedule for the regular back-up **of critical data**.
(b) Archive plans.
(c) A disaster recovery plan that includes off-site storage.

Part A: Information systems and the organisation

Passwords and logical access systems

5.19 Unauthorised persons may circumvent physical access controls. A **logical access system** that allocates each user a user-name and requires a password enables:

- Identification of the user
- Authentication of user identity
- Checks on user authority

Administrative controls

5.20 Measures to control personnel include the following.

- Careful recruitment
- Job rotation and enforced vacations
- Systems logs
- Review and supervision

5.21 **Segregation of duties** remains a core security requirement. This involves division of responsibilities into separate roles.

- Data capture and data entry
- Computer operations
- Systems analysis and programming

Audit trail

5.22 An **audit trail** is a record showing who has accessed a computer system and what operations he or she has performed. Audit trails are useful both for maintaining security and for recovering lost transactions.

5.23 An audit trail should be provided so that every transaction on a file contains a **unique reference** (eg a sales ledger transaction record should hold a reference to the customer order, delivery note and invoice).

Contingency controls

KEY TERM

A **contingency** is an unscheduled interruption of computing services that requires measures outside the day-to-day routine operating procedures.

5.24 The preparation of a contingency plan (also known as a disaster recovery plan) is one of the stages in the development of an organisation-wide security policy. A contingency plan is necessary in case of a major **disaster,** or if some of the **security measures** discussed elsewhere **fail**.

5.25 Any disaster recovery plan must therefore provide for:

(a) **Standby procedures** so that some operations can be performed while normal services are disrupted.

(b) **Recovery procedures** once the cause of the breakdown has been discovered or corrected.

(c) **Personnel management** policies to ensure that (a) and (b) above are implemented properly.

5.26 The contents of a disaster recovery (or contingency plan) will include the following.

Section	Comment
Definition of responsibilities	It is important that somebody (a manager or co-ordinator) is designated to take control in a crisis. This individual can then delegate specific tasks or responsibilities to other designated personnel.
Priorities	Limited resources may be available for processing. Some tasks are more important than others. These must be established in advance. Similarly, the recovery program may indicate that certain areas must be tackled first.
Backup and standby arrangements	These may be with other installations, with a company that provides such services (eg maybe the hardware vendor); or reverting to manual procedures.
Communication with staff	The problems of a disaster can be compounded by poor communication between members of staff.
Public relations	If the disaster has a public impact, the recovery team may come under pressure from the public or from the media.
Risk assessment	Some way must be found of assessing the requirements of the problem, if it is contained, with the continued operation of the organisation as a whole.

5.27 We look at the security issues surrounding the Internet in Chapter 7.

Chapter roundup

- An **information system** is an organisational and management solution, based on information technology, to any challenge posed by the environment.
- **Information** is a **valuable resource** that requires efficient management.
- Organisations **require information for** recording transactions, measuring performance, making decisions, planning and controlling.
- Strategic planning, management control and operational control may be seen as a **hierarchy** of planning and control decisions.
- **Strategic information** is used to **plan** the **objectives** of the organisation, and to **assess** whether the objectives are being met in practice.
- Tactical information is used to decide **how the resources of the business should be employed**, and to **monitor** how they are being and have been employed.
- Operational information is used to ensure that **specific operational tasks** are planned and carried out as intended.
- 'Good' information **aids understanding**. ACCURATE is a handy mnemonic for the qualities of good information.
- The **cost and value** of information are often not easy to quantify - but attempts should be made to do so.
- Information management entails:
    - Identifying current and future information needs
    - Identifying information sources
    - Collecting the information
    - Storing the information
    - Facilitating existing methods of using information and identifying new ways of using it
    - Ensuring information is communicated to those who need it
    - Ensuring information is not communicated to those who are not entitled to see it
- Organisations require different **types of information system** to provide **different levels** of information in a range of **functional areas**.
- There are six major types of Information Systems: Executive Support Systems (**ESS**), Management Information Systems (**MIS**), Decision Support Systems (**DSS**), Knowledge Work Systems (**KWS**), Office Automation Systems (**OAS**) and Transaction Processing Systems (**TPS**).
- The ease of which data flows from one system to another depends on the extent of **integration** between systems.
- Information is a valuable resource and a key tool in the quest for a competitive advantage. **Security controls**, **integrity controls** and **contingency controls** are used to protect data and information.

Quick quiz

1. List five uses of information.
2. List five characteristics of strategic information.
3. List five characteristics of tactical information.
4. List five characteristics of operational information.
5. Match the following abbreviations with the appropriate description.

    TPS, OAS, KWS, MIS, DSS, ESS.

    (a) Information systems that facilitate the creation and integration of new knowledge into an organisation

    (b) A system that pools data from internal and external sources and makes information available to senior managers in an easy-to-use form.

    (c) Computer systems designed to increase the productivity of data and information workers.

    (d) A system that converts data, mainly from internal sources into information (eg summary reports, exception reports).

    (e) A system that combines data and analytical models or data analysis tools to support semi-structured and unstructured decision making.

    (f) A system to perform and record routine transactions.

6. 'Full integration across all organisational information systems is vital.' Do you agree with this statement? Justify your answer (very briefly).

Part A: Information systems and the organisation

Answers to quick quiz

1. Planning, controlling, recording transactions, measuring performance and making decisions.

2. [Five of]

    Derived from both internal and external sources

    Summarised at a high level

    Relevant to the long term

    Concerned with the whole organisation

    Often prepared on an 'ad hoc' basis

    Both quantitative and qualitative

    Uncertain, as the future cannot be predicted accurately

3. [Five of]

    Primarily generated internally (but may have a limited external component)

    Summarised at a lower level

    Relevant to the short and medium term

    Concerned with activities or departments

    Prepared routinely and regularly

    Based on quantitative measures

4. [Five of]

    Derived from internal sources

    Detailed, being the processing of raw data

    Relevant to the immediate term

    Task-specific

    Prepared very frequently

    Largely quantitative

5. (a) Knowledge Work Systems (KWS).

    (b) Executive Support Systems (ESS).

    (c) Office Automation Systems (OAS).

    (d) Management Information Systems (MIS).

    (e) Decision Support Systems (DSS).

    (f) Transaction Processing Systems (TPS).

6. Disagree. A high degree of integration is usually desirable, but in all cases the costs of integration should be considered against the value of the expected benefits integration would bring.

Now try the questions below from the Exam Question Bank. Question 16 includes detailed guidance with the question and answer.

Number	Level	Marks	Time
12	Exam	10	18 mins
16 (b)	Exam	8	14 mins

Chapter 2

THE STRATEGIC ROLE OF INFORMATION SYSTEMS

Topic list	Syllabus reference
1 Strategic planning	3(a), 3(c)
2 Developing a strategy for information systems and information technology	1(a), 3(c)
3 PEST analysis	3(b)
4 PEST analysis and information systems strategic planning	3(b), 3(c)

Introduction

The role of information systems has changed from that of simply recording transactions and providing accounting information to the central and crucial role they now hold within almost all organisations.

In this chapter we look at the **strategic role** of information systems.

Study guide

3/4 – Strategic role of information systems

- Explain the strategic role of information systems
- Identify the major management challenges to building and using information systems in organisations *(Also see Chapter 8)*
- Describe the central and crucial role that information systems have within an organisation
- Evaluate information systems and the strategic planning process
- Identify opportunities for use in forecasting, analysing competition, scenario planning, generic strategies/business positioning, improving performance, measuring performance, opportunities for cost reduction, opportunities for service improvement, sales performance, evaluating proposals *(Also see Chapters 6 and 7)*

9 – Organisational requirements

- Evaluate linking information systems to the business plan
- Discuss the requirement to understand the business value of information systems

10 – Strategic analysis

- Evaluate the importance of Political, Economic, Social and Technological influences on organisations. PEST analysis as a tool for information systems strategic planning
- Apply PEST analysis to scenarios

11 – Strategic information systems

- Discuss the role of Strategic Information Systems as computer system within an organisation that enables changes to goals, processes, products, services or environmental relationships *(Also see Chapter 6)*

Part A: Information systems and the organisation

> **26 – Individual's information requirements**
> - Describe the design of Critical Success Factors *(Also see Chapter 8)*
> - Identify sources of data
> - Identify key performance indicators and how to measure performance
> - Identify how information systems can support the tasks of the manager *(Also see Chapter 9)*
>
> ## Exam guide
>
> Examination questions, particularly in Section A of the paper, are likely to include a strategic element. When reading the Part A Scenario, be aware of strategic issues such as integration of information systems with the business plan and the influence of the external environment.
>
> The Critical Success Factor approach and Porter's value chain are also likely to prove popular question topics.

1 STRATEGIC PLANNING

1.1 **Strategic planning** is a complex process which involves taking a view of the **organisation** and the **future** that it is likely to encounter, and then attempting to organise the structure and resources of the organisation accordingly.

> **KEY TERMS**
>
> **Strategy** can be defined as 'a course of action, including the specification of resources required, to achieve a specific outcome'.
>
> **Strategic planning** is the formulation, evaluation and selection of strategies for the purpose of preparing a long-term plan of action to attain objectives.

1.2 Three general levels of strategy can be identified: corporate, business and functional/operational.

Corporate strategy

1.3 **Corporate strategy** is concerned with what types of business the organisation is in. It denotes the most general level of strategy in an organisation.

Business strategy

> **KEY TERM**
>
> **Business strategy** is concerned with how an organisation approaches a particular product or market.

1.4 This can involve decisions as to whether, in principle, a company should:

(a) Segment the market and specialise in particularly profitable areas.
(b) Compete by offering a wider range of products.

1.5 Some large, diversified firms have separate **strategic business units** dealing with particular areas.

1.6 Characteristics of decisions relating to corporate and/or business strategy

Characteristic	Comment
Scope of activities	Products and markets – decisions might involve diversifying into a new line of business or into a new market. It might mean global expansion or contraction.
Environment	The organisation counters threats and exploits opportunities in the environment (customers, clients, competitors).
Capability	The organisation matches its activities to its resources: ie it does what it is able to do.
Resources	Strategy involves choices about allocating or obtaining resources now and in future.
Operations	Strategic decisions always affect operations.
Values	The value systems of people in power influence them to understand the world in a certain way.
Direction	Strategic decisions have a medium or long-term impact.
Complex	Strategic decisions involve uncertainty about the future, integrating the operations of the organisation and change.

Functional/operational strategies; information systems strategy

1.7 Information systems strategy is an example of a **functional/operational strategy** (although in some cases it may have strategic implications). Functional/operational strategies deal with specialised areas of activity.

Functional area	Comment
Information systems	A firm's information systems are becoming increasingly important, as an item of expenditure, as administrative support and as a tool for competitive strength.
Marketing	Devising products and services, pricing, promoting and distributing them, in order to satisfy customer needs at a profit.
Production	Factory location, manufacturing techniques, outsourcing etc.
Finance	Ensuring that the firm has enough financial resources to fund its other strategies.
Human resources	Secure personnel of the right skills in the right quantity at the right time.
R&D	New products and techniques.

Part A: Information systems and the organisation

1.8 The relationship between corporate, business and operational strategies is shown in the following diagram.

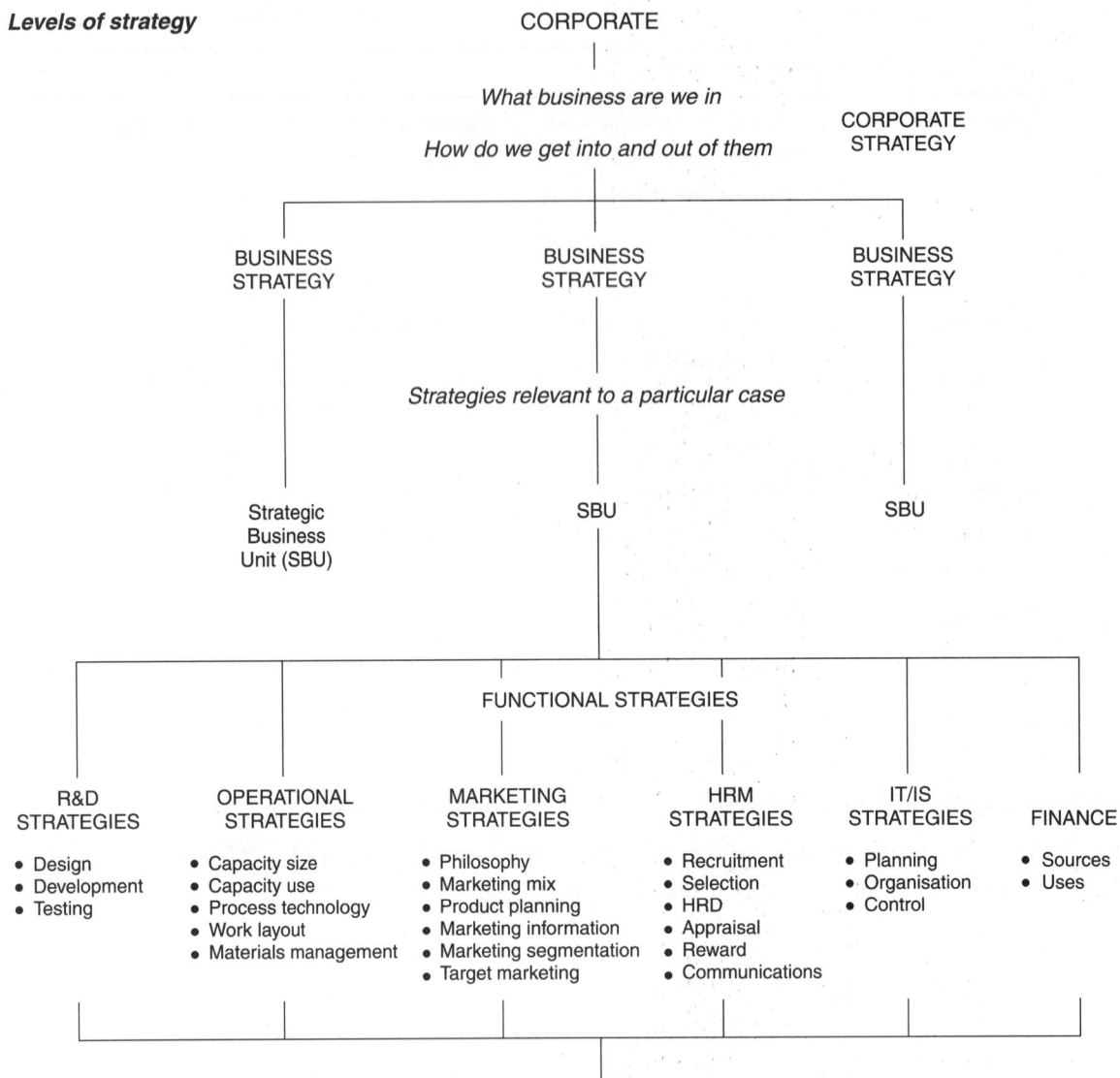

Formulating strategic business objectives: The rational model

1.9 Strategic planning divides into a number of different stages: strategic **analysis**, strategic **choice** and **implementation**.

(a) **Strategic analysis** involves the steps outlined in the following table (relevant models referred to are covered throughout this Text).

	Stage	Comment	Key tools, models, techniques
Step 1.	Mission and/or vision	Mission denotes values, the business's rationale for existing; vision refers to where the organisation intends to be in a few years time	• Mission statement
Step 2.	Goals	Interpret the mission to different stakeholders	• Stakeholder analysis
Step 3.	Objectives	Quantified embodiments of mission	• Measures such as profitability, time scale, deadlines
Step 4.	Environmental analysis	Identify opportunities and threats	• PEST analysis • Porter's 5 forces • Scenario building
Step 5.	Position audit or situation analysis	Identify strengths and weaknesses Firm's **current** resources, products, customers, systems, structure, results, efficiency, effectiveness	• Resource audit • Distinctive competence • Value chain • Product life cycle • Boston (BCG) matrix • Marketing audit
Step 6.	Corporate appraisal	Combines Steps 4 and 5	• SWOT analysis charts
Step 7.	Gap analysis	Compares outcomes of Step 6 with Step 3	• Gap analysis

Question 1

List five ways in which corporate and business strategy are relevant to the types of information system required in an organisation?

Answer

Five ways are shown below. You may have come up with others.

(a) Information is needed to shape corporate and business strategy.

(b) Information systems provide information that monitors progress towards strategic objectives.

(c) Business objectives are becoming increasingly customer focused. Good customer service requires good quality information available on demand.

(d) A strategy of growth will require a corresponding increase in the information system.

(e) A change of strategy may mean a new information system is required.

Part A: Information systems and the organisation

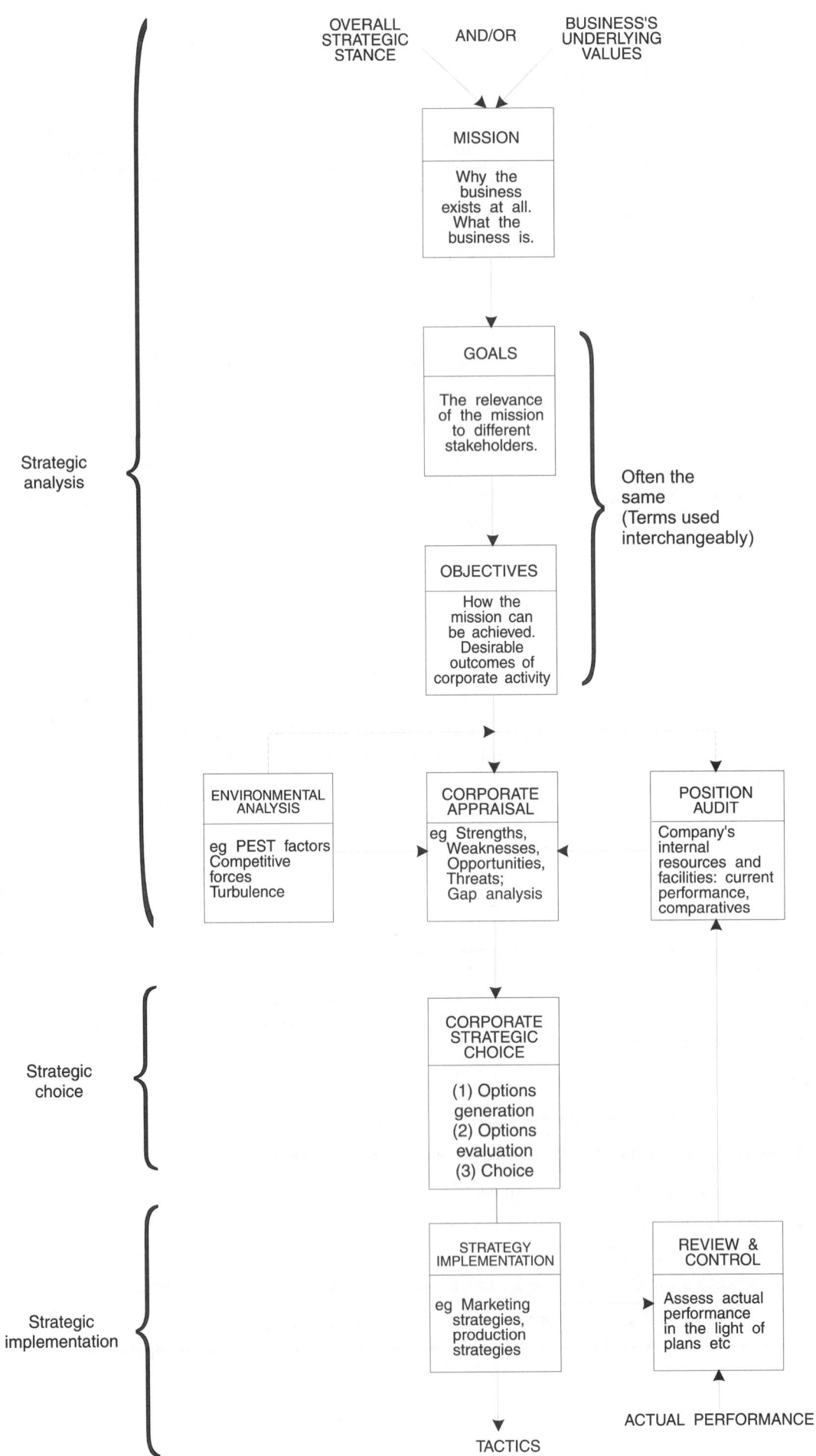

(b) **Strategic choice**

Stage	Comment	Key tools, models, techniques
Strategic options generation	Come up with new ideas: • How to compete (competitive advantage) • Where to compete • Method of growth	• Value chain analysis • Scenario building • Porter's generic strategic choices • Ansoff's growth vector • Acquisition vs organic growth
Strategic options evaluation	Normally, each strategy has to be evaluated on the basis of • Acceptability • Suitability • Feasibility • Environmental fit	• Stakeholder analysis • Risk analysis • Decision-making tools such as decision trees, matrices, ranking and scoring methods • Financial measures (eg ROCE, DCF)

Strategy selection involves choosing between the alternative strategies.

(i) The competitive strategies are the generic strategies for competitive advantage an organisation will pursue. They determine **how** you compete.

(ii) Product-market strategies (which markets you should enter or leave) determine **where** you compete and the direction of growth.

(iii) Institutional strategies (ie relationships with other organisations) determine the method of **growth**.

Case example

Strategic planning software packages

There are some software packages available designed to assist specifically with strategic planning.

Such packages are not used widely, probably because strategic decisions have to take into account so many different factors, and also because strategic decisions are seen as too important to be made by a software package.

One such package is Business Insight - an American package costing around £250. The system is built on rules that draw on concepts put forward by management and marketing experts such as Porter and Kotler.

Data is input under a series of headings such as 'Market Definition', 'Competition', 'Suppliers' and 'Financials'. The package produces a series of 'Observations', generated by comparing the input data with the rules in the system. For example one observation might be that the business could 'expect very strong competitive rivalry'.

The advantage of tools such as these is that they force managers to think about strategic issues, and they draw upon ideas that managers might not know about or realise the relevance of.

Disadvantages include; the package is only as good as the rules contained within it, 'standard' management rules may be of limited value in certain circumstances, the analysis depends on user judgements ('rate your business's ability to do X on a scale of 1 to 10').

(c) **Strategy implementation** is the conversion of the strategy into detailed plans or objectives for operating units. This involves:

- **Resource** planning (ie finance, personnel) involves assessing the key tasks
- **Operations** planning
- **Organisation** structure and control systems

Case example

Goold and Quinn (in *Strategic Control*) cite Ciba-Geigy, a Swiss-based global firm with chemicals and pharmaceuticals businesses, as an example of formal strategic control and planning processes.

(a) Strategic planning starts with the identification of strategic business sectors, in other words, areas of activity where there are identifiable markets and where profit, management and resources are largely independent of the other sectors.

(b) Strategic plans containing:

(i) Long term objectives
(ii) Key strategies
(iii) Funds requirements

are drawn up, based on a 'comprehensive analysis of market attractiveness', competitors etc.

(c) At corporate level, these plans are reviewed. Head office examines all the different plans and, with a 7-10 year planning horizon, the total risk, profitability, cash flow and resource requirements are assessed. Business sectors are allocated specific targets and funds.

Why have an IS/IT strategy?

1.10 A strategy for information systems and information technology is **justified** on the grounds that IS/IT.

- Involves **high costs**
- Is **critical to the success** of many organisations
- Is now used as part of the commercial strategy in the battle for **competitive advantage**
- Impacts on **customer service**
- Affects **all levels of management**
- Affects the way **management information** is created and presented
- **Requires effective management** to obtain the maximum benefit
- Involves many **stakeholders** inside and outside the organisation

IS/IT is a high cost activity

1.11 Many organisations invest large amounts of money in IS, but not always wisely.

1.12 The unmanaged proliferation of IT is likely to lead to expensive mistakes. Two key benefits of IT; the ability to **share** information and the **avoidance of duplication,** are likely to be lost.

1.13 All IT expenditure should therefore require approval to ensure that it enhances rather than detracts from the overall information strategy.

2: The strategic role of information systems

IS/IT is critical to the success of many organisations

1.14 When developing an IS/IT strategy a firm should assess **how important IT is** in the provision of products and services. The role that IT fills in an organisation will vary depending on the type of organisations. IS/IT could be:

- A **support** activity
- A **key** operational activity
- **Potentially** very important
- A **strategic** activity (without IT the firm could not function at all)
- A source of **competitive advantage**

Information and competitive advantage

1.15 It is now recognised that information can be used as a source of competitive advantage. Many organisations have recognised the importance of information and developed an **information strategy**, covering both IS and IT.

1.16 Information systems should be **tied in some way to business objectives**.

(a) The **corporate strategy** is used to plan functional **business plans** which provide guidelines for information-based activities.

(b) On a year-by-year basis, the **annual plan** would try to tie in business plans with information systems projects for particular applications, perhaps through the functioning of a **steering committee**.

IT can impact significantly on the business context

1.17 IT is an **enabling** technology, and can produce dramatic changes in individual businesses and whole industries. For example, the deregulation of US airline system encouraged the growth of computerised seat-reservation systems (eg SABRE, as used by American Airlines which always displayed American Airlines flights preferentially). IT can be both a **cause** of major changes in doing business and a **response** to them.

IT affects all levels of management

1.18 IT has become a routine feature of office life, **a facility for everyone to use**. IT is no longer used solely by specialist staff.

IT and its effect on management information

1.19 The use of IT has permitted the design of a range of information systems. Executive Support Systems (ESS), Management Information Systems (MIS), Decision Support Systems (DSS), Knowledge Work Systems (KWS) and Office Automation Systems (OAS) can be used to improve the quality of management information.

1.20 IT has also had an effect on **production processes**. For example, Computer Integrated Manufacturing (CIM) changed the methods and cost profiles of many manufacturing processes. The techniques used to **measure and record costs** have also adapted to the use of IT.

IT and stakeholders

1.21 Parties interested in an organisation's use of IT are as follows.

Part A: Information systems and the organisation

(a) **Other business users** - for example to facilitate Electronic Data Interchange (EDI).

(b) **Governments** – eg telecommunications regulation, regulation of electronic commerce.

(c) **IT manufacturers** looking for new markets and product development. User-groups may be able to influence software producers.

(d) **Consumers** - for example as reassurance that product quality is high, consumers may also be interested if information is provided via the Internet.

(e) **Employees** - as IT affects work practices.

Question 2

Babbage and Newman plc is a company with an established base of IT applications. The finance department has a fully computerised accounting system. The marketing department has developed a primitive customer modelling package. The production department 'does not need IT'.

The Finance Director is in charge of IT at Babbage and Newman. He proposes in the annual corporate budget a 10% increase in IT expenditure based on last year, for the relevant departments. This will enable system upgrades.

Comment briefly on the information strategy at Babbage and Newman.

Answer

There is no strategy at all. The Finance Director regards IT as a cost. Moreover the IT 'strategy' is directed to enhancing its existing base (eg in the accounts department) rather than areas where it might prove competitively valuable (eg in marketing).

Information systems and corporate/business strategy

1.22 It is widely accepted that an organisation's information system should **support** corporate and business strategy. In some circumstances an information system may have a greater influence and actually help **determine** corporate / business strategy. For example:

(a) IS/IT may provide a possible source of competitive advantage. This could involve new technology not yet available to others or simply using existing technology in a different way.

(b) The information system may help in formulating business strategy by **providing information** from internal and external sources.

(c) Developments in IT may provide **new channels** for distributing and collecting information, and /or for conducting transactions eg the Internet.

1.23 Some common ways in which IS/IT have had a major impact on organisations are explained below.

(a) **The type of products or services that are made and sold.** For example, consumer markets have seen the emergence of home computers, compact discs and satellite dishes for receiving satellite TV; industrial markets have seen the emergence of custom-built microchips, robots and local area networks for office information systems. Technological changes can be relatively minor, such as the introduction of tennis and squash rackets with graphite frames, fluoride toothpaste and turbo-powered car engines.

(b) **The way in which products are made.** There is a continuing trend towards the use of automation and computer aided design and manufacture. The manufacturing

environment is undergoing rapid changes with the growth of advanced manufacturing technology. These are changes in both apparatus and technique.

(c) **The way in which services are provided**. High-street banks encourage customers to use 'hole-in-the-wall' cash dispensers, or telephone or Internet banking. Most larger shops now use computerised **Point of Sale terminals** at cash desks. Many organisations use **e-commerce**: selling products and services over the Internet.

(d) **The way in which markets are identified**. Database systems make it much easier to analyse the market place.

(e) **The way in which employees are mobilised**. Computerisation encourages delayering of organisational hierarchies, and greater workforce empowerment and skills. Using technology frequently requires changes in working methods. This is a change in organisation.

(f) **The way in which firms are managed**. Computerisation encourages 'delayering' of organisational hierarchies (in other words, the reduction of management layers), but requires greater workforce skills. Using technology often requires changes in working methods.

(g) The means and extent of **communications** with customers.

1.24 Benefits of technological change might therefore be as follows.

- To **cut production costs** and so (probably) to **reduce sales prices** to the customer
- To develop **better quality** products and services
- To develop products and services that **did not exist before**
- To **provide** products or services to customers **more quickly or effectively**
- To **free staff** from repetitive work and to tap their creativity

1.25 An important role of the information technology and finance functions is to help ensure the agreed strategy is proceeding according to plan. The table below outlines the rationale behind this view.

	Traditional view	Strategic implications
Cost	The finance and information technology functions can be relatively expensive	Shared services and outsourcing could be used to capture cost savings
IT	IT has traditionally been transaction based	IT/IS should be integrated with business strategy
Value	The finance and IT functions do not add value	Redesign the functions
Strategy	Accountants and IT managers are seen as scorekeepers and administrators rather than as a business partner during the strategic planning process	Change from cost-orientated to market-orientated ie development of more effective strategic planning systems

The importance of managing technology

1.26 It is argued that **success or failure** of an organisation's use of technology is due largely not to the technology itself, but how its selection, implementation and use is **managed**. For example, information systems will fail for any of the following reasons.

(a) They are used to tackle the **wrong problem** (ie the use of IT has not been thought through in the context of the wider organisational context).

(b) Senior management are not interested.

(c) Users are ignored in design and development.

(d) No attention is given to behavioural factors in design and operation.

1.27 If an organisation develops and follows a realistic information strategy and information systems plan for information systems and technology then there is less chance that these problems will arise.

1.28 We look at common causes of information system failure in greater depth in Chapter 8.

1.29 Organisations should develop an **information systems plan** that supports their overall business plan. The plan should contain the following:

(a) Overall organisation goals.

(b) How information systems and information technology contributes to attaining these goals

(c) Key management decisions regarding hardware, software, data and telecommunications

(d) Specific dates and milestones relating to IS/IT projects

(e) Financial information such as a budget and cost-benefit analysis

2 DEVELOPING A STRATEGY FOR INFORMATION SYSTEMS AND INFORMATION TECHNOLOGY

> **KEY TERMS**
>
> The **Information Systems (IS) strategy** refers to the long-term plan concerned with exploiting IS and IT either to support business strategies or create new strategic options.
>
> **Strategic information systems** are systems at any level of an organisation that change goals, processes, products, services or environmental relationships with the aim of gaining competitive advantage.
>
> **Strategic-level systems** are systems used by senior managers for long-term decision making.

2.1 An IS/IT strategy should be developed with the aim of ensuring IS/IT is utilised as efficiently and effectively as possible in the pursuit of organisational goals and objectives.

2.2 The inputs and outputs of the IS/IT strategic planning process are summarised on the following diagram. (We explain SWOT analysis in the context of information systems strategy in Chapter 6.)

2: The strategic role of information systems

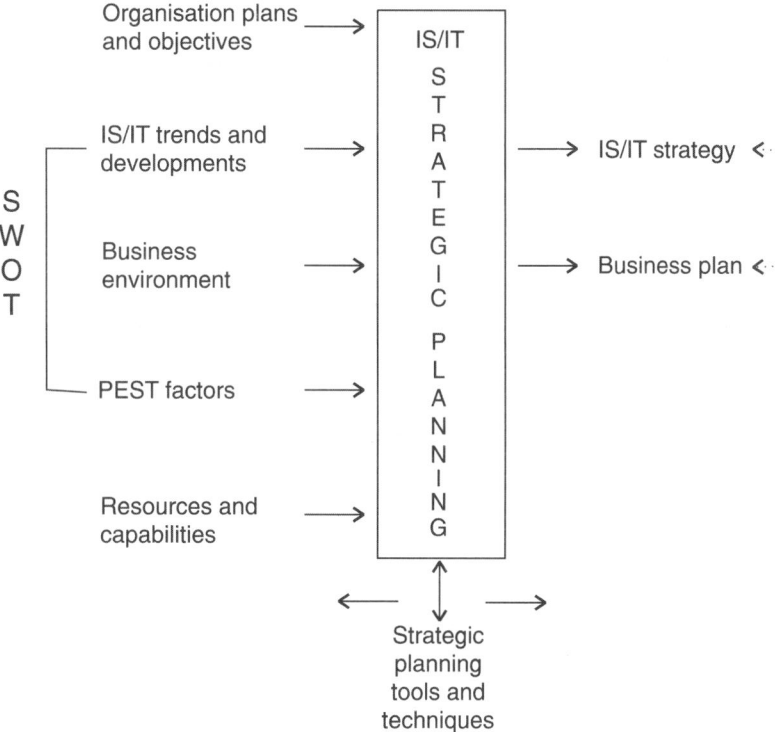

2.3 An IS strategy therefore deals with the integration of an organisation's information requirements and information systems planning with its **long-term overall goals** (customer service etc). IS strategy deals with what applications should be developed and where resources should be deployed.

2.4 The **information technology (IT) strategy** leads on from the IS strategy above. It deals with the **technologies** of:

- Computing
- Communications
- Data
- Application systems

2.5 This provides a framework for the analysis and design of the **technological infrastructure** of an organisation. This strategy indicates how the information systems strategies that rely on technology will be **implemented**.

Establishing organisational information requirements

2.6 The identification of organisational information needs and the information systems framework to satisfy them is at the heart of a strategy for information systems and information technology.

2.7 The IS and IT strategies should complement the overall strategy for the organisation. It follows therefore that the IS/IT strategy should be considered whenever the organisation prepares other long-term strategies such as marketing or production.

Earl's three leg analysis

2.8 The writer Earl devised a method for the development of IS strategies. His method identified three legs of IS strategy development:

Part A: Information systems and the organisation

- Business led (top down emphasis, focuses on **business plans and goals**)
- Infrastructure led (bottom up emphasis, focuses on **current systems**)
- Mixed (inside out emphasis, focuses on **IT/IS opportunities**)

A diagrammatic representation of the three legs follows.

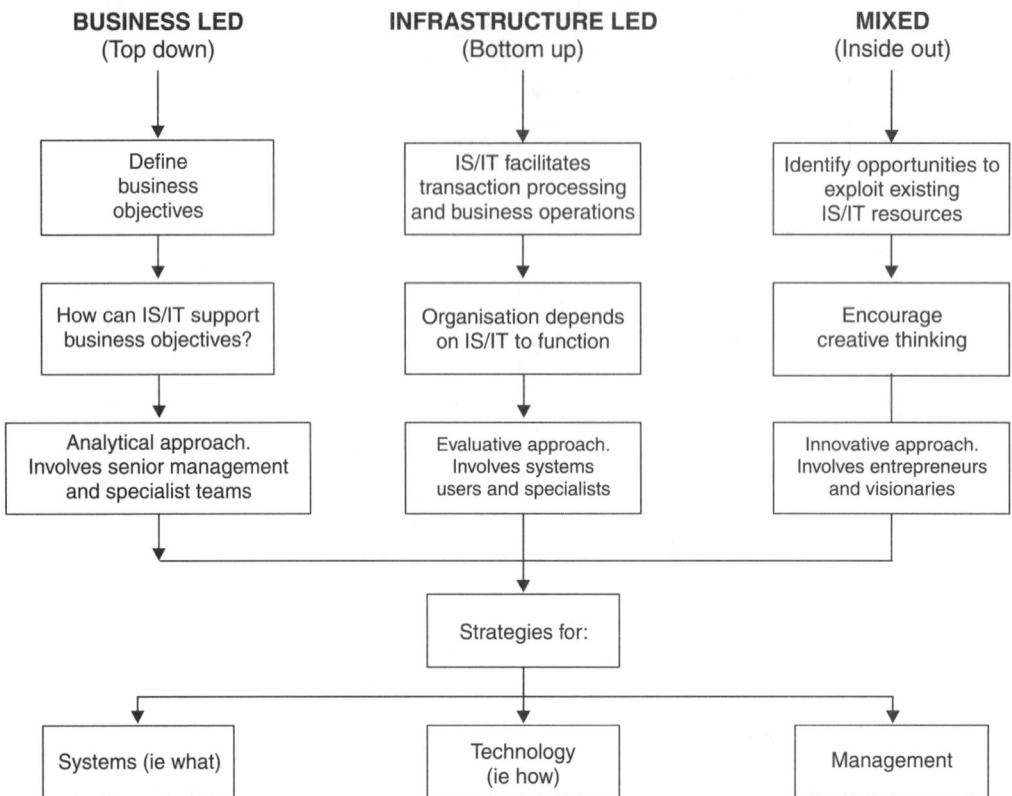

2.9 Earl's three leg analysis is explained in the following table.

Leg or approach	Comment
Business led (top down)	The overall objectives of an organisation are identified and then IS/IT systems are implemented to enable these objectives to be met. This approach relies on the ability to break down the organisation and its objectives to a series of business objectives and processes and to be able to identify the information needs of these.
	This is an analytical approach. The people usually involved are senior management and specialist teams.
Infrastructure led (bottom up)	Computer based transaction systems are critical to business operations. The organisation focuses on systems that facilitate transactions and other basic operations.
	This is an evaluative approach. The people usually involved are system users and specialists.
Mixed (inside out)	The organisation encourages ideas that will exploit existing IT and IS resources. Innovations may come from entrepreneurial managers or individuals outside the formal planning process.
	This is an innovative/creative approach. The people involved are entrepreneurs and/or visionaries.

2.10 We will now look at a number of other methodologies and frameworks that may be used as part of the information systems strategy development process.

2: The strategic role of information systems

Enterprise analysis

> **KEY TERM**
>
> **Enterprise analysis** involves examining the entire organisation in terms of structure, processes, functions and data elements to identify the key elements and attributes of organisational data and information.

2.11 Enterprise analysis is sometimes referred to as **business systems planning**. This approach involves the following steps.

Step 1. Ask a large sample of managers about:

- How they use information
- Where they get information
- What their objectives are
- What their data requirements are
- How they make decisions
- The influence of the environment

Step 2. Aggregate the findings from *Step 1* into subunits, functions, processes and data matrices. Compile a Process/data class matrix to show:

- What data classes are required to support particular organisational processes
- Which processes are the creators and users of data

Step 3. Use the matrix to identify areas that information systems should focus on, eg on processes that create data.

2.12

Enterprise analysis approach – strength	Comment
Comprehensive	The enterprise analysis approach gives a comprehensive view of the organisation and its use of data and systems.

2.13

Enterprise analysis approach – weaknesses	Comment
Unwieldy	The enterprise analysis approach results in a mountain of data that is expensive to collect and difficult to analyse.
Focussed on existing information	Survey questions tend to focus on how systems and information are currently used, rather than on how information that is needed could be provided. The analysis has tended to result in existing systems being automated rather than looking at the wider picture.

Critical success factors

2.14 The use of **critical success factors** (**CSF**s) can help to determine the information requirements of an organisation. CSFs are operational goals. If operational goals are achieved the organisation should be successful.

Part A: Information systems and the organisation

> **KEY TERM**
>
> **Critical success factors** are a small number of key operational goals vital to the success of an organisation. CSFs are used to establish organisational information requirements.

2.15 The CSF approach is sometimes referred to as the **strategic analysis** approach. The philosophy behind this approach is that managers should focus on a small number of objectives, and information systems should be focussed on providing information to enable managers to monitor these objectives.

2.16 **Two separate types** of critical success factor can be identified. A **monitoring** CSF is used to keep abreast of existing activities and operations. A **building** CSF helps to measure the progress of new initiatives and is more likely to be relevant at senior executive level.

- **Monitoring** CSFs are important for **maintaining** business
- **Building** CSFs are important for **expanding** business

2.17 One approach to **determining the factors** which are critical to success in performing a function or making a decision is as follows.

- List the organisation's **corporate objectives and goals**
- Determine **which factors are critical** for accomplishing the **objectives**
- Determine a small number of **key performance indicators** for each factor

2.18 EXAMPLE

One of the **objectives** of an organisation might be to maintain a high level of service direct from stock without holding uneconomic stock levels. This is first quantified in the form of a **goal**, which might be to ensure that 95% of orders for goods can be satisfied directly from stock, while minimising total stockholding costs and stock levels.

CSFs might then be identified as the following.

- **Supplier performance** in terms of quality and lead times
- Reliability of **stock records**
- **Forecasting** of demand variations

2.19 The determination of **key performance indicators** for each of these CSFs is not necessarily straightforward. Some measures might use **factual**, objectively verifiable, data, while others might make use of **'softer' concepts**, such as opinions, perceptions and hunches.

2.20 For example, the reliability of stock records can be measured by means of physical stock counts, either at discrete intervals or on a rolling basis. Forecasting of demand variations will be much harder to measure.

2.21 Where measures use quantitative data, performance can be measured in a number of ways.

- In **physical quantities**, for example units produced or units sold
- In **money terms**, for example profit, revenues, costs or variances
- In **ratios** and **percentages**

2: The strategic role of information systems

Data sources for CSFs

2.22 In general terms *Rockart* identifies four **general sources** of CSFs.

(a) The **industry** that the business is in.

(b) The **company** itself and its situation within the industry.

(c) The **environment**, for example consumer trends, the economy, and political factors of the country in which the company operates.

(d) Temporal organisational factors, which are **areas of corporate activity** which are currently **unacceptable** and represent a cause of concern, for example, high stock levels.

2.23 More specifically, possible internal and external data sources for CSFs include the following.

(a) **The existing system**. The existing system can be used to generate reports showing **failures to meet CSFs.**

(b) **Customer service department**. This department will maintain details of **complaints** received, **refunds** handled, **customer enquiries** etc. These should be reviewed to ensure all failure types have been identified.

(c) **Customers**. A survey of customers, provided that it is properly designed and introduced, would reveal (or confirm) those areas where **satisfaction** is high or low.

(d) **Competitors**. Competitors' operations, pricing structures and publicity should be closely monitored.

(e) **Accounting system**. The **profitability** of various aspects of the operation is probably a key factor in any review of CSFs.

(f) **Consultants**. A specialist consultancy might be able to perform a detailed review of the system in order to identify ways of satisfying CSFs.

2.24 The CSF approach to IS/IT planning is illustrated in the following diagram.

Part A: Information systems and the organisation

The critical success factor approach to IS/IT planning

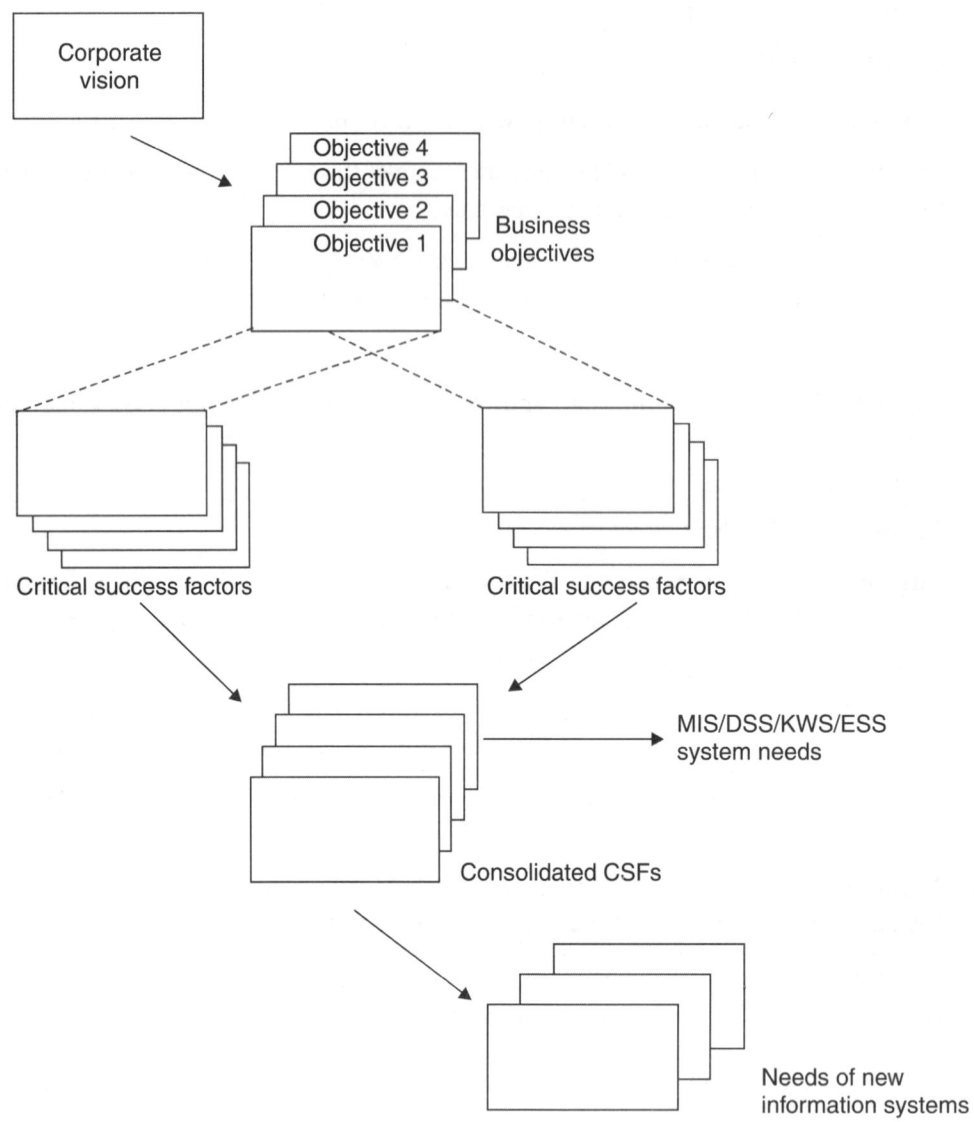

Source: IT Strategy for Business, Joe Peppard
Chapter 4, Garret Hickey

CSF approach: strengths and weaknesses

2.25

CSF approach - strengths	Comment
Takes into account environmental changes	The CSF approach requires managers to examine the environment and consider how it influences their information requirements.
Focuses on information	The approach doesn't just aim to establish organisational objectives. It also looks at the information and information systems required to establish and monitor progress towards these objectives.
Facilitates top management participation in system development	The clear link between information requirements and individual and organisational objectives encourages top management involvement in system (DSS, ESS) design.

2.26

CSF approach - weaknesses	Comment
Aggregation of individual CSFs	Wide-ranging individual CSFs need to be aggregated into a clear organisational plan. This process relies heavily on judgement. Managers who feel their input has been neglected may be alienated.
Bias towards top management	When gathering information to establish CSFs it is usually top management who are interviewed. These managers may lack knowledge of operational activities.
CSFs change often	The business environment, managers and information systems technology are subject to constant change. CSFs and systems must be updated to account for change.

Parson's six information systems strategies

2.27 The writer Parsons identified six possible generic Information System (IS) strategies. These are outlined in the following table.

Generic strategy for IS	Comment
Centrally planned	The logic of this approach is that those planning IS developments should have an understanding of the overall strategic direction. Business and IS strategy are viewed as being closely linked.
Leading edge	There is a belief that innovative technology use can create competitive advantage, and therefore that risky investment in unproven technologies may generate large returns. The organisation must have the motivation and ability to commit large amounts of money and other resources. Users must be enthusiastic and willing to support new initiatives.
Free market	This strategy is based on the belief that the market makes the best decisions. The IS function is a competitive business unit, which must be prepared to achieve a return on its resources. The department may have to compete with outside providers.
Monopoly	The direct opposite to the free market strategy. This strategy is based upon the belief that information is an organisational asset that should be controlled by a single service provider.
Scarce resource	This strategy is based on the premise that information systems use limited resources, and therefore all IS development requires a clear justification. Budgetary controls are in place and should be adhered to. New projects should be subject to Cost Benefit Analysis (CBA).
Necessary evil	IS/IT is seen as a necessary evil of modern business. IS/IT is allocated enough resource only to meet basic needs. This strategy is usually adopted in organisations that believe that information is not important to the business.

Part A: Information systems and the organisation

3 PEST ANALYSIS

3.1 Organisations exist within an **environment** which strongly influences what they do and whether they survive and develop. Strategic plans must take account of environmental influences if they are to be realistic and achievable. These environmental influences are shown in the following diagram.

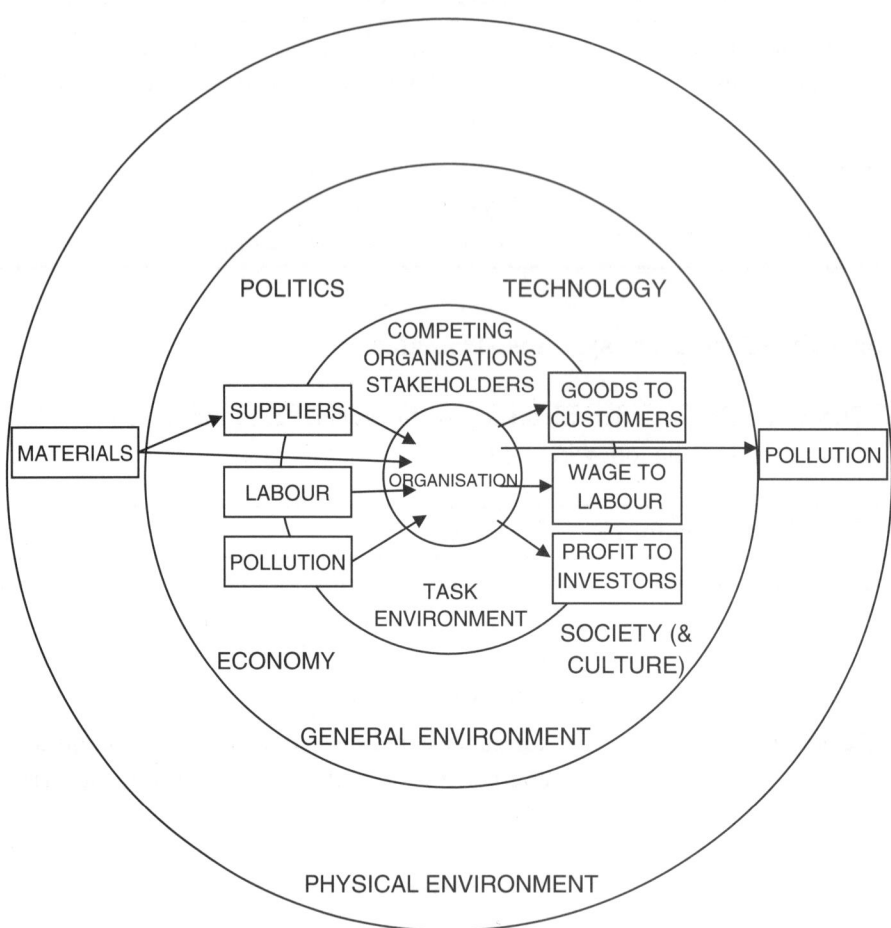

3.2 The **general environment** covers all the Political/legal, Economic, Social/cultural and Technological (PEST) influences in the countries an organisation operates in.

3.3 The **task environment** relates to factors of particular relevance to a firm, such as its competitors, customers and suppliers of resources.

3.4 One purpose of a strategy is to ensure **environmental fit**, relating a company to its environment.

3.5 Any strategy is made in conditions of **uncertainty**. The environment is a major source of this uncertainty.

(a) It contains **opportunities and threats** which may influence the organisation's activities and may even threaten its existence.

(b) The environment is so **varied** that many organisations will find it difficult to discern its effects on them.

(c) Firms can conduct **audits** and build models to identify which of the many different sorts of environmental factors have a significant influence.

3.6 Environmental issues may be of:

- **Long-term impact,** which can be dealt with in advance
- **Short-term impact,** which require crisis management

The political and legal environment

3.7 The **political environment** affects an organisation in a number of ways.

- Laws and legislation provide a legal framework
- Government policy may directly impact upon a business or industry
- The government's overall conduct of its economic policy is relevant

3.8 In the UK, laws include common law, parliamentary legislation and government regulations derived from it, and obligations arising out of EU membership and other treaties.

3.9 **Legal factors affecting all companies**

Factor	Example
General legal framework: contract, tort, agency	Basic ways of doing business, negligence proceedings, copyright laws, software licences.
Criminal law	Theft, insider dealing, bribery, deception.
Company law	Directors and their duties, reporting requirements, takeover proceedings, shareholders' rights, insolvency.
Employment law	Trade Union recognition, Social Chapter provisions, minimum wage, unfair dismissal, redundancy, maternity, Equal Opportunities.
Health and Safety	Fire precautions, safety procedures, workstation design.
Data protection	Use of information about employees and customers eg (UK) Data Protection Act (1998), privacy.
Marketing and sales	Laws to protect consumers (eg refunds and replacement, 'cooling off' period after credit agreements), what is or isn't allowed in advertising
Environment	Pollution control, waste disposal.
Tax law	Corporation tax payment, Collection of income tax (PAYE) and National Insurance contributions, VAT.

3.10 The political environment is not simply limited to legal factors. Governments are responsible for enforcing and creating a stable framework in which business can be done. The quality of government policy is important in providing the right:

- Physical infrastructure (eg transport, communications)
- Social infrastructure (education, a welfare safety net, law enforcement)
- Market infrastructure (enforceable contracts, policing corruption)

3.11 **Political change** complicates the planning activities of many firms The political risk in a decision is the risk that political factors will invalidate the strategy and perhaps severely damage the organisation. Examples are wars, political chaos, corruption and nationalisation.

Part A: Information systems and the organisation

The economic environment

3.12 Some of the major ways in which the economic environment influences organisations are outlined in the following table.

Economic factor	Impact
Overall growth or fall in Gross Domestic Product	Increased/decreased demand for goods and services.
Local economic trends	Type of industry in the area. Office/factory rents. Labour rates. House prices.
National economic trends:	
• Inflation	Low in most countries; distorts business decisions; wage inflation compensates for price inflation
• Interest rates	How much it costs to borrow money affects **cash flow**. Some businesses carry a high level of debt. How much customers can afford to spend is also affected as rises in interest rates affect people's mortgage payments.
• Tax levels	Corporation tax affects how much firms can invest or return to shareholders. Income tax and VAT affect how much consumers have to spend, hence demand.
• Government spending	Suppliers to the government (eg construction firms) are affected by spending.
• The business cycle	Economic activity may fluctuate between periods of growth followed by decline. In the past, the UK economy has been characterised by periods of 'boom' and 'bust'. Government policy can cause, exacerbate or mitigate such trends.

3.13 The **forecast state of the economy** will influence the planning process for organisations which operate within it. In times of boom and increased demand and consumption, the overall planning problem will be to **identify** the demand. Conversely, in times of recession, the emphasis will be on cost-effectiveness, continuing profitability, survival and competition.

3.14 The **impact of international factors** are shown in the following table.

Factor	Impact
Exchange rates	Cost of imports, selling prices and value of exports; cost of hedging against fluctuations
Characteristics of overseas markets. Different rates of economic growth, prosperity, taxation etc.	Desirable overseas markets (demand) or sources of supply. With the advent of the World Wide Web even the smallest organisation can have an international presence.
Capital, flows and trade	Investment opportunities, free trade, cost of exporting

Effect on the organisation

3.15 Particular economic factors may effect the organisation's operations.

(a) **Interest rates**

(i) A rise might increase the cost of any borrowing, thereby reducing profitability. It also raises the cost of capital. An investment project (eg a new information system) therefore has a higher hurdle to overcome to be accepted.

(ii) Interest rates also have a general effect on consumer confidence and liquidity, and hence demand.

(b) **Inflation**

(i) Inflation reduces the value of financial assets and the income of those on fixed incomes.

(ii) Inflation makes it hard for businesses to plan, owing to the uncertainty of future financial returns. Inflation and expectations of it encourages organisations to focus on the short-term ('short-termism').

(iii) Inflation requires high nominal interest rates to offer investors a real return..

3.16 **Exchange rate** volatility affects the cost of imports and the prices that can be charged to overseas customers. Many firms invest large sums of money in overseas production facilities.

The social and cultural environment

3.17 Social change involves changes in the nature, attitudes and habits of society. Social changes occur continually, and trends can be identified which may or may not be relevant to an organisation.

> **KEY TERM**
>
> **Demography** is the analysis of statistics on birth and death rates, age structures of populations, ethnic groups within communities etc.

3.18 Demography is important for these reasons.

- Labour is a factor of production
- People create demand for goods, services and resources
- It has a long-term impact on government policies
- There is a relationship between population growth and living standards

3.19 The following demographic factors are important to organisational planners.

Factor	Comment
Growth	The rate of growth or decline in a national population and in regional populations.
Age	Changes in the age distribution of the population. In the UK, there will be an increasing proportion of the national population over retirement age. In developing countries there are very large numbers of young people. Certain age groups may have a greater or lesser aptitude for technological developments such as the Internet.

Factor	Comment
Geography	The concentration of population into certain geographical areas.
Ethnicity	Different ethnic groups may display different purchasing patterns.
Household and family structure	A household is the basic social unit and its size might be determined by the number of children, whether elderly parents live at home etc. In the UK, there has been an increase in single-person households and lone-parent families.
Social structure	The population of a society can be broken down into a number of subgroups, with different attitudes and access to economic resources. Social class, however, is hard to measure (as people's subjective perceptions vary).
Employment	In part, this is related to changes in the workplace (eg IT has changed the nature of many jobs.) There has been some movement towards a more flexible workforce with greater numbers of workers on part-time or temporary contracts. However, despite some claims, most employees are in permanent, full-time employment.
Wealth	Rising standards of living lead to increased demand for many goods and services.

KEY TERM

In the context of the whole population, **culture** describes the beliefs, knowledge, attitudes and customs of people.

3.20 The culture of a society can affect an organisation in a number of ways.

(a) **Marketers** can adapt their products to suit cultural traits. (eg should websites be tailored for individual national markets?).

(b) **Human resource managers** may need to tackle cultural differences in recruitment and employment policies.

Case example

Consider the case of a young French employee of Eurodisney.

(a) The employee speaks the French language - part of the national culture - and has participated in the French education system etc.

(b) As a youth, the employee might, in his or her spare time, participate in various 'youth culture' activities. Music and fashion are emblematic of youth culture.

(c) As an employee of Eurodisney, the employee will have to participate in the corporate culture, which is based on American standards of service with a high priority put on friendliness to customers.

Technical issues

3.21 Any strategic view of information systems must take technical issues into account. For example, the proposed merger of two UK building societies was abandoned because of incompatibility between their computer systems. The cost of building a new system made the merger uneconomic.

3.22 Organisations that operate in an environment where the pace of technological change is fast must be flexible enough to adapt quickly and must **plan** for change and innovation. We look at the issues surrounding implementing change in Chapter 8.

Case example

Information Technology is helping the pub industry transform itself into a world of 'themed bars'. Complex mathematical analysis and software are helping the pub groups find locations with the right demographic profile for their brands. The software has helped in making detailed expansion plans.

Bass Leisure Retailing found out where to locate new pubs so that they have the least possible adverse effect on each other's business but admits that this technology cannot replace an experienced manager's 'gut feel' about a site.

Forecasting developments in technology

3.23 It is extremely difficult to forecast developments in technology beyond more than a few years. For example, many of the current developments in information technology would have seemed almost impossible a decade ago.

(a) **Futurology** is the science and study of sociological and technological developments, values and trends with a view to planning for the future.

(b) The **Delphi model** involves a panel of experts providing views on various events to be forecast such as inventions and breakthroughs, or even regulations or changes over a time period into the future.

(c) In some cases, instead of technical developments being used to predict future technologies, future social developments can be predicted, in order to predict future **customer needs.**

4 PEST ANALYSIS AND INFORMATION SYSTEMS STRATEGIC PLANNING

4.1 PEST analysis is a general technique that can be applied in a range of situations. The table below sets out some examples of how PEST factors may influence the strategic planning of information systems. The relevant factors will depend to a large extent on the actual situation or scenario.

PEST factor	Possible influence on IS strategic planning
Political	• Tax legislation; eg can the system cope with changes
	• Employment legislation; eg attitude to contractors
	• Data protection legislation; eg does the system comply, is it flexible
	• Nationalisation; eg is the company at risk and therefore should investment in the system proceed

Part A: Information systems and the organisation

PEST factor	Possible influence on IS strategic planning
	• General stability; eg is the business environment stable enough to justify further investment
	• Intellectual property laws; eg does the system comply, is our software protected
Economic	• Economic growth; eg the level of demand and volume of transactions
	• Relative strength of the national economy; eg relatively low economic growth in the home economy, compared with overseas, may lead to disparity in salary levels and a loss of skilled systems developers to other countries
	• Business partners; eg are those organisations we depend on for sales and supplies likely to be affected by economic trends
Social	• Relevant social attitudes; eg an information system for a pharmaceutical company conducting research using animals may need greater security
	• Demography; eg ageing population may mean a pension provider needs to build a system with spare capacity for future growth
	• Social acceptance of technology; eg is the cost of implementing an on-line purchasing facility justified
Technological	• Infrastructure development; eg are communications links of sufficient standard
	• Future developments; eg is a new technology imminent that would better meet our needs
	• Potential - are we utilising technology effectively eg instead of implementing a telephone banking system implement a system that facilitates telephone and Internet banking - and close under utilised branches
	• Existing systems; eg are we using what we already have, do we need a new system

Note: SWOT analysis may also be used as a tool to help the development of an effective strategy for information systems.

We cover SWOT analysis in the context of competitive position in Chapter 6.

Case example

Extracts from the International Management Accounting Practice Statement –

Strategic Planning for Information Resource Management (IRM)

An organisation's strategic plan describes how it will advance into the future. The IRM strategic plan should focus on how information and technology will support the goals and objectives outlined in the corporate strategy. IRM strategies must be creative and flexible to address current needs and potentially expanded future needs. There is a need for the organisation's IRM plan to mirror corporate strategy, eg if the enterprise's strategy emphasises customer service then the IRM plan must also.

IRM is an approach to strategic information systems planning that emphasises the importance of **information as a corporate resource**. It focuses on designing, implementing and maintaining a balanced, enterprise-wide system of information, processes and technology. In the IRM environment, technology is viewed as a means to assist the business to do things better, faster and cheaper - not as an end in itself.

Objectives of IRM

The fundamental objective of IRM is to ensure that an organisation's **information systems support its strategic direction** and business plans and enhance the quality, applicability, accessibility and value of the information resources of the enterprise. Its success in an organisation is dependent on the acceptance of four fundamental principles:

- Data is a valuable resource that requires proper management
- Most data is highly shareable
- The ability to share and use data more effectively is a **critical success factor** for most businesses
- Information systems should incorporate a broad view of the enterprise

An effective IRM program provides for continuously **scanning the environment** for opportunities that could drive the direction of an organisation's business. Information technology planners must have a strategic view on how information systems can increase the opportunities available to an organisation and also how to extend traditional business boundaries to include information resource links with customers and suppliers.

Organisations must emphasise strategic planning for IRM in order to gain a **competitive advantage** as they move into an era of increased automation and global competition. Information systems can help streamline business functions, improve managerial decision making, create new products and businesses and enhance relationships with suppliers and customers.

Developing the IRM strategic plan

The ultimate goal of an effective IRM strategic plan is the design, delivery and maintenance of a seamless, integrated information resource environment that responds successfully to the need for cross-functional flows of information while providing the flexibility and adaptability to respond to incessant business and technological change. The requirement is for a set of data transport capabilities and data management interfaces that are usable by each business function, but unique to and owned exclusively by none of them. Without a plan there are no objectives, no measures and, ultimately, no results.

There are three key steps involved in planning for the introduction of IRM practices into an organisation:

- Determine strategic information resource requirements
- Baseline the existing environment
- Design the IRM

Part A: Information systems and the organisation

Exhibit 1 **The Planning Process**

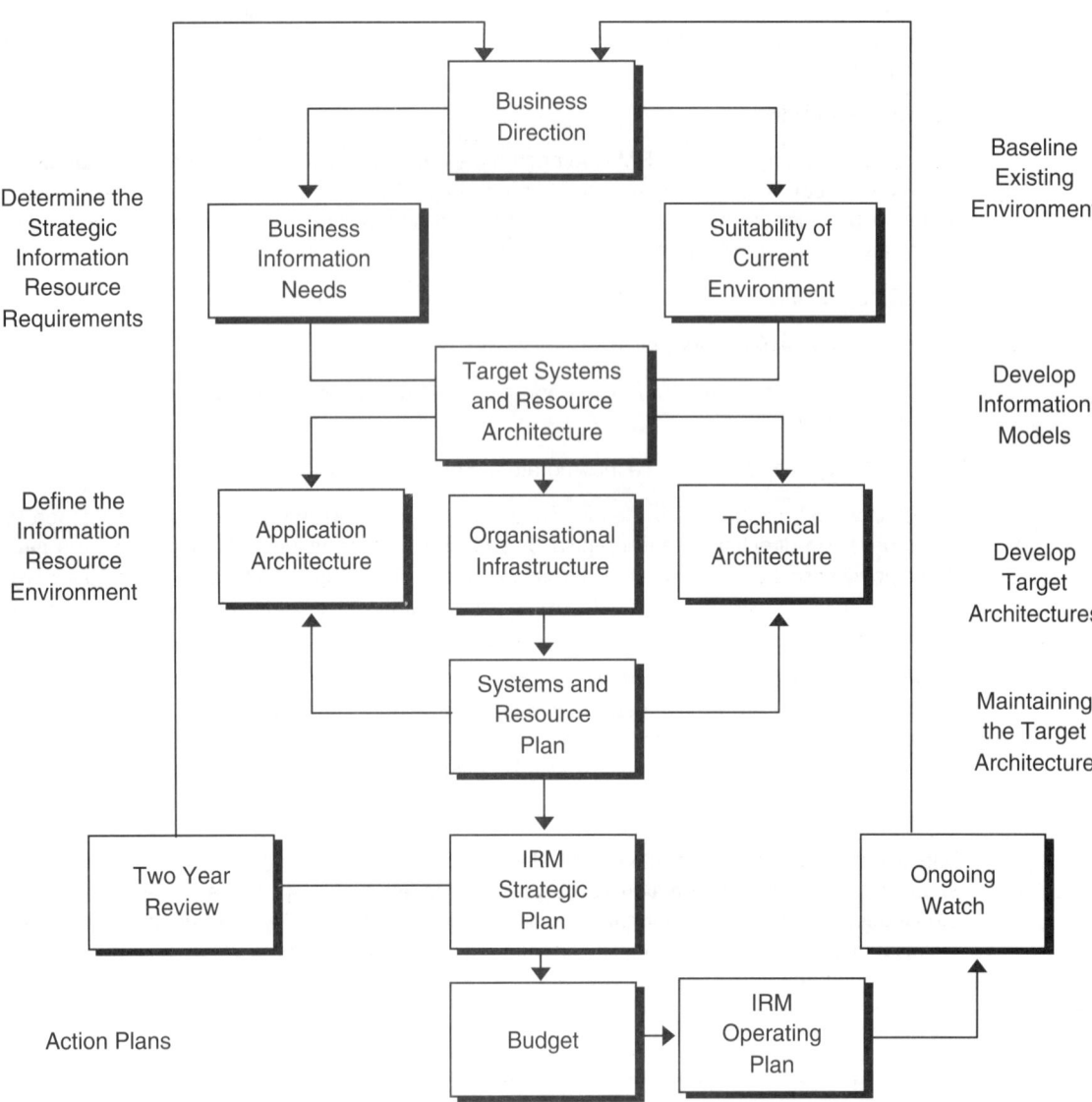

As shown in Exhibit 1, the planning process starts with a definition of the business direction, this is the foundation for all subsequent steps. The strategic business planning process ensures that an organisation understands its **critical success factors**, what it must do well to succeed and how it will measure success. Conversely, the strategic planning process provides an opportunity to identify areas of vulnerability, areas that may need to be monitored more closely and potentially subjected to stringent controls. Typical examples of what an organisation must do well to succeed in the next decade are customer service, new product development and cost control.

The business strategy drives the process of determining what information the business requires to **support its objectives** and how well the existing environment (systems, processes, information, organisational structure, etc.) supports, or has the potential to support, the achievement of the business objectives.

Technological issues are addressed in the third step, where a blueprint of the organisation's future computing infrastructure is designed. The blueprint takes the form of a set of 'target architectures,' ie systems and resource architecture, application architecture and the technical architecture, each of which describes a particular component of the infrastructure to be constructed. This is a plan, describing what hardware, software and databases are necessary to satisfy the strategic information requirements previously identified.

This set of target architectures supports the development of the IRM strategic plan, which, in turn, ensures the appropriate enabling technology and information infrastructure. It articulates how the organisation will make the most effective use of information, computers, database technology, decision support tools and telecommunications in combination with other resources to achieve its mission. The

2: The strategic role of information systems

IRM Plan reflects the organisation's business focus, mirroring its emphasis on customer service, becoming the least-cost provider, expansion, decentralisation goals and objectives and clearly states how the IRM organisation will support the business mission.

The following principles guide the development of an effective IRM strategy:

- It must be linked to the business strategy
- Cross-functional business processes are central to the planning dimension
- The technology infrastructure must represent a 'model of the business'

In the past, the focus of information systems planning may have been limited to determining how to apply technology to automate a task. Using the IRM approach more relevant questions might be: 'How do I apply technology to **competitive advantage**? How do I get the right information to the decision makers? Where are the best opportunities to add value through information resources?'

Exam focus point

In papers at Level 3, you must be able to apply knowledge in a variety of possible contexts. For example, in June 2003 a question required candidates to describe the importance of commitment, coordination and communication in the context of developing information systems. Some of the material covered in this chapter could have been applied to answer this question.

Part A: Information systems and the organisation

Chapter roundup

- **Strategic planning** is the formulation, evaluation and selection of strategies for the purpose of preparing a long-term plan of action to attain objectives.

- Information systems strategy is an example of a functional/operational strategy, although it often has **strategic implications**.

- A **strategy for information systems** and information technology is justified on the grounds that IS/IT:
    - Involves high costs
    - Is critical to the success of many organisations
    - Is now used as part of the commercial strategy in the battle for competitive advantage
    - Impacts on customer service
    - Affects all levels of management
    - Affects the way management information is created and presented
    - Requires effective management to obtain the maximum benefit
    - Involves many stakeholders inside and outside the organisation

- Organisations should develop an information systems plan that supports their overall business plan.

- There are a range of methodologies and frameworks for establishing the information requirements of an organisation including **Enterprise Analysis**, Critical Success Factors (**CSF**s), and **Earl's three leg analysis**.

- **Enterprise analysis** involves examining the entire organisation in terms of structure, processes, functions and data elements to identify the key elements and attributes of organisational data and information.

- **Critical success factors** are a small number of key operational goals vital to the success of an organisation.

- **Earl's three legs'** are:
    - Business led (focuses on business plans and goals)
    - Infrastructure led (focuses on current systems)
    - Mixed (focuses on IT/IS opportunities)

- Parsons wrote of six **generic strategies for information systems**:
    - Centrally planned
    - Leading edge
    - Free market
    - Monopoly
    - Scarce resource
    - Necessary evil

- Organisations exist within an environment which influences their activities. The general environment consists of **P**olitical/legal, **E**conomic, **S**ocial/cultural and **T**echnological (**PEST**) factors.

Quick quiz

1. The role that IT fills in an organisation will vary depending on the type of organisations. List five types of role IS/IT could fill.
2. Give another name for 'enterprise analysis' and another name for the 'CSF approach'.
3. List four general sources of CSFs.
4. Distinguish between an organisation's general environment and task environment.
5. What does IRM stand for?
6. Briefly explain the function of an Enterprise Resource Planning system.

Answers to quick quiz

1. Support activity

   Key operational activity

   Potentially very important

   Strategic activity

   A source of competitive advantage

2. Business systems planning; Strategic analysis
3. The industry that the business is in.

   The company itself and its situation within the industry.

   The environment, for example consumer trends and the economy.

   Specific internal measures, for example stock levels.
4. An organisation's general environment includes Political/legal, Economic, Social/cultural and Technological (PEST) influences. The task environment relates to factors of particular relevance to an organisation such as its competitors, customers and suppliers.
5. Information Resource Management. (Ensure you have read the *Case example* within this Chapter referring to the development of an IRM strategic plan.)
6. ERP systems are used for identifying and planning the enterprise-wide resources needed to record, produce, distribute, and account for customer orders.

Now try the questions below from the Exam Question Bank

Number	Level	Marks	Time
6	Exam	7	12 mins
7	Exam	8	14 mins
9	Exam	15	27 mins

Chapter 3

KNOWLEDGE MANAGEMENT

Topic list	Syllabus reference
1 Knowledge management	2(a), 7(a)(ii)
2 Databases	2(b)
3 Data warehousing and datamining	2(b)

Introduction

The modern business environment can be volatile. Businesses are increasingly reliant on good quality information and knowledge to anticipate and ensure an appropriate response to change. As the importance of information and knowledge has increased, organisations have come to realise that like any other valuable resource, **information and knowledge** must be **managed effectively**.

Study guide

6/7 – Knowledge management

- Discuss the difference between data workers and knowledge workers and the appropriate types of applications used by each (Also see Chapter 1)

    (i) Distribute knowledge: Office automation systems
    (ii) Share knowledge: Group collaboration systems
    (iv) Create knowledge: Knowledge work systems
    (v) Capture and codify knowledge: Artificial intelligence systems

7/8 Data management

- Explain the principles of Database Management Systems (DBMS)

- Describe the major characteristics of Integrity, Independence and Integration

- Discuss the difference between logical and physical data requirements. Describe logical models – hierarchical and relational

- Explain the principles of datamining and data warehousing

- Discuss datamining as the ability to analyse large pools of data to find patterns and rules that can be used by an organisation to guide decision making and predict future behaviour

- Discuss data warehousing as a database with reporting and query tools, that stores current and historical data extracted from various operational systems and consolidated for management reporting and analysis

22 Web-based technology

- Discuss and describe the uses of an extranet and an intranet (Also see Chapter 7)

Part A: Information systems and the organisation

> **Exam guide**
>
> Knowledge management is highly topical and therefore a prime candidate for examination questions. A detailed understanding of the technology is unlikely to be required. It is more important that you are aware of the capabilities of databases, datawarehouses, datamining and artificial intelligence techniques, and are able to recognise how the technologies could be applied to a range of business situations.

1 KNOWLEDGE MANAGEMENT

1.1 Studies have indicated that 20 to 30 percent of company resources are wasted because organisations are not aware of what **knowledge they already possess**. Lew Platt, Chief executive of Hewlett Packard, has articulated this in the phrase 'If only HP knew what HP knows, we would be three times as profitable'.

> **KEY TERMS**
>
> **Knowledge** is information within people's minds.
>
> **Knowledge management** describes the process of collecting, storing and using the knowledge held within an organisation.
>
> **Knowledge Work Systems (KWS)** are information systems that facilitate the creation and integration of new knowledge into an organisation.
>
> **Knowledge workers** are people whose jobs consist primarily of creating new information and knowledge. They are often members of a profession such as doctors, engineers, authors, lawyers and scientists.
>
> **Data workers** process and distribute information eg secretary, accounts clerk.

1.2 Knowledge is now commonly viewed as a sustainable source of **competitive advantage**. Producing unique products or services or producing products or services at a lower cost than competitors is based on superior knowledge.

1.3 Knowledge is valuable as it may be used to create new ideas, insights and interpretations and for decision making. However knowledge, like information, is of no value unless it is applied.

1.4 As the importance of knowledge increases the success of an organisation becomes increasingly dependant on its ability to gather, produce, hold and disseminate knowledge.

1.5 **Knowledge management** programmes are attempts at:

(a) Designing and installing techniques and processes to create, protect and use **explicit knowledge** (that is knowledge that the company knows that it has). Explicit knowledge includes facts, transactions and events that can be clearly stated and **stored in management information systems**.

(b) Designing and creating environments and activities to discover and release **tacit knowledge** (explained below).

1.6 **Tacit knowledge** is expertise held by people within the organisation that has not been formally documented. It is a difficult thing to manage because it is **invisible** and **intangible**.

3: Knowledge management

We do not know what knowledge exists within a person's brain, and whether he or she chooses to share knowledge is a matter of choice.

1.7 The **motivation to share** hard-won experience is sometimes low; the individual is 'giving away' their value and may be very reluctant to lose a position of influence and respect by making it available to everyone.

1.8 Organisations should encourage people to share their knowledge. This can be done through a culture of openness and rewards for sharing knowledge and information.

Where does knowledge reside?

1.9 There are various actions that can be taken to try to determine the prevalence of knowledge in an organisation.

1.10 One is the **identification and development of informal networks** and communities of practice within organisations. These self-organising groups share common work interests, usually cutting across a company's functions and processes. People exchange what they know freely and develop a shared language that allows knowledge to flow more efficiently.

1.11 It is then possible to **'map' a knowledge network** and make it available to others in the organisation. Knowledge maps are guides that assist employees to ascertain who knows what. Corporate **'yellow pages'**, skills inventories and expert databases are versions of maps.

1.12 Another means of establishing the prevalence of knowledge is to look at knowledge-related business **outcomes**. One example is **product development and service innovation**. While the knowledge embedded within these innovations is invisible, the products themselves are tangible.

1.13 Every day companies make substantial **investments in improving their employees' knowledge** and enabling them to use it more effectively. Analysis of these investments is a third way of making KM activities visible. For example how much technical and non-technical training are individuals consuming? How much is invested in competitive and environmental scanning, and in other forms of strategic research?

Knowledge creation

1.14 Japanese companies have a strong focus on **tacit knowledge**. They motivate knowledge creation through visions of products and strategies coupled with organisational cultures that promote sharing, transparency and proactive use of knowledge and innovation.

1.15 Human resource policies such as rotation of employees through different jobs and functions support the expansion of knowledge.

Organisational learning

1.16 The process by which an organisation develops its store of knowledge is sometimes called organisational learning.

1.17 A learning organisation is centred on the **people** that make up the organisation and the **knowledge** they hold. The organisation and employees feed off and into the central pool of knowledge. The organisation uses the knowledge pool as a tool to teach itself and its employees.

Part A: Information systems and the organisation

Knowledge management or information management?

1.18 There are dozens of **different approaches** to KM, including document management, information management, business intelligence, competence management, information systems management, intellectual asset management, innovation, business process design, and so on.

1.19 Many KM projects have a significant element of information management. After all, people need information about where knowledge resides, and to share knowledge they need to transform it into more or less transient forms of information.

1.20 But beyond that, KM does have two distinctive tasks: to facilitate the **creation** of knowledge and to **manage the way people share and apply it**. Companies that prosper with KM will be those that realise that it is as much about **managing people** as about information and technology.

Case example

How to facilitate knowledge sharing

The business trend for the new millennium might well be summed up as, 'Tradition is out, innovation is in.' World-class companies now realise that the best ideas do not necessarily come from the executive boardroom but from all levels of the company; from line workers all the way through to top management.

Companies that have cultures that **encourage best practice sharing** can unlock the rich stores of knowledge within each employee: sharing promotes overall knowledge, and facilitates further creativity. World-class companies are innovatively implementing best practice sharing to shake them of out of the rut of 'the way it's always been done.' Programs such as General Electric's Work-Out sessions or Wal-Mart's Saturday meetings help employees challenge conventions and suggest creative new ideas that drive process improvement, increased efficiency, and overall, **a stronger bottom line**.

The fundamental goal of **knowledge management** is to capture and disseminate knowledge across an increasingly global enterprise, enabling individuals to avoid repeating mistakes and to operate more intelligently - striving to create an entire **learning organisation** that works as efficiently as its most seasoned experts.

Best Practices recently updated report, '*Knowledge Management of Internal Best Practices*', profiles innovative methods used by world-class companies to communicate best practices internally. The study provides recommendations for how to create a best practice-sharing culture through all levels of the organisation, how to use both external and internal sources to find best practices and how to capture that knowledge and communicate it to all employees.

Best Practices, LLC contacted over fifty leading companies at the vanguard of knowledge management to compile its report. Some of the vital issues these thought leaders addressed include **measurement and management of intellectual assets**, best practice identification and recognition systems, best practice prioritisation systems, communication of best practices, and **knowledge sharing through technology**. For example, in the area of best practice communications, the report examines how General Electric spreads best practices with **regular job rotations**.

Adapted from Chapel Hill, N.C. (Business Wire) Feb 2000 via News Edge Corporation

Systems that aid knowledge management

1.21 Information systems play an important role in knowledge management, helping with **information flows** and helping formally **capture** the knowledge held within the organisation.

1.22 Any system that encourages people to work together and share information and knowledge will aid knowledge management. Examples are shown in the following table.

What the systems facilitate	Examples
Knowledge distribution	**Office automation systems** • Word processing • Electronic schedulers • Desktop databases • Web publishing • Voice mail • E-mail
Knowledge sharing	**Group collaboration systems** • Groupware • Intranets • Extranets
Knowledge creation	**Knowledge work systems** • CAD • Virtual Reality • Investment workstations
Knowledge capture and codification	**Artificial intelligence systems** • Expert systems • Neural Nets • Fuzzy logic • Intelligent agents (See Chapter 9)

Distributing knowledge

Office automation systems (OAS)

1.23 As we learnt in Chapter 1, an OAS is any application of information technology that increases productivity within an office.

1.24 Knowledge work is dependant on the efficient production and distribution of documents and other forms of communication such as voice messaging systems.

1.25 Document imaging systems convert documents and images to digital form, reducing the amount of paper required. Electronic information should be easier to retrieve as electronic searches should be quicker than hunting through a mountain of paper.

Knowledge sharing

Groupware

> **KEY TERM**
>
> **Groupware** is a term used to describe software that provides functions for the use of collaborative work groups.

Part A: Information systems and the organisation

1.26 Typically, groups utilising groupware are small project-oriented teams that have important tasks and tight deadlines Perhaps the best-known groupware product at present is **Lotus Notes**. However, there are many related products and technologies.

1.27 Features might include the following.

(a) A **scheduler** (or diary or calendar), allowing users to keep track of their schedule and plan meetings with others.

(b) An electronic **address book** to keep personal and business contact information up-to-date and easy to find. Contacts can be sorted and filed in any way.

(c) **To do** lists. Personal and business to-do lists can be kept in one easy-to-manage place, and tasks can quickly be prioritised.

(d) A **journal,** which is used to record interactions with important contacts, record items (such as e-mail messages) and files that are significant to the user, and record activities of all types and track them all without having to remember where each one was saved.

(e) A **jotter** for jotting down notes as quick reminders of questions, ideas, and so on.

1.28 There are clearly advantages in having information such as this available from the desktop at the touch of a button, rather than relying on scraps of paper, address books, and corporate telephone directories. However, it is when groupware is used to **share information** with colleagues that it comes into its own. Here are some of the features that may be found.

(a) **Messaging**, comprising an **e-mail** in-box which is used to send and receive messages from the office, home, or the road and **routing** facilities, enabling users to send a message to a single person, send it sequentially to a number of people (who may add to it or comment on it before passing it on), or sending it to every one at once.

(b) Access to an **information database,** and customisable **'views'** of the information held on it, which can be used to standardise the way information is viewed in a workgroup.

(c) **Group scheduling**, to keep track of colleagues' itineraries. Microsoft Exchange Server, for instance offers a 'Meeting Wizard', which can consult the diaries of everyone needed to attend a meeting and automatically work out when they will be available, which venues are free, and what resources are required.

(d) **Public folders**. These collect, organise, and share files with others on the team or across the organisation.

(e) One person (for instance a secretary or a stand-in during holidays or sickness) can be given **'delegate access'** to another's groupware folders and send mail on their behalf, or read, modify, or create items in public and private folders on their behalf.

(f) **Conferencing**. Participation in public, online discussions with others.

(g) **Assigning tasks**. A task request can be sent to a colleague who can accept, decline, or reassign the task. After the task is accepted, the groupware will keeps the task status up-to-date on a task list.

(h) **Voting** type facilities that can, say, request and tally responses to a multiple-choice question sent in a mail message (eg 'Here is a list of options for this year's Christmas party').

(i) **Hyperlinks** in mail messages. The recipient can click the hyperlink to go directly to a Web page or file server.

(j) **Workflow management** (see below) with various degrees of sophistication.

1.29 **Workflow** is a term used to describe the defined series of tasks within an organisation to produce a final outcome. Sophisticated workgroup computing applications allow the user to define different **workflows** for different types of jobs. For example, in a publishing setting, a document might be automatically routed from writer to editor to proofreader to production.

1.30 At **each stage** in the workflow, **one individual** or group is **responsible** for a specific task. Once the task is complete, the workflow software ensures that the individuals responsible for the **next** task are notified and receive the data they need to do their stage of the process.

1.31 Workflow systems can be described according to the type of process they are designed to deal with. There are three common types.

(a) **Image-based workflow systems** are designed to automate the flow of paper through an organisation, by transferring the paper to digital "images". These were the first workflow systems that gained wide acceptance. These systems are closely associated with 'imaging' (or 'document image processing' (DIP)) technology, and help with the routing and processing of digitised images.

(b) **Form-based workflow systems** (formflow) are designed to route forms intelligently throughout an organisation. These forms, unlike images, are text-based and consist of editable fields. Forms are automatically routed according to the information entered on them. In addition, these form-based systems can notify or remind people when action is due.

(c) **Co-ordination-based workflow systems** are designed to help the completion of work by providing a framework for **co-ordination** of action. Such systems are intended to improve organisational productivity by addressing the issues necessary to **satisfy customers**, rather than automating procedures that are not closely related to customer satisfaction.

Intranets

> **KEY TERM**
>
> An **intranet** is an internal network used to share information. Intranets utilise Internet technology and protocols. The firewall surrounding an internet fends off unauthorised access.

1.32 The idea behind an 'intranet' is that companies set up their own **mini version of the Internet.** (We look at the Internet in detail in Chapter 7). Intranets use a combination of the organisation's own networked computers and Internet technology. Each employee has a browser, used to access a server computer that holds corporate information on a wide variety of topics, and in some cases also offers access to the Internet.

1.33 Potential applications include company newspapers, induction material, online procedure and policy manuals, employee web pages where individuals post up details of their activities and progress, and **internal databases** of the corporate information store.

1.34 Most of the **cost** of an intranet is the **staff time** required to set up the system.

1.35 The **benefits** of intranets are diverse.

(a) Savings accrue from the **elimination of storage, printing** and **distribution** of documents that can be made available to employees on-line.

(b) Documents on-line are often **more widely used** than those that are kept filed away, especially if the document is bulky (eg manuals) and needs to be searched. This means that there are **improvements in productivity** and **efficiency**.

(c) It is much **easier to update** information in electronic form.

(d) Wider access to corporate information should open the way to **more flexible working patterns,** eg material available on-line may be accessed from remote locations..

Extranets

KEY TERM

An extranet is an intranet that is accessible to authorised outsiders.

1.36 Whereas an intranet resides behind a firewall and is accessible only to people who are members of the same company or organisation, an extranet provides various levels of accessibility to outsiders.

1.37 Only those outsiders with a valid username and password can access an extranet, with varying levels of access rights enabling control over what people can view. Extranets are becoming a very popular means for **business partners to exchange information**.

1.38 Extranets therefore allow better use of the knowledge held by an organisation - by facilitating access to that knowledge.

Creating knowledge

Knowledge work systems (KWS)

1.39 Knowledge Work Systems (KWS) are information systems that facilitate the creation and integration of new knowledge into an organisation. They provide knowledge workers with tools such as:

- Analytical tools
- Powerful graphics facilities
- Communication tools
- Access to external databases
- A user-friendly interface

1.40 The workstations of knowledge workers are often designed for the specific tasks they perform. For example, a design engineer would require sufficient graphics power to manipulate 3-D Computer Aided Design (**CAD**) images; a financial analyst would require a powerful desktop computer to access and manipulate a large amount of financial data (an **investment workstation**).

1.41 The components of a KWS are shown in the following diagram.

Knowledge work system

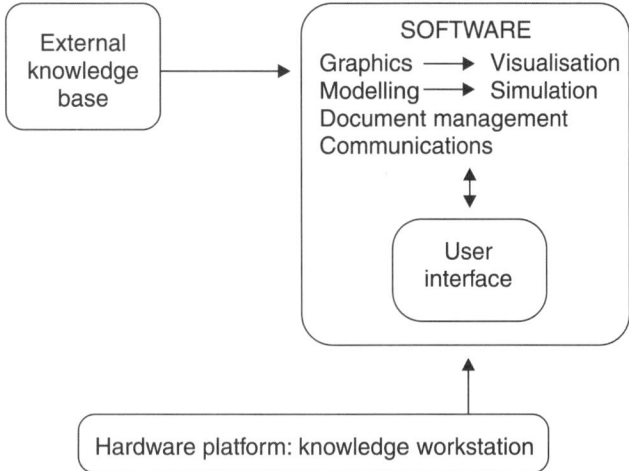

1.42 **Virtual reality systems** are another example of KWS. These systems create computer generated simulations that emulate real-world activities. Interactive software and hardware (eg special headgear) provide simulations so realistic that users experience sensations that would normally only occur in the real world.

Case examples

Virtual reality

Burger King have used virtual reality stores to test new store designs.

Volvo have used virtual reality test drives in vehicle development.

Capturing and codifying knowledge

Artificial intelligence (AI)

> **KEY TERM**
>
> **Artificial intelligence** (AI) is the development of computer-based systems designed to behave as humans. Artificial intelligence systems are based on human expertise, knowledge and reasoning patterns.

1.43 The field of AI includes:
- Robotics
- 'Natural language' programming tools
- Perceptive systems
- Expert systems

1.44 The main commercial applications of AI have involved **expert systems**.

Part A: Information systems and the organisation

> **KEY TERM**
>
> An **expert system** is a computer program that captures human expertise in a limited domain of knowledge.

1.45 Expert system software uses a knowledge base that consists of facts, concepts and the relationships between them on a particular domain of knowledge and uses pattern-matching techniques to 'solve' problems.

1.46 Rules of thumb or ('heuristics') are important. A simple example might be 'milk in first' when making a cup of tea: this is a rule of thumb for tea making that saves people having to rethink how to make a cup of tea every time they do so. A simple business example programmed into a credit check may be: 'Don't allow credit to a person who has no credit history and has changed address twice or more within the last three years'.

1.47 For example, many financial institutions now use expert systems to process straightforward **loan applications**. The user enters certain key facts into the system such as the loan applicant's name and most recent addresses, their income and monthly outgoings, and details of other loans. The system will then:

(a) **Check the facts** given against its database to see whether the applicant has a good previous credit record.

(b) **Perform calculations** to see whether the applicant can afford to repay the loan.

(c) **Make a judgement** as to what extent the loan applicant fits the lender's profile of a good risk (based on the lender's previous experience).

(d) Suggest a decision.

1.48 A decision is then suggested, based on the results of this processing. This is why it is now often possible to get a loan or arrange insurance **over the telephone**, whereas in the past it would have been necessary to go and speak to a bank manager or send details to an actuary and then wait for him or her to come to a decision.

1.49 Other applications of expert systems include:

(a) **Legal** advice.

(b) **Tax** advice.

(c) **Forecasting** of economic or financial developments, or of market and customer behaviour.

(d) **Surveillance**, for example of the number of customers entering a supermarket, to decide what shelves need restocking and when more checkouts need to be opened, or of machines in a factory, to determine when they need maintenance.

(e) **Diagnostic systems**, to identify causes of problems, for example in production control in a factory, or in healthcare.

(f) **Education and training** (diagnosing a student's or worker's weaknesses and providing or recommending extra instruction as appropriate).

3: Knowledge management

> **Exam Focus Point**
>
> An exam question could ask you to explain how an expert system could help with the activities of a company described in a scenario. Give some thought to this for different sorts of organisation, for example a local authority, a transport company, a manufacturer of fast-moving consumer goods, a firm of accountants and so on.

1.50 An organisation can use an expert system when a number of conditions are met.

　(a) The problem is **well defined**.
　(b) The expert can define **rules** by which the problem can be solved.
　(c) The **investment** in an expert system is cost-justified.

1.51 The knowledge base of an expert system must be kept up-to-date.

1.52 Expert systems are not suited to high-level unstructured problems as these require information from a wide range of sources rather than simply deciding between a few known alternatives.

1.53 A diagram of an expert system follows.

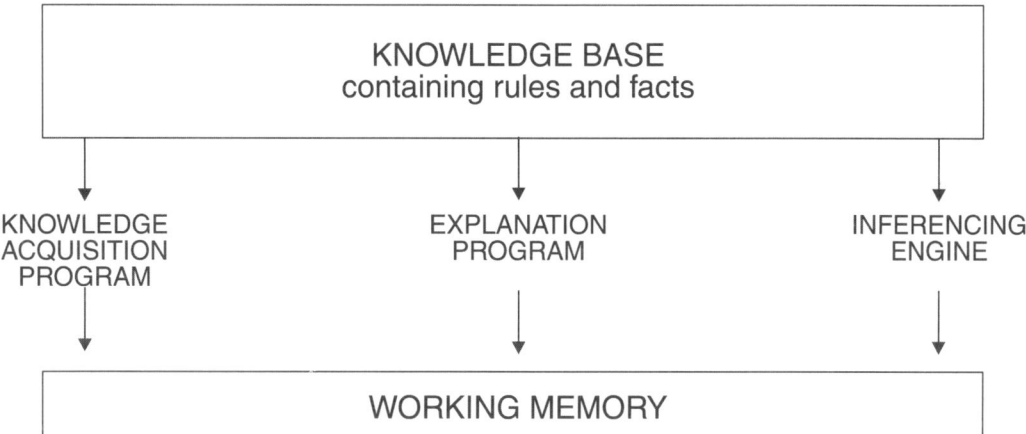

　(a) The **knowledge base** contains facts and rules from past experience.

　(b) The **knowledge acquisition program** is a program which enables the expert system to incorporate new knowledge and rules.

　(c) The **working memory** stores the facts and rules being used by the current enquiry, and the current information given to it by the user.

　(d) The **inferencing engine** is the software that executes the reasoning. It decides which rules apply, and allocates priorities.

Question 1

Why do you think organisations wish to automate reasoning or decision-making tasks which humans are naturally better able to perform than computers?

Answer

The primary reason has to do with the relative cost of information. A human expert builds up a specialised body of knowledge over time. This knowledge has a commercial value. With human resource 'time is money'. Expert systems aim to use this expertise without requiring the human expert

Part A: Information systems and the organisation

to spend time making the decision. The system also protects the organisation against loss of this expertise should the human expert leave the organisation.

Capturing knowledge in a computer system means that this wisdom can be accessed by more people. Thus, the delivery of complicated services to customers, decisions whether or not to extend credit and so forth, can be made by less experienced members of staff if the expert's knowledge is available to them.

If a manufacturing company has a complicated mixture of plant and machinery, then the repair engineer may accumulate a lot of knowledge over a period of time about the way it behaves: if a problem occurs, the engineer will be able to make a reasoned guess as to where the likely cause is to be found. If this accumulated expert information is made available to less experienced staff, it means that some of their learning curve is avoided.

An expert system is advantageous because it saves time, and therefore costs less. It is particularly useful as it possesses both knowledge and a reasoning ability.

1.54 **Advantages** of expert systems include the following.

(a) AI and expertise is **permanent**, whereas human experts may leave the business.

(b) AI is **easily copied**.

(c) AI is **consistent**, whereas human experts and decision makers may not be.

(d) AI can be **documented**. The reasoning behind an expert recommendation produced by a computer will be recorded.

(e) Depending on the task the computer may be much **faster** than the human being.

1.55 **Disadvantages** of expert systems include the following:

(a) Systems are **expensive**.

(b) The technology is still relatively new. Systems will probably need extensive testing and debugging.

(c) People are naturally **more creative**.

(d) Systems have a very **narrow focus**.

Neural networks

1.56 Neural networks are another application of AI, seen by some as the 'next step' in computing. Neural computing is modelled on the biological processes of the human brain.

1.57 Neural networks can **learn from experience**. They can analyse vast quantities of complex data and **identify patterns** from which predictions can be made. They have the ability to cope with incomplete or 'fuzzy' data, and can deal with previously unspecified or **new situations**.

1.58 Neural techniques have been applied to similar areas as expert systems eg credit risks. Neural techniques are more advanced in that they don't rely on a set of hard rules, but develop a 'hidden' layer of experience and come to a decision based on this hidden layer.

1.59 A diagram showing a neural network follows.

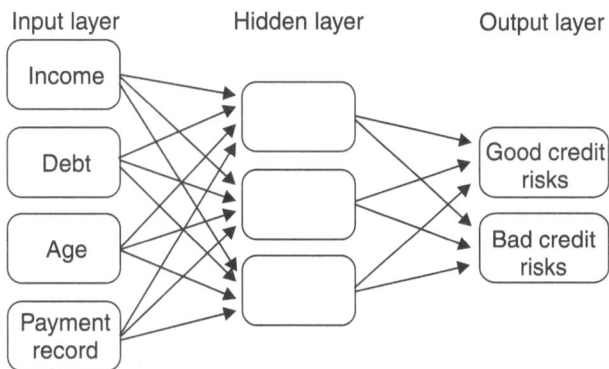

Fuzzy logic

1.60 Artificial intelligence applications are increasingly making use of 'fuzzy logic'. Traditionally computer programs have required precision such as 'yes' or 'no'.

1.61 Fuzzy logic involves using more complex rules than the traditional IF-THEN statements. For example, a traditional statement may say '*IF room temperature is less than 60 degrees THEN raise the heat*'.

1.62 A system using fuzzy logic would have a range of membership functions which are less precise than rules. A membership function may say '*If the temperature is warm or hot and the humidity is high lower the temperature and humidity.*'

1.63 The parameters for *warm, hot, high, low* etc would be defined elsewhere in the system (and may overlap). The program would combine the function readings and using weightings decide on the required course of action.

2 DATABASES

2.1 The way in which data is held on a system affects the ease with which the data is able to be accessed and manipulated.

> **KEY TERMS**
>
> A **database** is a collection of data organised to service many applications. The database provides convenient access to data for a wide variety of users and user needs.
>
> A **database management system** (**DBMS**) is the software that centralises data and manages access to the database. It is a system which allows numerous applications to extract the data they need without the need for separate files.
>
> The **logical structure** of a database refers to how various application programs access the data. The **physical structure** relates to how data is organised within the database.
>
> The independence of data items from the programs which access them is referred to as **data independence**.
>
> Duplication of data items is referred to as **data redundancy**.
>
> In a database environment, the ease with which applications access the central pool of data is referred to as **integration**.

> **Integrity** relates to data accuracy and consistency. Data independence and integration should reduce data redundancy resulting in improved data integrity.

The characteristics of a database system

2.2 A database system has the following characteristics.

(a) **Shared**. Different users are able to access the same data for their own processing applications. This removes the need for duplicating data on different files.

(b) **Controls** to preserve the **integrity** of the database. Users should not be able to alter the data on file so as to **spoil** the database records for other users. However, users must be able to make **valid** alterations to the data.

(c) **Flexibility.** The database system should provide for the **needs of different users**, who each have their own processing requirements and data access methods. The database should be capable of **evolving** to meet **future** needs.

Database structures

2.3 There are three logical database models.
- The **hierarchical** model
- The **network** model
- The **relational** model

The hierarchical model

2.4 The hierarchical model is an example of **a logical database model**. It shows data in a tree-like format. Upper segments of the model are connected to lower segments in a parent-child relationship. A parent can have more than one child, but a child can have only one parent. Such relationships can be expressed conveniently in a **hierarchy**. Each data item is related to only one item above it in the hierarchy, but to any number of data items below it.

2.5 In a customer database, for example, the hierarchical model might be used to show customers and customer orders. An extract from a **parts department database** might be structured as follows.

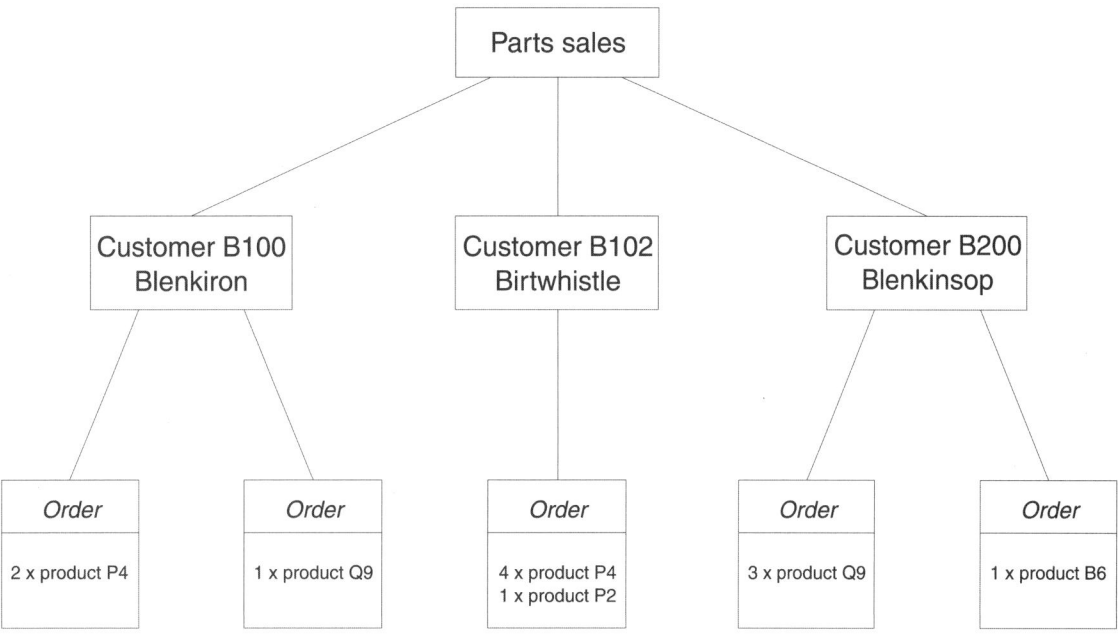

2.6 In the diagram above, the starting point (Part sales) is known as the **root segment**. Three child segments are shown below the root and further child segments below these.

2.7 The hierarchical nature of the model makes it **unsuitable for situations involving many-to-many relationships**.

2.8 For example, say we wish to model a purchases system using a Part code number as the root segment. If we buy Part X from three suppliers (A, B and C) the root segment (X) will have three children (A, B and C). The hierarchical model can show this relationship effectively. However, if we also buy another part (Y) from supplier A, a separate model would be needed to show this relationship – as a child (A) can have only one parent (X). If a hierarchical model was used in this situation, supplier A data would have to be held in more than one location (data redundancy).

2.9 Hierarchical structures are appropriate when systems must handle large numbers of routine requests for information eg an airline reservation system.

The network model

2.10 The network model is **another logical database model**. Whereas a hierarchical data structure only allows a **one-to-many** relationship between data items, a **network** database allows **many-to-many** relationships. In other words, parents can have many children and children can have many parents.

2.11 The relationship between courses run by an educational institution (such as BPP) and students (such as you) can be shown in a network data model. A student could take many courses and a course will (hopefully) have many students.

Part A: Information systems and the organisation

Network Data Model

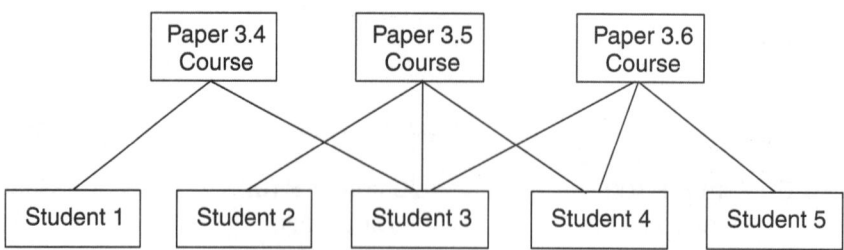

2.12 The data in the diagram above could be structured hierarchically but this would require data redundancy as student details would have to be stored separately for each course enrolled in.

2.13 Returning to our Part sales example, a network model is shown below.

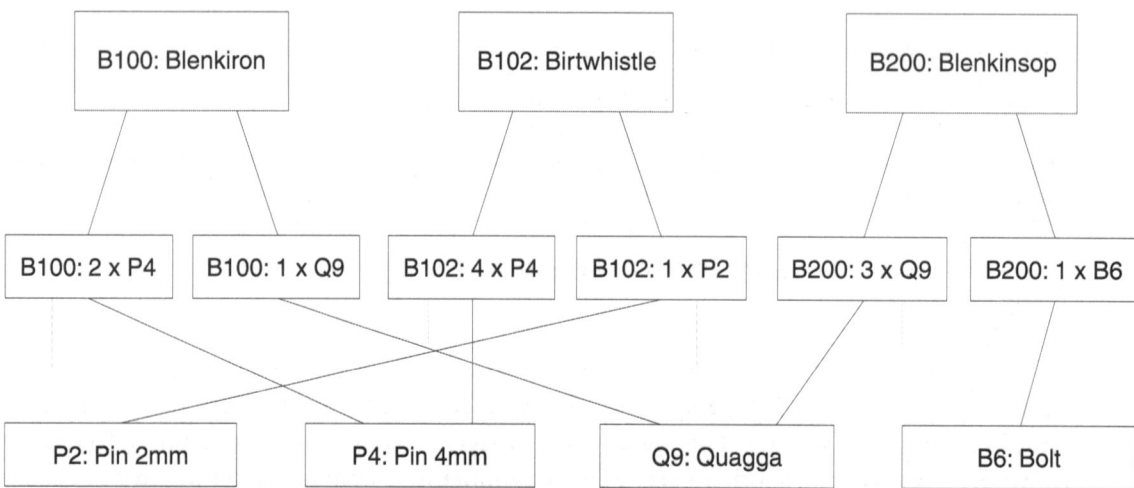

2.14 Using the network structure allows student details to be stored just once and should provide quicker response time to queries. To facilitate this, network databases require widespread use of **pointers**. Pointers are data elements attached to record segments on disk giving the location of related records. Hierarchical databases also use pointers but not to the extent they are required in network databases.

The relational model

2.15 The relational model is the third type of logical database model, designed to overcome some of the limitations of the other two models. A relational model organises data elements in a series of **two-dimensional tables** consisting of rows and columns. A row represents a record, and columns represent part of a record.

2.16 In a **relational data structure** the relationships between different entity types have been determined at the outset, and are not embodied in the records themselves. A relational database thus does not have to navigate through other data before reading the required record.

2.17 Any data element can be recognised by its record number or field name. The **primary key** is used to identify a record. Data redundancy is eliminated.

Customer table

B100	Blenkiron
B102	Birtwhistle
B200	Blenkinsop

Product table

B6	Bolt
P2	Pin 2mm
P4	Pin 4mm
Q9	Quagga

Order table

B100	P4	2
B100	Q9	1
B102	P4	4
B102	P2	1
B200	Q9	3
B200	B6	1

2.18 Using the DBMS, data from these tables can be extracted and combined to produce reports, provided that any two share a common data element. For example, the customer code could be used to link the *Customer table* with the *Order table*.

2.19 Instead of pointers, three basic operations are used to develop useful sets of data.

- Select - creates a subset of rows (records) based on stated criteria
- Join - combines tables to provide more information
- Project - creates new tables containing only the columns required

The advantages and disadvantages of database systems

2.20 The **advantages** of a database system are as follows.

(a) **Avoidance of unnecessary duplication of data**

It recognises that data can be used for many purposes but only needs to be input and stored once.

(b) **Multi-purpose data**

From (a), it follows that although data is input once, it can be used for several purposes.

(c) **Data for the organisation as a whole, not just for individual departments**

The database concept encourages management to regard data as a resource that must be **properly managed** just as any other resource. Database systems encourage management to analyse data, relationships between data items, and how data is used in different applications.

(d) **Consistency**

Because data is only held once, it is easier to ensure that it is up-to-date and consistent across departments.

(e) **New uses for data**

Data is held independently of the programs that access the data. This allows greater flexibility in the ways that data can be used. New programs can be easily introduced to make use of existing data in a different way.

(f) **New applications**

Developing new application programs with a database system is easier as a central pool of data is already available to be drawn upon.

(g) **Flexibility**

Relational systems are extremely flexible, allowing information from several different sources to be combined and providing answers to ad-hoc queries.

Part A: Information systems and the organisation

2.21 The **disadvantages** of a database systems relate mainly to security and control.

(a) There are potential problems of **data security** and **data privacy**. Administrative procedures for data security should supplement software controls.

(b) Since there is only one set of data, it is essential that the data should be **accurate** and free from corruption. A back-up routine is essential.

(c) Initial **development costs** may be high.

(d) For hierarchical and network structures, the access paths through the data must be **specified in advance**.

(e) Both hierarchical and network systems require intensive **programming** and are **inflexible**.

Database alternatives

2.22 The following table compares the three database alternatives we have looked at.

Type	Programming effort required	User-friendliness	Processing efficiency	Flexibility
Hierarchical	High	Low	High	Low
Network	High	Low to medium	Medium to high	Low to medium
Relational	Low	High	Low (improving)	High

Databases and planning

2.23 Planning will always involve an element of risk – as it deals with the future. Databases can at least ensure that information we have about the present and the past is available to aid planning. Organised data retrieval techniques make the data available in an effective way. In a world in which decisions must be ever more rapid, it is crucial to be able to access diverse, complex, multiple data bits and to analyse them to rapidly and correctly extract the knowledge they contain.

3 DATA WAREHOUSING AND DATAMINING

3.1 Two techniques designed to utilise the ever increasing amounts of data held by organisations are **data warehousing** and **datamining**.

Data warehousing

> **KEY TERM**
>
> A **data warehouse** consists of a database, containing data from various operational systems, and reporting and query tools.

3.2 A data warehouse contains data from a range of internal (eg sales order processing system, nominal ledger) and external sources. One reason for including individual transaction data in a data warehouse is that if necessary the user can drill-down to access transaction level

3: Knowledge management

detail. Data is increasingly obtained from newer channels such as customer care systems, outside agencies or websites.

3.3 Data is copied to the data warehouse as often as required – usually either daily, weekly or monthly. The process of making any required changes to the format of data and copying it to the warehouse is usually automated.

3.4 The result should be a coherent set of information available to be used across the organisation for management analysis and decision making. The reporting and query tools available within the warehouse should facilitate management reporting and analysis.

3.5 The reporting and query tools should be flexible enough to allow multidimensional data analysis, also known as on-line analytical processing (**OLAP**). Each aspect of information (eg product, region, price, budgeted sales, actual sales, time period etc) represents a different dimension. OLAP enables data to be viewed from each dimension, allowing each aspect to be viewed and in relation to the other aspects.

Features of data warehouses

3.6 A data warehouse is subject-oriented, integrated, time-variant, and non-volatile.

(a) **Subject-oriented**

A data warehouse is focussed on data groups not application boundaries. Whereas the operational world is designed around applications and functions such as sales and purchases, a data warehouse world is organised around major **subjects** such as customers, supplier, product and activity.

(b) **Integrated**

Data within the data warehouse must be consistent in format and codes used – this is referred to as **integrated** in the context of data warehouses.

For example, one operational application feeding the warehouse may represent **gender** as an 'M' and an 'F' while another represents **gender** as '1' and '0'.

While it does not matter how **gender** is represented in the data warehouse (let us say that 'M' and 'F' is chosen), it **must** arrive in the data warehouse in a **consistent integrated** state. The data import routine should 'cleanse' any inconsistencies.

(c) **Time-variant**

Data is organised by time and stored in 'time-slices'.

Data warehouse data may cover **a long time horizon**, perhaps from five to ten years. Data warehouse data tends to deal with **trends** rather than single points in time. As a result, each data element in the data warehouse environment must carry with it the time for which it applies.

(d) **Non-volatile**

Data **cannot be changed** within the warehouse. Only load and retrieval operations are made.

3.7 Organisations may build a single central data warehouse to serve the entire organisation or may create a series of smaller **data marts**. A data mart holds a selection of the organisation's data for a specific purpose.

Part A: Information systems and the organisation

3.8 A data mart can be constructed more quickly and cheaply than a data warehouse. However, if too many individual data marts are built, organisations may find it is more efficient to have a single data warehouse serving all areas.

Advantages of data warehouses

3.9 Advantages of setting up a datawarehouse system include the following.

(a) Decision makers can access data without affecting the use of operational systems.

(b) Having a wide range of data available to be queried easily encourages the taking of a wide perspective on organisational activities.

(c) Datawarehouses have proved successful in some businesses for:

   (i) Quantifying the effect of marketing initiatives.
   (ii) Improving knowledge of customers.
   (iii) Identifying and understanding an enterprise's most profitable revenues streams.

3.10 Some organisations have found they have invested considerable resources implementing a datawarehouse for little return. To benefit from the information a datawarehouse can provide, organisations need to be flexible and prepared to act on what they find. If a warehouse system is implemented simply to follow current practice it will be of little value.

3.11 The components of a data warehouse are shown in the following diagram.

Components of a data warehouse

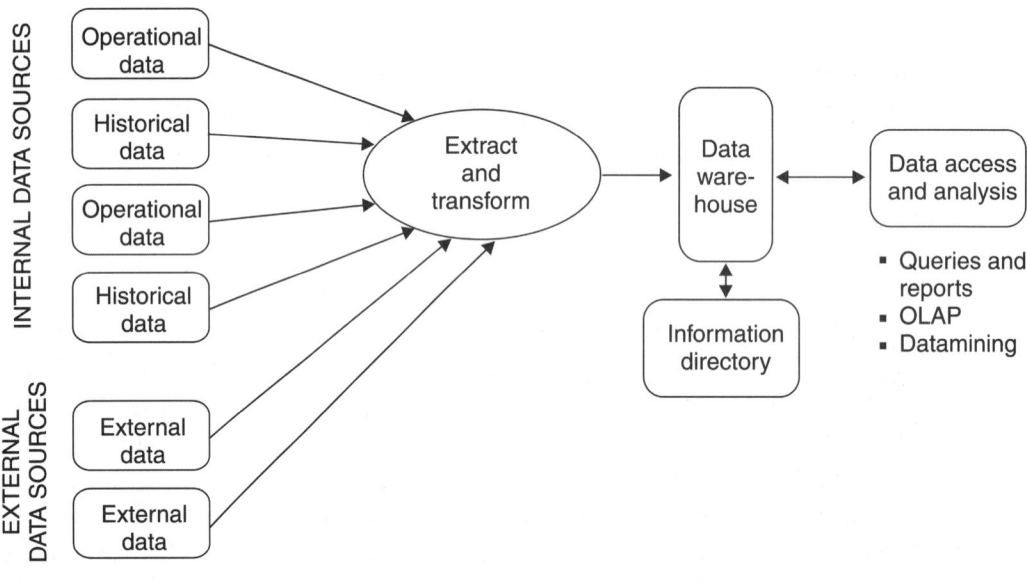

Case example: Seven steps to bring your systems into the 21st century

Step One. Implement a data warehouse

A data warehouse is a computer loaded with a database product such as Oracle or Microsoft SQL server. **This database is configured to hold the key information** you want to look at and is interfaced with the 'transaction processing' systems.

For larger volumes of data a toolset has been developed called **OLAP (on-line analytical processing)** which allows **summary information** to be created and stored across the different business performance metrics. As a consequence of this, on-line and instant enquiries can potentially be made on the balances of any combination of customer/product/regional performance by date/period range.

3: Knowledge management

The performance of the transaction-processing systems will not be affected by heavy use of the data warehouse for a complex set of enquiries, as you will not be working with the live information.

Once this warehouse has been set up, information can be combined from the different operations systems into a consistent format and can be accessed by a wide variety of reporting/analysis/web tools.

Step Two. Reporting tools

Time and time again finance directors say that their key IT issue is lack of reporting capabilities in the systems they are using. Reporting problems tend to fall into three categories.

First, the **inability to access the source data**. This is either because it is in a format that cannot be accessed by PC technology or it is held in so many places that its structure is incomprehensible to a member of the finance team.

Second, the **tools to make the enquiries** or produce the reports are often **difficult to use** and do not produce the reports in a 'user friendly' format with 'drill down' capabilities.

Third, there is the issue of **consistency of information** across systems. In order to get an overall picture of your organisation's performance you will usually need to access data from different operation applications. All too often the data is not the same across these systems.

The argument for replacing what you have is well rehearsed. New systems promise the latest technology for reporting and enquiries. **Enterprise Resource Planning (ERP)** packages promise to integrate your different applications smoothly and give you a single point of access to all data. **Customer Relationship Management (CRM)** software has been added to this recipe to give this approach a better chance of happening.

There are a myriad of reporting tools costing from a few pounds to hundreds of thousands of pounds. One that is regularly overlooked is the **spreadsheet**. Excel is the product most commonly used by accountants. With the advent of Microsoft Office 2000 there is a bewildering array of features to present information on your desktop or paper. **Pivot tables** are starting to be used more widely for multi-dimensional analysis and can be combined with the increasingly powerful **graphical capabilities** of Excel. Spreadsheets are much underrated and it is surprising how many organisations go out and buy expensive new knowledge-management tools when they already have a product on their computer that will deliver all the reporting/enquiry performance they require.

So, see how far your spreadsheet will take you and see if you can avoid the cost of another new IT tool.

Step Three. Intranet enable reporting/enquiries

Larger companies have by now started to implement a **corporate intranet**. This typically holds information on employee phone and contact details, standard forms for holiday requests, terms and conditions of employment and so on.

It is possible now to integrate financial reporting into an intranet. The leading web page development tools allow the display of information from a data warehouse. Excel has facilities to post spreadsheets and pivot table information straight to a web page and for users to drill down to the detail from a summary level. There are a number of **benefits** to this.

First, the information is presented in a **user-friendly** format and can be made 'idiot proof' for non-IT literate staff.

Second, the benefit of using a web browser is that it allows for **remote access** to the information quickly and easily. This means that people working at different parts of the organisation or away from the office can access this data rapidly.

Third, the web browser technology is becoming an **industry standard** and as such is well supported and increasingly reliable.

So start to use a web browser to access your reports and **publish these to your intranet** server rather than printing them out.

Step Four. Client/supplier access to information

So you have implemented the above and have your core business data from your different systems in **a single data warehouse**. You will be using PC tools like Excel to access this and will have developed part of your intranet so that staff can access key information quickly and easily wherever they are.

Part A: Information systems and the organisation

Why not consider making **some of this information available to your business partners**? For example, if you have customer sales order information in your data warehouse, why not make it available to your customers and even suppliers? If you have internal information on the products and services that you sell, why not do likewise?

This is where the Internet can really start to bite and give your organisation real commercial benefit.

Step Five. Streamlined transaction processing

The next step is to look at the possibility of **streamlining your business processes**. How many times are you capturing your transactions in your organisation?

Why not allow customers to generate their own orders via the web? If the data warehouse holds information on the clients, the products and services you sell, it could be relatively straightforward to create an order front-end with a web browser to this information.

You could populate the data warehouse with these incoming orders and use this to upload your core transaction processing systems. Most packages now have data import modules and this process may be more straightforward than you think and a lot cheaper and easier than replacing your core business systems. Why not extend this to allowing your employees and even customers to 'self service' the information in your systems and keep it up-to-date themselves.

Clearly there are lots of caveats to this option. **Security** is always a concern, as is the resilience of the IT infrastructure necessary to support on-line order processing by clients. However, a number of forward-thinking businesses have achieved this without replacing all their systems.

Step Six. Train staff in what you already have

Do your staff really understand the features of your accounting and business systems? Are they familiar with what the web can offer your organisation? Put together a **comprehensive training programme**.

Step Seven. Get board buy-in

A note of caution to conclude on: **you MUST get board and senior management buy-in to what you are planning**.

Source: Adapted from an article by John Tate, Management Accounting, April 2000

Datamining

> **KEY TERM**
>
> **Datamining** software looks for hidden patterns and relationships in large pools of data.

3.12 True datamining software discovers **previously unknown relationships**. Datamining provides insights that can not be obtained through OLAP. The hidden patterns and relationships the software identifies can be used to guide decision making and to **predict future behaviour**.

Case examples: Datamining

(1) The American retailer Wal-Mart discovered an unexpected relationship between the sale of **nappies** and **beer!** Wal-Mart found that both tended to sell at the same time, just after working hours, and concluded that men with small children stopped off to buy nappies on their way home, and bought beer at the same time. Logically therefore, if the two items were put in the same shopping aisle, sales of both should increase. Wal-Mart tried this and it worked.

The Wal-Mart system, tracking sales by store, item and date, required a **4 terabyte** (4000 gigabyte) database. Even this enormous quantity of data will not support the market analysis techniques that Wal-Mart anticipates using in the future, which will require data on each sales transaction.

3: Knowledge management

(2) Some credit card companies have used datamining to predict which customers are likely to switch to a competitor in the next few months. Based on the datamining results, the bank can take action to retain these customers.

3.13 Datamining uses statistical analysis tools as well as neural networks, fuzzy logic and other **intelligent techniques**.

3.14 The types of relationships or patterns that datamining may uncover may be classified as follows.

Relationship\Discovery	Comment
Classification or cluster	These terms refer to the identification of patterns within the database between a range of data items. For example, datamining may find that unmarried males aged between 20 and 30, who have an income above £50,000 are more likely to purchase a high performance sports car than people from other demographic groups. This group could then be targeted when marketing material is produced/distributed.
Association	One event can be linked or correlated to another event – such as in Wal-Mart example (1) above.
Forecasting	Trends are identified within the data that can be extrapolated into the future.

Case example: Datamining software

Datamining software

The following is extracted from marketing material for a Datamining product called the NeoVista Decision Series.

Understand The Patterns In Your Business and Discover The Value In Your Data

Within your corporate database resides extremely valuable information - information that reflects how your business processes operate and how your customers behave. Every transaction your organisation makes is captured for accounting purposes, and with it, a wealth of potential knowledge.

When properly analysed, organised and presented, this information can be of enormous value. Conventional 'drill down' database query techniques may reveal some of these details, but much of the valuable **knowledge content will remain hidden**.

The NeoVista Decision Series is a suite of knowledge discovery software specifically designed to address this challenge. Analysing data without any preconceived notion of the patterns it contains, the Decision Series **seeks out relationships and trends**, and presents them in easy-to-understand form, enabling better business decisions. The Decision Series is being used today by leading corporations to discover the hidden value in their data, providing them with major competitive advantages and organisational benefits.

A Large Multi-National Retailer uses the Decision Series **to refine inventory stocking levels**, by store and by item, to dramatically reduce out-of-stock or overstocking situations and thereby improve revenues and reduce forced markdowns.

A Health Maintenance Group uses the Decision Series to **predict which of its members are most at risk** from specific major illnesses. This presents opportunities for timely medical intervention and preventative treatment to promote the patient's well-being and reduce the healthcare provider's costs.

An International Retail Sales Organisation uses the Decision Series to **optimise store and department layouts**, resulting in more accurate targeting of products to maximise sales within the scope of available resources.

NeoVista's unique software can be applied to a wide range of business problems, allowing you to:

Part A: Information systems and the organisation

Determine the **relationships** that lie at the heart of your business.

Make reliable **estimates of future behaviour** based on sophisticated analyses of past events.

Make **business decisions with a higher degree of understanding** and confidence.

Datamining is renowned for exposing important facts and anomalies within data warehouses. The NeoVista Decision Series' knowledge discovery methodology has the proven ability to expose the patterns that are not merely interesting, but which are critical to your business. These patterns provide you with an advantage through insight and knowledge that your competition may never discover.

Summary diagram

3.15 Some of the major issues and relationships covered in the first three chapters are shown in the following diagram. (You don't need to learn this diagram, its purpose is to encourage you to think about possible relationships and links between different topics.)

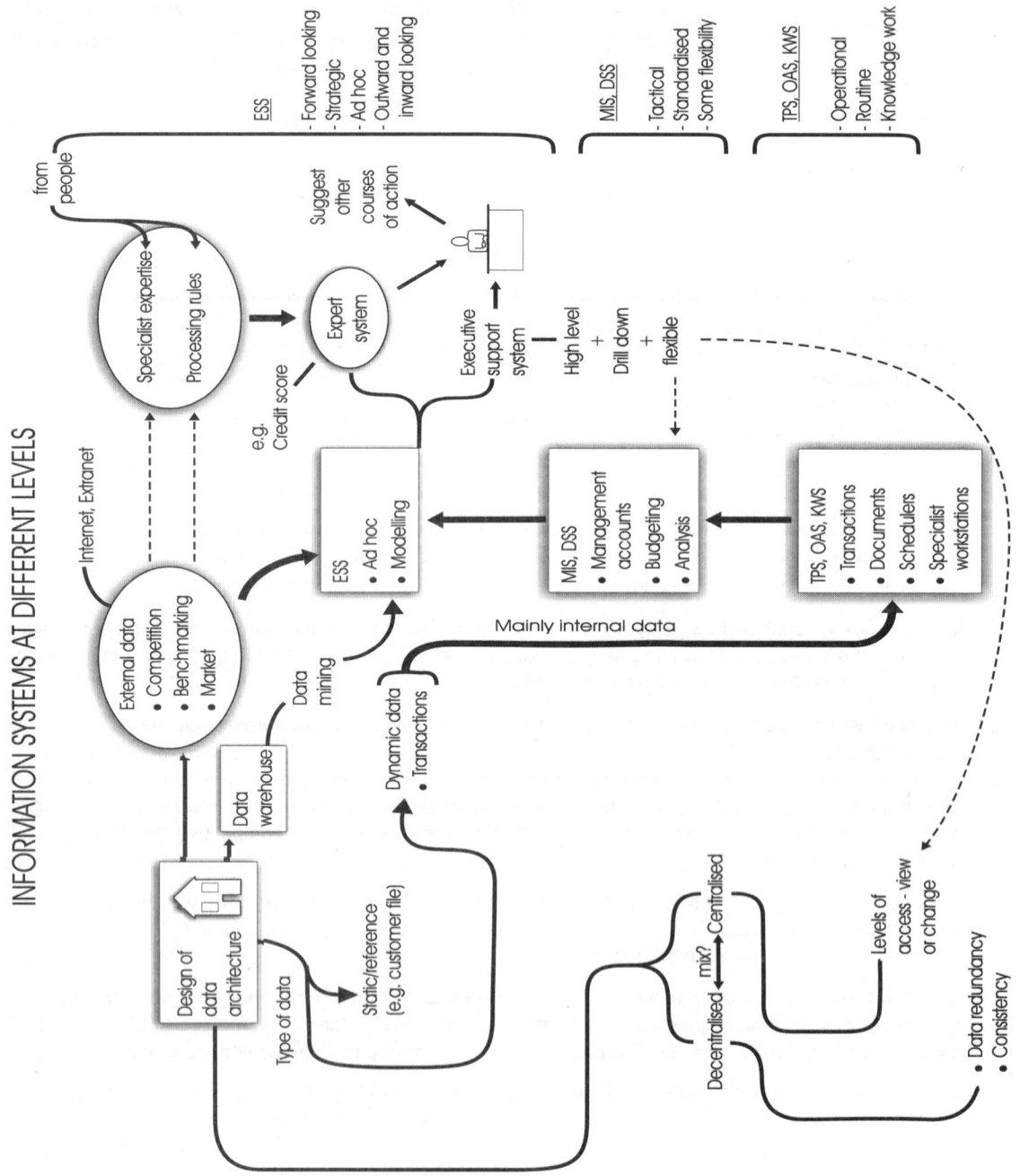

Chapter roundup

- **Knowledge management** describes the process of collecting, storing and using the knowledge held within an organisation.
- Knowledge is now commonly viewed as a sustainable source of competitive advantage. Producing unique products or services or producing products or services at a lower cost than competitors is based on superior knowledge.
- **Tacit knowledge** is expertise held by people within the organisation that has not been formally documented.
- **Knowledge workers** are people whose jobs consist primarily of creating new information and knowledge. They are often members of a profession such as doctors, engineers, authors, lawyers and scientists.
- **Data workers** process and distribute information eg secretary, input clerk.
- Information systems play an important role in knowledge management, helping with **information flows** and helping formally **capture** the knowledge held within the organisation.
- Office automation systems are used for knowledge **distribution**.
- Group collaboration systems are used for knowledge **sharing**.
- Knowledge work systems are used for knowledge **creation**.
- Artificial intelligence systems are used for knowledge **capture and codification**.
- A database is a collection of data organised to service many applications. The database provides convenient access to data for a wide variety of users and user needs.
- A database management system (**DBMS**) is the software that centralises data and manages access to the database. It is a system which allows numerous applications to extract the data they need without the need for separate files.
- There are three types of database structures; **hierarchical**, **network** and **relational**.
- **Advantages of a database system** include the avoidance of data duplication, management is encouraged to manage data as a valuable resource, data consistency across the organisation, and the flexibility for answering ad-hoc queries.
- **Disadvantages of a database system** include initial development costs and the potential problems of data security.
- A **data warehouse** consists of a database, containing data from various operational systems, and reporting and query tools.
- Organisations may build a single central data warehouse to serve the entire organisation or may create a series of smaller **data marts**.
- **Datamining** software looks for **hidden** patterns and relationships in large pools of data. Datamining uses **statistical analysis tools** as well as **neural networks**, **fuzzy logic** and other **intelligent techniques**.

Part A: Information systems and the organisation

Quick quiz

1. Distinguish between explicit knowledge and tacit knowledge.
2. Match the following types of system (left column) with how they help knowledge management (right column).

Knowledge work systems	Knowledge distribution
Artificial intelligence systems	Knowledge sharing
Office automation systems	Knowledge creation
Group collaboration systems	Knowledge capture and codification

3. What is groupware?
4. List five features of groupware.
5. Artificial intelligence and expert systems are the same thing. TRUE or FALSE?
6. What is a database management system (DBMS)?
7. Which logical database model does not use 'pointers'?
8. Distinguish between a data warehouse and a data mart.
9. List four business applications of datamining.

Answers to quick quiz

1. Explicit knowledge is knowledge that an organisation already stores in formal systems. It includes facts, transactions and events that can be clearly stated and stored in information systems.

    Tacit knowledge is expertise held by people within the organisation that has not been formally documented.

2.
Knowledge work systems	Knowledge creation
Artificial intelligence systems	Knowledge capture and codification
Office automation systems	Knowledge distribution
Group collaboration systems	Knowledge sharing

3. Groupware is a term used to describe software that provides functions for the use of collaborative work groups.

4. A scheduler (or diary or calendar) allowing users to keep track of their schedule and plan meetings with others.
    An electronic address book containing contact information.
    To do lists enabling tasks to be prioritised.
    A journal to record significant interactions and activities.
    A jotter for jotting down notes as quick reminders of questions, ideas, and so on.

5. FALSE. Artificial intelligence (AI) is the development of computer-based systems designed to behave as humans. Artificial intelligence systems are based on human expertise, knowledge and reasoning patterns. An expert system is one example of AI. Expert systems are computer programs that capture human expertise in a limited domain of knowledge.

6. A database management system (DBMS) is the software that manages access to a database. It is a system which allows numerous applications to extract the data they need without the need for separate files.

7. Relational databases do not use pointers. Hierarchical and network databases have pointers attached to record segments giving the location of related records. Instead of pointers, relational databases use three basic operations to develop useful sets of data; Select, Join and Project.

3: Knowledge management

> 8   A data warehouse consists of a database, containing data from various operational systems, and reporting and query tools. Organisations may build a single central data warehouse to serve the entire organisation or may create a series of smaller data marts. A data mart holds a selection of the organisation's data for a specific purpose.
>
> 9   Some examples include:
>
> Predicting what each website visitor is most interested in seeing.
> Predicting which customers are likely to switch to competitors.
> Identifying common characteristics of customers.
> Determining which products are often purchased together.
> Identifying which transactions are most likely to be fraudulent.

Now try the questions below from the Exam Question Bank. Question 15 includes detailed guidance with the question and answer.

Number	Level	Marks	Time
15 (b)	Exam	10	18 mins
15 (c)	Exam	4	7 mins

96

Part B
Business systems, systems analysis and business case development

Chapter 4

BUSINESS SYSTEMS AND SYSTEMS THINKING

Topic list	Syllabus reference
1 Systems thinking: Hard and soft properties	4(a), 4(b)
2 Hard systems approach	4(a)
3 Soft systems approach	4(b)
4 Business systems	4(c)
5 Business automation, rationalisation and re-engineering	4(c)
6 Automate, informate and transformate	4(c)

Introduction

It is becoming increasingly common to view organisations as systems, and to apply systems theory to organisational and business problems. This chapter contains much theoretical information. Remember to keep in mind how the theory could be applied to real world (or examination) scenarios.

Study guide

13 – Business strategy

- Describe the stages in the development of business systems and strategies *(Also see Chapter 1)*
- Explain the concept of business automation
- Explain the concept of business rationalisation
- Evaluate and discuss the principles of business process engineering

14 – Hard systems approach

- Evaluate the structured systems lifecycle emphasising the deliverables from each stage, clarifying the importance of these from a management perspective

15 – Soft systems approach

- Evaluate the principles of Checkland's soft systems methodology
- Apply the major tools employed in Checkland's soft systems methodology: Root definitions, CATWOE, conceptual models

Exam guide

The soft systems approach provides a way of ensuring human issues are included when analysing a business system or situation. Soft systems methodology is new to the ACCA syllabus and is therefore highly examinable.

Part B: Business systems, systems analysis and business case development

1 SYSTEMS THINKING: HARD AND SOFT PROPERTIES

1.1 Systems theory explores the nature of systems and the characteristics of systems and approaches that are suited to different situations. **Organisations** are social systems. All social systems are open to a wide range of influences, which means they are sensitive to a wide variety of environmental factors and are often exposed to **unstructured problems**.

1.2 Unstructured problems are sometimes referred to as 'soft' problems. Different people might have different views of **what the problem that needs to be addressed is**, and a solution might have to satisfy a variety of different objectives.

1.3 On the other hand, a 'hard' approach is based on structured, logical problems, where the objective is clear.

1.4 A **hard** approach is suitable in circumstances when:

- The problem can be clearly defined
- Objectives are clear
- The problem is self-contained
- Information needs are known
- A solution can be recognised
- Standard solution techniques are applicable

1.5 A **soft** approach is suitable in circumstances when:

- The problem is difficult to define
- Tastes, values, judgement and opinions are involved
- It is not clear what is known and what is needed
- It is not clear what the solution should achieve
- The problem is 'people' oriented
- There are no standard solution techniques available

1.6 Many problems or situations have both hard and soft properties, for example an information systems project. Properties can be classified as either hard or soft – although in practise the two will, in some circumstances, be **related**.

1.7 The hard properties would include the **specifications** of the system, for example processing speeds, the **space required** to accommodate the system and the **budget** available to develop the system. Soft properties are usually **people** related.

2 HARD SYSTEMS APPROACH

2.1 Different approaches to systems development place differing emphasis on hard or soft areas. Early systems development approaches, such as the systems lifecycle, tended to be 'harder' in their approach than more modern approaches.

2.2 In the early days of business computing, computers were used to **automate processing activities**. To a large extent, the systems which were developed simply **matched previous manual procedures**. However, the process of managing information systems development has moved on from being a matter of technical control over a few computer programmers to being a **major management operation** involving large parts of an organisation and elements of its environment.

Systems lifecycle

2.3 The systems lifecycle (sometimes referred to as the Systems Development Lifecycle or SDLC) is a traditional method of building information systems. This **disciplined approach** to systems development identifies several stages of development. (Note than the number and name of the stages varies depending on the author or organisation referred to – but the principle of a structured approach is consistent.)

> **KEY TERM**
>
> The term **'systems lifecycle'** describes the stages a system moves through from inception until it is discarded or replaced.

Stage	Comment
Project definition	Involves an **investigation** and analysis of the organisation's information requirements to decide if a new or modified information system is required. If a new project is identified its **objectives**, **scope** and **project plan** are developed.
Feasibility study	This involves a review of the existing system and the identification of a range of possible alternative solutions. A feasible (technical, operational, economic, social) solution will be selected – or a decision not to proceed made. Findings are usually contained in a **feasibility study report** which describes the activities required in the remaining lifecycle phases.
Design	The logical and physical design specifications are produced in a **detailed specification** of the new system.
Programming or software selection	If bespoke software is to be produced, analysts work with programmers to prepare **program specifications** and then the **programs**. If off-the-shelf software is suitable, packages are evaluated (perhaps in a report) and **selected**.
Installation	Steps are taken to put the system into operation. **Testing**, file conversion and user **training** are carried out. A **formal conversion plan** is developed.
Post-implementation	The system is used and evaluated. A formal **post-implementation audit** determines how well the system has met its objectives and whether any modifications are required.

Drawbacks of the lifecycle approach

2.4 The systems lifecycle is considered a **hard systems approach** as it has a narrow focus. The approach efficiently automates **existing procedures** within easily defined processing requirements. The resulting systems are modelled on the manual systems they are replacing.

2.5 Sequential models (such as the lifecycle model) **restrict user input** throughout much of the process. (A sequential model is one where a stage is not started until the previous stage is complete.) This often results in substantial and costly modifications late in the development process. It becomes increasingly difficult and expensive to change system requirements the further a system is developed.

2.6 Time overruns are common. The sequential nature of the process meant a hold-up on one stage would stop development completely – contributing to time overruns. Time pressures and **lack of user involvement** often resulted in a poor quality system.

2.7 Because of these drawbacks the lifecycle approach is not as widely used today as in the past. However, it is still used with success for building systems where requirements are **highly structured** and well-defined eg large transaction processing systems.

3 SOFT SYSTEMS APPROACH

3.1 The soft systems approach to systems development aims to take into account the **soft properties** of the implementation – this approach looks at the wider picture. Some examples of soft properties that should be considered during systems development and implementation are described in the following paragraphs.

Job security and status

3.2 Employees might think that a new system will **put them out of a job**, because the computer will perform routines that are currently done manually, and so reduce the need for human intervention.

3.3 A new system might make some staff, experienced in the existing system, feel that all their experience will be worthless when the new system goes live, and so they will **lose 'status'** within the office.

3.4 In some cases, the resistance to a new system might stem from a fear that it will result in a loss of status for the **department** concerned. For example, the management of the department concerned might believe that a computer system will give 'control' over information gathering and dissemination to another group.

Career prospects

3.5 Managers and staff might think that a new system will damage their career prospects by reducing the requirement for **middle managers** and therefore reducing opportunities for promotion.

Social change

3.6 New systems might disrupt the established **social system** in the office. Individuals who are used to working together might be separated into different groups, and individuals used to working on their own might be expected to join a group.

Bewilderment

3.7 It is easy for individuals to be confused and bewildered by change. The systems analyst must **explain the new system fully,** clearing up doubts, inviting and answering questions, etc from a very early stage in systems investigation onwards through the design stage to eventual implementation.

Fear of depersonalisation

3.8 Staff may be afraid that the computer will 'take over' and they will be **reduced to being operators** chained to the machine, losing the ability to introduce the 'human touch' to the work they do. This is not wholly unrealistic.

4: Business systems and systems thinking

3.9 Dysfunctional behaviour might manifest itself in the **antagonism of staff** towards specialists who are employed to design and introduce a computer system. It might take the form of:

(a) An **unwillingness to explain** the details of the current system, or to suggest weaknesses in it that the new system might eradicate. Since development staff need information from and participation by the operating staff to develop an efficient system, any such antagonism would impair the system design.

(b) A **reluctance to be taught** the new system.

(c) A **reluctance to help** with introducing the new system.

3.10 Another fear is that the new system will expose how inefficient previous methods of information gathering and information use had been. Individuals feel that they are being criticised by the revelation of any such deficiencies.

3.11 To **overcome the human problems** with systems design and implementation, management and systems analysts must recognise them, and do what they can to resolve them.

(a) **Keeping staff informed**

Employees should be kept fully informed about plans to install the new system, how events are progressing and how the new system will affect what people do. If there are to be job losses, or a redeployment of staff, these should be arranged in full consultation with the people concerned.

(b) **Explanations**

It should be explained to staff why the change is 'for the better'.

(c) **Participation**

User department employees should be encouraged to participate fully in the design of the system. Participation should be genuine.

(d) **Skills**

Employees will learn new skills which will make them more attractive candidates either for internal or external positions.

(e) **Training**

A training programme should be planned in advance of the implementation.

(f) **Work patterns**

Careful attention should be given to:

(i) The design of work organisation.
(ii) The developments or preservation of 'social work groups'.
(iii) The inter-relationship between jobs and responsibilities in the new system.

(g) **Planning**

Change should be planned and managed.

(h) **The analyst**

The systems analyst should:

(i) Produce changes gradually, giving time for personnel to accept the changes.
(ii) Try to build up good working relationships.
(iii) Work towards getting employees to accept change as a matter of course.
(iv) Be willing to **listen**.

Part B: Business systems, systems analysis and business case development

(i) **Management commitment**

The system must be committed to by all involved.

Checkland's Soft Systems Methodology (SSM)

3.12 The soft systems approach is represented by *Checkland's* **Soft Systems Methodology** (SSM). SSM is a way of analysing situations in systems - such as an organisation. It provides an organised approach which can be used **to tackle unstructured and poorly defined problems**.

3.13 The underlying theme of SSM is that the world contains many **complex relationships** and therefore situations can not be easily defined scientifically. The real world consists of an individual's derived experience-based view of it. This means that requirements for action/improvement are not constant, but evolve as the differing view of individuals change and as actions are taken.

3.14 Much traditional systems design is concerned with how to complete a given task. The nature of the task, the 'what', has already been defined. In many situations however, a manager will not know what the problem is. It can be demonstrated that being a manager involves not only deciding how to go about a task, but **deciding what the task is** as well.

3.15 SSM is based on **a number of assumptions**.

Meaning

3.16 Human beings will attempt to place a **meaning** on their observations and experiences. This is 'human nature'. The meaning which an individual attributes to an event or situation is that individual's **interpretation** of the event or situation. This **interpretation** is derived from experience of the real world.

Intention

3.17 Once an interpretation has been placed on experience, it is possible to form intentions. An intention represents a decision to **follow a particular course of action**.

Action

3.18 When an individual has decided to follow a particular course of action, he or she can be described as taking **purposeful action**. This is any action which is deliberate. Purposeful action has the effect of changing the world. This in turn means that the event or situation upon which an interpretation was placed is altered, creating a cycle of activity.

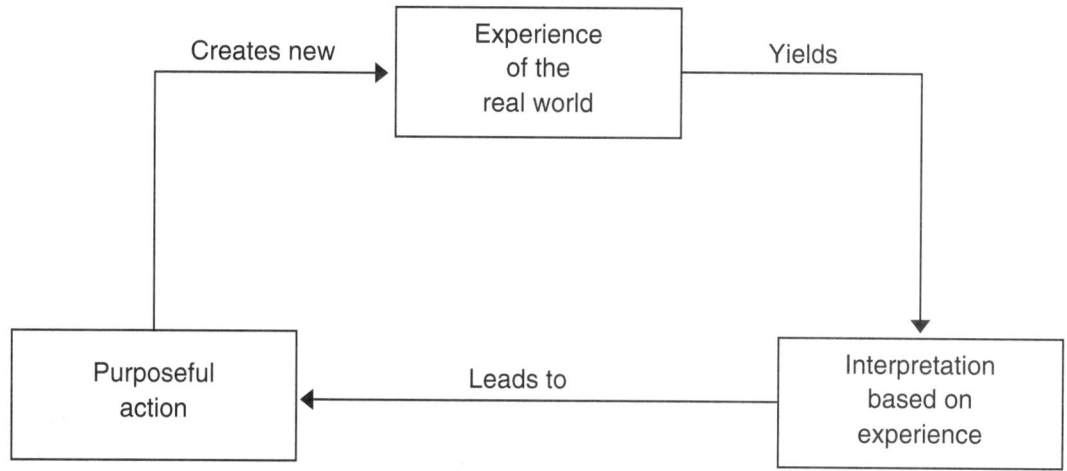

3.19 The purpose of SSM, therefore, is to enhance understanding of complex human situations. It attempts to deal with complex social situations which entail **many divergent perspectives**. There is no such thing as the 'real world', just different perspectives on it.

3.20 SSM involves a process of enquiry which leads to action, but this action is not ever regarded as an end point unless the participants in the process choose to make it one. SSM recognises that **taking action changes the problem situation**: this means that enquiry can continue in a learning process that remains open for new findings.

The 'stages' of SSM

3.21 The learning process of SSM cycles between learning and action and follows a set of seven stages.

(a) In the first stage the **problematic situation** is identified and entered into.

(b) Secondly, the problem situation is **expressed in three analytical steps** (intervention, prevalent culture, and power relationships).

(c) The third stage involves developing a set of '**root definitions**' (explained later in this section) for systems thought to be relevant to the problem situation.

(d) **Conceptual models** are built in stage four. The verbal concepts previously defined are logically structured, by use of arrows, to form relevant combinations of an operational and a monitoring and control system.

(e) By **comparing** models and reality (real-world actions) stage five aims at inducing learning steps in the group. This often leads to a reiteration of the preceding stages.

(f) The purpose of the sixth stage is to achieve a **common understanding** regarding possible improvements to the real-world situation.

(g) The last stage of SSM is concerned with **taking action** and putting the changes in place – thus changing the problem situation itself and restarting the cycle.

3.22 This approach tended to lead to the (restricting) belief that SSM was a stage-by-stage process, which is not intended. The representation of SSM developed by Checkland is shown in the following diagram.

Part B: Business systems, systems analysis and business case development

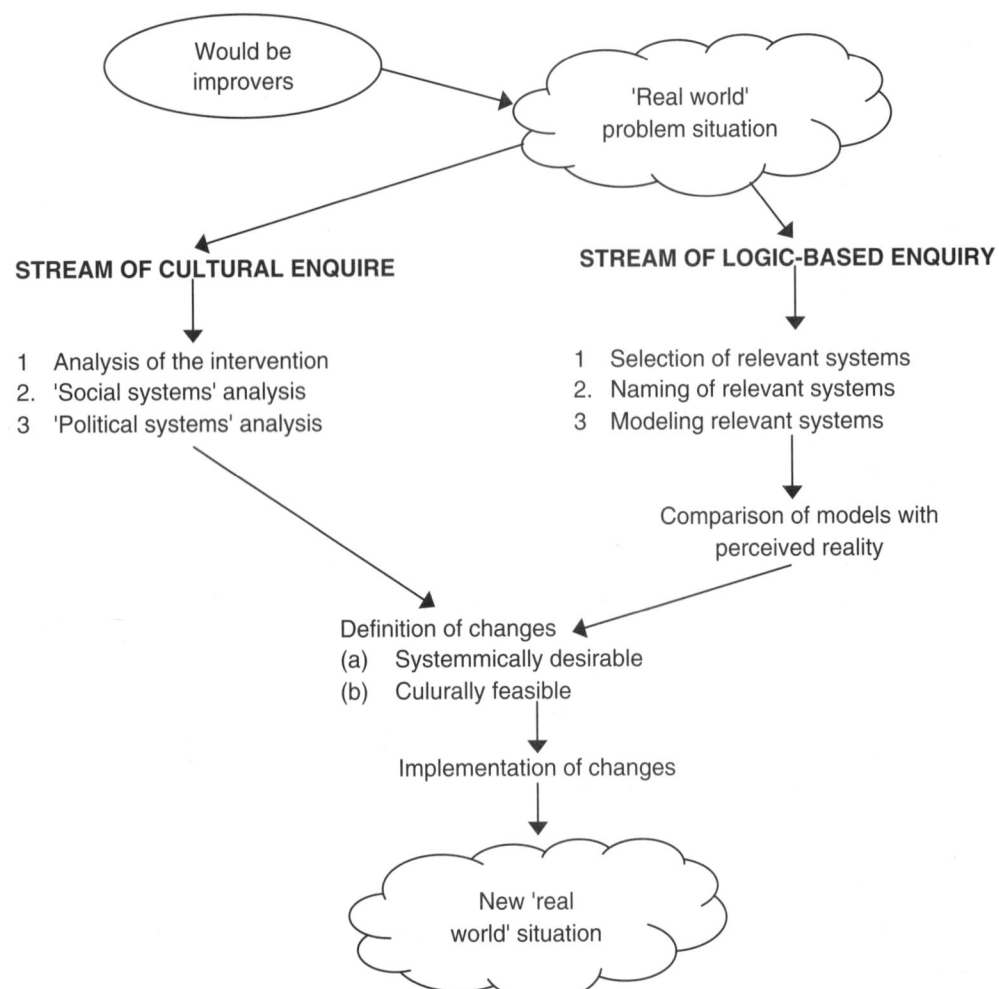

3.23 SSM entails two related **streams of enquiry**: the logic-driven stream of enquiry and the cultural stream of enquiry.

The logic-driven stream of enquiry

3.24 The logic-driven stream of enquiry uses models of 'human activity systems' to analyse the problem situation. Under the logic-driven stream of enquiry the **core purpose** of the system is established. This is known as the **root definition**.

KEY TERM

The **root definition** is a concise description of a human activity system that states what the system is and what the system does.

3.25 One approach to formulating the root definition is to consider the mnemonic CATWOE. This has the following elements.

(a) **Customers.** These are the people or groups who benefit or suffer from the system.

(b) **Actors.** Actors are those who will carry out the transformation process.

(c) **Transformation process.** This is the conversion of input to output.

(d) **Weltanschauung.** This is the 'world view' which underlies the assumptions behind the root definition.

4: Business systems and systems thinking

(e) **Owners.** These are people who could stop the transformation process.

(f) **Environmental constraints.** These are fixed elements outside the system.

Case example

Root definitions can vary. For example, a root definition for a prison could be any of the following.

A system to punish criminals.
A system to deter possible future criminals.
A system to rehabilitate offenders.
A system to provide justice for victims.

Root definitions frequently utilise the same 'a system to ... by ... in order to' structure.

3.26 Once the core purpose of the system has been established a **conceptual model** of the relevant system is created.

> **KEY TERM**
>
> A **conceptual model** is a systematic account of a human activity system built on the basis of the system root definition.

3.27 Conceptual models need to be logically possible, but do not purport to describe existing situations.

3.28 The steps involved in building a conceptual model from a root definition are outlined below (the sequence should be used flexibly):

Step 1. Use the root definition and CATWOE elements to form an impression of the system carrying out a **transformation process**.

Step 2. Decide on a **number of key verbs** which describe the fundamental activities necessary in the system.

Step 3. Structure **key related activities** in groups.

Step 4. Connect the groups of activities by arrows which indicate **logical dependencies**.

Step 5. Check that the root definition and conceptual model together give a clear impression of what the system **is** and what the system **does**.

Case example

This example of a conceptual model is based on an example in *Peter Checkland's Systems Thinking, Systems Practice.*

For a software producer to prosper the firm must develop technically and commercially innovative products and **protect** its innovations and income by means of international copyright law.

The **root definition** of a system designed to protect the firms intellectual property could be:

'A system that aims to ensure the firms intellectual property is managed to ensure the best possible contribution to business success.'

The CATWOE elements could be:

Customers. The software company as a whole.

Actors. Those within the firm responsible for protecting intellectual property eg company secretary.

Part B: Business systems, systems analysis and business case development

Transformation process. To take in knowledge of the firm's business and potential intellectual property and to use these inputs to generate action concerning intellectual property which makes the best possible contribution to business success.

World view. That the firm is operating in a world that is concerned about enforcing intellectual property rights.

Owners. Senior management of the firm – who could decide not to attempt to defend intellectual property, and would therefore not require the system eg issue software as 'shareware'.

Environmental constraints. International intellectual property law.

A conceptual model of the system described in the root definition follows.

Conceptual model

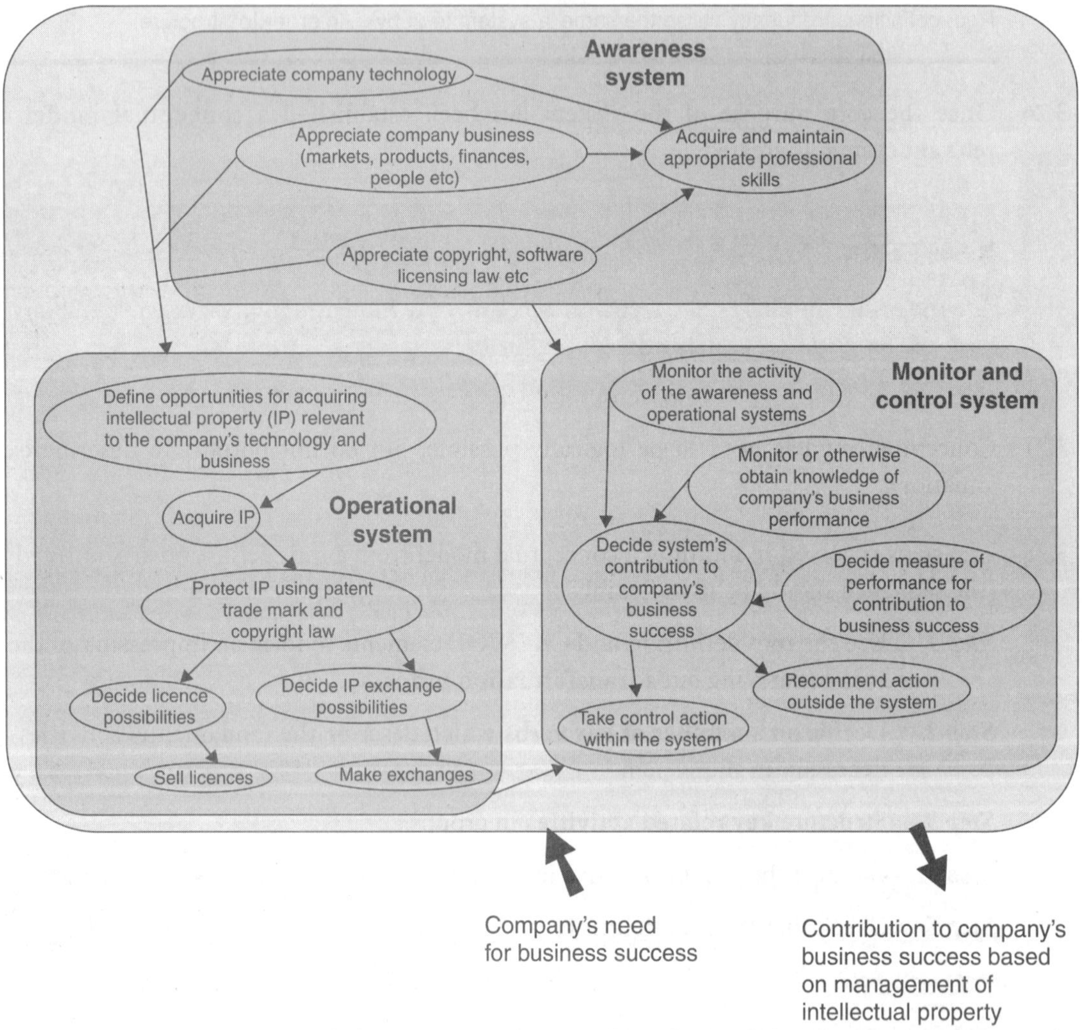

3.29 The success or failure of the transformation process in the model is assessed by reference to three factors.

(a) **Efficacy**. This checks whether the means chosen produces the required output.

(b) **Efficiency**. This ensures that the process uses the minimum amount of resources possible to produce the desired results.

(c) **Effectiveness**. This tests whether long-term objectives are being met.

3.30 Although the model does not set out to document the current situation, it is often useful to **compare it to the real world**. This should stimulate debate among the participants as to whether the model improves the current situation and should highlight areas that may require adjustment. The comparison process could involve:

(a) **Formal questioning**, asking questions about the situation based on the model.

(b) **Informal discussion**, asking how the model differs from the current situation.

(c) **Event reconstruction**, considering what might have happened in the past using the system modelled.

(d) **Model overlay**, comparing the model with a conceptual model of the existing system.

The cultural stream of enquiry

3.31 Under the cultural stream of enquiry, three analyses are carried out. **Analysis One** is an analysis of the relationship between three groups.

(a) The **client** is the person or group who initiated the study.

(b) The **would-be problem solver,** who may be the client, wishes to take some action in respect of the problem situation.

(c) The **problem owner** is the person or group most affected by the problem.

3.32 **Analysis Two** considers the evolving set of relationships between roles, norms and values. A role may be defined formally, for example 'information systems manager' or informally, for example 'office joker'. The behaviour expected from a person in a particular role is the norm. Behaviour of a person in a particular role is assessed by reference to values, which are the local yardsticks of performance measurement.

3.33 **Analysis Three** considers the political dimension. The focus is on understanding how power is expressed.

3.34 A **rich picture** is developed which shows the relevant relationships and attempts to provide the 'feel' of the situation by incorporating value judgements.

> **KEY TERM**
>
> A **rich picture** is a diagrammatic representation of a situation compiled through examining elements of structure, process and the situation climate.

3.35 There are no hard and fast rules for drawing rich pictures. They use simple but meaningful symbols and text to give an overview of major flows and structures. There is no need for expert drawing skills: for instance, people or groups can be 'stick' people; the distribution department may be shown as a primitive drawing of a van; conflicts are usually shown by the crossed swords symbol; agreement by shaking hands. Three aspects of information systems are usually shown.

(a) **Structural elements** such as departmental boundaries, physical or geographical layout and product types and activities.

(b) **Process elements**, indicating what actually takes place in the system.

(c) **Relationships**, indicated by arrows and symbols (such as the 'crossed swords' symbol).

An example (adapted from *Mathiassen and Nielsen*) follows.

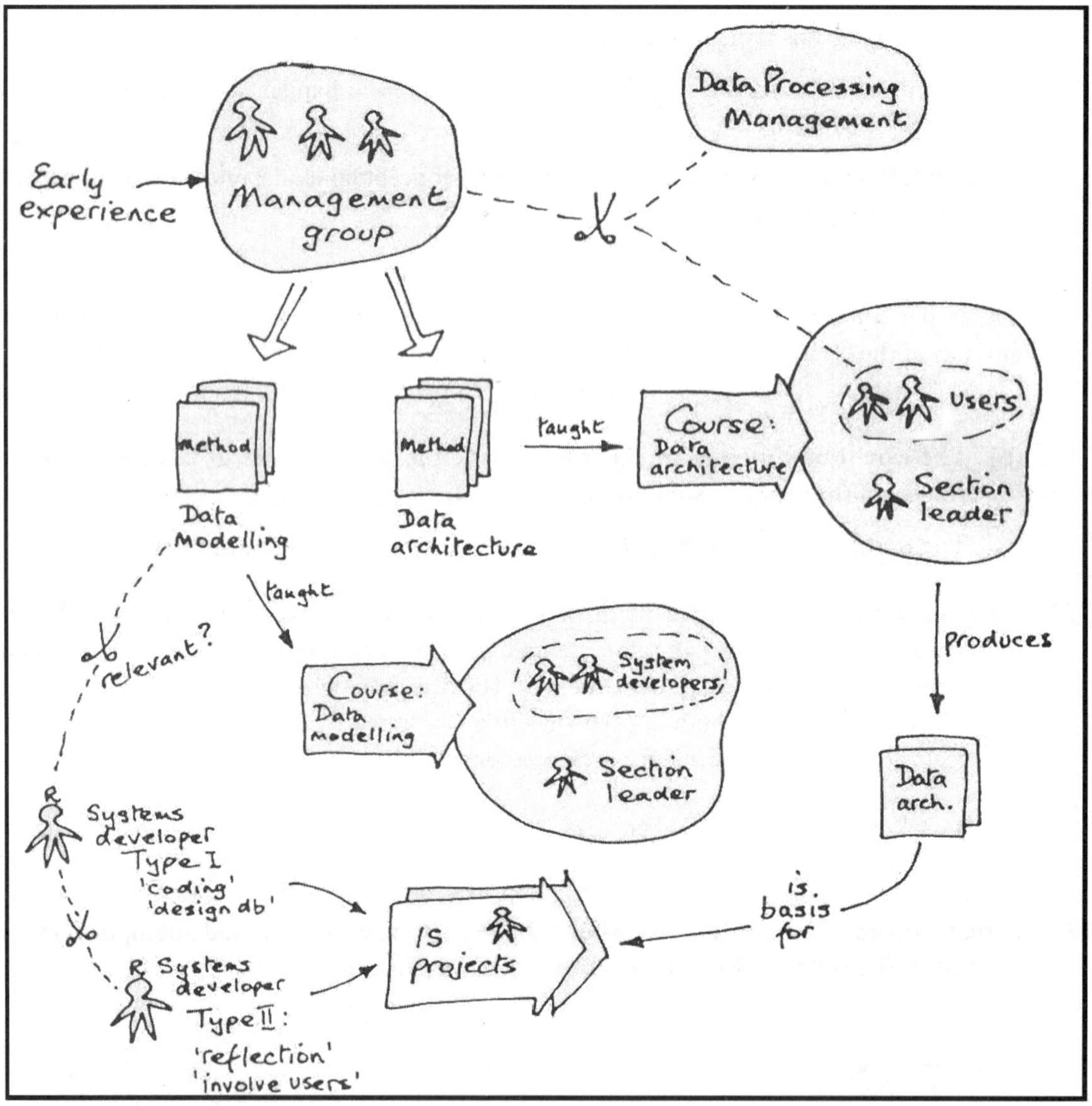

Part B: Business systems, systems analysis and business case development

[Diagram showing Management group, Data Processing Management, methods for Data Modelling and Data architecture, courses taught to users/section leader and system developers, producing Data arch. which is basis for IS projects, with Systems developer Type I ('coding', 'design db') and Type II ('reflection', 'involve users').]

3.36 Once the two streams of enquiry have been followed, it is necessary to **define the changes** which would improve the problem situation and **implement** measures to effect these changes.

4 BUSINESS SYSTEMS

The systems approach to developing business strategies

4.1 Organisations such as businesses can be viewed as a system. **Inputs** are received and **processed** to produce **outputs** of goods and services. The **objectives** of the organisation are thereby fulfilled.

> **KEY TERMS**
>
> A **system** is a set of interacting components that operate together to accomplish a purpose.
>
> A **business system** is a collection of people, machines and methods organised to accomplish a set of specific functions.

4: Business systems and systems thinking

4.2 The systems approach uses three steps.

Step 1. Identify what the whole system is.
Step 2. Identify the overall **objectives** of the system as a whole.
Step 3. Make **plans** with these objectives in mind.

4.3 For example, in a business, the total system is the **business as a whole**. Its objective might be to **maximise profits**. The plans for the business should then be made with this objective in view.

4.4 To achieve system objectives, it is usually necessary to set objectives and targets for **individual parts** of the system. The systems approach involves development of plans and controls for subsystems within the framework of the overall objectives of the total system.

4.5 However, the organisation must also remain sensitive to its **external environment**. It must respond to threats and opportunities, restrictions and challenges posed by markets, consumer trends, competitors, the government and so on.

Hierarchy of systems

4.6 The organisation as system can be viewed as being composed of subsystems arranged in a **system hierarchy**.

Corporate level

4.7 Corporate systems support the organisation as a whole. They are concerned with its **strategic** outlook and its relationship with the external elements and systems in the environment. Systems at this level might include business and economic **forecasting** systems and corporate **financial planning** systems.

Divisional level

4.8 Many organisations are divided into a number of distinct units which may operate in different industrial sectors, provide different services or sell different products. Legally, these units may be divisions of a single company or separate subsidiary companies or a combination of the two. Systems at this level might include **market analysis** systems and **industry performance** forecasting systems.

Departmental level

4.9 At departmental level, the emphasis is on the implementation of the organisation's strategy. This involves managing available resources within the constraints imposed. Systems at this **tactical** level include **credit control** and **quality control** systems.

Operational level

4.10 At **operational** level, the emphasis is on the control of day-to-day operations. The systems usually found at this level are **transaction processing systems**, such as sales order processing or production control systems.

Socio-technical systems

4.11 Another point of view suggests that an organisation is a 'structured **sociotechnical** system', that is, it consists of at least three sub-systems.

(a) A structure.

(b) A technological system (concerning the work to be done, and the machines, tools and other facilities available to do it).

(c) A social system (concerning the people within the organisation, the ways they think and the ways they interact with each other).

4.12 We look at the concept of socio-technical design in relation to employee/employer relations in Chapter 9.

5 BUSINESS AUTOMATION, RATIONALISATION AND RE-ENGINEERING

5.1 Information technology can have a major effect on business systems. The following diagram shows **four types of change encouraged by information technology** that have implications for organisation structure, work flows, relationships, products and services. Each change carries different potential rewards and risks.

Forms of organisational change

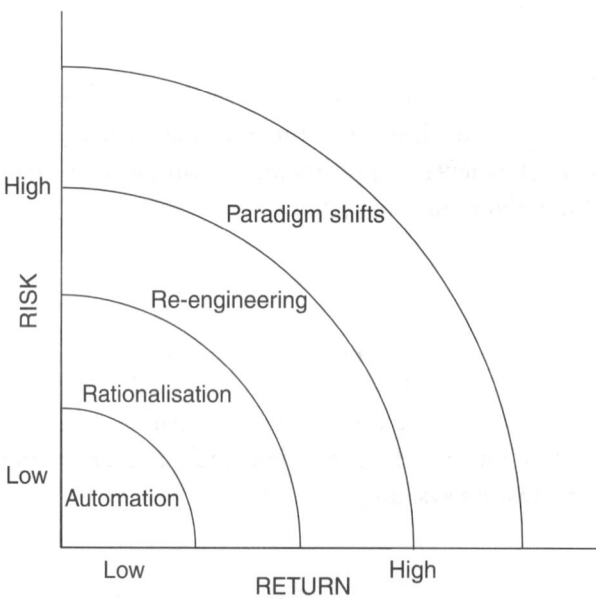

KEY TERMS

Business automation is the use of computerised working methods to speed up the performance of existing tasks.

Business rationalisation is the streamlining of operating procedures to eliminate obvious inefficiencies. Rationalisation usually involves automation.

5.2 Automation and rationalisation are relatively the most common forms of organisational change. They usually offer modest returns and little risk.

5.3 **Automation** usually involves assisting employees to carry out their duties more efficiently – for example introducing a computerised accounting package.

5.4 **Rationalisation** involves not only the automation of a process but also efficient process design. For example, before computerisation it was not necessary for all bank account numbers to follow a consistent structure (eg nine numeric characters) and account balances may not have been calculated daily.

5.5 An automated banking system requires the standardisation of account number structure and standard rules for calculating daily account balances – in this situation automation encouraged a certain amount of rationalisation.

5.6 **Business process re-engineering** (BPR) involves considering how **business processes** could be redesigned or re-engineered to improve efficiency. (Business process re-engineering is sometimes referred to simply as **business process engineering.** Strictly speaking, business process engineering has a slightly wider focus as it looks at business processes in general – not only existing processes in a specific business.)

5.7 BPR reorganises work flows, eliminating waste. It can lead to **fundamental changes** in the way an organisation functions. It is more ambitious than rationalisation and therefore carries greater risk.

5.8 The following definition is taken from Hammer and Champy's *Re-engineering the Corporation*.

> **KEY TERM**
>
> **Business Process Re-engineering** is the fundamental rethinking and radical redesign of business processes to achieve dramatic improvements in critical contemporary measures of performance, such as cost, quality, service and speed.

5.9 The key words here are '**fundamental', 'radical', 'dramatic' and 'process'**.

(a) **Fundamental** and **radical** indicate that BPR is somewhat akin to zero base budgeting: it starts by asking basic questions such as 'why do we do what we do', without making any assumptions or looking back to what has always been done in the past.

(b) '**Dramatic**' means that BPR should achieve 'quantum leaps in performance', not just marginal, incremental improvements.

(c) '**Process**' is explained in the following paragraphs.

> **KEY TERM**
>
> A **process** is a collection of activities that takes one or more kinds of input and creates an output.

5.10 For **example,** order fulfilment is a process that takes an order as its input and results in the delivery of the ordered goods. Part of this process is the manufacture of the goods, but under BPR the aim of manufacturing is **not merely to make** the goods. Manufacturing should aim to **deliver the goods that were ordered,** and any aspect of the manufacturing process that hinders this aim should be re-engineered. The first question to ask might be 'Do they need to be manufactured at all; should they be purchased from outside?'

Part B: Business systems, systems analysis and business case development

5.11 A re-engineered process has certain **characteristics**.

- Often several jobs are **combined** into one
- Workers often **make decisions**
- The **steps** in the process are performed in **a logical order**
- **Work** is performed where it **makes most sense**
- Checks and controls may be reduced, and **quality 'built-in'**
- One manager provides a **single point of contact**
- The advantages of **centralised and decentralised** operations are combined

5.12 EXAMPLE: BPR

This scenario is based on a problem at Ford.

A company employs 25 staff to perform the standard accounting task of matching goods received notes with orders and then with invoices. About 80% of their time is spent trying to find out why 20% of the set of three documents do not agree.

One way of improving the situation would have been to computerise the existing process to facilitate matching. This would have helped, but BPR went further: why accept any incorrect orders at all?

What if all the orders are entered onto a computerised database? When goods arrive at the goods inwards department they either agree to goods that have been ordered or they don't. It's as simple as that. Goods that agree to an order are accepted and paid for. Goods that are not agreed are sent back to the supplier. There are no files of unmatched items and time is not wasted trying to sort out these files.

The re-engineering of the process resulted in gains for the company: less staff time wasted, quicker payment for suppliers, lower stocks, and lower investment in working capital.

Principles of BPR

5.13 Hammer presents **seven principles** for BPR.

(a) Processes should be designed to achieve a desired **outcome** rather than focusing on existing **tasks.**

(b) Personnel who use the **output** from a process should **perform** the process. For example, a company could set up a database of approved suppliers; this would allow personnel who actually require supplies to order them themselves, perhaps using on-line technology, thereby eliminating the need for a separate purchasing function.

(c) Information processing should be **included** in the work which **produces** the information. This eliminates the differentiation between information gathering and information processing.

(d) Geographically **dispersed** resources should be treated as if they are **centralised.** This allows the benefits of centralisation to be obtained, for example, economies of scale through central negotiation of supply contracts, without losing the benefits of decentralisation, such as flexibility and responsiveness.

(e) Parallel activities should be **linked** rather than **integrated.** This would involve, for example, co-ordination between teams working on different aspects of a single process.

(f) 'Doers' should be allowed to be **self-managing.** The traditional distinction between workers and managers can be abolished: decision aids such as expert systems can be provided where they are required.

4: Business systems and systems thinking

(g) Information should be captured **once** at **source**. Electronic distribution of information makes this possible.

Is there a BPR methodology??

5.14 Davenport and Short prescribe a **five-step approach to BPR**.

Step 1. Develop the **business vision and process objectives**. BPR is driven by a business vision which implies specific business objectives such as cost reduction, time reduction and quality improvement.

Step 2. **Identify the processes** to be redesigned. Most firms use the High-Impact approach which focuses on the most important processes or those that conflict most with the business vision. Lesser number of firms use the Exhaustive approach that attempts to identify all the processes within an organisation and then prioritise them in order of redesign urgency.

Step 3. Understand and **measure the existing processes**. So old mistakes are not repeated and to provide a baseline for future improvements.

Step 4. **Identify IT levers**. Awareness of IT capabilities can and should influence process design. The role of IT is expanded on in the next section.

Step 5. Design and **build a prototype** of the new process. The actual design should not be viewed as the end of the BPR process - it should be viewed as a prototype, with successive alterations. The use of a prototype enables the involvement of customers.

IT and BPR

5.15 Simply **throwing IT at a problem does not cause it to be re-engineered**. Merely computerising existing ways of doing things is not necessarily the best solution. For technology to deliver value, it must help enact the processes that satisfy business requirements.

5.16 IT is not the solution in itself, it is an enabler. BPR uses IT to allow a business to do things that it is not doing already. For example, teleconferencing does not only reduce the cost of travelling to meetings - a re-engineering approach takes the view that teleconferencing allows more frequent meetings.

As Hammer and Champy put it, 'It is this disruptive power of technology, its ability to break the rules that limit how we conduct our work, that makes it critical to companies looking for competitive advantage.'

5.17 We look in detail at how technology has changed they way work is conducted in Chapter 9. Some examples are also provided below:

(a) **Shared databases** allow information to be viewed simultaneously from many locations.

(b) **Expert systems** enable generalists to do the work of an expert (in some circumstances).

(c) **Telecommunications networks** allow businesses to combine centralised and decentralised structures.

(d) **Decision-support tools** have resulted in decision making being passed lower down the organisation hierarchy.

(e) **Wireless data communication and portable computers** enable field staff to send and receive information wherever they are.

(f) **Interactive websites** mean that personal contact with buyers can be replaced by **effective** contact with buyers.

(g) **Automatic identification and tracking technology** allows closer monitoring of an object's whereabouts.

(h) **High performance computing** facilitates instant revision of plans and reports rather than periodic updates.

Why focus on processes?

5.18 Many businesses recognise that value is delivered **through processes,** but still define themselves in terms of their functional roles. To properly harness the resources within a business a clear agreement of the management and implementation of processes is needed. **Without this focus** on processes:

(a) It is **unclear how value is achieved** or can continue to be achieved.

(b) The **effects of change** on the operation of the business are **hard to predict**.

(c) There is no basis to achieve **consistent business improvement**.

(d) **Knowledge is lost** as people move around or out of the business.

(e) Cross-functional interaction is not encouraged.

(f) It is **difficult to align the strategy** of an organisation with the people, systems resources through which that strategy will be accomplished.

5.19 The relationship between **strategy, processes, people** and **technology** is shown below.

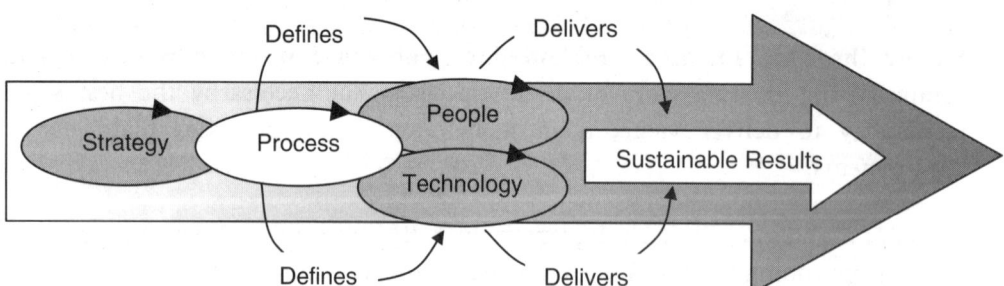

Problems with BPR

5.20 There are concerns that BPR has become misunderstood. According to an independent study of 100 European companies BPR has become allied in manager's minds with narrow targets such as **reductions in staff numbers and cost-cutting measures**.

5.21 Champy suggests that management itself should be re-engineered. Managers are not used to thinking in systems terms, so, **instead of looking at the whole picture** (which might affect their own jobs), they tend to **seize on individual aspects** of the organisation, such as re-engineering of processes.

5.22 It is argued that process re-engineering is really only a part of the **wider picture**. A report in the *Financial Times* (extracts below) on an unnamed company suggested four sets of changes as important to the transformation from a company which **satisfies** customers, to a company that **delights** them - and from a company which is **competent** to a company which is the **best** in its industry. Extracts from the report follow.

4: Business systems and systems thinking

'... **first, breaking down barriers** between its different disciplinary specialists and national units by a series of procedural and structural steps, of which the re-engineering of cross-unit processes is only one;

second, developing an explicit set of values and behaviour guidelines which are subscribed to (or 'shared') by everyone in the organisation;

third, redefining the role of management in order to foster much more empowerment, responsibility and decisiveness at every level.

All this requires the creation of the **fourth factor: an unprecedented degree of openness** and trust among managers and employees'.

Case example

Workflow systems / process re-engineering

Work design, whether it is related to work in the factory or at the desk, is a process of arriving at the most efficient way of completing tasks and activities that minimises effort and reduces the possibility of mistakes. It is the primary element involved in increasing productivity and efficiency whilst maintaining or improving quality standards.

Today work design is often referred to as process re-engineering and has a bad press because the perceived outcome is reduced employee numbers or downsizing. As we move increasingly to a computerised workplace the use of workflow systems is growing and changing the nature of work from one of social contact to service to the system.

A workflow system is a system that organises work and allocates it to particular workstations for the attention of the person operating the workstation. The system usually also incorporates a document-management facility and presents data on large-format screens in the form of the finished document. There are three main forms in which workflow systems operate. These are on the **casework basis**, the **flowline basis** or an **ad hoc basis**.

The **casework** basis functions by knowing the individual caseload of staff and directs existing cases to the appropriate caseworker and new cases or customers are allocated on the basis of equalising caseload.

The **flowline** approach allocates a small number of tasks to each operator and the case flows along the line from screen to screen. The ad hoc system works on the basis of equalising workload, regardless of who may have dealt with the case previously. The choice depends on the particular circumstances of the business and the approach taken to customer service.

In one large Australian insurance company the **ad hoc** approach was initially chosen for equalising caseload. The belief was that the system would have all the information concerning each customer readily available for each operator. After a period of time it transpired that customers were not happy with this arrangement and wanted to speak to the person who 'looks after our business'. They then, with some difficulty, transferred to the casework approach, which has worked very well.

Workflow management provides supervisors with information on screen about the workloads of individuals and information on their processing capabilities with statistics for average time taken to deal with a case, errors detected by the system as a percentage of cases, and so on. This information is intended to ensure that staff receive appropriate support and training, but can be and is used for bonus payments and league tables of performance.

In one organisation where workflow has been used in sales-order processing, the use of the management statistics has become quite draconian and the average period of employment of sales-order staff is three months.

The **advantages** and benefits of workflow systems come mainly from improvements in productivity and efficiency and better or speedier services to customers. It is usually very easy and quick to access customer information.

Offset against these benefits are the **disadvantages** stemming from the way that workflow systems are implemented and managed.

A list of the **benefits from the employer's point of view** would be:

- More efficient office procedures
- Providing workflow management

- Equalising of workloads
- Monitoring of operator performance
- Better security
- Ensuring work gets done when it should get done

The **dangers** lie in the segmentation or specialisation in a small number of tasks before passing the work on to the next person's screen, almost like a production line. This **de-skilling** of work increases boredom and leads to high staff turnover. It also reduces social contact to a minimum and the contact that does exist takes place via the system.

So far the casework approach, where staff deal with cases as a 'one stop shop', is the most empowering and beneficial for staff. The skills needed are high and there is a greater sense of completion and satisfaction for operators. In the flowline approach people are demoralised at the repetitive nature of the work. Ad hoc approaches seem to fall between two stools - there is work satisfaction to a degree and no sense of continuing customer contact. Perhaps one of the key difficulties in introducing workflow systems successfully goes back to work design.

Work design - a forgotten art

It seems to me that there is a need to return to basics:

- Work design as a key to productivity
- Work design and worker satisfaction
- Work design and performance
- Work design - the path to quality

I have consistently returned to these four basic requirements in my work with organisations. I believe there are six golden rules of work design.

The golden rules of work design

- Ensure that the end product/output of the work is clearly defined, unambiguous, and fully understood by the operator.

- Ensure that the steps/tasks to be performed to achieve the required end product/output are clearly defined in the appropriate sequence and are fully understood by the operator.

- Ensure that operators know and understand where their responsibility starts and finishes in the work process.

- Ensure that the tools, facilities and information needed to perform the work are readily available to and fully understood by the operator.

- Ensure that there is a process whereby operators can signal possible improvements in the work design and exercise initiative in implementing them.

- Always **involve operators** in the work design process.

Adapted from: 'Computer talk' - Workflow systems Trevor Bentley - CIMA Articles database

---

6 AUTOMATE, INFORMATE AND TRANSFORMATE

6.1 The implementation and development of information systems can impact upon an organisation in different ways. Automation, rationalisation and re-engineering provide one framework for analysing and explaining this impact. The writer *Zuboff* devised a similar framework, using the terms **automate**, **informate** and **transformate**. These terms are explained in the following table.

Stage/term	Comment
Automate	This involves the automation of repetitive manual tasks. Automate type changes typically take place during the initial introduction of information systems and information technology into an organisation. The new system replaces or speeds up previously manual tasks. (Corresponds to the automation stage in the **automation**, rationalisation, re-engineering framework.)
Informate	Some processes are redesigned to exploit the potential of information technology. Operating procedures are streamlined and the organisation infrastructure becomes more integrated, for example linking the order processing system with the stock control system. (Corresponds to the **rationalisation** stage in the automation, rationalisation, re-engineering framework.)
Transformate	Information systems and information technology are used to change the way the organisation operates and the way business is done. Systems are utilised that allow the organisation to conduct business in a way that was previously not possible. Transformate type changes may involve significant changes in organisation structure. This is a more risky strategy, which goes much further than rationalisation of processes. A traditional retail business moving to web-based e-commerce could be viewed as a fundamental change. Transformate type changes may bring competitive advantage. (Corresponds to the **re-engineering** stage in the automation, rationalisation, re-engineering framework.)

Exam focus point

The December 2002 exam required candidates to 'explain, with examples the terms Automate, Informate and Transformate'.

In June 2003, a question required knowledge of a 'Business Process Re-engineering approach'.

Chapter roundup

- Organisations are social systems that are exposed to a wide range of influences and environmental factors. Organisations are often exposed to **unstructured** or '**soft**' **problems**.
- In the early days of business computing, computers were used to **automate** processing activities. Systems were developed that matched previous manual procedures.
- The **Systems Development Lifecycle** (SDLC) is a **disciplined**, **hard** approach to systems development which identifies several stages of development.
- The soft systems approach to systems development aims to take into account the **soft properties** of the implementation – this approach looks at the wider picture.
- Checkland's **Soft Systems Methodology** (SSM) is a way of analysing situations in systems - such as an organisation. It provides an organised approach which can be used to tackle **unstructured** and poorly defined problems.
- The purpose of SSM is to **enhance understanding** of complex social situations which entail many divergent perspectives.
- The learning process of SSM cycles between learning and action and follows a set of seven stages.
- In SSM the **root definition** is a concise description of a human activity system that states **what** the system **is** and what the system **does**. The root definition is established using the mnemonic **CATWOE**.
    - **C** ustomers
    - **A** ctors
    - **T** ransformation process
    - **W** eltanschauung or 'world view'
    - **O** wners
    - **E** nvironmental constraints
- A **conceptual model** is a systematic account of a human activity system built on the basis of the systems root definition.
- A **rich picture** is a diagrammatic representation of a situation compiled through examining elements of structure, process and the situation climate.
- Organisations such as **businesses can be viewed as a system**. A business system is a collection of people, machines and methods organised to accomplish a set of specific functions. Inputs are received and processed to produce outputs of goods and services.
- The organisation as system can be viewed as being composed of subsystems arranged in a system **hierarchy**.
    - Corporate level
    - Divisional level
    - Departmental level
    - Operational level
- Another point of view suggests that an organisation is a 'structured **sociotechnical** system', that is, it consists of at least three sub-systems; a structure, a technological system and a social system
- Business **automation** is the use of computerised working methods to speed up the performance of existing tasks.
- Business **rationalisation** is the streamlining of operating procedures to eliminate obvious inefficiencies. Rationalisation usually involves automation.
- **Business Process Re-engineering** is the **fundamental** rethinking and **radical** redesign of business processes to achieve **dramatic** improvements in **critical** contemporary measures of performance, such as cost, quality, service and speed.
- Simply throwing IT at a problem does not cause it to be re-engineered. BPR uses IT to allow a business to do things that it is **not doing already**.
- The **automate**, **informate** and **transformate** framework is very similar to **automation**, **rationalisation** and **re-engineering**.

4: Business systems and systems thinking

Quick quiz

1. List five characteristics of problems or situations that would make a hard approach to problem solving suitable.
2. List five characteristics of problems or situations that would make a soft approach to problem solving suitable.
3. The term 'systems lifecycle' describes the stages a system moves through from inception until it is discarded or replaced. What are the six stages of the lifecycle?
4. List five examples of soft properties that should be considered during the development and implementation of an information system.
5. Although SSM is not intended to follow a rigid sequential approach, some writers have identified 'stages of SSM'. Briefly outline these seven stages.
6. List the steps involved in building a conceptual model from a root definition.
7. The systems approach to developing business strategies involves three steps. List them.
8. Distinguish between business automation and business rationalisation.
9. Business process re-engineering involves computerising tasks previously done by people. TRUE or FALSE?

Answers to quick quiz

1. Any five of those given below. You may have thought of others.

   Objectives are clear
   The problem is self-contained
   The problem can be clearly defined
   Information needs are known
   A solution can be recognised
   Standard solution techniques are applicable

2. Any five of those given below. You may have thought of others.

   Tastes, values, judgement and opinions are involved
   It is not clear what is known and what is needed
   The problem is difficult to define
   It is not clear what the solution should achieve
   The problem is 'people' oriented
   There are no standard solution techniques available

3. The model used in this Text has the stages Project definition; Feasibility study; Design; Programming or software selection; Installation and Post-implementation.

4. Five are given below. You may have thought of others.

   Employee job security and status
   Damage to career prospects
   Disrupted social interactions
   Staff morale – fear of change
   Training requirements

5. Stage 1. The problem situation is entered into.

   Stage 2. The problem situation is expressed in three analytical steps (intervention, prevalent culture, and power relationships).

   Stage 3. Involves devising a set of 'root definitions' for systems thought to be relevant to the problem situation.

   Stage 4. Conceptual models are built. Verbal concepts are logically structured to form relevant combinations of an operational and a monitoring and control system.

   Stage 5. The aim of this stage is to induce learning by comparing models and reality, which may lead to a reiteration of the preceding stages.

Part B: Business systems, systems analysis and business case development

Stage 6. The purpose of the sixth stage is to achieve a common understanding of possible

Stage 7 is concerned with taking action and putting the changes in place – thus changing the problem situation itself and restarting the cycle.

6 Step 1. Use the root definition and CATWOE elements to form an impression of the system carrying out a transformation process.

Step 2. Decide on a number of key verbs which describe the fundamental activities necessary in the system.

Step 3. Structure key related activities in groups.

Step 4. Connect the groups of activities by arrows which indicate logical dependencies.

Step 5. Check that the root definition and conceptual model together give a clear impression of what the system is and what the system does.

7 Step 1. Identify what the whole system is.

Step 2. Identify the overall objectives of the system as a whole.

Step 3. Make plans with these objectives in mind.

8 Business automation is the use of computerised working methods to speed up the performance of existing tasks. Business rationalisation is the streamlining of operating procedures to eliminate obvious inefficiencies. Rationalisation usually involves automation.

9 FALSE. BPR uses IT to allow a business to do things that it is not doing already.

Now try the questions below from the Exam Question Bank

Number	Level	Marks	Time
1	Exam	20	36 mins
14 (b)	Exam	10	18 mins

Chapter 5

GAP ANALYSIS AND BUSINESS CASE DEVELOPMENT

Topic list	Syllabus reference
1 Business case development	5(b)
2 Business analysis	5(a), 5(c)
3 Gap analysis	5(b)

Introduction

In this chapter we look at how to develop a business case to justify investment in a particular course of action, such as spending on a new or improved information system. The emphasis is on **strategic issues**, which requires the wider issues regarding how information systems impact on the organisation's operations and strategy to be considered.

Study guide

17 – Business analysis

- Discuss the need for a general framework for the development of a business case
  Where we are W^2R
  Where we want to be W^3B
  Going to get there $(GT)^2$

- Discuss Business Analysis vs Systems Analysis in terms of: A framework for business analysis, exploring and expressing problem situations, understanding what people do and why they do it, modelling the current situation, the notion of gap analysis, modelling the required situation (*Also see Chapter 4*)

18 – Business case development

- Discuss the major elements of business case development concentrating on the strategic issues of: Estimating costs and timescales, estimating benefits, benefit realisation dependencies, sensitivity analysis and business justification

19 – Gap analysis

- Discuss applications portfolio/IT investment decisions

- Evaluate Portfolio analysis; risks and benefits. An analysis of the portfolio of potential applications within a firm to determine the risks and benefits and select among alternatives for IS

- Scoring model

- Describe determining the best fit with the current system

Part B: Business systems, systems analysis and business case development

> # Exam guide
>
> The syllabus is geared towards encouraging you to think of a business as a system. This concept could be examined in the Part A scenario, with questions requiring you to draw on knowledge of gap analysis, business case development together with soft system concepts (covered in Chapter 4).
>
> System/software selection is a popular topic for examination. Remember the portfolio analysis and the scoring model may be relevant to those questions.

1 BUSINESS CASE DEVELOPMENT

> **KEY TERM**
>
> A **business case** is a justification for a project or particular course of action (an investment) to be undertaken.

General framework

1.1 A business case aims to convince decision-makers within an organisation that an investment is justified. The case should provide a clear understanding of the implications of proceeding with the proposed investment.

1.2 Many organisations have a general framework under which all competing business cases are submitted. Using a standard framework enables comparisons to be made between different types of investments to be made more easily.

1.3 The syllabus includes a generic framework for business case development with three basic stages. We look at each of these stages in the table below – in the context of an investment in an improved information system.

	Stage	Comment
1	W²R *(Where we are)* The present	A business case starts by establishing **what the current position is**. The person (or people) responsible for authorising the investment will use this information to develop an understanding as to why the new information system is being proposed. Documenting the current system may involve systems analysis techniques such as interviews, observations and system modelling. As the aim is to justify the investment in the context of the organisations overall operations and strategy an environmental analysis should also be undertaken (eg SWOT, PEST). The information compiled during this stage should provide a clear picture of where the organisation is at present.

5: Gap analysis and business case development

	Stage	Comment
2	W³2B *(Where we want to be)* The future	This stage involves devising a statement of where the organisation would like to be (**the desired position**), and a justification (maybe a cost-benefit analysis) showing why the position described is desirable.
		The statement may be broken down into more detailed objectives for the investment. These objectives are in effect what the investment hopes to achieve (the benefits) – decision-makers can compare these against the cost when assessing the investment.
3	(GT)² *(Going to get there)* The plan	This stage focuses on the actual work that needs to be undertaken to move from W²R to W³2B. In an information system installation this would include Work Breakdown Structure and Network Analysis.
		A clear plan of exactly **what is involved in the project** should be developed.

Exam focus point

The examiner has referred to other stages of gap analysis in addition to those specified in the syllabus. These are:

W^3 (Where we were) – the past

W^4 (Where we went wrong) – the review

If an examination question suits these additional stages, then refer to them in your answer.

Business case justification

1.4 **Cost-benefit analysis** is a key part of a business case justification. All costs and benefits (financial, commercial, strategic etc) should be summarised. For example, a supermarket chain may find that implementing on-line shopping with free delivery is not cost-effective when viewed in isolation, but is necessary to maintain market share. You should be familiar with the methods of evaluating the **financial viability** of a project from your earlier studies. Three common techniques are outlined below:

Method	Comment
Payback period	Calculates the length of time a project will take to recoup the initial investment; in other words how long a project will take to pay for itself. The method is based on **cash flows**.
Accounting rate of return (ARR)	This method, also called **return on investment**, calculates the profits that will be earned by a project and expresses this as a percentage of the capital invested. The higher the rate of return, the higher a project is ranked. This method is based on **accounting** results rather than cash flows.
Internal rate of return (IRR)	**Internal rate of return (IRR)** involves comparing the rate of return expected from the project calculated on a discounted cash flow (NPV) basis with the rate used as the cost of capital. Projects with an IRR higher than the cost of capital are worth undertaking.

Part B: Business systems, systems analysis and business case development

1.5 Cost-benefit analysis of information systems is complicated by the fact that many of the system cost elements are poorly defined and that benefits can often be highly qualitative and **subjective** in nature.

1.6 An added complication is that the benefits or returns are not certain – there is a **risk** that the benefit will not eventuate. Probabilities can be assigned to different levels of return and an **expected value** of the return established. We look at risk analysis later in this chapter.

The costs of a proposed system

1.7 The costs of a new system will include costs in a number of different categories.

Cost	Example
Hardware costs	• Computers and peripherals
Installation costs	• New buildings (if necessary) • The computer room (wiring, air-conditioning if necessary) • Desks, security systems etc
Development costs	These include costs of measuring and analysing the existing system and costs of looking at the new system. They include **software**/consultancy work and systems analysis and programming. Changeover costs, particularly file conversion, may be very considerable.
Personnel costs	• Staff training • Staff recruitment/relocation • Staff salaries and pensions • Redundancy payments • Overheads
Operating costs	• Consumable materials (tapes, disks, stationery etc) • Maintenance • Accommodation costs • Heating/power/insurance/telephone • Standby arrangements, in case the system breaks down
Intangible costs	Some costs are **harder to quantify**. • 'Learning curve' – staff will work slower until they become familiar with the new system • Staff morale may suffer from the enforced changes • Investment opportunities forsaken – the opportunity cost • Incompatibility with other systems may mean an unforeseen change is required elsewhere in the organisation

Capital and revenue costs

1.8 The distinction between capital costs and revenue costs is important. Capital items will be capitalised and then depreciated, and revenue items will be expensed as incurred as a regular annual cost.

Question 1

Draw up a table with three headings: capital cost items, one-off revenue cost items and regular annual costs. Identify at least three items to be included under each heading.

Answer

Capital cost items	'One-off' revenue cost items	Regular annual costs
Hardware purchase costs	Consultancy fees	Operating staff salaries/wages
Software purchase costs	Systems analysts' and programmers' salaries	Data transmission costs
Purchase of accommodation (if needed)	Costs of testing the system (staff costs, consumables)	Consumable materials
Installation costs (new desks, cables, physical storage etc)	Costs of converting the files for the new system	Power
		Maintenance costs
	Staff recruitment fees	Cost of standby arrangements
		Ongoing staff training

The benefits of a proposed system

1.9 The benefits from a proposed new system must also be evaluated. These consist of direct and indirect or intangible benefits.

1.10 **Direct benefits**

(a) Savings because the old system is no longer operating. These include savings in staff salaries and other operating costs such as consumable materials.

(b) Efficiency savings resulting in less overtime and possibly increased turnover.

(c) Extra savings or revenue benefits because of the improvements or enhancements that the new system should bring:

(i) Possibly more sales revenue and so additional contribution.

(ii) Operational efficiencies such as better stock control (with a new stock control system) and so fewer stock losses from obsolescence and deterioration, or reduced bad debts from a new debtors system.

(d) Possibly, some one-off revenue benefits from the sale of equipment which the existing system uses, but which will no longer be required. Second-hand computer equipment does not have a high value, however! It is also possible that the new system will use **less office space,** and so there will be benefits from selling or renting the spare accommodation.

1.11 Many of the benefits are **intangible,** or impossible to give a money value to.

(a) Greater **customer satisfaction** and **loyalty,** arising from better customer service.

(b) Improved **staff morale** from working with a more efficient system.

(c) Automating routine decisions and tasks should provide **more time for planning**.

(d) More informed **decision making**.

(e) Further savings in staff time, resulting perhaps in **reduced future staff growth**.

(f) Benefits accruing from gaining **competitive advantage**.

Part B: Business systems, systems analysis and business case development

1.12 The fact that so many of the benefits a new information system provides are intangible means that it is difficult to construct a meaningful cost benefit analysis. There are three possible approaches to dealing with this problem.

Approach	Comment
Calculate a value for the benefits	We could estimate the worth of each of the intangible benefits and allocate an appropriate cash value.
	The problem with this approach is that realistically it is nothing more than **guesswork**.
Ignore the 'too intangible' benefits	Allocate a value to those intangible benefits we are able to estimate a realistic value for. Ignore the other intangible benefits.
	This approach will significantly **undervalue** the system.
Adopt a qualitative approach	Find a reasonable non-financial way of stating intangible benefits. For example customer satisfaction ratings could be established through questionnaires – as could staff time savings and staff morale. Market share could be used to assess competitive advantage.
	The problems with this approach are: • Much of the information would only be available **after** the system had been implemented • Determining **appropriate measures** • **Isolating the effect** of the information system from other factors

Sensitivity analysis

1.13 One way of taking into account the uncertainty of possible benefits is to use **sensitivity analysis**. This involves:

(a) **Identifying** the main factors or variables that the benefits the system could bring are dependent upon (eg staff acceptance, budgetary control, effective programming, integration with other systems etc)

(b) **Assessing** the effect on the benefits if the variable was amended by x% up or down.

1.14 Sensitivity analysis involves asking 'what if?' questions. By changing the value of different variables in the model, a number of different **scenarios** for the future will be produced.

1.15 This will highlight those variables which are most likely to have a significant effect on realising the benefits expected from the system. Once the most critical variables have been established, management then can:

(a) Apply the most stringent **controls** to the most critical variables.

(b) **Alter the plans** so that the most critical variables are no longer as critical. For example, if management is worried that existing staff do not possess the skills and motivation to operate the new system new employees with the required skills may be recruited.

(c) Choose a **lower-risk** plan. For example, instead of outsourcing all IS/IT operations an organisation may decide to maintain a small IS/IT team to liase with the facilities management company and oversee operations and developments.

Business case report

1.16 The business case should be presented to the decision-makers in report format. The report should **summarise** the findings of the activities carried out under the stages of the general framework. If detailed analyses are included they should be appended to the report as appendices.

1.17 The report should contain:

- An introduction stating the terms of reference
- An outline of the current position highlighting problem areas
- The relevant objectives from the organisation's information system strategy
- A gap analysis (this will be explained later in this chapter)
- Different options explored and a summary of the cost-benefit analyses
- A conclusion, and a recommended course of action

2 BUSINESS ANALYSIS

2.1 The term 'business analysis' does not have a strict meaning. Many techniques that analyse and explore business processes, relationships and performance fall under the business analysis umbrella.

2.2 We will be looking at business analysis in the context of the relationship between information systems and business operations and performance.

Business analysis and systems analysis

2.3 Systems analysis has a narrower focus than business analysis. In the context of an information system, systems analysis would focus on the system itself using techniques such as a systems audit.

2.4 Systems analysis is more interested in the operation of the system rather than the surrounding business issues.

2.5 Business analysis views the information system in the context of the organisation's operations and strategy. Techniques such as resource analysis would take into account all aspects of the organisation's information systems and how they fit into the overall strategy.

2.6 When building a business case, business analysis is likely to be more effective than systems analysis as the decision makers are interested in the 'big picture'.

2.7 We will now look at two ways of modelling a business situation centred on an information system. Firstly we look at a systems analysis approach (information audit), followed by a business analysis approach (resource analysis).

2.8 An **information audit** aims to establish the information needs of users and decide how these needs could be met. The audit has three stages.

Part B: Business systems, systems analysis and business case development

	Stage	Comment
1	Information needs assessment	This stage involves gathering information, usually through interviews and questionnaires.
		Information users are asked what information they require, why they require it, when they require it and the preferred format.
		People should be encouraged to think laterally about what information would help them do their job, rather than simply listing the information they currently receive.
		To encourage wide-ranging thought, users should be asked to state the information they would like in an 'ideal world'. Unrealistic and uneconomic needs can be rejected (tactfully) at a later stage.
2	Information analysis	This stage focuses on the information provided by the existing information system. Both the quantity and the quality of the information are analysed. For example, the timing of information may reduce the quality of otherwise excellent information as it is provided too late to influence decision-making. Slightly less accurate information, provided earlier, may be more desirable.
3	Gap analysis	This stage compares the information needs identified in stage 1 with the information identified as being provided in stage 2. Gaps between what is required and what is currently provided are identified.
		'Information gaps' are analysed to evaluate the costs and benefits of closing the gap.

2.9 An information system **resource analysis** involves a review of **all** information systems and information technology used within an organisation. The review includes all aspects of hardware, software, communications devices, network topologies, systems development methodologies, maintenance procedures, contingency plans and IS/IT personnel. The review looks at all of these aspects in the context of the organisation's overall strategy and the IS/IT strategy.

2.10 Resource analysis is sometimes called **Current Situation Analysis (CSA)**. The analysis establishes the current status of IS/IT within the organisation.

2.11 The CSA has similar problems to that of a cost-benefit analysis in that it relies on the **subjective judgements** of information users. A group of people using the same system for the same purpose may come up with different ratings for system efficiency and user-friendliness.

2.12 Two techniques that could be useful when conducting a CSA are **Earl's grid** and the **applications portfolio**.

Earl's grid

2.13 Earl suggests a grid to analyse an organisation's current use of information systems. Current systems are plotted on the following grid.

5: Gap analysis and business case development

	Low Technical Quality	High Technical Quality
Business Value High	Renew	Maintain, enhance
Business Value Low	Divest	Reassess

(a) A system of poor quality and little value should be **disposed of** (divest).

(b) A system of high business value and low technical quality should be **renewed** (invested in). An important system of low quality carries a high business risk.

(c) A system of high quality but low business value should be **reassessed**. Is the system meeting an information need? Why is it under-utilised?

(d) High quality systems with a high business value should be **maintained** to preserve the high quality, and if possible **enhanced** in the quest for competitive advantage.

2.14 Establishing where to place systems on the grid is the difficult part. Consultation with system users and those for formulating and implementing information system strategy would be undertaken to form an opinion of each system. Again, judgements are subjective.

The strategic grid

2.15 The importance of IS/IT to an organisation was studied by McFarlan and McKenney back in the early 1980s.

2.16 They devised a matrix designed to show the level of dependence on IS/IT within an organisation. The grid classifies four levels of dependence.

	Low Strategic importance of current information systems	High Strategic importance of current information systems
Strategic importance of planned information systems High	Turnaround	Strategic
Strategic importance of planned information systems Low	Support	Factory

2.17 Organisations in the **strategic** quadrant currently depend on IS/IT for competitive advantage, and expect to continue to do so.

2.18 Organisations in the **turnaround** quadrant do not currently view IS/IT as having strategic importance, but expect IS/IT will be strategically important in the future.

2.19 Organisations in the **support** quadrant see no strategic value in IS/IT.

2.20 Organisations in the **factory** quadrant sees IS/IT as strategically significant at the moment, but predict this will not be the case in the future.

Part B: Business systems, systems analysis and business case development

Applications portfolio

2.21 Peppard developed this strategic grid into the applications portfolio. This is used to analyse the strategic impact of individual applications within an organisation.

	Low	High
High *Strategic importance of individual applications in the predicted **future** competitive environment*	High potential	Strategic
Low	Support	Key operational

*Strategic importance of individual applications in the **current** competitive environment*

2.22 **Support applications** are not critical to business success, but do not improve management effectiveness. Examples include an accounting system and legally required systems.

2.23 **Key operational applications** support established core business activities. A production planning system is a good example, inventory control is another example.

2.24 **Strategic applications** are vital to the organisation's future success. Finance/service companies are becoming increasingly dependent on information systems and technology.

2.25 **High potential applications** are applications likely to have a significant impact in the future environment. They are often innovative. A supermarket on-line ordering application is an example, an expert system is another example.

3 GAP ANALYSIS

> **KEY TERM**
>
> **Gap analysis** involves the comparison of the desired (or planned) position with actual and predicted progress, and the identification of how the gap might be filled.

3.1 Gap analysis may be applied to a range of business situations. The purpose of gap analysis is to establish the following.

(a) What are the organisation's targets for achievement over the planning period?

(b) What would the organisation be expected to achieve if it 'did nothing' - ie simply carried on in the current way.

This difference is the 'gap'. New strategies will then have to be developed which will close this gap, so that the organisation can expect to achieve its targets over the planning period.

3.2 Some relevant definitions are outlined below.

> **KEY TERMS**
>
> A **projection** is an expected future trend pattern.
>
> **Extrapolation** is the technique of determining a projection by statistical means.

5: Gap analysis and business case development

> A **simple gap** occurs where the current position does not meet the current expectation level.
>
> A **continuous gap** occurs where the predicted position does not meet the predicted expectation level.

3.3 Gap analysis has traditionally been used most often to identify the **profit gap**. The profit gap is the difference between the target profits and the profits on the forecast.

3.4 Strategies that may be considered to close the profit gap may include entering new markets or developing new products or services.

3.5 Strategies to close the gap may, in many cases, expose the organisation to greater **risk:** - in many cases a higher return can equate to a higher risk.

3.6 The same basic technique of gap analysis can be used as a starting point for formulating any particular strategy.

Gap analysis for information systems strategy

3.7 In the context of information systems strategy, gap analysis could be used to identify whether the organisation's information systems meet the current and/or predicted organisational information requirements.

3.8 Traditionally, gap analysis is shown using a graph-style diagram. It is unlikely that such a diagram would be required when conducting gap analysis for information strategy. However, the graph below provides a useful illustration of the theory behind gap analysis.

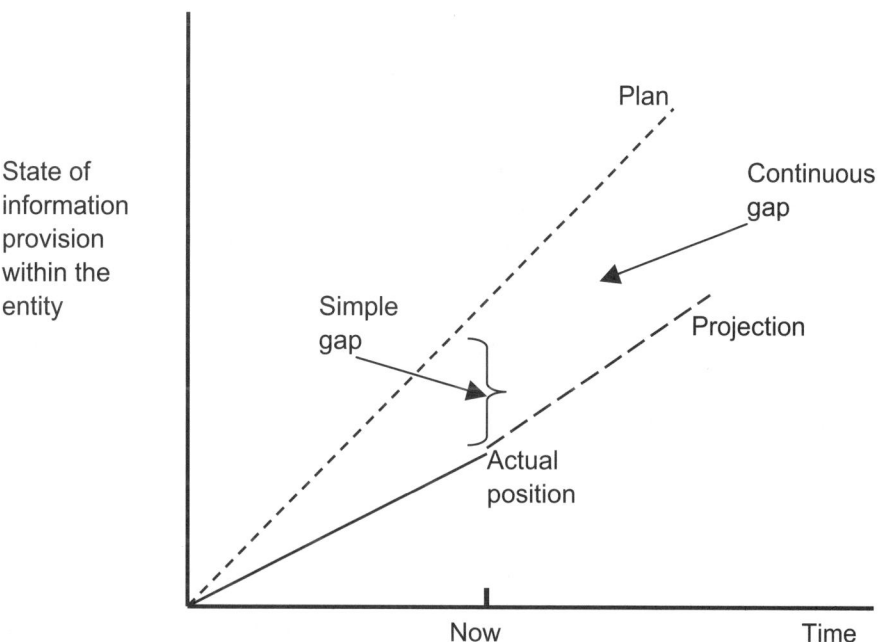

Gap analysis: Information systems strategy

3.9 The gap could be established as follows.

(a) The **actual position** could be established by way of a current situation analysis.

(b) The **projection** would be obtained by taking the current position and projecting forward using a revised plan of imminent IS projects. (In traditional gap analysis, such

Part B: Business systems, systems analysis and business case development

as the profit gap, this projection would be obtained though extrapolation, which involves statistical techniques.)

(c) The **plan** line (sometimes referred to as the **expectation line**) would be obtained from objectives stated in the organisation's information strategy plan.

Closing the information systems gap

3.10 It is not possible to close the simple gap - the gap between the current state and the current expectation level - as time can not stand still. Investigations should try to establish how the gap between the future projection and the expectation levels specified in the IS plan may be closed.

3.11 The identification and evaluation of options may involve a range of techniques such as the applications portfolio, feasibility studies, business case development, cost-benefit analyses and, depending on the scope of the action proposed, SWOT and PEST analyses.

3.12 Actions that may be taken to close the IS gap could include:

- Systems development projects in areas of information deficiency
- The adoption of new technologies such as the Internet
- The implementation of a data warehouse and data mining
- A decision to outsource IS/IT service provision
- A decision to decentralise the IS function
- The adoption of groupware and knowledge management principles

Selecting strategies and projects to close the IS gap

3.13 The range of options open to an organisation to close the IS gap can be considered as a portfolio of potential applications. After strategic analyses have established the overall direction of systems development **portfolio analysis** can be used to select between alternatives.

> **KEY TERM**
>
> **Portfolio analysis** aims to facilitate selection between potential applications an organisation may implement through considering the risks and benefits.

3.14 The potential benefits of applications or IS projects should be considered against the likely risks. A portfolio analysis grid can be used to illustrate the risk and benefit profile of applications. The courses of action suggested by the gird are self-explanatory.

Portfolio analysis grid

		High risk	Low risk
Potential benefits	*High*	Cautiously examine	Identify and develop
	Low	Avoid	Routine projects

Project risk

5: Gap analysis and business case development

3.15 The **benefits** an information system could bring are explained throughout this Text. The **risks** could include:

(a) The system does not perform to the standard required.

(b) **Cost** exceeds budget.

(c) The system proves unworkable and is **scrapped**.

(d) The system is **late**.

(e) **Staff** are unable to operate the system.

(f) 'Bugs' may hinder operation and may lead to the provision of **flawed information** and poor decision-making.

3.16 The level of risk that is acceptable to an organisation will depend on the type of business and the competitive environment. Organisations that require cutting edge information systems for competitive advantage may pursue a range of relatively risky projects that potentially could bring high rewards.

3.17 Firms with a low reliance on information systems are more likely to implement high-benefit, low-risk systems.

Exam focus point

A question in June 2003 required candidates to describe the use of gap analysis and its use of an applications portfolio approach in the context of developing information systems.

3.18 Another method used to choose between alternative systems is a **scoring model**.

KEY TERM

A **scoring model** uses a system of ratings for selected objectives to choose between alternative applications or systems.

3.19 Scoring models enable the suitability of alternative systems to be compared with each other through a single score based on the relevant objectives used in the model.

Case example

An organisation must chose between three office automation systems.

Option 1 An IBM AS/400 client/server system with proprietary software.

Option 2 A Unix based client/server system using an Oracle database.

Option 3 A Windows NT/2000 client/server system using Windows and Lotus Notes.

The decision-makers within the organisation have decided on the relevant criteria and weightings that will be used to judge the systems. This information is shown in the following model, together with the scores that have been allocated to each system.

Part B: Business systems, systems analysis and business case development

Scoring model							
Scoring scale: 1 = low, 5 = high		AS/400		Unix		Windows 2000	
Criteria	Weight	Score	Weighted score	Score	Weighted score	Score	Weighted score
User needs met	0.40	2	0.8	3	1.2	4	1.6
Cost	0.20	1	0.2	3	0.6	4	0.8
Financing	0.10	1	0.1	3	0.3	4	0.4
Maintenance	0.10	2	0.2	3	0.3	4	0.4
Chance of success	0.20	3	0.6	4	0.8	4	0.8
	1.00	Final score	1.9	Final score	3.2	Final score	4.0

The model shows that an office automation system based on Windows 2000 appears to best meet the organisation's needs.

Adapted from Loudon and Loudon.

3.20 Subjective techniques such as the scoring model require many **qualitative judgements** in the selection of the criteria, the weightings applied to the criteria and the scores allocated to the systems. These judgements must be made by people who have a good understanding of the organisation and of the technology involved.

Determining the best fit

3.21 Systems or applications very rarely operate in isolation. They will need to **integrate** directly or indirectly with other systems used in the firm. Systems should also **fit** with organisation strategy, culture and current systems.

3.22 If a system is proposed that is considered important to the future prosperity of the organisation, yet it does not fit well with existing systems, culture and staff skills, then a decision has to be made regarding business and information **strategy**.

3.23 For example, a traditional high street bookseller losing market share to Amazon.com may consider implementing an e-commerce enabled website. However, such a system is **unlikely to fit** well with existing systems (and culture) which are geared to over the counter sales. The organisation could decide to:

(a) Implement book selling over the web, and overhaul existing systems and staffing to fit the new environment.

(b) Enter into a strategic partnership with an organisation to run a separate book selling operation via the web.

(c) Ignore the web. Try to entice customers back into stores through improved décor and coffee shop ambience.

Chapter roundup

- A **business case** is a justification for a project or particular course of action (an investment) to be undertaken.

- The **general** framework for business case development has four stages:

    1. Where we are W^2R
    2. Where we want to be W^32B
    3. Going to get there $(GT)^2$
    4. Justification

- **Cost-benefit analysis** is a key part of a business case justification. Cost-benefit analysis of information systems is complicated by the fact that many of the system cost elements are poorly defined and that benefits are **subjective** in nature.

- One way of taking into account the uncertainty of possible benefits is to use **sensitivity analysis**.

- **Business analysis** views the information system in the context of the organisation's operations and strategy.

- An **information audit** aims to establish the information needs of users and decide how these needs could be met.

- An information system **resource analysis**, or Current Situation Analysis (**CSA**), reviews all aspects of hardware, software, communications devices, network topologies, systems development methodologies, maintenance procedures, contingency plans and IS/IT personnel. The review looks at all of these aspects in the context of the organisation's overall strategy and the IS/IT strategy.

- **Earl** suggests a **grid** to analyse an organisation's current use of information systems. A system of poor quality and little value should be **disposed** of. A system of high business value and low technical quality should be **renewed**. A system of high quality but low business value should be **reassessed**. High quality systems with a high business value should be maintained and if possible **enhanced**.

- **Gap analysis** may be used to identify whether the organisation's information systems meet the current and/or predicted organisational information requirements.

- **Portfolio analysis** aims to facilitate selection between potential applications an organisation may implement through considering the risks and benefits. The level of risk that is acceptable to an organisation will depend on the type of business and the competitive environment.

- A **scoring model** is used to score alternative applications against relevant objectives.

- When selecting information systems another relevant consideration is determining the **best fit** with existing systems.

Part B: Business systems, systems analysis and business case development

Quick quiz

1. List five categories of costs related to the implementation of an information system.
2. List five intangible benefits that may be realised from a new system.
3. Which has a narrower focus, systems analysis or business analysis?
4. Fill in the gaps. Under portfolio analysis…

   (a) Projects that carry a high risk and high potential benefits should be cautiously e……… .

   (b) Projects that carry a low risk and low potential benefits should be considered r…… .

   (c) Projects that carry a high risk and low potential benefits should be a…… .

   (d) Projects that carry a low risk and high potential benefits should be identified and d……… .

5. What is a scoring model?

Answers to quick quiz

1. [Five of]

   Hardware costs
   Installation and site costs
   Development costs
   Personnel costs
   Overheads
   Operating costs
   Maintenance
   Contingency arrangements
   Intangible costs

   You may have thought of other classifications.

2. [Five of]

   Greater customer satisfaction and loyalty, arising from better customer service.
   Improved staff morale from working with a more efficient system.
   Automating routine decisions and tasks should provide more time for planning.
   More informed decision making.
   Further savings in staff time, resulting perhaps in reduced future staff growth.
   Benefits accruing from gaining competitive advantage.
   You may have thought of others.

3. Systems analysis has a narrower focus than business analysis.

4. (a) Examined
   (b) Routine
   (c) Avoided
   (d) Developed

5. A scoring model uses a system of ratings for selected objectives to choose between alternative applications or systems.

Now try the question below from the Exam Question Bank

Number	Level	Marks	Time
14(a)	Exam	10	18 mins

Part C
Using information competitively

Chapter 6

INFORMATION SYSTEMS AND COMPETITIVE POSITION

	Topic list	Syllabus reference
1	SWOT analysis	6(a)
2	Integrating IS/IT and business objectives	3(a), 3(c), 6(c)
3	The effect of IS/IT on an industry	3(a), 3(c), 6(c)
4	Using IS/IT for competitive advantage	3(a), 3(c), 6(c)
5	Outsourcing	6(b)
6	Bespoke software or an 'off the shelf' package?	6(b)

Introduction

In this chapter we explore issues surrounding the strategic value of information systems. You will have encountered SWOT analysis in previous studies. In this chapter we look at how SWOT analysis can be used in the context of information system strategy.

The later part of the chapter focuses on the various options available to manage the IS/IT function, including outsourcing.

We finish the chapter with an evaluation of the relative merits of packaged software and bespoke solutions.

Study guide

3/4 – Strategic role of information systems

- Identify opportunities for use in forecasting, analysing competition, scenario planning, generic strategies/business positioning, improving performance, measuring performance, opportunities for cost reduction, opportunities for service improvement, sales performance, evaluating proposals (*Also see Chapters 2 and 7*)

11 – Strategic information systems

- Discuss the role of strategic information systems, as computer systems within an organisation that enables changes to goals, processes, products, services or environmental relationships (*Also see Chapter 2*)

- Discuss the alignment with business strategy. Using IS to create Focus, support Linkages and develop Information Leadership

12 – Strategic impact of information systems

- Evaluate Porter's value chain

- Apply Porter's value chain to scenarios

Part C: Using information competitively

> **20 – Competitive position analysis**
> - Evaluate Strengths, Weaknesses, Opportunities and Threats (SWOT) analysis as a technique for identifying opportunities for information systems development
> - Apply SWOT analysis to scenarios
>
> **21 – Linking business strategy and information systems strategy**
> - Identify and discuss the links between Business Strategy and Information Systems Strategy using IS/IT as an enabler: Analysis of external (competitive) environment, SWOT output, identify drivers for change, agree guiding principles, infrastructure standards and planning
> - Discuss the potential advantages and disadvantages of IS/IT management partnership - internal/outsourcing (in all its forms), facilities management
> - Evaluate advantages of package solutions versus bespoke solutions
>
> ## Exam guide
>
> SWOT analysis is an examination favourite in many papers. Be sure you are aware of the meaning and requirements of SWOT analysis in the context of identifying opportunities for information systems development.

1 SWOT ANALYSIS

1.1 The general management technique of **SWOT analysis** can be applied to the development of information systems strategy.

> **KEY TERM**
>
> **SWOT analysis**, when used as a technique for identifying opportunities in information systems development, aims to determine:
>
> What **Strengths** does our (overall) information system have? (How can we take advantage of them?)
>
> What **Weaknesses** does the system have? (How can we minimise them?)
>
> What **Opportunities**, outside the information system, are there in the organisation or beyond? (How can we capitalise on them?)
>
> What **Threats**, outside the information system, might prevent us operating or improving the information system? (How can we protect ourselves from them?)

1.2 The **strengths** and **weaknesses** analysis has an **internal** focus. The identification of shortcomings in a system could lead to a decision to enhance the current system or to purchase a new system.

1.3 Opportunities and threats are considered as part of an **external appraisal**, or **environmental scan**.

1.4 The internal and external appraisals of SWOT analysis will be brought together. The analysis aims to ensure that a strategy is not followed without considering the wider implications.

(a) Major **strengths** and profitable opportunities can be **exploited** especially if strengths and opportunities are matched with each other.

6: Information systems and competitive position

(b) Major **weaknesses** and threats should be **countered**, or a contingency strategy or corrective strategy developed.

1.5 The elements of the SWOT analysis can be summarised and shown on a **cruciform chart**. The following chart relates to a proposal to install a new computerised accounting system.

1.6 EXAMPLE: NEW COMPUTERISED ACCOUNTING SYSTEM

STRENGTHS	WEAKNESSES
£1 million of funds allocated	Workforce has very limited experience of computerised systems
Willing and experienced workforce	Seems to be an expectation that the new system will 'do everything'

THREATS	OPPORTUNITIES
The software vendor is rumoured to be in financial trouble and may 'disappear'	Chance to introduce compatible systems in other departments at a later date
System failure, particularly at month or year end, would be costly	Later integration with e-commerce functions is possible

Potential strategy

Significant benefits could be obtained from implementing the system, which should be able to achieve its aims within the £1 million budgeted.

Assurances should be sought from the software vendor as to their future plans and profitability. Contractual obligations should be obtained in regard to this. If the rumours are justified, either another supplier should be approached or the possibility of employing the original vendor's staff on a contract basis could be explored. (*This is an example of an alternative strategy coming out of the SWOT analysis.*)

The end users of the system must be involved in all aspects of system design. Training of staff must be thorough and completed before the system 'goes live'. Management and users must be educated as to what the system will and will not be able to do.

A contingency plan should be in place for repairing or even replacing hardware at short notice.

1.7 The application of SWOT analysis to an information systems scenario is shown in the following question.

Question 1

Scenario

Bargos plc operates 150 retail stores nation-wide. Each store sells a wide variety of consumer goods including kitchenware, clothing, electrical appliances, computers and peripherals, sporting goods, toys and hardware.

Very few goods are displayed in Bargos stores. Customers choose items they wish to purchase from copies of the Bargos catalogue. Customers write the product code on order slips and take completed slips to sales counter staff to complete the sale.

Part C: Using information competitively

Most goods are held at the back of the service area, enabling customers to take their items with them when leaving the store. Larger, or out-of-stock items are delivered within 48 hours to the customer's address.

Bargos has been established for over 50 years and has developed a reputation as an efficient, reputable retailer of good quality goods.

However, sales have stagnated over the last three years. Senior management believe sales are being lost to competitors, particularly those that offer customers on-line purchasing using an Internet website.

Bargos are now considering an investment of £10 million pounds in a system that would provide on-line purchasing to customers over the Internet. Much of the £10 million is necessary to replace existing back-office systems that would not be able to integrate with the web-based system.

Required

Produce a brief SWOT analysis relevant to the proposed new system at Bargos plc.

Answer

Strengths

- **£10 million** is available for the new system
- **Existing** warehouses and delivery infrastructure could be used with the new system
- Although Bargos has no experience of web technology, the organisation is **IT literate**

Weaknesses

- The amount of extra sales the site will generate is **unclear**
- Bargos has no in-house **web expertise**
- **Stock holding levels** may need to be higher to ensure prompt delivery
- The **on-going costs** of staff time and expertise to keep the site operational and up-to-date

Opportunities

- E-commerce provides a **new sales channel** and revenue stream
- **Partnerships with suppliers** may be forged allowing delivery direct from the factory
- The use of 'cookies', database and data mining technology to establish more profitable **customer relationships**

Threats

- The **security** implications of establishing Internet links
- Timing – Bargos has missed 'first-mover' advantage
- Consumer **resistance** to on-line purchasing

The possibility of losing Bargos' **distinct** catalogue-based market position (becoming just another retailer with a web-site).

1.8 The following general points may be of use when applying SWOT analysis to a particular information systems scenario.

Economic/industry context

1.9 IT is an **enabling technology**, and can produce dramatic changes in individual businesses and whole industries, especially where there are other major forces for change.

Stakeholders

1.10 Stakeholders are affected by an organisation's use of IT.

6: Information systems and competitive position

(a) **Customers and suppliers** have preferences as to how IT should be used (eg electronic data interchange, extranet).

(b) **Governments** have an interest in the legal aspects of copyright, data protection, security and e-commence.

(c) **IT manufacturers** pioneer the development and use of new technology.

(d) **Consumers:** both their expectations of IT and their willingness to use it are important for its success.

(e) **Employees** and other internal users are interested as IT affects work practices.

Technical issues

1.11 A strategic view of IT must take detailed **technical issues** into account. For example, two UK building societies abandoned a merger because of incompatibility between their computer systems.

1.12 The **security** of IT-based systems must be considered.

The importance of management

1.13 Success or failure in implementing IS/IT depends on the systems themselves and the management effort behind them. An implementation or strategy will fail if:

(a) The system is designed to tackle the wrong problem, that is, the use of IT has not been thought through in the wider organisational context.

(b) If senior management are not interested in, and do not appreciate the significance of, IT based choices.

(c) If users are ignored in design and development.

(d) When no attention is given to behavioural factors in design and operation.

Case example

An example of the importance of the wider organisational processes for the success of information technology is provided by the *Taurus project*.

This was a project, funded by various institutions in the City of London and managed by the Stock Exchange, to computerise certain aspects of share trading and registration. There was an existing computer system, Talisman, but for various reasons it was regarded as being no longer suitable.

(a) A new system was felt to be necessary to cope with increased trading volumes.

(b) Stock markets and bourses elsewhere in Europe already used computerised settlement systems, giving increased competition to London as a financial centre.

However, the plans to develop a computer system failed, at a substantial cost to City institutions and damage to London's reputation as a financial centre. What went wrong? There was nothing inherently impossible about the task: automated settlement has been achieved in other financial centres. A number of reasons were suggested.

(a) Poor project management with inadequate control.

(b) The system was designed to *replicate* existing structures. Rather than use *one* central database, it was decided to use a system of separate but linked databases. Not to do so would have taken away business (and profits) from *share registrar* companies. The design was made unnecessarily complex in order to cater for all the vested interests. This then is an instance of the neutralisation of technology's possible benefits by wider social and organisational choices.

Part C: Using information competitively

2 INTEGRATING IS/IT AND BUSINESS OBJECTIVES

2.1 A firm's IS/IT strategy should support the overall strategy of the business. We explained why an organisation should have an IS/IT strategy, and the development of an IS/IT strategy in Chapter 2.

2.2 IS/IT can be considered a functional strategy, but might also be viewed as an aspect of **corporate or business strategy**: The strategy for information systems deals with the deployment of a crucial resource throughout the whole business.

2.3 A representation of IS/IT strategy development is given in the following diagram.

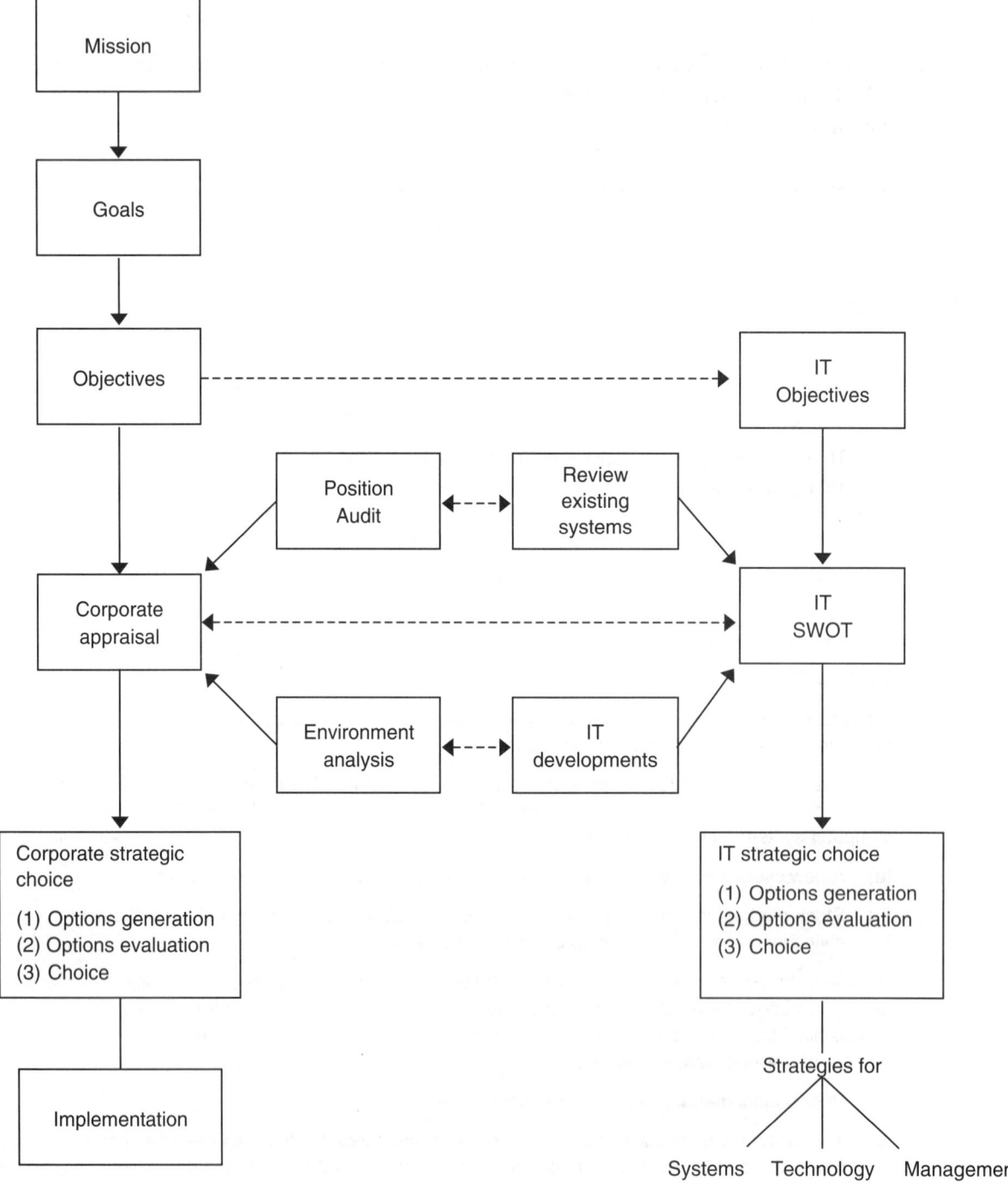

6: Information systems and competitive position

Business objectives and IS/IT resources

2.4 The **identification of business needs** and the information technology framework to satisfy them is at the **heart of a strategy for information systems** and information technology. This is not always feasible, especially if an organisation's use of IS/IT has grown in a haphazard fashion. The purpose of the strategy in this situation may be to impose some sort of order on a disorganised situation.

2.5 The ability to use information and/or information systems to provide better quality information, or to facilitate more efficient processes and therefore establish competitive advantage, is referred to as **information leadership**.

2.6 We discussed **critical success factors** (CSFs) in the preparation of resource plans in Chapter 2. CSFs can translate business objectives into IS/IT objectives - they function as linking pins between IS/IT and business planning. The process is as follows.

(a) **Define business objectives** (eg raise earnings per share, develop new businesses).

(b) **Identify the CSFs** whose success is necessary for the organisation to flourish (eg new markets, new products, core activities).

(c) **Develop the information systems to support the CSFs** (eg develop customer information systems, improve the financial control reporting system).

2.7 **EXAMPLE**

A bank hopes to persuade its customers to buy more of its products.

Step 1. Business objective: **increase profit.**

Step 2. Strategies to increase profit are cutting costs per customer and increasing revenue per customer.

Step 3. A critical success factor for increasing revenue per customer is **getting customers to buy other services.**

Step 4. A key task in getting customers to buy other services is to identify those customers who are most likely to be receptive to new products. A customer **database** could help here.

Evolution of IS/IT

2.8 Organisations that had previously paid little attention to IS/IT may be forced into radical changes in strategy and operations to enable them to embrace technology. On the other hand, organisations that keep up to date with IS/IT developments are able to implement changes more gradually.

2.9 *Richard Nolan's* **stage hypothesis,** outlined below, attempts to model the stages organisations go through in their use of IS/IT. (Nolan's stage hypothesis is sometimes referred to as Nolan's Six Stage Growth Model

Stage 1: Initiation

2.10 The firm begins its involvement with IS/IT.

(a) **Applications.** The objective is to discover to identify suitable applications (eg **payroll**), and to **save money** on clerical processing. There are a number of separate IS/IT applications that carry out restricted, well-defined tasks.

Part C: Using information competitively

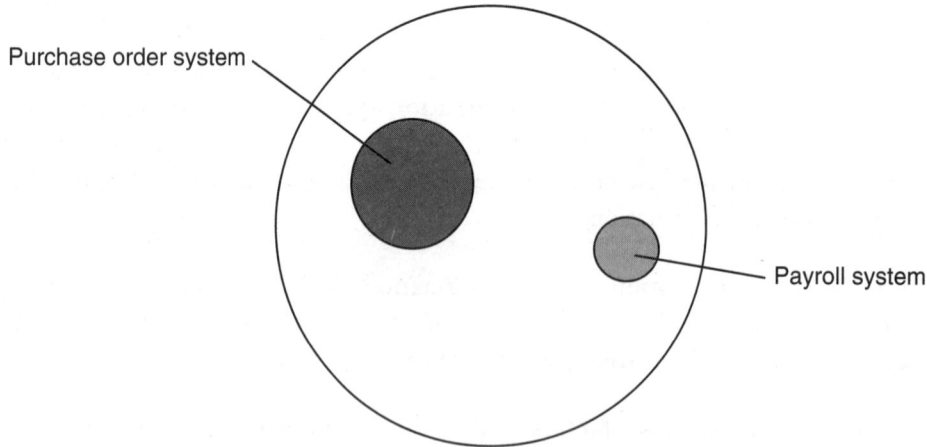

(b) **IS/IT** is a distinctly separate department, for technical experts.

(c) **Control:** there are computer controls, but few management controls and little planning.

(d) **Users** have little involvement.

Stage 2: Contagion

2.11 The use of IS/IT spreads over time.

(a) **Applications.** Many more applications are developed, but a lot of time is spent updating old ones. This is a period of unplanned, haphazard growth.

(b) **Organisation.** The IS/IT department is still centralised, but end-users begin to influence what it does. Programmers become more sensitive to user needs.

(c) **Controls** are still very lax. IS/IT is a corporate overhead, and budgetary control over IS/IT expenditure is limited. Furthermore, there are few checks over requests for more applications.

(d) **User awareness.** Users are enthusiastic about IS/IT, but have little understanding as to its benefits and drawbacks.

Stage 3: Control

2.12 The excesses of the contagion stage (too many applications not providing value for money, overspend) lead to tight management controls.

(a) **Applications.** There are restrictions on the development of new systems; existing applications are consolidated. Users might feel frustrated.

(b) **Organisation.** The IS/IT function is properly organised and headed by a manager, who has to justify expenditure, just as is the case with other departments.

(c) **Control.** Financial, quality and other controls (eg steering committees) are introduced over projects and purchases. User departments begin to be charged for the IS/IT resource, as a way of controlling costs. However, controls are mainly exercised in and over the IS/IT department.

(d) **Users** begin to understand IS/IT.

Stage 4: Integration

2.13 The role of IS/IT in the business and the controls over it are greatly clarified. **IS/IT begins to be considered as integral to business issues.**

(a) **Applications** begin to cross the boundaries of each business function (eg integrating sales order processing and stock control). However, data is often duplicated, so there is an attempt to integrate information and accounting systems. A **management information system** enables managers to get information about many of the firm's activities from a database.

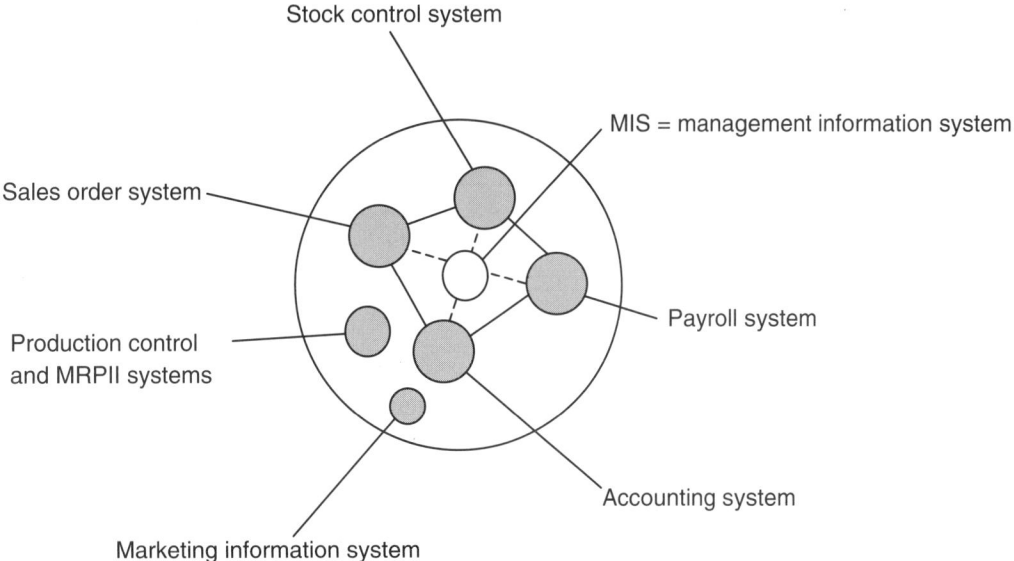

(b) **Organisation:** perhaps a higher profile for IS/IT?

(c) **Controls.** More planning is introduced to IS/IT.

(d) **User involvement** in policy and project management increases.

Stage 5: Data administration

2.14 The organisation gains confidence in managing IS/IT. Information is seen as a resource. **Information requirements, not the technology** which supports it, is the focus of management attention.

(a) **Applications.** The organisation seeks to develop a single integrated database serving organisational needs, and applications are devised to use the database.

(b) **Organisation.** A database administrator is appointed.

(c) **Control.** Data rather than the systems which process it, is the subject of control. To avoid duplication, data definitions, coding systems, file layouts and so on are standardised.

(d) **Users** become more accountable themselves for the integrity and correct use of information.

Stage 6: Maturity

2.15 **Information flows reflect the real life requirements of the organisation.** An organisation's information systems and databases become a sort of mirror in which the workings of the organisation can be scrutinised, modelled and analysed, in a way that was not possible before.

Part C: Using information competitively

(a) **Applications.** In theory, data about all the organisation's activities find their way into an information system, which can be interrogated in a variety of ways. If the information is analysed with sufficient rigour it may be possible to discover those areas in the organisation's **value chain** where savings can be made or advantages delivered.

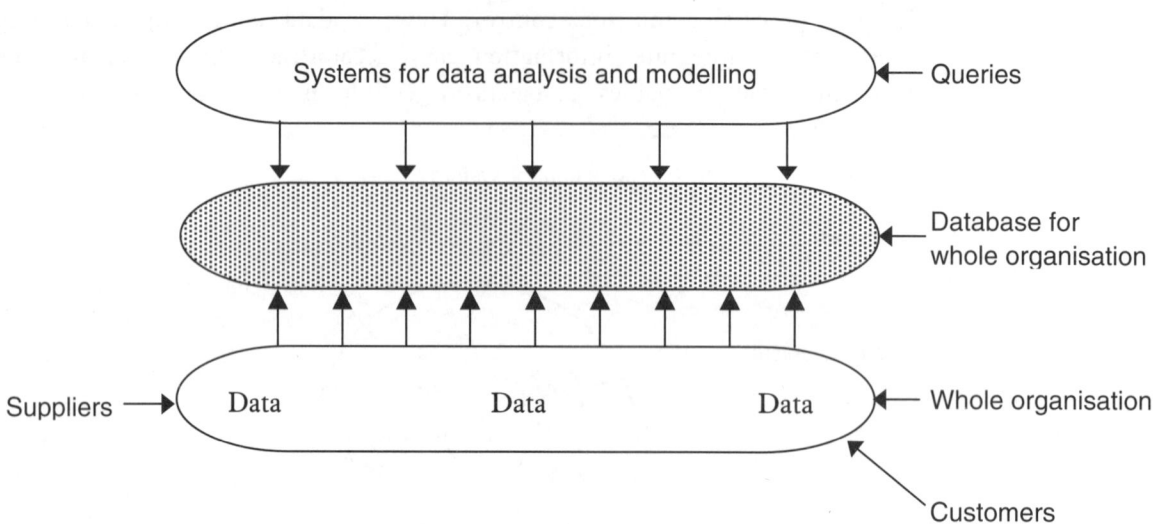

(b) Information is now able to be used as **a source of competitive advantage**. There is an emphasis on **strategic issues**.

(c) Control data is used flexibly.

(d) There is heavy involvement by **users** and management. IS/IT professionals act more as advisors and support staff: systems developments are user driven.

Case example

The South Bank Arts Centre in London has used *Concentrics*, a system which covers 'everything from space allocation to the timely supply of fireworks for a performance of Tchaikovsky's 1812 Overture'.

At the same time, the planning system is used as a marketing tool. Customer details are entered into the system, so that the firm can tailor its direct mailshots, and thus save money on advertising.

The accounting system is also to be integrated with the other systems to enable 'open access to the accounting system to non-financial departments, giving them responsibility for their own budgeting and report writing'.

The electronic diary and scheduling system will streamline the production process. The aim is to control overheads so as to maintain artistic budgets.

2.16 The **value** of the stage hypothesis is that it is:

(a) **Diagnostic:** managers might be able to make sense of IS/IT's current position in the organisation and where it might be headed.

(b) **Prescriptive:** it suggests remedies which IS/IT managers in the business can prescribe to correct any problems.

2.17 **Problems** with the stage hypothesis include those described below.

(a) **Dated.** First developed in 1974, it preceded PCs, Windows, networks, the Internet, client/server architecture etc.

(b) **Linearity.** Some organisations' uses of IS/IT have the characteristics of several of the stages.

6: Information systems and competitive position

(c) **Size and cost.** IS/IT is now cheaper than when the hypothesis was developed. The management issues do not really arise for many of the smaller businesses running PC-based office automation software.

2.18 Key **lessons** of the stage hypothesis

- An organisation's use of IS/IT must be **planned** and **managed**
- **Users** are empowered by IS/IT

2.19 The stage model was devised during the data processing (DP) era, when the focus was very much on data and transaction processing. *Earl* describes the differences between the DP era and the IT/IS era as follows.

	DP era	IT/IS era
Money spent on IT is...	a cost	an investment
The role of IT in business is...	support	critical
IT applications are...	tactical	strategic
IT's social impact is...	limited	pervasive
Technologies...	computing	multiple
Management of IT...	delegated	leadership

2.20 The future management problems of IS/IT will no longer be those of control and cost-efficiency. Future management effort will concentrate on configuring IS/IT at those places in the value chain where it can **deal with weaknesses** and **enhance competitive performance;** and on ensuring that the firm manages the **risks** of IS/IT appropriately.

2.21 Nolan's stage hypothesis described what was essentially an **emergent strategy**.

(a) IS/IT was adopted by departments according to their operational needs without any real idea of what wider overall implications there might be.

(b) Organisations ended up with a number of different IS/IT systems which may or may not have been compatible.

2.22 With IS/IT, more than with other functional strategies, **conscious planning**, not crafting strategies after the event, is necessary to ensure that IS/IT's potential is maximised and that pitfalls are avoided. Issues of systems **compatibility** and **design** are at the heart of the overall value of the system to an organisation.

2.23 That said, it is short-sighted to go back to a planning model that ignores the value and **creativity** of emergent strategies.

- Opportunities for the use of IT cannot always be identified in advance
- Creative thinking should be encouraged.
- There should be many inputs as possible to the planning process
- End-user development is increasingly viable as IT literacy and technology develop

2.24 **Successful IT development tendencies**

- **User-driven**, with the active support of superiors in user departments
- **Evolutionary** developments of existing approaches, rather than revolutionary change
- Developed outside the information system function
- Marketed extensively throughout the organisation and to customers
- Developed in consultation with **customers**

Part C: Using information competitively

3 THE EFFECT OF IS/IT ON AN INDUSTRY

3.1 Porter and Millar state that IS/IT has the potential to change the **nature of competition** within an industry in three ways. IS/IT can:

- Change the industry structure
- Create new businesses and industries
- Be used to create competitive advantage

Sections three and four of this chapter look at these three areas.

Changing the industry structure

3.2 Porter's five forces model can be used to analyse the effect of IS/IT on an industry. **Porter** identified **five competitive forces** operating in a competitive environment.

(a) The threat of **new entrants**.
(b) The bargaining power of **suppliers**.
(c) The bargaining power of **customers**.
(d) The threat of **substitute** products/service.
(e) The **existing competitive rivalry** in the industry.

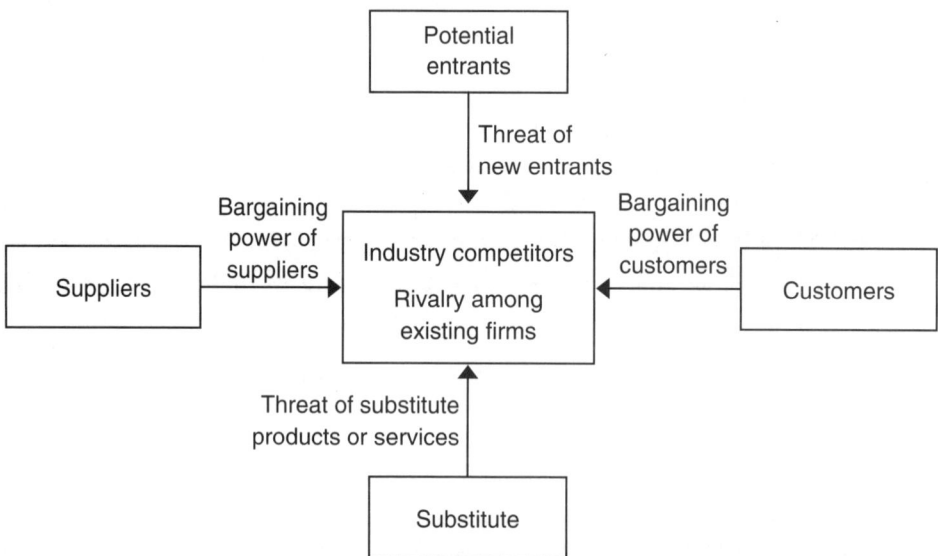

New entrants

3.3 IS/IT can have two possible roles in relation to **barriers to entry**.

(a) **Defensively**, IS/IT can increase economies of scale, raise the capital cost of entry (by requiring a similar investment in IS/IT) or effectively colonising distribution channels by tying customers and suppliers into the supply chain or distribution chain.

(b) **Offensively**, IS/IT can leap over entry barriers. An example is the use of telephone banking, which sometimes obviates the need to establish a branch network.

Suppliers

3.4 **Supplier power** can derive from various factors such as geographical proximity and the fact that the organisation requires goods of a certain standard in a certain time. The bargaining power of suppliers can be **eroded** by IS/IT in three ways.

6: Information systems and competitive position

(a) By **increasing competition** between suppliers. IS/IT can provide a purchases database, which enables easy scanning of prices from a number of suppliers.

(b) Suppliers' power can be **shared**. An example is using CAD and so forth to **design components in tandem with suppliers**. Such relationships might be developed with a few key suppliers. The supplier and the organisation both benefit from performance improvement.

(c) Suppliers can be **integrated**, in purely administrative terms, by a system of **electronic data interchange**.

Case example

Some German companies have reported losing lucrative home markets because the Internet has made it easier for customers to access and compare prices from other suppliers.

Geographical price discrimination is becoming harder to sustain in an age where 'a shopper with a credit card and computer can sit at home and order from around the world'. The Internet has therefore increased competition, and is used by many organisations as a competitive weapon.

Customers

3.5 The bargaining power of **customers** can be affected by using IS/IT to '**lock them in**'.

(a) IS/IT can **raise switching costs** (in both cash terms, and in terms of operational inconvenience). An example is where IS/IT provides a distribution channel for certain services (eg airline tickets). Another example comes from the computer industry itself. Until the advent of the PC, most computers were run with proprietary software: in other words, you could not run ICL software, say, on IBM mainframes. This made any switch in supplier (of hardware or software) too much trouble to contemplate.

(b) Customer information systems can enable a **thorough analysis of marketing information** so that products and services can be **tailored to the needs** of certain segments.

Substitutes

3.6 IT has the following relationship to existing and substitute products and services.

(a) In some cases IT/IS itself **is the 'substitute'**. PC-based word processing packages are a substitute for typewriters, e-commerce is a substitute for a high street shop.

(b) IT is the basis for **new leisure activities** (eg computer games). Alternatively, IT based systems can imitate existing goods (eg electronic keyboards imitating pianos).

(c) IT can **add value to existing services** by allowing **more detailed analysis** (as in a geographical information system), by generating **cost advantages,** or by **extending the market**.

   (i) The **cost advantages** of microprocessors massively extended the market for computing.

   (ii) Earl quotes the example of an econometrics firm, whose innovation enabled PC users to access its database, broadening the reach of the company's services.

Part C: Using information competitively

Rivalry

3.7 IT can be used to compete – as a source of **competitive advantage**. This is covered later in this chapter.

3.8 Alternatively, IT can be used as a **collaborative venture**, perhaps to set up new communications networks. An example is the perceived threat that IT-based firms like Reuters pose to stock exchanges and commodities exchanges. A communications network soon becomes something that can be marketed. Some competitors in the financial services industry share the same ATM network. (Also see the following section.)

3.9 Porter's five forces model has come in for criticism in recent years.

    (a) The model relies on a **static picture of the competition** and therefore plays down the role of innovation.

    (b) It overemphasises the importance of the **wider environment** and therefore ignores the significance of possible individual company advantages with regard to resources, capabilities and competence.

IT as a collaborative venture

3.10 Companies have been using computerised networks for many years to exchange information about ordering, invoicing and delivery with their main customers and suppliers. Until recently (ie before widespread use of the Internet - which we look at in Chapter 7) the main examples were **Electronic Data Interchange (EDI)** and **Value Added Network Services (VANS)**. Although these methods require close co-operation with other organisations, the ultimate aim is still to gain a competitive advantage.

Case example

Wickes, the timber, building materials and home improvement products group has made electronic trading a core part of the company's IT operations.

Wickes started by approaching larger suppliers to pilot the receipt of electronic orders and now uses EDI to send over 10,000 orders a month to over 75% of its suppliers. The retail sites provide order information on a daily basis for consolidation at the company's computer centre. The consolidated orders are then transmitted to suppliers overnight and are ready for processing the following morning. Order lead times are reduced, slower paper-based ordering is eliminated and accuracy is better.

Wickes also receives around 60% of its invoices electronically. Early receipt of invoices via EDI into the company's in-house invoice processing application allows prompt identification of problems and mismatches.

Creating new businesses and industries

3.11 There have been many examples in the last decade of IT affecting the competitive business environment by creating new businesses. This may take the form of a completely new business or a significant change to an existing business.

3.12 For example, the Internet Service Provider industry is a completely **new industry** resulting from technological change. The publishing industry provides a good example of an **existing industry** affected by IS/IT. Encyclopaedia publishers such as Encyclopaedia Britannica have moved in recent years from solely paper-based products to paper and CD-ROM, and then again to a hybrid CD-ROM\Web-based product.

3.13 The **nature of competitors** can also be influenced by developments in technology. For example, Encyclopaedia Britannica now has to compete not only against traditional encyclopaedia producers, but also against software companies such as Microsoft (with Microsoft Encarta).

3.14 Technology has increased the amount of information that can be collected. For example, the use of bar-code scanners in retail outlets means accurate sales data is available across all product ranges. This data is then available for further analysis, perhaps against customer profiles obtained under 'customer loyalty' schemes. This information could be **used internally**, and/or could be **offered for sale** to producers or other interested parties.

Question 2

Think about the role of Information Systems (IS) and Information Technology (IT) in achieving business objectives and securing an advantage over competitors. Try to think of an example of each of the following.

(a) The use of IT to 'lock out' competitors.
(b) The use of IS/IT to reduce the likelihood of customers changing suppliers.
(c) The use of IS/IT to secure a performance advantage.
(d) How IT may generate a new product or service.

Answer

(a) An example is an organisation that invests so heavily in technology that potential competitors lack both the expertise and the funds to compete successfully. Microsoft has not completely locked competitors out of the office software market but its domination is increasing.

(b) Once a bank customer has gone to the effort of installing a home banking system, he or she is unlikely to make a decision to change banks.

(c) Accurate stock systems that facilitate Just-In-Time (JIT) stock management, and organisations participating in Electronic Data Interchange (EDI) are two examples of how IT can increase efficiency and facilitate better service - providing an advantage over competitors. (They may also make an organisation more dependent on existing suppliers therefore discouraging the changing of suppliers.)

(d) Internet Service Providers (ISPs) did not exist before the advent of the Internet.

4 USING IS/IT FOR COMPETITIVE ADVANTAGE

4.1 As the importance of information has increased over the last two decades, organisations have realised that **Information Systems (IS)** and **Information Technology (IT)** can be used as a source of **competitive advantage**.

KEY TERM

Competitive advantage is a profitable and sustainable position. It exists in the minds of customers, who believes the value they will receive from a product or service is greater than both the price they will pay and the value offered by competitors.

Part C: Using information competitively

Generic strategies for competitive advantage

4.2 Porter proposes **three generic strategies** for achieving competitive advantage.

(a) **Cost leadership** means being the lowest-cost producer in the industry as a whole. A cost leadership strategy seeks to achieve the position of lowest-cost producer in the industry.

(b) **Differentiation** is the exploitation of a product or service which the industry as a whole believes to be unique. A differentiation strategy assumes that competitive advantage can be gained through **particular characteristics** of a product or service.

(c) **Focus** involves a restriction of activities to only part of the market (a segment or niche) through:

   (i) Providing goods and/or services at lower cost **to that segment** (**cost-focus**).

   (ii) Providing a differentiated product or service to that segment (**differentiation-focus**).

4.3 Cost leadership and differentiation are **industry-wide** strategies. Focus involves segmentation - pursuing **within the segment** a strategy of cost leadership or differentiation.

4.4 Examples of how IS/IT can support each of these strategies are shown in the following table.

Strategy	How IS/IT can support the strategy
Cost-leadership	By facilitating reductions in cost levels, for example by reducing the number of administration staff required.
	Allowing better resource utilisation, for example by providing accurate stock information allowing lower 'buffer' inventories to be held.
	Using IT to support just-in-time and advanced manufacturing systems.
Differentiation	Differentiation can be suggested by IT, perhaps in the product itself or in the way it is marketed.
	The publishing example quoted earlier provides evidence of this – with the move from paper-based products to electronic.
Focus	IT may enable a more customised or specialised product/service to be produced.
	IT also facilitates the collection of sales and customer information that identifies targetable market segments.

Porter's value chain

4.5 Michael Porter analyses the various activities of an organisation into a **value chain**. This is a model of value activities (which procure inputs, process them and add value to them in some way, to generate outputs for customers) and the relationships between them.

4.6 The value chain can be used to design a competitive strategy, by deploying the various activities strategically. The two examples that follow are based on two different supermarket chains.

6: Information systems and competitive position

(a)

		Minimum corporate HQ			
Firm infrastructure					
Human resource management		De-skilled store-ops	Dismissal for checkout errors		
Technology development	Computerised warehousing		Checkouts simple		
Procurement	Branded only purchases big discounts	Low cost sites			Use of concessions
	Bulk warehousing	1,000 lines only Price points Basic store design		Low price promotion Local focus	Nil
	INBOUND LOGISTICS	OPERATIONS	OUTBOUND LOGISTICS	MARKETING & SALES	SERVICE

(b)

		Central control of operations and credit control			
Firm infrastructure					
Human resource management	Recruitment of mature staff	Client care training	Flexible staff to help with packing		
Technology development		Recipe research	Electronic point of sale	Consumer research & tests	Itemised bills
Procurement	Own label products	Prime retail positions	Adverts in quality mags & poster sites		
	Dedicated refrigerated transport	In store food halls Modern store design Open front refrigerators Tight control of sell-by dates	Collect by car service	No price discounts on food past sell-by dates	No quibble refunds
	INBOUND LOGISTICS	OPERATIONS	OUTBOUND LOGISTICS	MARKETING & SALES	SERVICE

Question 3

One of these chains is concentrating on low prices, the other differentiated on quality and service. Which is which?

Answer

The value chain in (a) is based on that of Kwik Save, a 'discount' chain which sells on price, pursuing a cost-focus strategy. The value chain in (b) is based on Marks and Spencer foods, which seeks to differentiate on quality and service.

4.7 Value chain analysis can be used to assess the impact of IS/IT, and to identify **processes where IT could be used to add value**.

4.8 IT can be used to **automate** and improve physical tasks in the **manufacturing** sector. It also, provides **extra information** about the process.

Part C: Using information competitively

(a) **Process** control. Computer systems enable tighter control over production processes.

   (i) It is possible to **measure** many aspects of the production process.
   (ii) A variety of control techniques are available.

(b) **Machine tool control.** Machine tools can be automated and, it is hoped, be made more precise.

   (i) **Numerical control**: information to operate the machine tool is prepared in advance to generate a set of instructions.
   (ii) **Computer numerical control** is where the computer produces the instructions.
   (iii) **Direct numerical control** is where the computer is linked directly to the machine tool.

(c) **Robots** can automate some of the process.

(d) **Computer aided manufacturing** (CAM) involves a variety of software modules.

   - Production control, supervisory systems
   - Materials requirement planning (MRP) and MRP II
   - Capacity requirements planning

(e) **Computer Integrated Manufacturing** (CIM) integrates all aspects of an organisation's manufacturing activities. 'IT cannot solve basic organisational problems, but the essence is the use of the IT to provide integration though communication, effectiveness and efficiency'. Flexible manufacturing systems include:

   - Machine tools
   - Materials handling conveyor sets
   - Automatic guided vehicles

(f) **Enterprise Resource Planning** (ERP) systems take MRP II systems a step further, and are not restricted to certain types of organisation. ERP systems are used for identifying and planning the **enterprise-wide** resources needed to record, produce, distribute, and account for customer orders.

4.9 In both **inbound** logistics and **outbound** logistics IT can have an impact.

(a) The use of IT in **inbound logistics** includes stock control systems such as MRP, MRPII, ERP and JIT.

(b) **Warehousing**. The use of barcodes can increase knowledge about the quantity and nature of stock in hand.

(c) It is possible to create computer models, or **virtual warehouses,** of stock actually held at **suppliers**. For example an organisation with several outlets might have each connected to a system which indicates the total amount of stock available at different sites.

4.10 **Marketing and services** can be made more effective by **customer databases** enabling market segmentation.

(a) Buying and analysing a mailing list is a more precise method of targeting particular groups of consumers than television advertising.

(b) A variety of market research companies use IT to **monitor consumers' buying habits**.

(c) Supermarkets can use automated **EPOS** systems to have a precise hour-by-hour idea of how products are selling to enable speedy ordering and replenishments.

4.11 **Customer relationship management (CRM)** describes the methodologies, software, and usually Internet capabilities that help an enterprise manage customer relationships.

4.12 For example, an enterprise might build a database about its customers that described relationships in sufficient detail so that management, salespeople, service staff, and maybe the customer, could access information, match customer needs with product plans, remind customers of service requirements and know what other products a customer had purchased.

CRM consists of:

(a) Helping an enterprise to identify and target their best customers, manage marketing campaigns with clear goals and objectives, and generate quality leads.

(b) Assisting the organisation to improve telesales, account, and sales management by **optimising information shared**, and streamlining existing processes (for example, taking orders using mobile devices).

(c) Allowing the formation of relationships with customers, with the aim of improving customer satisfaction and maximising profits; identifying the most profitable customers and providing them with the highest level of service.

(d) Providing employees with the information and processes necessary to know their customers, understand their needs, and effectively build relationships between the company, its customer base, and distribution partners.

4.13 As far as **support** activities are concerned IT has some impact.

(a) **Procurement**. IT can automate some purchasing decisions. Paperwork can be saved if the organisation's purchase systems are linked directly to the sales order systems of some suppliers (eg by electronic data interchange).

(b) **Technology development.** Computer automated design (**CAD**) is, in a number of areas, an important influence.

   (i) **Drafting**. CAD produces engineer's drawings, component design, layout (eg of stores, wiring and piping) and electronic circuit diagrams in complex systems.

   (ii) **Updating**. It is easy to change design in CAD systems and to assess ramifications of any changes. Some CAD systems have archive data (eg for reference).

   (iii) CAD enables modelling to be **checked** without the necessity of producing working prototypes. Some 'stress testing' can be carried out on the model.

(c) There is perhaps less impact on **human resources.** However, the HR applications include the maintenance of a skills database, staff planning (eg using network analysis), computer based training, time attendance systems, payroll systems, pension systems.

Case example

Fast-growing firms say IT's their edge

The fastest-growing companies in the United States attribute their competitive advantage to an edge in IT. A PricewaterhouseCoopers survey found that 52% of the 436 CEOs interviewed said that their companies have a competitive edge in computer and information technology. The companies are identified as the fastest-growing U.S. businesses over the last five years.

The 'trendsetter' companies 'with an IT advantage are reaping the benefits,' Jim Atwell, global private equity director at Pricewaterhouse, said in a statement. 'Their composite revenues have grown 20-fold over the past 5 years, 45% faster growth than their counterparts without an IT edge. And they also tend to be larger - with 58% higher revenues and 56% more employees.'

Part C: Using information competitively

> The study found that service firms lead product vendors in claiming an IT advantage, 58% compared to 46%. 57% of the companies surveyed report having financial analysis/cash management systems; 52% have sales information systems; 37% have sales/customer service systems; 28% have marketing systems; and 24% have customer 'end user' systems. In addition, 47% report the Internet as being very important to their business. *(BPP note: This figure is likely to have increased significantly since the survey date - late 1998.)*
>
> Nearly all of the CEOs of the companies studied (97%) rated computers and information technology as important to their company's profitable business growth over the past two years, with 80% rating them as extremely or very important.
>
> Companies that rated IT as extremely important to their business have grown their revenues ten-fold over the past five years, or 72% faster than those who did not rate it as highly. Likewise, 96% of the CEOs said computers and IT have generally lived up to their expectations for increased business productivity. 60% rated IT as performing extremely or very well against their original expectation.
>
> Although a majority of the companies studied praised IT as a business necessity, 84% of growing companies' CEOs now express concern about information security, an increase of 7 points from a similar study done two years ago. 31% say security is a major concern, with this high degree of discomfort more prevalent among service than product firms. To address this issue, more than half of the CEOs of these companies have documented disaster recovery plans in place for IT emergencies.
>
> Looking ahead over the next year, 32% of the companies surveyed said they are planning to increase their levels of investment in computers and information technology, while only 11% are cutting back. About 55% expect to continue with current IT spending levels, and the remaining 2% are uncertain.
>
> *Adapted from an article posted on CNET News.com*

IS/IT and competitive advantage - other writers

4.14 Ward and Griffiths suggested four ways that IS/IT could be used for competitive advantage:

(a) **Linking the organisation to customers or suppliers**, eg EDI, website, VAN, extranet.

(b) Creating **effective integration** of the use of information in a value-adding process, eg data-mining, ERM.

(c) Enabling the organisation to **develop, produce, market and distribute new products or services**, eg CAD, CRM.

(d) Giving **senior management information** to help develop and implement strategy, eg knowledge management.

4.15 Moriarty and Swartz provide an example of how the application of IS/IT can generate a competitive advantage in relation to the sales and marketing function. They explain how technology can **increase productivity** through providing better marketing information (eg databases), and more efficient sales and marketing tools (eg direct mail, websites).

4.16 To be classed as a competitive advantage the increased productivity **would not be available to others**. This is unlikely unless the technology is too expensive (entry barrier), or competitors are unaware of how to utilise it.

4.17 Increased productivity may lead to **reduced fixed costs**. For example, fewer sales and marketing staff may be required, allowing a move to smaller premises. The effect of reduced fixed costs is shown in the following diagram.

6: Information systems and competitive position

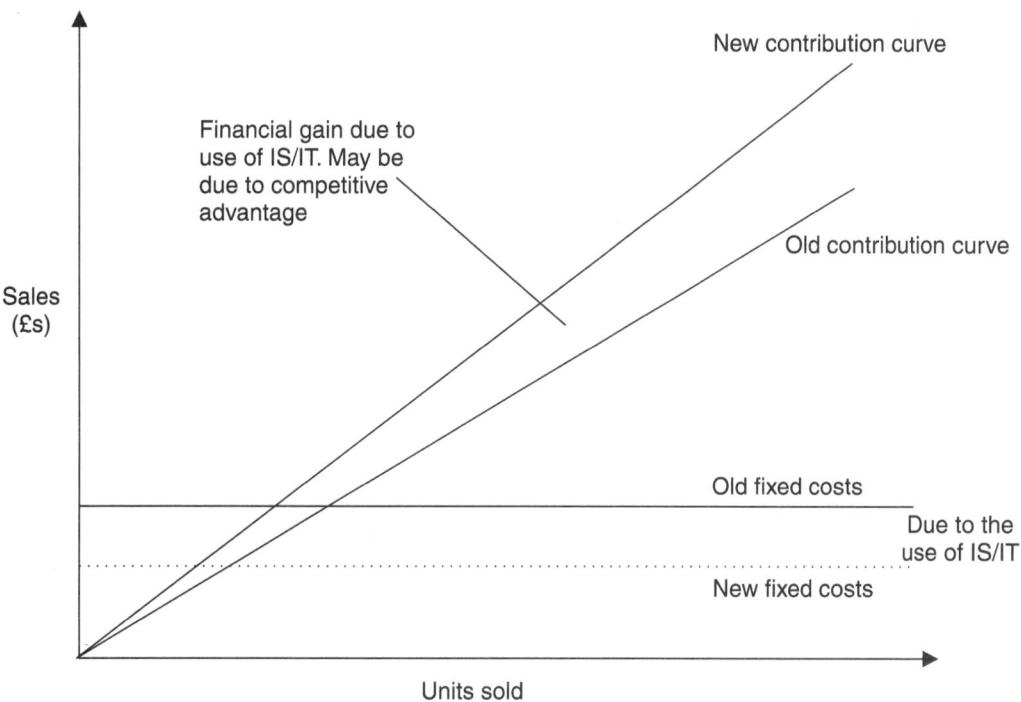

4.18 Peppard summarises the ways in which IS/IT can be used for competitive advantages as:

- Establishing entry barriers
- Affecting the cost of switching operations
- Differentiating products/services
- Limiting access to distribution channels
- Ensuring competitive pricing
- Decreasing supply costs
- Increasing cost efficiency
- Using information as a product
- Building closer relationships with supplies and customers

Case example

Competitive Advantage through IT - Information Technology at OTIS

Otis' success derives from being an effective user of information technology. The company's competitive advantage stems from three main developments – OTISLINE, REM and the use of fuzzy logic.

OTISLINE

The 'freephone' OTISLINE, in addition to its original purpose of improving customer service, has helped in areas like elevator maintenance, new equipment sales, marketing of elevator services. Otis has used OTISLINE in foreign markets to **increase the barriers to entry for its competitors** seeking to enter those same markets.

Otis now possesses the ability to access service information from both independent service companies and its own regional offices. This serves as a **database for customer files** as well as a **depository for all maintenance activities** for elevators under service contracts.

REM

REM is a PC-based system designed to monitor elevator performance from a distant location, 24 hours a day, that controls selected standard functions in order to spot problems in advance and to **avoid breakdowns**.

It is a **preventive** system that is programmed with predefined parameters that when deviated from initiates a warning signal which if unattended, could lead to a breakdown. Otis is able to recognise potential problems without alerting the customer and perform the necessary maintenance quickly.

Part C: Using information competitively

Technicians **can access elevator maintenance information as they are working** upon the problem without having to completely shut down the elevator beforehand.

Fuzzy Logic

Neural networks and artificial intelligence are used to identify peak hours of usage and the elevator can respond accordingly. Using weight and frequency, **elevators decide for themselves** where they should be at certain times of the day, thus greatly **reducing waiting time** (2 minutes to 30 seconds).

As a technology-based development, fuzzy logic is **copied relatively easily by competitors**, thus effectively eliminating Otis' competitive advantage in this area.

5 OUTSOURCING

KEY TERM

Outsourcing is the contracting out of specified operations or services to an external vendor.

Types of outsourcing

5.1 There are four **broad classifications** of outsourcing.

Classification	Comment
Ad-hoc	The organisation has a short-term requirement for increased IS/IT skills. An example would be employing programmers on a short-term contract to help with the programming of bespoke software.
Project management	The development and installation of a particular IS/IT project is outsourced. For example, a new accounting system. (This approach is sometimes referred to as **systems integration**.)
Partial	Some IT/IS services are outsourced. Examples include hardware maintenance, network management or ongoing website management.
Total	An external supplier provides the vast majority of an organisation's IT/IS services. Eg a third party owns or is responsible for IT equipment, software and staff.

Levels of service provision

5.2 The degree to which the provision and management of IS/IT services are transferred to the third party varies according to the situation and the skills of both organisations.

(a) **Time-share**. The vendor charges for access to an external processing system on a time-used basis. Software ownership may be with either the vendor or the client organisation.

(b) **Service bureaux** usually focus on a specific function. Traditionally bureaux would provide the same type of service to many organisations eg payroll processing. As organisations have developed their own IT infrastructure, the use of bureaux has decreased.

(c) **Facilities management (FM)**. The terms 'outsourcing' and 'facilities management' are sometimes confused. Facilities management traditionally involved contracts for premises-related services such as cleaning or site security.

In the context of IS/IT, facilities management involves an outside agency managing the organisation's IS/IT facilities. All equipment usually remains with the client, but the responsibility for providing and managing the specified services rests with the FM company.

5.3 The following table shows the main features of each of the outsourcing arrangements described above.

Feature	Outsourcing arrangement		
	Timeshare	Service bureaux	Facilities Management (FM)
Management responsibility	Mostly retained	Some retained	Very little retained
Focus	Operational	A function	Strategic
Timescale	Short-term	Medium-term	Long-term
Justification	Cost savings	More efficient	Access to expertise; higher quality service provision. Enables management to concentrate on the areas where they do possess expertise.

Organisations involved in outsourcing

Facilities management companies

5.4 FM arrangements have been covered in paragraph 5.2(c).

Software houses

5.5 Software houses concentrate on the provision of 'software services'. These services include feasibility studies, systems analysis and design, development of operating systems software, provision of application program packages, 'tailor-made' application programming, specialist systems advice, and so on. For example, a software house might be employed to write a computerised system for the London Stock Exchange.

Consultancy firms

5.6 Some consultancy firms work at a fairly high level, giving advice to management on the general approach to solving problems and on the types of system to use. Others specialise in giving more particular systems advice, carrying out feasibility studies and recommending computer manufacturers/software houses that will supply the right system. When a consultancy firm is used, the terms of the contract should be agreed at the outset.

5.7 The use of consultancy services enables management to learn directly or indirectly from the experience of others. Many larger consultancies are owned by big international accountancy firms; smaller consultancies may consist of one or two person outfits with a high level of specialist experience in one area.

5.8 The following categories of **consulting activity** have been identified by Beaumont and Sutherland.

Part C: Using information competitively

(a) **Strategic studies**, involving the development of a business strategy or an IS strategy for an organisation.

(b) **Specialist studies**, where the consultant provides a high level of expertise in one area, for example Enterprise Resource Management software.

(c) **Project management**, involving supervision of internal and external parties in the completion of a particular project.

(d) **Body-shopping**, where the necessary staff, including consultants, project managers, systems analysts and programmers, for a project are identified.

(e) **Recruitment**, involving the supply of permanent or temporary staff.

Hardware manufacturers and suppliers

5.9 Computer manufacturers or their designated suppliers will provide the **equipment** necessary for a system. They will also provide, under a **maintenance contract**, engineers who will deal with any routine servicing and with any breakdown of the equipment.

Case example

The retailer Sears outsourced the management of its vast information technology and accounting functions to Accenture. First year *savings* were estimated to be £5 million per annum, growing to £14 million in the following year, and thereafter. This is clearly considerable, although re-organisation costs relating to redundancies, relocation and asset write-offs are thought to be in the region of £35 million. About 900 staff were involved: under the transfer of undertakings regulations (which protect employees when part or all of a company changes hands), Accenture was obliged to take on the existing Sears staff. This provided new opportunities for the staff who moved, while those who remained at Sears are free to concentrate on strategy development and management direction.

Developments in outsourcing

5.10 Outsourcing arrangements are becoming increasingly flexible to cope with the ever-changing nature of the modern business environment. Three trends are:

(a) **Multiple sourcing**. This involves outsourcing different functions or areas of the IS/IT function to a range of suppliers. Some suppliers may form alliances to present a stronger case for selection.

(b) **Incremental approach**. Organisations progressively outsource selected areas of their IT/IS function. Possible problems with outsourced services are solved before progressing to the next stage.

(c) **Joint venture sourcing**. This term is used to describe an organisation entering into a joint venture with a supplier. The costs (risks) and possible rewards are split on an agreed basis. Such an arrangement may be suitable when developing software that could be sold to other organisations.

(d) **Application Service Providers (ASP)**. ASPs are third parties that manage and distribute software services and solutions to customers across a Wide Area Network. ASP's could be considered the modern equivalent of the traditional computer bureaux.

Managing outsourcing arrangements

5.11 Managing outsourcing arrangements involves deciding **what** will be outsourced, **choosing and negotiating** with suppliers and managing the supplier **relationship**.

5.12 When considering whether to outsource a particular service the following questions are relevant.

(a) Is the system of **strategic importance**? Strategic IS are generally not suited to outsourcing as they require a high degree of specific business knowledge that a third party IT specialist can not be expected to possess.

(b) Can the system be relatively isolated? Functions that have only **limited interfaces** are most easily outsourced eg payroll.

(c) Do we know enough about the system to manage the outsourced service agreement? If an organisation knows very little about a technology it may be difficult to know what constitutes good service and value for money. It may be necessary to recruit additional **expertise** to manage the relationship with the other party.

(d) Are our requirements likely to **change**? Organisations should avoid tying themselves into a long-term outsourcing agreement if requirements are likely to change.

5.13 A key factor when **choosing and negotiating** with external vendors is the contract offered and subsequently negotiated with the supplier. The contract is sometimes referred to as the **Service Level Contract** (SLC) or **Service Level Agreement** (SLA).

5.14 The key elements of the contract are described below.

Contract element	Comment
Service level	The contract should clearly specify **minimum levels of service** to be provided. Penalties should be specified for failure to meet these standards. Relevant factors will vary depending on the nature of the services outsourced but could include: • Response time to requests for assistance/information • System 'uptime' percentage • Deadlines for performing relevant tasks
Exit route	Arrangements for an exit route, addressing how transfer to another supplier, or the move back in-house would be conducted.
Timescale	When does the contract expire? Is the timescale suitable for the organisation's needs or should it be renegotiated?
Software ownership	Relevant factors include: • Software licensing and security • If the arrangement includes the development of new software who owns the copyright?
Dependencies	If related services are outsourced the level of service quality agreed should group these services together.
Employment issues	If the arrangement includes provision for the organisation's IT staff to move to the third party, employer responsibilities must be specified clearly.

5.15 After a supplier has been selected, and the contact negotiated and signed, the contact provides the framework for the **relationship** between the organisation and the service provider.

Part C: Using information competitively

5.16 The nature of the relationship between the organisation and the service provider will depend on the service that has been outsourced and the preferences and personalities of the people involved.

5.17 If full facilities management is involved, and almost all management responsibility for IT/IS lies with the entity providing the service, then a close relationship between the parties is necessary (a '**partnership**'). Factors such as organisation culture need to be considered when entering into such a close and critical relationship.

5.18 On the other hand, if a relatively simple function such as payroll were outsourced, such a close relationship with the supplier would not be necessary. A 'typical' supplier - customer relationship is all that is required. (Although issues such as confidentiality need to be considered with payroll data.)

5.19 Regardless of the type of relationship, a legally binding contract is the key element in establishing the obligations and responsibilities of all parties.

Question 4

Do any organisations with which you are familiar use outsourcing? What is the view of outsourcing in the organisation?

Answer

One view is given below.

A survey conducted by the PA Consulting Group found that 'on average the top five strategic outsourcers out-performed the FTSE by more than 100 per cent over three years; the bottom five under-performed by more than 66%'.

However the survey revealed that of those organisations who have opted to outsource IT functions, only five per cent are truly happy with the results. A spokesman for the consultants said that this is because most people fail to adopt a proper strategic approach, taking a view that is neither long-term nor broad enough, and taking outsourcing decisions that are piecemeal and unsatisfactory.

This lack of prescience is compounded by a failure to take a sufficiently rigorous approach to selection, specification, contract drafting and contract management.

The survey found that a constant complaint among many of those interviewed is the lack of ability of outsourcing organisations to work together.

Twenty-five per cent of those asked would bring the functions they had outsourced back in-house if it were possible.

Advantages of outsourcing arrangements

5.20 The **advantages** of outsourcing are as follows.

(a) Outsourcing can remove uncertainty about **cost,** as there is often a long-term contract where services are specified in advance for a **fixed price**. If computing services are inefficient, the costs will be borne by the FM company. This is also an incentive to the third party to provide a high quality service.

(b) Long-term contracts (maybe up to ten years) encourage **planning** for the future.

(c) Outsourcing can bring the benefits of **economies of scale**. For example, a FM company may conduct research into new technologies that benefits a number of their clients.

6: Information systems and competitive position

(d) A specialist organisation is able to retain **skills and knowledge**. Many organisations would not have a sufficiently well-developed IT department to offer IT staff opportunities for career development. Talented staff would leave to pursue their careers elsewhere.

(e) New skills and knowledge become available. A specialist company can **share** staff with **specific expertise** (such as programming in HTML to produce Web pages) between several clients. This allows the outsourcing company to take advantage of new developments without the need to recruit new people or re-train existing staff, and without the cost.

(f) **Flexibility** (contract permitting). Resources may be able to be scaled up or down depending upon demand. For instance, during a major changeover from one system to another the number of IT staff needed may be twice as large as it will be once the new system is working satisfactorily.

An outsourcing organisation is more able to arrange its work on a **project** basis, whereby some staff will expect to be moved periodically from one project to the next.

Disadvantages of outsourcing arrangements

5.21 Some possible **drawbacks** are outlined below.

(a) It is arguable that information and its provision is **an inherent part of the business and of management**. Unlike office cleaning, or catering, an organisation's IS services may be too important to be contracted out. Information is at the heart of management.

(b) A company may have highly **confidential information** and to let outsiders handle it could be seen as **risky** in commercial and/or legal terms.

(c) Information strategy can be used to gain **competitive advantage**. Opportunities may be missed if a third party is handling IS services, because there is no onus upon internal management to keep up with new developments and have new ideas. Any new technology or application devised by the third party is likely to be available to competitors.

(d) An organisation may find itself **locked in** to an unsatisfactory contract. The decision may be very difficult to reverse. If the FM company supplies unsatisfactory levels of service, the effort and expense the organisation would incur to rebuild its own computing function or to move to another provider could be substantial.

(e) The use of FM does not encourage awareness of the potential costs and benefits of IS/IT within the organisation. If managers cannot manage in-house IS/IT resources effectively, then it could be argued that they will not be able to manage an arrangement to outsource effectively either.

Insourcing

5.22 Outsourcing involves purchasing specific services or expertise from outside the organisation. Several factors have led some to believe this is not the best solution in today's environment.

(a) Many organisations have found there is often a shortage of qualified candidates with the skills they require.

(b) The **cost** of acquiring people with high-tech expertise and business skills fluctuates due to factors affecting supply and demand.

Part C: Using information competitively

(c) Third, there is increasing recognition that IT professionals require an understanding of the **business principles** behind the systems that they develop and manage.

5.23 In relation to IS/IT, insourcing involves recruiting IS/IT staff internally, from other areas of the business, and teaching these business-savvy employees about technology. The logic behind the idea is that it is easier (and cheaper) to **teach technical skills to business people** than to teach business skills to technical people.

5.24 Supporters of insourcing believe it has the potential to:

(a) Create a better quality workforce that combines both technical and business skills.
(b) Reduce costs.
(c) Improve relationships and communication between IT staff and other departments.
(d) Increase staff retention through providing an additional career path.

5.25 Possible disadvantages include:

(a) The risk that non-technical employees will not pick up the IS/IT skills required.
(b) Finding staff willing to make the change.
(c) Replacing staff who do make the switch.

6 BESPOKE SOFTWARE OR AN OFF-THE-SHELF PACKAGE?

6.1 An organisation has a range of options when sourcing software for information systems. The four main options are described in the following table.

Source	Comment
Standard off-the-shelf package	This is the simplest option. The organisation purchases and installs a ready-made solution.
Amended standard package	A standard package is purchased, but some customisation is undertaken so that the software meets the organisations requirements. This may require access to the source code.
Standard package plus additions	The purchased standard package is not amended itself, but additional software that integrates with the standard package is developed. This also may require access to the source code.
Bespoke package	Programmers write an application to meet the specific needs of the organisation. This can be a time-consuming and expensive process.

6.2 In this section we discuss the relative advantages of the two main options - purchasing an application off-the-shelf and developing a bespoke solution. The other two options include elements of both of these two main options.

KEY TERMS

Bespoke software is designed and written either 'in-house' by the IS department or externally by a software house.

An **off-the-shelf package** is one that is sold to a wide range of users. The package is written to handle requirements that are common to a wide range of organisations.

Bespoke software

6.3 **Advantages** of having software specially written include the following.

(a) If it is well-written, the software should meet the organisation's specific needs.

(b) Data and file structures may be chosen by the organisation rather than having to meet the structures required by standard software packages.

(c) The company may be able to do things with its software that competitors cannot do with theirs. In other words it is a source of competitive advantage.

(d) Similar organisations may wish to purchase the software.

(e) The software should be able to be modified to meet future needs.

6.4 Key **disadvantages** are.

(a) As the software is being developed from scratch, there is a risk that the package may not perform as intended.

(b) There is a greater chance of 'bugs'. Widely used off-the-shelf software is more likely to have had bugs identified and removed.

(c) Development will take longer than purchasing ready-made software.

(d) The cost is considerable when compared with a ready-made package.

(e) Support costs are also likely to be higher than with off-the-shelf software.

Overcoming the risks of bespoke development

6.5 Building a bespoke software application involves much time, effort and money. The risks associated with such an undertaking are that the resulting software:

- Does not meet user needs
- Does not interact as intended with other systems
- Is produced late
- Is produced over-budget

6.6 These risks can be minimised or overcome by:

(a) Good project management.

(b) Involving users at all stages of development.

(c) Ensuring in-house IT staff are able to maintain and support bespoke systems supplied from outside parties.

(d) Ensuring the ITT document includes details of all file structures required, and details of interfaces with other systems.

Off-the-shelf packages

6.7 **Advantages** of an off-the-shelf package

(a) The software is likely to be available immediately.

(b) A ready-made package will almost certainly cheaper because it is 'mass-produced".

(c) The software is likely to have been written by software specialists and so should be of a high quality.

(d) A successful package will be continually updated by the software manufacturer.

(e) Other users will have used the package already, and a well-established package should be relatively free of bugs.

(f) Good packages are well-documented, with easy-to-follow user manuals or on-line help.

(g) Some standard packages can be customised to the user's specific needs (see below).

6.8 The **disadvantages** of ready-made packages are as follows.

(a) The organisation is purchasing a standard solution. A standard solution may not be well suited to the organisation's particular needs.

(b) The organisation is dependent on the supplier for maintenance of the package - ie updating the package or providing assistance in the event of problems. It is unlikely that the supplier would give access to the code that would allow organisations with the relevant expertise to amend the software themselves.

(c) Competitors may well use the same package, removing any chance of using IS/IT for competitive advantage.

Customised versions of standard packages

6.9 Standard packages can be customised so that they fit an organisation's specific requirements. This can be done by purchasing the source code of the package and making modifications in-house, or by paying the producer of the package to customise it.

6.10 **Advantages** of customisation are similar to those of producing a bespoke system, with the additional advantages that:

(a) Development time should be much quicker, given that most of the system will be written already.

(b) If the work is done in-house the organisation gains considerable knowledge of how the software works and may be able to 'tune' it so that it works more efficiently with the company's hardware.

6.11 **Disadvantages** of customising a standard package include the following.

(a) It may prove more costly than expected, because new versions of the standard package will also have to be customised.

(b) Customisation may delay delivery of the software.

(c) Customisation may introduce bugs that do not exist in the standard version.

(d) If done in-house, the in-house team may have to learn new skills.

(e) If done by the original manufacturer disadvantages such as those for off-the-shelf packages may arise.

Add-ons and programming tools

6.12 Two other ways of trying to give a computer user more flexibility with packages are:

(a) The sale of 'add-ons' to a basic package, which an organisation may purchase if the add-ons suit their particular needs.

(b) The provision of programming tools (such as fourth generation languages) with a package, which allows users to write amendments to the software (without having to be a programming expert).

6: Information systems and competitive position

Software contracts and licences

6.13 The agreement to supply bespoke software should be formally laid out in a contract. The contract to supply the software is likely to include terms relating to:

(a) The cost, and what this figure does and does not include.

(b) Delivery date.

(c) Ownership of the source code, sometimes referred to as ownership rights.

(d) Right to make copies.

(e) Number of licensed users.

(f) Performance criteria, such as what the software will and will not do, processing speed.

(g) Warranty period.

(h) Support available.

(i) Arrangements for upgrades.

(j) Maintenance arrangements (maintenance is discussed in Chapter 14).

Software licences

6.14 Packaged software generally has a licence, the terms of which users are deemed to have agreed to the moment the package is unwrapped or a seal is broken.

6.15 A licence typically covers matters such as:

(a) How many users can use the software.

(b) Whether it can be modified without the manufacturer's consent.

(c) In what circumstances the licence is terminated.

(d) A limitation of liability should the software contain bugs or be mis-used (in an 'exclusion clause'). This is a complex area that is still developing. The representations that the software supplier makes regarding the package's capabilities would also be taken into account in any legal dispute.

6.16 When a user purchases software they are merely buying the rights to use the software in line with the terms and conditions within the licence agreement. The licence will be issued with the software, on paper or in electronic form. It contains the terms and conditions of use, as set out by the software publisher or owner of the copyright. A breach of the licence conditions usually means the owners' copyright has been infringed. In the UK, computer software is defined as a Literary Work in the Copyright, Designs and Patents Act (1988).

6.17 The unauthorised copying of software is referred to as software piracy. If an organisation is using illegal copies of software, the organisation may face a civil suit, and corporate officers and individual employees may have criminal liability. In the UK, remedies for civil copyright infringement may include damages to compensate the copyright owners for damage caused to their business, including reputation, and for loss of sales. Criminal penalties can include unlimited fines and two years' imprisonment or both.

6.18 The most common type of software piracy in a business setting is referred to as Corporate Over-Use. This is the installation of software packages on more machines than there are licences for. For example if a company purchases five single-user licences of a software program but installs the software on ten machines, then they will be using five infringing

Part C: Using information competitively

copies. Similarly, if a company is running a large network and more users have access to a software program than the company has licences for, this too is Corporate Over-Use.

6.19 A grey area is the installation of programs on portable or laptop computers for use off-site. Generally speaking, if a person has a program installed on their desktop in the office and the same person has the same program on their laptop for off-site use, then this usually counts as one user under the licence rather than two. However, the terms in different licences may differ.

6.20 To ensure they do not infringe copyright organisations should:
- Make sure they receive and keep licences - these are valuable documents
- Track the number of users with access to licensed programs
- Periodically check all computers for unlicensed software
- Buy from reputable dealers
- Get a written quote listing hardware/software specification and version
- Require an itemised invoice giving details of all hardware and software supplied

6.21 In the UK, the Copyright, Designs and Patents Act 1998 specifically allows the making of back-up copies of software, but only providing it is for lawful use.

Case example: Reports of corporate under licensing on the rise
Federation Against Software Theft reports 12% increase

Reports of corporate under licensing are on the rise according to the latest figures issued by industry watchdog, the Federation Against Software Theft (FAST). In the year 2000 the organisation received in excess of 380 reports of under licensing within the business community, an annual increase of 12%.

According to FAST the figures indicate a number of trends year on year not least the increased impact of the organisation's awareness campaigns. These campaigns, aimed at educating everyone within the workforce, have increasingly focused on the criminality of under licensing and the impact it can have on business.

Over the past couple of years FAST and other trade bodies associated with protecting copyright, have made it far easier to report the illegal use of software within the business community. This has included a new Hotline facility, greater anonymity for those reporting under licensing and even the ability to report via the FAST web site.

Commenting on the rise in reports made to the Federation, Geoff Webster, CEO said: 'We believe these figures reflect a positive change in attitude towards how organisations in general are viewing software piracy as a serious business issue. Particularly within large organisations, board level executives are realising that software piracy can have a huge financial impact on the business if not dealt with properly.'

He continued: 'It is an interesting point to note that while software piracy and under licensing is in general in decline, according to the latest figures from the Business Software Alliance (BSA), the number of reports is on the rise. This can to my mind solely be attributed to a general increase in awareness of the issue. FAST believes that its educational and enforcement roles are working in tandem and working effectively.'

FAST, January 2001

End-user development

6.22 End-user computing has been fuelled by the introduction of **PCs** to user departments, by **user-friendly software,** and by **greater awareness** of computers and what they can do.

6: Information systems and competitive position

> **KEY TERM**
>
> **End-user development** is the direct, hands-on development of computer systems by users.

6.23 Staff such as accountants often design and use complex **spreadsheet models** – this is an example of end-user computing.

6.24 Modern spreadsheet packages allow the use of macros and other 'programming' techniques which allow users to develop their own fairly complex applications. Often the people building these models have little or no formal training in programming and system design, and the methods used are personal to each user.

6.25 While these programs may work well, they are likely to be very **difficult to modify**. Often only the person who developed the model fully understands it. Such models are rarely documented. This is risky from the organisation's viewpoint: systems are developed with little control, and the organisation becomes dependant upon those individuals who developed the system.

6.26 Other disadvantages are as follows:

(a) The risk from the elimination of the **separation of the functions of user and analyst**.

(b) The risk from **limits on user ability** to identify correct and complete requirements for an application.

(c) The risk from **lack of user knowledge and acceptance of application quality assurance procedures** for development and operation.

(d) The risk from **unstable user systems**.

(e) The risk from encouraging **private information systems**.

(f) The risk from permitting **unstructured information systems development**.

User groups

6.27 The concept of user groups has existed in the computer industry for some time.

> **KEY TERM**
>
> A **user group** is a forum for users of particular hardware or, more usually, software, so that they can **share ideas and experience**.

6.28 User groups are usually set up either by the software manufacturers themselves (who use them to **maintain contact** with customers and as a source of **new product ideas**) or by groups of users. The term is used most commonly with users of packaged software.

6.29 Users of a particular package can meet, or perhaps exchange views over the **Internet** to discuss solutions, ideas or 'short cuts' to improve productivity. An (electronic) newsletter service might be appropriate, based on views exchanged by members, but also incorporating ideas culled from the wider environment by IT specialists.

Part C: Using information competitively

6.30 Sometimes user groups are set up **within** individual organisations. Where an organisation has written its own application software, or is using tailor-made software, there will be a very **small knowledge base** initially, and there will obviously not be a national user group, because the application is unique.

6.31 'Interested parties', including, as a minimum, representatives from the **IT department** and **users** who are familiar with different parts of the system can attend monthly or quarterly **meetings** to discuss the **operation** of the system, make **suggestions for improvements** (such as the production of new reports or time-tabling of processing) and raise any **queries**.

Question 5

Trends in IT such as distributed processing, increased use of PCs and wide availability of sophisticated general purpose packages have resulted in more responsibility for information systems being transferred to end-users. What problems may this result in for organisations?

Answer

Here are some suggestions.

(a) Lack of formal training could result in inefficient or even 'faulty' systems.

(b) User requests for assistance that overwhelm the IS/IT department.

(c) Lack of user knowledge or concern may lead to inadequate controls being built into the system.

(d) Lack of integration across the organisation with many users developing systems to suit themselves.

(e) Poor maintainability of user-developed systems as only the person that developed it understands it

(f) Lack of centralised management of resources.

(g) A lack of understanding of the organisations use of IS/IT may develop – it becomes difficult to see the 'big picture'

Summary diagram

6.32 The following diagram shows one example of how a wide range of syllabus areas may be relevant to how an organisation uses information. (You don't need to learn this diagram, its purpose is to encourage you to think about possible relationships and links between different topics.)

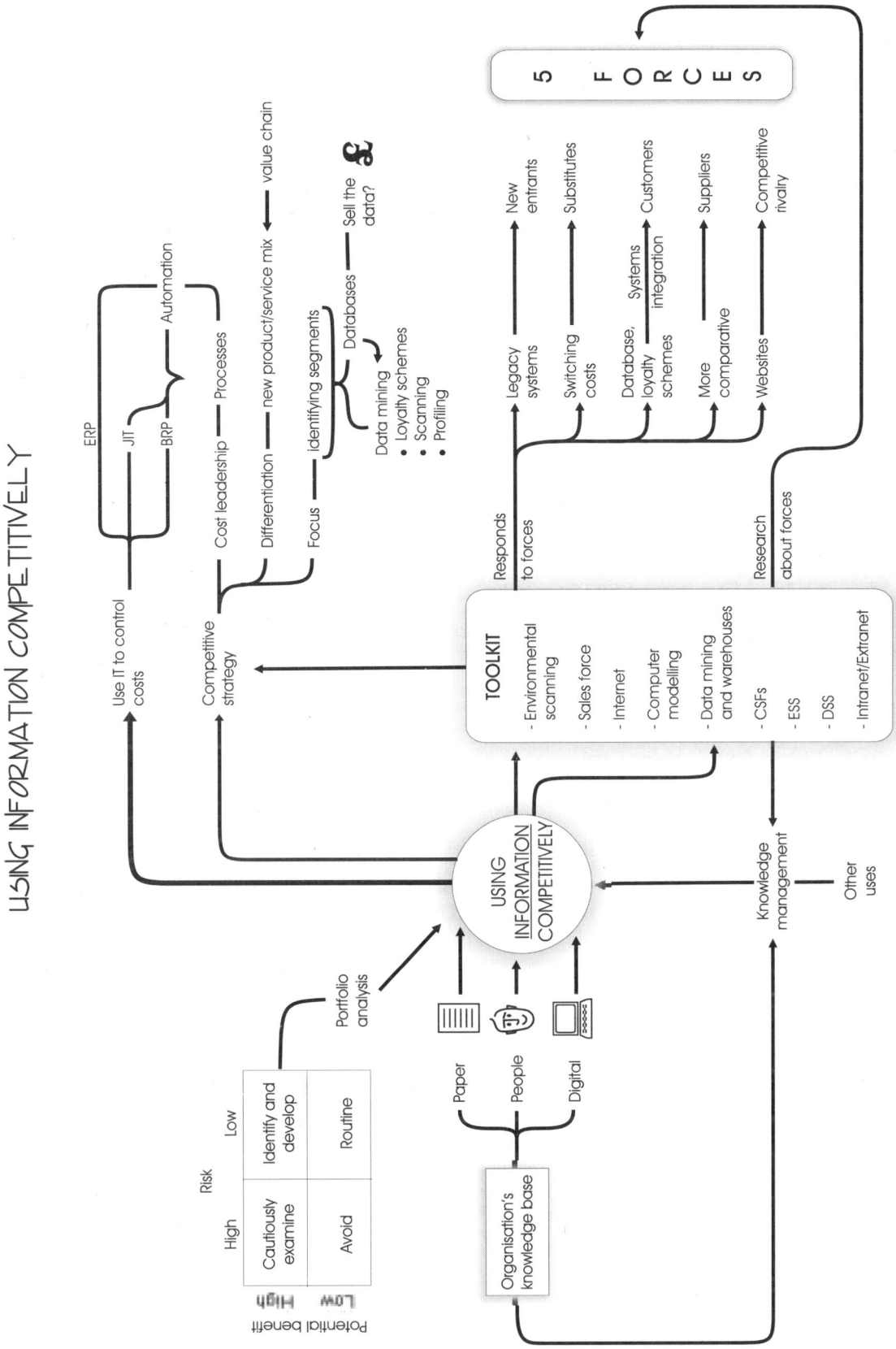

Chapter roundup

- The general management technique of **SWOT** analysis can be applied to the development of **information systems strategy**.

- The identification of **business needs** and the information **technology framework** to satisfy them is at the heart of a strategy for information systems and information technology.

- Critical success factors (**CSFs**) function as linking pins between IS/IT and business planning. The process is as follows.

    Step 1. Define business objectives.

    Step 2. Identify the CSFs whose success is necessary for the organisation to flourish.

    Step 3. Develop the information systems to support the CSFs.

- Richard Nolan's **stage hypothesis** attempts to model the stages organisations go through in their use of IS/IT. A key lesson of the stage hypothesis is that an organisation's use of IS/IT must be **planned** and **managed**.

- Porter and Millar state that IS/IT has the potential to change the **nature of competition** within an industry in three ways. IS/IT can:
    - Change the industry structure
    - Create new businesses and industries
    - Be used to create competitive advantage

- Porter's **five forces model** can be used to analyse the effect of IS/IT on an industry. Porter identified five competitive forces operating in a competitive environment:
    - The threat of new entrants
    - The bargaining power of suppliers
    - The bargaining power of customers
    - The threat of substitute products/service
    - The existing competitive rivalry in the industry

- Porter proposes three **generic strategies** for achieving competitive advantage:
    - Cost leadership
    - Differentiation
    - Focus (either cost or differentiation)

- Michael Porter's **Value Chain** models activities (inputs, process and add value to generate outputs for customers) and the relationships between them. The value chain can be used to design a competitive strategy.

- Ways in which IS/IT can be **used for competitive advantage** include:
    - Establishing entry barriers
    - Differentiating products/services
    - Ensuring competitive pricing
    - Increasing cost efficiency
    - Building closer relationships with supplies and customers
    - Affecting the cost of switching operations
    - Limiting access to distribution channels
    - Decreasing supply costs
    - Using information as a product

- The **management of IS and IT** involves many interrelated issues and options, including:
    - Organisation structure
    - Power and privacy
    - Legacy system
    - **Outsourcing**
    - Constant change
    - Backward compatibility
    - Open systems and interoperability
    - Whether to develop **bespoke** software or buy an existing package **off-the shelf**

6: Information systems and competitive position

Quick quiz

1. What does SWOT analysis, when used as a technique for identifying opportunities in information systems development, aim to determine?
2. List Porter's five competitive forces operating in a competitive environment.
3. Provide an example of how IS/IT can support each of Porter's generic strategies.
4. What does ERP stand for?
5. Define 'interoperability'.
6. What is an ASP?
7. What would you say is the main advantage of bespoke software?
8. What is the main disadvantage of bespoke software?
9. Define 'Corporate Over-Use'.

Answers to quick quiz

1. What Strengths does our (overall) information system have? (How can we take advantage of them?)

    What Weaknesses does the system have? (How can we minimise them?)

    What Opportunities, outside the information system, are there in the organisation or beyond? (How can we capitalise on them?)

    What Threats, outside the information system, might prevent us operating or improving the information system? (How can we protect ourselves from them?)

2. The threat of new entrants.

    The bargaining power of suppliers.

    The bargaining power of customers.

    The threat of substitute products/service.

    The existing competitive rivalry in the industry.

3. Try to think of your own examples. Some are provided in paragraph 4.4.
4. Enterprise Resource Planning.
5. Interoperability is the concept of systems facilitating the sharing and exchange of information between parties, regardless of the service provider and technology platform.
6. Application Service Providers (ASPs) are third-party entities that manage and distribute software-based services and solutions to customers across a Wide Area Network.
7. As it is written for a specific purpose it should match user requirements very closely.
8. It's expensive when compared to off-the-shelf software.
9. The installation or use of software by more users than the organisation is licenced for.

Now try the questions below from the Exam Question Bank

Number	Level	Marks	Time
2	Exam	20	36 mins
3	Exam	20	36 mins
4	Exam	20	36 mins
11	Exam	12	21 mins

Chapter 7

THE INTERNET AS A STRATEGIC BUSINESS TOOL

Topic list	Syllabus reference
1 The Internet – an overview	7(a)
2 Internet security issues	7(a)
3 Electronic commerce	7(b)
4 Developing a strategy for the Internet and e-commerce	7(b)
5 Globalisation	7(a)

Introduction

The Internet is potentially the most **significant business and social development** since the advent of the telephone.

As with any new technology the Internet provides both opportunities and risks. In this chapter we look at how the **Internet can be exploited** to provide enhanced value to businesses and their customers. We also cover the **security issues** associated with the Internet and e-commerce.

We end this chapter with a discussion of globalisation, and how information systems can support an organisation's global business strategy.

Study guide

3/4 – Strategic role of information systems

- Identify opportunities for use in forecasting, analysing competition, scenario planning, generic strategies/business positioning, improving performance, measuring performance, opportunities for cost reduction, opportunities for service improvement, sales performance, evaluating proposals (Also see Chapters 2 and 6)

22 – Web-based technology

- Discuss the business impact of the Internet
- Identify good practice requirements, infrastructure required, and change of business functions/ strategy
- Understand the Internet as a system
- Explain how to integrate with existing systems (Also see Chapter 2)
- Evaluate the problems associated with using web-based technology and the issue of security

23 – Electronic commerce

- Discuss the impact of globalisation on business strategy
- Describe the implications of globalisation in terms of: management and control in a global marketplace, competition in world markets, global work groups, and global delivery systems

Part C: Using information competitively

> ## Study guide (continued)
>
> **23 – Electronic commerce (continued)**
>
> - Describe Virtual Supply Chain (VSC)
> - Discuss electronic marketing
>
> ## Exam guide
>
> The Internet is a '**hot topic**' in both the academic and business worlds – so ensure you understand the issues raised in this chapter.

1 THE INTERNET- AN OVERVIEW

> ### KEY TERMS
>
> The **Internet** is a global network connecting millions of computers (and other compatible devices).
>
> The **World Wide Web** (WWW) is a system of Internet servers that support specially formatted documents. Most documents on the web are formatted in HTML (HyperText Markup Language) that supports links to other documents, as well as graphics, audio, and video files.
>
> A group of documents accessed from the same base web address is known as a **website**.

1.1 The Internet is the name given to the technology that allows any computer (or other device) with a telecommunications link to **send and receive information** from any other suitably equipped device.

1.2 Connection to the Internet is made via an Internet Service Provider (ISP). ISPs, such as AOL and Virgin, provide their own information services in addition to Internet access and e-mail capability.

1.3 The Internet is viewed through interface programs called **browsers**. The most widely used are Microsoft Internet Explorer and Netscape Navigator. Searching the web is done using a **search engine** such as Google, Yahoo!, Lycos or Alltheweb.

1.4 Most organisations now have a **website** on the Internet. A website address will typically be given in the format of a **U**niversal **R**esource **L**ocator (**URL**). eg http://www.bbc.co.uk

URL element	Explanation
http://	'http' tells the browser to use the HyperText Transfer Protocol when retrieving the document from the Internet server. The two forward slashes after the colon introduce a 'host name' such as www.
www	This stands for **World Wide Web**. As noted before, to put it simply the web (via its use of HTML), is what makes the Internet user-friendly.

URL element	Explanation
bbc	This is the **domain name** of the organisation or individual whose site is located at this URL
co	This indicates the type of organisation concerned, in this case a company. Other designations include: .com — Commercial .ac or .edu — Educational and research .org — Usually non-commercial institutions .net or .biz — Inconsistent, an 'overflow' from .com and .org .mil — Military .gov — Government agencies
uk	This indicates that the organisation is located in the UK. For a full list of country codes used on the web visit; www.dundee.ac.uk/english/url-jav.htm

Current uses of the Internet

1.5 The scope and potential of the Internet are still developing. Its uses already embrace the following:

(a) **Dissemination of information.**

(b) Product/service development - through almost instantaneous **test marketing**.

(c) **Transaction processing** - both business-to-business (B2B) and business-to-consumer (B2C).

(d) **Relationship enhancement** - between various groups of stakeholders, but principally (for our purposes) between consumers and product/service suppliers.

(e) **Recruitment** and job search - involving organisations worldwide.

(f) **Entertainment** - including music, humour, games and some less wholesome pursuits!

Growth of the Internet

1.6 It is estimated that 60% of households in the USA and 50% of households in the UK will have Internet access by the end of 2003.

(a) Many households are now establishing multiple Internet access points eg Digital TV set, PCs, WAP phones.

(b) **Changes in the telecoms market** are likely to mean that Internet connection time will become cheaper.

(c) Digital television and WAP enabled mobile phones permit the Internet to be accessed without the necessity to use a personal computer.

(d) For many, the preferred Internet interface is not the PC but the **PDA (Personal Digital Assistant).**

(e) Internet kiosks are becoming increasingly common in shopping centres, train stations and cafes.

1.7 A critical factor in the long-run expansion of the Internet is its use today by children, the adult consumers of tomorrow.

Part C: Using information competitively

1.8 The Internet is not expanding at the same rate in every sphere of business. The rate of growth is influenced by:

   (a) The degree to which the customer can be persuaded to believe that using the Internet will **deliver some added-value** - in terms of quickness, simplicity and price.

   (b) Whether there are 'costs' which the **customer** has to bear - not exclusively 'costs' in the financial sense, but also such psychological 'costs' as the isolated on-line shopping experience.

   (c) The **market segment** to which the individual belongs. The Internet is largely the preserve of younger, more affluent, more technologically competent individuals with above-average amounts of disposable income.

   (d) The frequency of supplier/customer contact required.

   (e) The availability of **incentives** which might stimulate Internet acceptance. For example, interest rates on bank accounts which are higher than those available through conventional banks (Egg), the absence of any charges (Freeserve), the creation of penalties for over-the-counter transactions (Abbey National), and the expectations of important customers (IBM's relationships with its suppliers).

1.9 Arguably, the most profitable pure Internet companies, as well as the most influential, will be **business-to-business 'infomediaries'** (the term coined by John Hagel of McKinsey), because they can exploit the Internet's most salient characteristics.

   (a) **The Internet shifts power from sellers to buyers by reducing switching costs.** Buyers may feel overwhelmed by this power, but they typically want one-stop shopping, with information they believe and advice they can trust. Sellers cannot be believed or trusted - but infomediaries may.

   (b) **The Internet reduces transaction costs and thus stimulates economic activity.** According to one US calculation, a banking transaction via the Internet costs 1 cent, 27 cents at an ATM (automated teller machine) and 52 cents over the telephone. Infomediaries can enable significant savings to be enjoyed by small-scale or even single customers.

   (c) **The speed, range and accessibility of information on the Internet, and the low cost of capturing and distributing it, create new commercial possibilities.** Infomediaries can focus on particular product/service supply issues; by doing so, they attract specialised buyers and sellers; in turn they acquire more expertise which generates continued customer loyalty and participation.

1.10 The major growth so far in the field of e-commerce has concentrated on the **Business to Business** (B2B) sector.

   (a) **Major companies** are setting themselves up as e-businesses. In November 1999, both Ford and General Motors announced that they were switching a major portion of their procurement and supply chain management to the web.

   (b) IBM now requires **all its suppliers to quote and invoice electronically** - no paper documentation is permitted.

   (c) Many firms are using the Internet to exploit the **transparency of supplier prices**, and to maximise their purchasing benefits from the availability of world-wide sourcing. Robert Bosch, the German kitchen appliance manufacturer, **requires all its suppliers to have web-based catalogues** and prices.

   (d) Companies are also increasing their customer service through the web. Dell, the computer company, has created **extranets for its major business customers**, enabling

them to receive personalised customer support, their own price lists, and some free value-added services.

Case example
Business and the Internet

The Internet has the potential to turn business upside down and inside out, to fundamentally change the way companies operate, whether in high-tech or metal-bashing. This goes far beyond buying and selling over the Internet, or e-commerce, and deep into the processes and culture of an enterprise.

Some companies are using the Internet to make direct connections with their customers for the first time. Others are using secure Internet connections to intensify relations with some of their trading partners, and using the Internet's reach and ubiquity to request quotes or sell off perishable stocks of goods or services by auction.

The Internet is helping companies to lower costs dramatically across their supply and demand chains, take their customer service into a different league, enter new markets, create additional revenue streams and redefine their business relationships.

Some writers argue that companies can be either '**brick**' or '**click**' businesses, but they can't be both: if they are a 'brick' operation - ie they have real premises, real shops, real factories and warehouses - then their culture will make it impossible for them fully to assimilate the drastic changes required in order to operate successfully in a 'click' environment. It is no accident, therefore, that companies like Prudential Assurance have initiated their Internet activities through stand-alone enterprises, using newly-recruited people situated in geographically-distinctive locations.

1.11 The Internet provides opportunities to automate tasks which would previously have required more costly interaction with the organisation. These have often been called low-touch or zero-touch approaches.

1.12 Tasks which a website may automate include:

(a) **Frequently-Asked Questions (FAQs)**: carefully-structured sets of answers can deal with many customer interactions.

(b) **Status checking**: major service enquiries (Where is my order? When will the engineer arrive? What is my bank balance?) can also be automated, replacing high-cost human service processes, and also providing the opportunity to proactively offer better service and new services.

(c) **Keyword search**: the ability to search provides web users with opportunities to find information in large and complex websites.

(d) **Wizards (interview style interface) and intelligent algorithms**: these can help diagnosis, which is one of the major elements of service support.

(e) **E-mail and systems to route and track inbound e-mail**: the ability to route and/or to provide automatic responses will enable organisations to deal with high volumes of e-mail from actual and potential customers.

(f) **Bulletin boards**: these enable customers to interact with each other, thus facilitating self-activated customer service and also the opportunity for product/service referral. Cisco in particular has created communities of Cisco users who help each other - thus reducing the service costs for Cisco itself.

(g) **Call-back buttons**: these enable customers to speak to someone in order to deal with and resolve a problem; the more sophisticated systems allow the call-centre operator to know which web pages the users were consulting at the time.

(h) **Transaction processing**: the taking of orders and payment on-line.

Part C: Using information competitively

Problems with the Internet

1.13 To a large extent the Internet has grown **without any formal organisation**. There are specific communication rules, but it is not **owned** by any one body and there are no clear guidelines on how it should develop.

1.14 Inevitably, the **quality** of much of the information on the Internet leaves much to be desired.

1.15 Speed is a major issue. Data only downloads onto the user's PC at the speed of the slowest telecommunications link - downloading data can be a time-consuming procedure. However, future developments will mean that speeds will improve.

1.16 A number of **faster services** have recently become available, but cost is preventing widespread installation of these technologies by consumers.

(a) **Integrated Services Digital Network (ISDN)** is an international communications standard for sending voice, video, and data over digital telephone lines or normal telephone wires. ISDN supports data transfer rates three times faster than modems.

(b) **ADSL** (Asymmetric Digital Subscriber Line)) is offers data transfer rates of up to **8 Mbps**, considerably faster than ISDN. ADSL allows information to be sent out over ordinary copper wires and simultaneous use of the normal telephone service.

1.17 So much information and entertainment is available that employers worry that their **staff will spend too much time** browsing through non-work-related sites.

1.18 **Security** is perhaps the biggest worry of all; this is covered in the next section.

1.19 The following diagram shows how the different elements of the Internet fit together.

7: The Internet as a strategic business tool

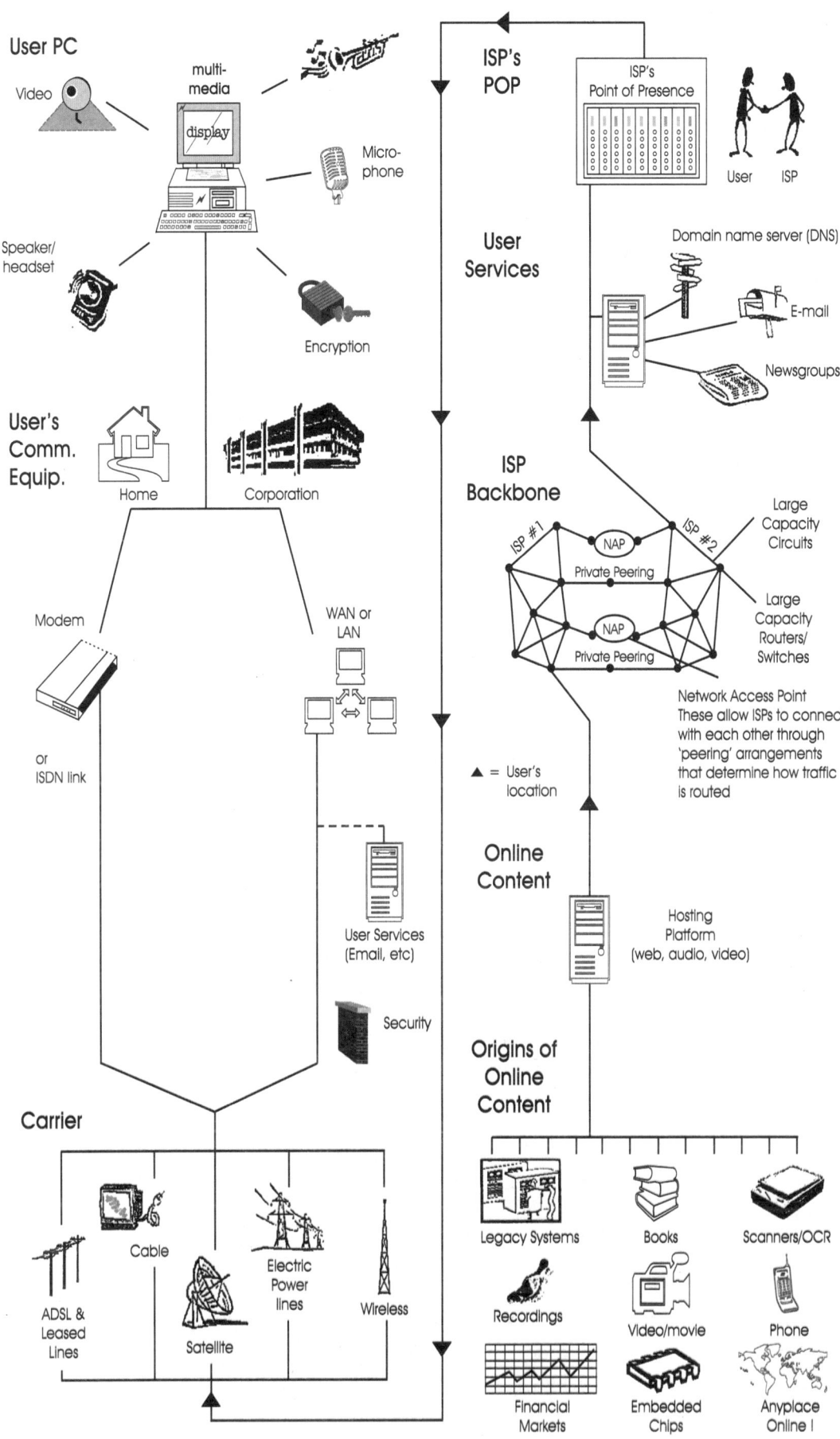

Part C: Using information competitively

2 INTERNET SECURITY ISSUES

2.1 Establishing organisational links to the Internet brings numerous security dangers.

   (a) Corruptions such as **viruses** on a single computer can spread through the network to all of the organisation's computers. (Viruses are described at greater length later in this section.)

   (b) Disaffected employees have much greater potential to do **deliberate damage** to valuable corporate data or systems because the network could give them access to parts of the system that they are not really authorised to use.

   (c) If the organisation is linked to an external network, persons outside the company (**hackers**) may be able to get into the company's internal network, either to steal data or to damage the system.

   (d) Employees may **download inaccurate information** or imperfect or **virus-ridden software** from an external network. For example 'beta' (free trial) versions of forthcoming new editions of many major packages are often available on the Internet, but the whole point about a beta version is that it is not fully tested and may contain bugs that could disrupt an entire system.

   (e) Information transmitted from one part of an organisation to another may be **intercepted**. Data can be 'encrypted' (scrambled) in an attempt to make it unintelligible to eavesdroppers, this is covered later in this section.

   (f) The **communications link itself may break down or distort data**. The worldwide telecommunications infrastructure is improving thanks to the use of new technologies, and there are communications 'protocols' governing the format of data and signals transferred.

Hacking

2.2 Hacking involves attempting to gain unauthorised access to a computer system, usually through telecommunications links.

2.3 Hackers require only limited programming knowledge to cause large amounts of damage. The fact that billions of bits of information can be transmitted in bulk over the public telephone network has made it **hard to trace** individual hackers, who can therefore make repeated attempts to invade systems. Hackers, in the past, have mainly been concerned to **copy** information, but a recent trend has been their desire to **corrupt it**.

2.4 Phone numbers and passwords can be guessed by hackers using **electronic phone directories** or number generators and by software which enables **rapid guessing** using hundreds of permutations per minute.

2.5 **Default passwords** are also available on some electronic bulletin boards and sophisticated hackers could even try to 'tap' messages being transmitted along phone wires (the number actually dialled will not be scrambled).

Encryption and other safety measures

2.6 **Encryption** aims to ensure the security of data during transmission. It involves the translation of data into secret code. To read an encrypted file, you must have access to a secret key or password that enables you to decrypt it. Unencrypted data is called plain text; encrypted data is referred to as cipher text.

7: The Internet as a strategic business tool

> **KEY TERM**
>
> **Encryption** involves scrambling the data at one end of the line, transmitting the scrambled data, and unscrambling it at the receiver's end of the line.

2.7 **Authentication** is a technique of making sure that a message has come from an authorised sender. Authentication involves adding an extra field to a record, with the contents of this field derived from the remainder of the record by applying an algorithm that has previously been agreed between the senders and recipients of data.

2.8 Systems can have **firewalls** (which disable part of the telecoms technology) to prevent unwelcome intrusions into company systems, but a determined hacker may well be able to bypass even these.

2.9 **Dial-back security** operates by requiring the person wanting access to the network to dial into it and identify themselves first. The system then dials the person back on their authorised number before allowing them access.

2.10 All attempted **violations of security** should be automatically **logged** and the log checked regularly. In a multi-user system, the terminal attempting the violation may be automatically disconnected.

Viruses

> **KEY TERM**
>
> A virus is a piece of software which infects programs and data and possibly damages them, and which replicates itself.

2.11 Viruses need an **opportunity to spread**. The programmers of viruses therefore place viruses in the kind of software which is most likely to be copied. This includes:

(a) Free software (for example from the Internet).
(b) Pirated software (cheaper than original versions).
(c) Games software (wide appeal).
(d) **E-mail attachments**. E-mail has become the most common means of spreading the most destructive viruses. The virus is often held in an attachment to the e-mail message. Recent viruses have been programmed to send themselves to all addresses in the user's electronic address book.

2.12 The main types of viruses (and related programs) are explained in the following table.

Type of virus/program	Explanation/Example
File viruses	File viruses infect program files. When you run an infected program the virus runs first, performs an unauthorised act and copies itself to another file or to another location (replicating itself).
Dropper	A dropper is a program that installs a virus while performing another function.

Type of virus/program	Explanation/Example
Boot sector or 'stealth' viruses	The boot sector is the part of every hard disk and diskette which is read by the computer when it starts up. These 'stealth' viruses hide from virus detection programs by hiding themselves in boot records or files. If the boot sector is infected, the virus runs when the machine starts.
Trojan	A Trojan (or Trojan Horse) is a small program that performs an unexpected function. The trojan is hidden inside a 'valid' program. Trojans therefore act like a virus, but they aren't classified as a virus as they don't replicate themselves.
Logic bomb	A logic bomb is a program that is executed when a specific act is performed. The logic bomb then performs an unexpected function, often designed to cause damage.
Time bomb	A time bomb is a logic bomb activated at a certain time or date, such as Friday the 13th or April 1st.
Worm	A worm is a type of virus that can replicate (copy) itself and use memory, but cannot attach itself to other programs.
Macro viruses	A macro virus is a piece of self-replicating code written in an application's 'macro' language. Many applications have macro capabilities including all the programs in **Microsoft Office**. The distinguishing factor which makes it possible to create a virus with a macro is the existence of **auto-execute events**. Auto-execute events are opening a file, closing a file, and starting an application. Once a macro is running, it can copy itself to other documents, delete files, and create general havoc. Melissa was a well publicised macro virus.

Protecting against viruses

2.13 The main protection against viruses is **anti-virus software** such as McAfee or Nortons. This software searches systems for viruses and removes any that are found. The programs are periodically updated by downloading upgrades that include profiles of new known viruses. Very new viruses won't be detected by anti-virus software (until the anti-virus software vendor updates their package - and the organisation installs the update).

2.14 Additional precautions include disabling floppy disk drives to prevent viruses entering an organisation via floppy disk. However, this can disrupt work processes. At the very least, organisations should ensure all files received via floppy disk and e-mail are virus checked.

2.15 External e-mail links can be protected by way of a **firewall** that may be configured to virus check all messages, and may also prevent files of a certain type being sent via e-mail (eg .exe files, as these are the most common means of transporting a virus).

Case example

COMPUTER VIRUS TIMELINE

1981 Apple Viruses 1, 2, and 3 are some of the first viruses in the public domain. Found on the Apple II operating system, the viruses spread via pirated computer games.

1983 Fred Cohen, while working on his dissertation, formally defines a computer virus as 'a computer program that can affect other computer programs by modifying them in such a way as to include a (possibly evolved) copy of itself.'

7: The Internet as a strategic business tool

1986 Two programmers replace the executable code in the boot sector of a floppy disk with their own code designed to infect each floppy accessed on any drive.

1988 One of the most common viruses, Jerusalem, is unleashed. Activated every Friday the 13th, the virus affects both .EXE and .COM files and deletes any programs run on that day.

1990 Symantec launches Norton AntiVirus, one of the first anti-virus programs developed by a large company.

1991 Tequila is the first polymorphic virus to cause significant damage. Polymorphic viruses make detection difficult for virus scanners by changing their appearance with each new infection.

1992 1300 viruses are in existence, an increase of 420% from December 1990. The Michelangelo scare predicts 5 million computers will crash, but only 5,000–10,000 actually do crash.

1994 The 'Good Times' e-mail hoax is widespread. The hoax warns of a virus that will erase an entire hard drive by opening an email with the subject line 'Good Times'. The hoax, or a modified version, often resurfaces.

1999 The Melissa virus executes a macro in a document attached to an e-mail, which forwards the document to 50 addresses from the user's Outlook address book. The virus also infects other Word documents and subsequently mails them out as attachments. Melissa spread faster than any other previous virus.

2000 In May The Love Bug worm shut down e-mail systems around the world. The 'Stages' virus, disguised as a joke email about the stages of life, spreads across the Internet. Unlike previous viruses, Stages is hidden in an attachment with a false '.txt' extension, making it easier to lure recipients into opening it.

2001 The Anna Kournikova virus which masquerades as a picture of tennis star Anna Kournikova, spreads by sending copies of itself to the entire address book in Microsoft Outlook. It is believed that this virus was created with a so-called virus creation kit, a program which can enable even a novice programmer to create a virus. The Code Red worm attacked computer networks in July and August, affecting over 700,000 computers. Code Red took advantage of a vulnerability in Microsoft's Windows 2000 and Windows NT server software.

2002 Early in January LFM showed up as the first virus to infect Shockwave Flash (.SWF) files. It was named for the message it displays while it's infecting: 'Loading.Flash.Movie...'. In May the Javascript worm SQLSpider was released. It was unique in that it attacked installations running Microsoft SQL Server (and programs that use SQL Server technology).

Hoaxes

2.16 There are a number of common hoaxes, the most common of these is **Good Times**. This hoax has been around for a few years, and usually takes the form of a virus warning about viruses contained in e-mail. People pass along the warning because they are trying to be helpful, but they are wasting the time of all concerned.

2.17 The security issues surrounding e-commerce, particularly regarding making payment over the Internet are covered later in this chapter.

3 ELECTRONIC COMMERCE

> **KEY TERM**
>
> **Electronic commerce** means conducting business electronically via a communications link.

3.1 An older technology that is covered under the electronic commerce umbrella is Electronic Data Interchange (EDI).

Part C: Using information competitively

Electronic Data Interchange (EDI)

3.2 EDI is a form of computer-to-computer data transfer. For instance instead of sending a customer a paper invoice through the post the data is sent over telecommunications links. This offers savings and **benefits** to organisations that use it.

(a) It reduces the **delays** caused by postal paper chains.

(b) It avoids the need to **re-key** data and therefore saves time and reduces errors.

(c) It provides the opportunity to reduce administrative **costs** eg the costs associated with the creation, recording and storage of paper documents.

(d) It facilitates shorter **lead times** and reduced stock holdings which allow reductions in working capital requirements (eg Just-In-Time policies).

(e) It provides the opportunity to improve **customer service**.

3.3 The general concept of having one computer talk directly to another might seem straightforward enough in principle, but **difficulties** may arise.

(a) Businesses hold records in computer files to their own **file structure** specifications. A translation mechanism may be required to allow transfer between the systems.

(b) The problem of **compatibility** between different makes or types of computer was a serious one in the past, and some form of interface between the computers had to be devised to enable data interchange to take place.

(c) Businesses often work to differing **time** schedules and time-zones. Organisations may conduct system maintenance late at night thinking this will not affect business. However, an overseas company in a different time zone, may need to access the system.

(d) As the number of trading partners grows the number of one-to-one links eventually becomes **unmanageable**.

E-commerce and the web

3.4 Over the last few years, electronic commerce or **e-commerce** has increasingly been used to describe the use of the Internet and websites in the sale of products or services. A simple definition is that 'e-commerce is the process of trading on the Internet'.

3.5 The Internet allows businesses to reach potentially millions of consumers worldwide and extends trading time to seven days, around the clock. Electronic commerce worldwide is valued at US$12 billion, and is set to reach US$350-500 billion by 2002. The OECD forecasts global e-commerce to be worth $1 trillion by 2003-05.

3.6 An e-business **start-up** has a considerable advantage over more established companies working in the same business area, because it does not have to take existing systems into account. This gives the start-up the agility and flexibility to launch new services far more quickly and cheaply than established rivals.

3.7 For established companies e-commerce reduces expensive sales and distribution workforces, and offers new marketing opportunities.

Distribution

3.8 The Internet can be used to get certain products **directly into people's homes**. Anything that can be converted into **digital form** can simply be uploaded onto the seller's site and

then **downloaded** onto the customer's PC at home. The Internet thus offers huge opportunities to producers of text, graphics/video, and sound-based products. Much computer software is now distributed in this way.

Electronic marketing

3.9 Besides its usefulness for tapping into worldwide information resources businesses are also using it to **provide information** about their own products and services.

3.10 For **customers** the Internet offers a **speedy and impersonal** way of getting to know about the services that a company provides. For **businesses** the advantage is that it is much cheaper to provide the information in electronic form than it would be to employ staff to man the phones on an enquiry desk, and much more effective than sending out mailshots that people would either throw away or forget about when they needed the information.

3.11 Companies will need to develop new means of promoting their wares through the medium of the Internet, as opposed to shop displays or motionless graphics. Websites can provide **sound and movement** and allow **interactivity,** so that the user can, say, drill down to obtain further information or watch a video of the product in use, or get a virtual reality experience of the product or service.

3.12 For many companies this will involve a rethink of current promotional activity.

Case example

Peapod.com is an online supermarket and one of the more sophisticated recorders and users of customers' personal data and shopping behaviour. With over 200,000 customers in various US cities, Peapod's website sells groceries that are then delivered to customer's homes. a list of previous purchases (including brand, pack size and quantity purchased) is kept on the site, so the customer can make minor changes from week to week, saving time and effort.

Peapod creates a database on each shopper that includes their purchase history (what they bought), their online shopping patterns (how they bought it), questionnaires about their attitudes and opinions, and demographic data (which Peapod buys from third parties). A shopper's profile is used by the company to determine which advertisement to show and which promotions/electronic coupons to offer. Demographically identical neighbours are thus treated differently based on what Peapod has learned about their preferences and behaviours over time.

Shoppers seem to like this high-tech relationship marketing, with 94% of all sales coming from repeat customers. Manufacturers like it too. the more detailed customer information enables them to target promotions at customers who have repeatedly bought another brand, thereby not giving away promotion dollars to loyal customers.

Collecting information about customers

3.13 People who visit a site for the first time may be asked to **register,** which typically involves giving a name, physical address and post code, e-mail address and possibly other demographic data such as age, job title and income bracket.

3.14 When customers come to the site on subsequent occasions they either type their (self-chosen) username and password or more usually now, if they are using the same computer, the website recognises them using a **cookie,** which is a small and **harmless** file containing a string of characters that uniquely identify the computer.

Part C: Using information competitively

3.15 From the initial registration details the user record may show, say, that the user is male, aged 20 to 30 and British. The **website can respond** to this by displaying products or services likely to appeal to this segment of the market.

Clickstreams

3.16 As users visit the site more often, more is learned about them by **recording what they click on,** since this shows what they are really interested in. On a news site for instance, one user may always go to the sports pages first, while another looks at the TV listings. In a retail sense this is akin to physically following somebody about the store recording everything they do (including products they pick up and put back) and everything they look at, whether or not they buy it.

Virtual companies and virtual supply chains (VSC)

> **KEY TERMS**
>
> A **virtual company** is a collection of separate companies, each with a specific expertise, who work together, sharing their expertise to compete for bigger contracts/projects than would be possible if they worked alone.
>
> A traditional **supply chain** is made up of the physical entities linked together to facilitate the supply of goods and services to the final consumer.
>
> A **Virtual Supply Chain** (VSC) is a supply chain that is enabled through e-business links (eg the web, extranets or EDI).

3.17 The **virtual company** concept has been around since the mid-1990s. Initially, companies attempted to work together using fax and phone links. The concept only really became a reality when technology such as extranets came into common usage. Companies are now able to work together and exchange information on-line. For example, engineers from five companies could design a product together on the Internet.

3.18 Many companies have become, or are becoming, more 'virtual'. They are developing into looser affiliations of companies, organised as a supply network.

3.19 Virtual Supply Chain networks have two types of organisation: producers and integrators.

(a) **Producers** produce goods and services. They have core competencies in production schedule execution. Producers must focus on delivery to schedule and within cost. The sales driver within these companies is on ensuring that their capacity is fully sold through their networking with co-ordinators. Producer are often servicing multiple chains, so managing and avoiding capacity and commercial conflicts becomes key.

(b) **Integrators** manage the supply network and effectively 'own' the end customer contact. The focus of the integrating firms is on managing the end customer relationship. Their core competence is in integrating and controlling the response of the company to customer requirements. This includes the difficult task of synchronising the responses and performance of multi-tiered networks, where the leverage of direct ownership is no longer available, and of often outsourced services such as warehousing and delivery.

3.20 Many of the most popular Internet companies are integrators in virtual company's eg Amazon.com and Lastminute.com. These organisations 'own' customer contact and manage customer relationships for a range of producers.

How does the Internet and e-commerce challenge traditional business thinking?

3.21 There are several features of the Internet which make it radically different from what has gone before.

(a) It **challenges traditional business models** - because, for example, it enables product/service suppliers to interact directly with their customers, instead of using intermediaries (like retail shops, travel agents, insurance brokers, and conventional banks).

(b) Although the Internet is global in its operation, its benefits are not confined to large (or global) organisations. **Small companies** can move instantly into a global market place, either on their own initiative or as part of what is known as a 'consumer portal'. For example, Ede and Ravenscroft is a small outfitting and tailoring business in Oxford: it could easily promote itself within a much larger 'portal' called OxfordHighStreet.com, embracing a comprehensive mixture of other Oxford retailers.

(c) It offers a **new economics of information** - because, with the Internet, much information is free. Those with Internet access can view all the world's major newspapers and periodicals without charge.

(d) It supplies an almost incredible **level of speed** - virtually instant access to organisations, plus the capacity to complete purchasing transactions within seconds. This velocity, of course, is only truly impressive if it is accompanied by equal speed so far as the delivery of tangible goods is concerned.

(e) It has created **new networks of communication** - between organisations and their customers (either individually or collectively), between customers themselves (through mutual support groups), and between organisations and their suppliers.

(f) It stimulates the appearance of **new intermediaries** and the disappearance of some existing ones. Businesses are finding that they can cut out the middle man, with electronic banking, insurance, publishing and printing as primary examples.

(g) It has led to **new business partnerships** through which small enterprises can gain access to customers on a scale which would have been viewed as impossible a few years ago. For example, a university can put its reading list on a website and students wishing to purchase any given book can click directly through to an on-line bookseller such as Amazon.com. The university gets a commission; the on-line bookseller gets increased business; the student gets a discount. Everyone benefits except the traditional bookshop.

(h) It promotes **transparent pricing** - because potential customers can readily compare prices not only from suppliers within any given country, but also from suppliers across the world.

(i) It facilitates **personalised attention** - even if such attention is actually administered through impersonal, yet highly sophisticated IT systems and customer database manipulation.

(j) It provides sophisticated **market segmentation** opportunities. Approaching such segments may be one of the few ways in which e-commerce entrepreneurs can create **competitive advantage**. As **Management Today** (March 2000) puts it:

Part C: Using information competitively

'The starting point must be a neat niche, a funky few, a global tribe. You need to understand your particular tribe better than anyone else. The tribe is the basic unit of business... The good news is that there are lots of tribes out there - and some are enormous. It's just a question of identifying them, understanding them and meeting their needs better than anyone else.'

(k) The web can either be a **separate** or a **complementary** channel.

(l) A new phenomenon is emerging called **dynamic pricing**. Companies can rapidly change their prices to reflect the current state of demand and supply.

3.22 These new trends are creating **pressure** for companies. The main threat facing companies is that **prices will be driven down by consumers' ability to shop around**.

Case example

(1) Airlines

The impact of the web is seen clearly in the transportation industry. Airlines now have a more effective way of bypassing intermediaries (ie travel agents) because they can give their customers immediate access to flight reservation systems. British Airways aims to sell at least half of its tickets on-line by the end of 2003; one of the new low-cost airlines in the UK, EasyJet, has become the first airline to have over half of its bookings made on-line.

(2) Travel agents

The web has also produced a new set of on-line travel agents who have lower costs because of their ability to operate without a High Street branch network. Their low-cost structure makes them a particularly good choice for selling low margin, cheap tickets for flights, package holidays, cruises and so forth.

These low-cost travel agents have been joined, furthermore, by non-travel-agents who simply specialise in opportunistic purchasing (eg lastminute.com).

(3) Tesco

In another arena, Tesco is already the UK's largest Internet grocery business, but other companies are rapidly developing new initiatives. Waitrose@work allows people to order their groceries in the morning (typically through their employer's Intranet communication system) and then have them delivered to the workplace in the afternoon: this approach achieves significant distribution economies of scale so far as Waitrose is concerned.

(4) Financial services

The impact of the Internet is especially profound in the field of financial services. New intermediaries enable prospective customers to compare the interest rates and prices charged by different organisations for pensions, mortgages and other financial services. This means that the delivering companies are losing control of the marketing of their services, and there is a downward pressure on prices, especially for services which can legitimately be seen as mere commodities (eg house and contents insurance).

Disadvantages of e-commerce

3.23 E-commerce involves an unusual mix of people – security people, web technology people, designers, marketing people – and this can be very difficult to manage. The e-business needs supervision by expensive specialists.

3.24 In spite of phenomenal growth the market is still fuzzy and undefined. Many e-businesses have only recently reported making any **profit**, the best-known example being **Amazon.com** the Internet book-seller.

3.25 Unless the e-business is one started completely from scratch, any new technology installed will **need to link up with existing business systems,** which could potentially take years of programming. Under-estimating the time and effort involved is a common obstacle.

7: The Internet as a strategic business tool

3.26 The international availability of a website means that the laws of all countries that transactions may be conducted from have to be considered. The legal issues surrounding e-commerce are complex and still developing.

Lack of trust

3.27 Above all, however, the problem with e-commerce is one of **trust**. In most cultures, consumers grant their trust to business parties that have a close **physical presence**: buildings, facilities and people to talk to. On the Internet these familiar elements are simply not there. The seller's reputation, the size of his business, and the level of customisation in product and service also engender trust.

3.28 Internet merchants need to elicit consumer trust when the level of **perceived risk** in a transaction is high. However, research has found that once consumers have built up trust in an Internet merchant such concerns are reduced.

3.29 Internet merchants need to address issues such as fear of **invasion of privacy** and abuse of customer information (about their **credit cards**, for example) because they stop people even considering the Internet as a shopping medium.

Cryptography, keys and signatures

3.30 The parties involved in e-commerce need to have confidence that any communication sent gets to its target destination **unchanged**, and **without being read by anyone else**.

3.31 One way of providing electronic signatures is to make use of what is known as **public key** (or asymmetric) **cryptography**. Public key cryptography uses **two keys – public and private**. The **private key** is only known to its owner, and is used to scramble the data contained in a file.

3.32 The 'scrambled' data is the electronic signature, and can be checked against the original file using the **public key** of the person who signed it. This confirms that it could only have been signed by someone with access to the private key. If a third party altered the message, the fact that they had done so would be easily detectable.

3.33 An alternative is the use of encryption products which support **key recovery,** also known as **key encapsulation.** Such commercial encryption products can incorporate the public key of an agent known as a **Key Recovery Agent (KRA).** This allows the user to recover their (stored or communicated) data by approaching the KRA with an encrypted portion of the message. In both cases the KRA neither holds the user's private keys, nor has access to the plain text of their data.

Case example

E-commerce dangers and benefits

For some the Internet is a necessary evil - others browse and surf the net with that obsessive drive that is peculiar to any new technology. But the Internet is not just any new technology. It is the most important communications development since the advent of the telephone, and like the telephone it has created its own culture and given birth to new businesses and new possibilities.

Early confusion about the Internet meant that many companies came to us having built their own websites after learning the rudiments of HTML. They had registered their company name and done everything by the book. The website went on-line and they all waited with baited breath. Nothing happened. No new business arrived and nothing changed, and they couldn't understand why.

Part C: Using information competitively

E-commerce is a tidal wave; if you choose to participate you either 'sink or swim'. You must be daring enough in design to achieve something quite different from the ways things have been done in the past.

A website is a shopfront that must be located in the centre of town in the full gaze of everyone. A good one can make a small business as powerful and competitive as some of the largest players. It just needs flair and commitment to succeed. But to do so there are some measures that must be used. Marketing outside the web, in the press or even on the radio can alert the market to the website. The site itself should be properly identified by name, registered competently with the appropriate search engines and it must look good.

> **WEBSITE ESSENTIALS**
> - Integration with all company systems (ie back office)
> - Speedy implementation
> - Quick and easy updating by own staff to retain topicality
> - Self producing audit records
> - Promotion via the internet
> - Press and PR for website
> - Attractive design but appropriate for the web
> - Scope to interact with visitors
> - Planned structure to include profitable business concept
> - Control and maintenance by owner, without developer involvement

The appearance of a website is extremely important. Attractive and easy to fill interactive forms can lure a sales prospect into being a buyer. One has seconds in which to achieve this end. Too many graphics slow down the procedure. The experience of visiting and browsing through the shop and responding to the goods on offer must be clever, intriguing, quick and efficient. Millions of pounds worth of business is lost on the Internet every day as a result of so-called interactive websites that are difficult to operate and dull.

The **key to success**, and the true working system is to be found in the **back office**. This invisible component is frequently overlooked. You can have the most seductive website in the world, but without a robust, secure, integrated back office system it's worth nothing. The website designer makes the shop window look good but cannot be expected to address the back office system.

Installing e-commerce can bring about overall improvements in accounting and management systems across the board. One bookseller never realised that he had fundamental problems in terms of dispatching stock and warehouse management. This is now being solved by the introduction of an integrated website that will interact with his financial and accounting system.

There are so many new possibilities and ventures created by this new technology, and the most inspired e-commerce enterprises will empower small and medium sized concerns to compete as never before.

Adapted from *Management Accounting*, February 2000

Customer service on the web

3.34 Effective, competent and acceptable customer service through the web is a combination of the following factors:

(a) **Rapid response time**. If the website is not fast, the transient potential shopper will simply click on to another. These 'fickle' visitors to a website will only allow around five to eight seconds: if the site has not captured their attention in that time-frame, they will move elsewhere.

(b) **Response quality**. The website must be legible, with appropriate graphics and meaningful, relevant information supplied. Generally speaking, website visitors are not interested in the company's history and size: they are much more concerned about what the company can offer them.

7: The Internet as a strategic business tool

(c) **Navigability**. It is important to create a website which caters for every conceivable customer interest and question. Headings and category-titles should be straightforward and meaningful, not obscure and ambiguous.

(d) **Download times**. Again, these need to be rapid, given that many Internet shoppers regard themselves (rightly or otherwise) as cash-rich and time-poor.

(e) **Security/Trust**. One of the biggest barriers to the willingness of potential Internet customers actually to finalise a transaction is their fear that information they provide about themselves (such as credit card details) can be 'stolen' or used as the basis for fraud.

(f) **Fulfilment**. Customers must believe that if they order goods and services, the items in question will arrive, and will do so within acceptable time limits (which will generally be much faster than the time limits normally associated with conventional mail order). Equally, customers need to be convinced that if there is a subsequent need for service recovery, then speedy and efficient responses can be secured either to rectify the matter or to enable unsatisfactory goods to be returned without penalty.

(g) **Up-to-date**. Just as window displays need to be constantly refreshed, so do websites require frequent repackaging and redesign.

(h) **Availability**. Can the user reach the site 24 hours a day, seven days a week? Is the down-time minimal? Can the site always be accessed?

(i) **Site effectiveness and functionality**. Is the web site intuitive and easy to use? Is the content written in a language which will be meaningful even to the first-time browser (ie the potential customer)?

Question 1

Up to now, many companies have ignored e-commerce. They have watched as a succession of much-publicised ventures have failed to get off the ground and even the best have struggled to translate success into profits. This has created an impression that the Internet is a confusing and dangerous sales channel that can, for now, be left to others.

Why, do you think, is this view increasingly untenable?

Answer

Relevant points include:

(a) The likely scale and speed of development is immense: in 2002 Internet business between, for example, US businesses, was estimated at $300bn, rising from only $4.5bn in 1997.

(b) Every part of the value chain is up for grabs. Any participant in the value chain could usurp the role of any other participant.

 (i) The free flow of information about buyers and sellers undermines the role of intermediaries.

 (ii) A book publisher could bypass retailers or distributors and sell directly.

 (iii) A book seller could decide to publish books, based on the information it has obtained about readers' interests.

(c) Net pioneers can secure important advantages over latecomers. They can use information about their customers to tailor their offerings and they may even be able to foster a sense of community among users. For example, part of the appeal of Amazon (the Internet bookseller) is the book reviews posted by other readers.

Part C: Using information competitively

4 DEVELOPING A STRATEGY FOR THE INTERNET AND E-COMMERCE

4.1 Four broad approaches a company may adopt towards the Internet are:

(a) Do not sell products through the Internet at all, and if distribution is conducted through resellers, prevent them from doing so. Provide only product **information** on the Internet. This may be an appropriate strategy where products are **large, complex and highly customised**, such as aircraft manufacturing.

(b) **Leave the Internet business to resellers** and do not sell directly through the Internet (ie do not compete with resellers). This can be appropriate, for instance, where manufacturers have already assigned exclusive territories to resellers.

(c) The manufacturer can **restrict Internet sales exclusively to itself**. The problem with this is that most large manufacturers do not have systems that are geared to dealing with sales to end users who place numerous, irregular small orders.

(d) Open up Internet sales to everybody and **let the market decide** who it prefers to buy from.

4.2 On a more detailed level, in an article for *IT Consultancy* magazine, Laurence Holt offered 18 potential strategies for e-commerce.

Strategy	Comment
Outsource to your customers	What do we do for our customers that they would rather do for themselves and could probably do better? Examples: *www.cisco.com*, *www.dell.com*.
Cannibalise your own business	If there were an Amazon.com in our market, what would it be doing? Examples: *www.barnesandnoble.com*, *www.egghead.com*.
Host your competitors	How can we create a marketplace that includes our competitors, but that we own? Examples: *www.sabre.com*, *www.jewellery.com*.
Build one-to-one customer relationships	How can we make each customer feel that we built our organisation just for them? Examples: *www.My.yahoo.com*, *www.netgrocer.com*.
Make first contact	What is the first step our customers take in the chain of events that leads them to buy from us? How can we make contact with them? Examples: *www.autobytel.com*.
Be a process integrator	What other things do customers need or do when they buy from us? Examples: *www.autobytel.com*.
Catch rites of passage	What major life changes are customers going through when they come into contact with us? How can we help? Examples: *www.usnews.com*, *www.citibank.com*.
Create a community	What interests do our customers share? How can we create a place that people with those interests will keep coming back to? Examples: *www.yahoo.com*.
Create a niche portal	How can we make our site the portal our customers go to first? Examples: *www.ft.com*.
Pirate your value chain	How can we take over the roles of others in our value chain? Examples: *www.dell.com*.
Re-intermediate on information value	How can we boost the value we add through information? Examples: *www.britannica.com*.

Strategy	Comment
Go pure cyberspace	What if we made the digital world our first priority and the physical world second? Examples: *www.tiscali.com*.
Be a fast follower	What are our competitors doing that looks likely to be successful? How can we do the same thing faster? Examples: *www.barnesandnoble.com*.
Think dream not transaction	What dream do our customers start with that leads them to buy from us? How can we realise that dream? Examples: *www.expedia.com*.
Beat the physical world	What can we do in the digital world that would be impossible or not feasible in the physical world? Examples: *www.benjerry.com*.
Leverage the froth	What simple ideas would capture most media and public attention, even if short-lived? Examples: *www.travelocity.com*, *www.lastminute.com*.
Change the pricing model	Would our customers benefit from a different way of pricing, perhaps micro-payments or auctions? Examples: *www.priceline.com*.
Convert atoms to bits	What physical world core competencies do we have that could be applied to the digital world? Examples: *www.ups.com*.

4.3 If the decision is made to enter into e-commerce, an e-business venture needs **support and long-term commitment from high-level management**. Ideally such a project should be 'sponsored' by the chief executive or a board-level director.

Guidelines for establishing an Internet sales/marketing capability

4.4 An organisation's sales/marketing Internet capability may, at the outset, solely **dispense information** (operating like a product catalogue), but may eventually become **transactional** (so that individuals can place orders) and/or **interactive** (dealing with queries, complaints and other kinds of customer communications).

The context

4.5 To put these guidelines into context, a survey (late 2000) by Booz Allen & Hamilton and the Economist Intelligence Unit, involving 600 executives, sought views on the strategic significance of the Internet.

(a) 61 per cent believed the Internet would help them to achieve business goals.

(b) 30 per cent said the Internet had already forced them to overhaul their existing business strategies.

(c) On the other hand, only 28 per cent had generated income from the Internet.

4.6 The same survey highlighted seven **megatrends** which, coupled with the Internet, are changing the face of organisations:

(a) New **distribution channels**, revolutionising sales and brand management.

(b) The continued **shift of power** towards the consumer.

(c) **Growing competition** locally, nationally, internationally and globally.

(d) An acceleration in the **pace of business**.

(e) The **transformation of companies** into 'extended enterprises' involving 'virtual teams of business, customer and supplier' working in collaborative partnerships.

(f) A re-evaluation of how companies, their partners and competitors **add value** not only to themselves but in the wider environmental and social setting.

(g) Recognition of '**knowledge**' as a strategic asset.

4.7 Most observers and experts agree that a successful strategy for e-commerce cannot simply be bolted on to existing processes, systems, delivery routes and business models. Instead, management groups have, in effect, to start again, by asking themselves such **fundamental questions** as:

(a) What do customers want to buy from us?
(b) What business should we be in?
(c) What kind of partners might we need?
(d) What categories of customer do we want to attract and retain?

4.8 In turn, organisations can visualise the necessary changes at three interconnected levels.

Level 1 The simple **introduction of new technology** to connect electronically with customers and suppliers through a website or intranet.

Level 2 **Re-organisation** - of the workforce, processes, systems and strategy - in order to make best use of the new technology.

Level 3 **Re-positioning** of the company in order to enable it to fit into the emerging e-economy.

4.9 So far, very few companies have gone beyond levels (1) and (2). Instead, pure Internet businesses such as Amazon.com and AOL have emerged from these new rules: unburdened by physical assets, their competitive advantage lies in knowledge management and customer relationships.

Ten key steps to constructing an effective strategy for e-commerce

Step 1. Upgrade customer interaction

4.10 The first thing for the organisation to do is to **upgrade the interaction with its existing customers**.

(a) Create automated responses for the FAQs (Frequently Asked Questions) posed by customers, so that customers become conditioned to electronic communication. Automated responses, perhaps surprisingly in view of their impersonal nature, can help to improve customer confidence and trust.

(b) Set fast response standards, at least to match anything offered by the competition.

(c) Use e-mail in order to confirm actions, check understanding, and reassure the customer that their business is being taken forward.

(d) Establish ease of navigation around your website and enhance the site's 'stickiness' so that there is a measurably reduced likelihood that actual or potential customers will migrate elsewhere.

4.11 A study conducted by Rubic Inc in the USA ('Evaluating the 'Sticky' Factor of E-Commerce Sites') found that the majority of websites fail to communicate effectively with customers. Only 40 per cent had a strategy of personalisation for their e-mail messages to customers; when customers responded to follow-up offers, only one quarter of websites recognised the fact that they were dealing with a repeat customer; 40 per cent of e-mail enquiries went unanswered despite promises of replies within two days.

Step 2. Understand customer segments

4.12 The organisation preparing its e-commerce strategy should **understand its customer segments** and classify each segment against the likelihood that it will be receptive to an Internet business route.

   (a) Some will be eager to transfer to the new technology, others will do so if persuaded (or incentivised), and residual groups will prefer to remain as they are.

   (b) Once the degree of profitability-per-customer has been established, efforts should be made to automate the provision of customer service and transaction capability so far as low-value customers are concerned.

   (c) The organisation may establish personalised service relationships with key (ie high profit-generating) customers.

Step 3. Understand service processes

4.13 The organisation must **understand its customer service processes** in order to disentangle those processes which can safely be put on to the Web and those which have to be delivered in other ways.

   (a) Typically, organisations serving customers may find that there are between five and ten generic transaction types which describe their relationships with these customers (eg information query, complaint, and so forth).

   (b) This analysis is essential for addressing such questions as: Which of these processes is appropriate for low-touch automation? Which of these processes will work better, from the customer's standpoint, if put on the web?

   (c) Transaction costs also need to be investigated, again from the perspective of the organisation and its overheads, and also taking into account the transaction costs incurred by the customer. These may involve money, but customers are often more conscious about time and timeliness. Getting on to the Internet takes longer than a telephone call (though this may not always be the case), so the customer, behaving rationally, will want more value from the process.

   (d) On the other hand, a short simple transaction is often better conducted over the telephone.

Step 4. Define the role

4.14 The organisation needs to **define the role for live interaction with its customers**.

   (a) Live interaction may be very useful if there is scope for cross-selling and the conversion of enquiries into sales.

   (b) The availability of service supplied by human intervention can also be appropriate if the organisation needs to build trust (eg it is a new brand which must work hard to establish confidence) and secure diagnostic information from the customer before any product or service can be delivered.

   (c) E-mail may not be sufficient as a communications route, especially if it involves a delay before replies or acknowledgements are forthcoming.

   (d) Live interaction can be essential for customers who have a strong preference for human contact.

Part C: Using information competitively

Step 5. Decide technology

4.15 **Making the key technology decisions** involves some tough choices. Given the pace of change and innovation in this arena, it is difficult to know whether to initiate a pilot programme immediately, with the full IT and people investment scheduled for later, or whether to go for full integration at once. The risk with a pilot programme is that the organisation can be overtaken by pioneering competitors; the risk with full integration is that new systems can be inadequate or may even collapse completely, causing irretrievable havoc with customers.

Step 6. Deal with the tidal wave

4.16 There is much evidence that offering an Internet-based service can lead to a major increase in customer interaction, and so organisations need to develop strategies for **dealing with the tidal wave**. This might involve:

(a) Ensuring sufficient capacity is available for worst-case scenarios.
(b) Using low-touch technologies and system design.
(c) Setting targets for low-touch interaction.
(d) Ensuring facilities are scaleable if demand rapidly outstrips supply.

Step 7. Create incentives

4.17 The organisation may have to **create incentives for use of the lowest-cost channels**, with savings passed on the customer through discounts. The alternatives are:

(a) To create **incentives** to switch to the lowest-cost channels, through financial inducements, training and additional benefits.

(b) To introduce **disincentives** for continuing to use existing channels. Thus Abbey National has implemented a £5 charge for customers who pursue over-the-counter cash transactions in their branches. Such tactics almost invariably generate very hostile reactions from customers themselves and from consumer groups.

Step 8. Decide on channel choices

4.18 The eighth consideration involves the decision about **which channel choices to offer**, and whether, for instance, to confine operations to the 'click' route or whether to simultaneously maintain the 'brick' presence through a branch network. There are two crucial questions:

(a) **Whether to offer the customer a choice of channels**, eg face-to-face, post, phone and Internet. Many banks offer all four; some have single-channel accounts (phone or Internet only), whilst others (like **egg**) allow constrained choice: **egg** (the Internet and telephone banking arm of the Prudential Assurance Company) will allow telephone and Internet customer interaction, but only permits new customers to enrol via the web.

(b) **How to balance the costs of different channels whilst managing the Customer Relationship Management (CRM) database**. In most customer service environments, the quality and scope of the CRM database is central to the successful delivery of service, so it becomes desirable not to operate each customer-communication channel separately, but to integrate existing channels around a single CRM database.

(c) One reason why Charles Schwab (specialists in stock and share dealing) is able to charge much bigger fees than some of its rivals is that it combines an on-line service with a low-cost branch network and a telephone service. They have recognised the web has certain virtues and weaknesses. The web is lousy if you have a complex question. Likewise, it does not allow for people's need for relationships. Not everyone feels happy about sending a cheque to a broker they have never seen.

Step 9. Exploit the Internet

4.19 The organisation should **exploit the Internet in order to create new relationships and an experience**.

(a) It is desirable to create **tailor-made service** sites for significant customers.

(b) Proactive **product/service offerings** should be regularly incorporated into the website architecture.

(c) **Communities of users** and/or customers (depending on whichever is appropriate) should be facilitated, since these generate additional business through referral and may well undertake a large proportion of the customer-service activity among themselves. Such communities may also stimulate product/service innovation, new uses for existing products and services, and product/service extensions.

(d) Deliberate mechanisms need to be developed in order to **turn browsers into buyers**, and transform one-off customers into repeat purchasers.

(e) Any successful e-commerce strategy presupposes the likelihood that the product/service supplier can engage the potential customer **emotionally** despite the technology which surrounds Internet availability.

4.20 It is necessary for the strategist to visualise the **extended experience** that customers encounter when they carry an Internet transaction through from initiation to completion. It is vital for organisations to place themselves in the shoes of customers and ask the question: what are our customers really buying? The answer, 99 times out of 100, is that customers are buying benefits whilst companies are selling features. Further, if the transaction lacks any emotional commitment, then it also lacks any real likelihood of voluntary customer retention.

Step 10. Implement

4.21 No strategy is worth the paper is written on if it simply remains a document, gathering dust: as Peter Drucker once pointed out, 'Strategy is nothing until it degenerates into work'.

Important aspects of strategy implementation for e-commerce

4.22 **Organisation and culture**. When organisations move into an electronic age, some people (and functions) increase their corporate influence, whilst others move into the shadows. The increasing use of technology is unsettling, especially for senior people (ironically, employees lower down the hierarchy are likely to be much more comfortable about technological innovation). The Internet promotes freedom of information, both upwards and downwards; this, for some managers, is equated with a loss of authority.

4.23 **Systems and infrastructure**. Implementation of e-commerce often requires integration of service systems, particularly call centres, the web, and CRM processes. This in turn may require a company to review its whole decision-making patterns and make some difficult choices about existing 'legacy' procedures.

Part C: Using information competitively

4.24 **Training**. Effective e-commerce implementation requires both staff and customers to be trained. Dealing with electronic interaction demands different skills from those which are appropriate to staff who focus on voice communications. Dealing simultaneously with written and verbal interaction is likely to call for a new skill set.

4.25 **Looking to the customers**. This is well summarised by Mike Harris, Chief Executive of Egg, explaining the need to avoid rehearsed, scripted and bureaucratic approaches which give the impression that technology is driving the interaction rather than the need to relate to people.

4.26 Conventional thinking says that a company should pay no more to bring in a customer than the net present value of the stream of profits that the customer will subsequently generate. Yet in the e-commerce context, investors have often rewarded companies for customer acquisition without asking any questions about how quickly those customers may disappear.

4.27 Similar turbulence is affecting the B2B world. Traditional manufacturing companies around the world, sensing the potential benefits from automating transactions with suppliers and customers, have rushed into e-commerce. Many have formed alliances to create their own on-line market place, especially in the automobile, aerospace and chemicals industries. By pooling their buying power, the organisations behind these alliances hope to have more control over their activities - and this leaves the small, purely Internet-based commodity/component exchanges struggling to attract the volume of transactions needed to make them viable.

Case example

E-technology - fuelling or fooling customer strategies?

One of the most important challenges the modern enterprise has is to find ways to increase value from its customers, rather than from its products, so as to get long-lasting growth rather than short-term gains. Research and practice forcefully demonstrate that e-technology can facilitate this - but not if e-technology is simply used to cut costs in order to drive market share of core products or services and so perpetuate past strategies.

Increased and sustained growth from customers can only come to firms that know how to 'lock-in' their customers. This means customers want them as their dominant or sole choice because they get ongoing superior value at low cost.

Enterprises get this lifelong customer value when they push boundaries to create new 'market spaces' which link benefits otherwise separated by industry or companies providing users with results or outcomes rather than just what they happen to make, have in stock, or be promoting at a moment in time. Contrast for instance: cars v personal mobility; books v information and knowledge discovery; PCs v global networking capability; audio-visual equipment v integrated home 'edutainment' - to see the difference.

In new market spaces, working together with a network of partners, the object is to provide an integrated experience for customers over their activity cycles: 'pre' the experience, when customers are deciding what to do; 'during' the experience, when they are doing it, and 'post' the experience, when they are keeping it going, reviewing, updating, and renewing. If value gaps or discontinuities happen in the customer activity cycle, companies (even industries) become vulnerable: other players (usually outsiders) get in, build relationships and capture the new wealth. Which is what happened to IBM in the late 1980s and why Amazon took the book retailers by storm.

There are four levels for which e-technology is currently being used.

Level 1: Tell. At its most basic, the object here is to create presence on the web for customers who come to the site in search of information about the company and its products or services. The result is a website catalogue or brochure..

Level 2: Sell. Here the Internet is used as an alternative channel or tool to promote and sell a firm's wares on-line, typically what food retailers are doing, or alternatively to sell others' wares. The problem here is that the enterprise is playing the same game: frequently what is delivered is just what is kept in stock, and emphasis often goes to supply management to save costs. When combined with savings on conventional infrastructures price competition is created - resulting in a commodity spiral which inevitably ends up in poor service where no-one gains, including customers.

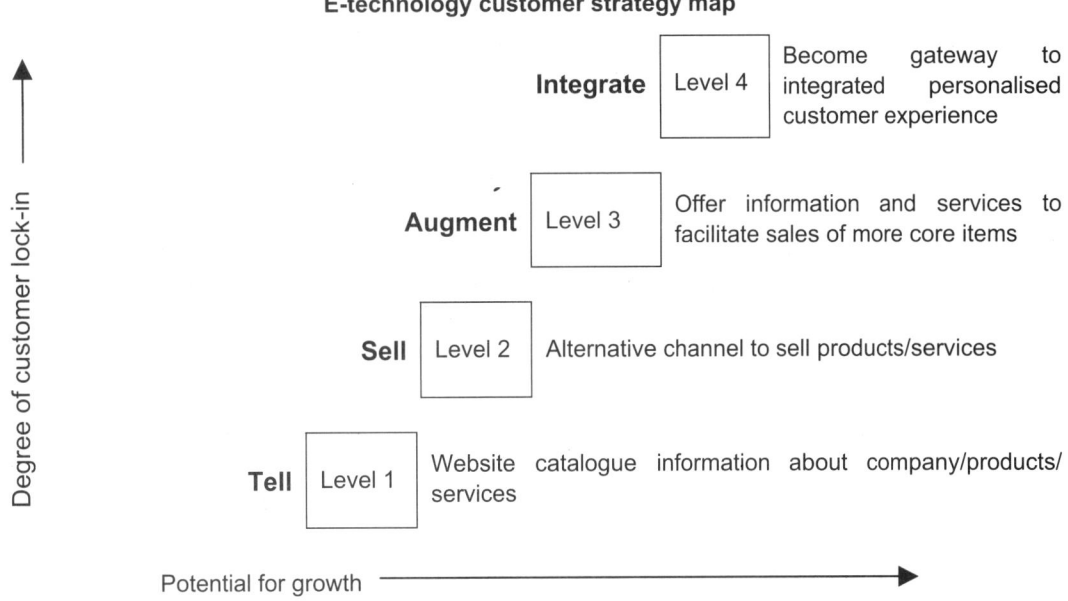

Level 3: Augment. At a more advanced level, through e-technology a firm can offer information, choice or services like remote diagnostics, as Dyson Appliances is doing. But the goal is still transactional - sell more core items, either directly or through distributors or retailers. The offering is augmented to differentiate the company in order to get customer loyalty and retention, to increase transactions and decrease transactional costs. This is often accompanied by customer relationship management tools: using databases to learn about what customers buy, in what quantities, where, and how often, as well as promotional devices like loyalty cards, typical of banks and airlines, but all too easy to emulate. Such CRM approaches do not really consider who these customers are, or interact with them to deliver ongoing, superior, personalised value.

Level 4: Integrate. In order to achieve that value, we need to move to level 4 on the e-technology customer strategy map. Here the enterprise becomes the gateway to customers, providing them with an integrated experience across product, industry, company, country and even brand, over time - sometimes lifetime/ Customer relationships are managed interactively in a highly personalised way so as to achieve the 'lock-in', which happens because the enterprise knows more about the customer than anyone else and uses this information and knowledge to build offerings which are proactive and precise.

The intangibles - ideas, information and knowledge - which become the key component of the offering - are easy to assimilate, codify and disseminate using e-technology. And while the internet is a mass medium, customers can be handled in a highly personalised way at extremely low, if not zero, marginal cost.

What protects the enterprise here is that, once Level 4 has been reached, customer lock-in becomes self reinforcing: the more information and knowledge customers share with the firm, the more proactive and precise offerings become, the more customers lock-in, and the more ideas, information and knowledge they share.

With its powerful and pervasive effects, e-technology allows the enterprise to excel with customers in ways never before imagined. The e-technology strategy map may help managers position themselves and make better decisions so that e-technology can fuel, rather than fool, their customer strategy.

Strategy Magazine, May 2000

Part C: Using information competitively

Building an investment case for e-commerce

4.28 There is still opposition in some organisations to the necessary investment required for e-commerce. Reasons for this opposition often include:

(a) Straightforward **resistance to change**, coupled with **fear of the unknown**. Even stories about Internet successes elsewhere may be viewed with caution on the grounds that they may not easily be transferable.

(b) Existence of the belief that even if new entrants were able to take advantage of the fashionable popularity of the Internet, others coming along behind - 'laggards' - will not be able to do so.

(c) The evidence that many 'dot.com' enterprises remain **unable to achieve sustained profitability** or indeed any profitability at all.

4.29 On the other hand, companies still experiencing doubts should put themselves in the shoes of a potential Internet competitor - and ask themselves: *How might they attack us?* The evidence from experience gained so far in the field of electronic commerce suggests the following scenarios:

(a) They would ignore the unattractive, expensive channels through which your product or service is currently delivered. If your business is banking, they will not establish a branch network; if you are a retailer, they will not operate a chain of shops.

(b) They will **cherry-pick** the more profitable customer segments. Again, if you are a bank, the new entrant will seek to entice away your credit-worthy customers with expensive tastes and unrestricted consumption habits.

(c) They will create highly **differentiated customer segments**, possibly customised for specific individuals. In other words, they will offer a degree of personalised attention which you may find difficult to match.

(d) They will deliberately choose to supply products and services where their presence on the World Wide Web will **add value** - both for themselves and for their customers.

(e) They will offer **shared services** - so that they operate, in effect, as a one-stop shop for, say, a whole repertoire of financial services or in-home entertainment products.

(f) They will capture **intermediary roles** - and benefit from the savings because their costs will not include commission paid to travel agents.

(g) They can use the strength of their website as a **portal** - generating even more business for themselves through the provision of allied, complementary or even virtually identical services.

(h) They can create **affiliate programmes** - equipping them with the capacity for organising comprehensive options. Thus, for example, an on-line grocer may develop relationships with up-market catering companies which cook and serve meals for dinner parties in customers' own homes.

(i) They may **offer incentives** - in the form of reduced prices, discounts, cashback offers, lower interest rates, or higher investment returns. Some of these incentives may be tax-free if they are operated outside any given country's tax regime.

7: The Internet as a strategic business tool

Case example

E-business and what it means for accountants

Electronic business refers to aspects of business being conducted electronically throughout the entire value chain. Figures suggest companies that have commenced trading electronically with their supplies are experiencing a 20% reduction in costs.

In today's business environment, organisations are looking for accountants to act as business partners in delivering value to shareholders, manage financial risks, while still maintaining financial control. We speculate that tomorrow's winners will be those companies that possess accountants who have full understanding of their industry's long-term growth patterns, corporate profiles, together with an understanding of the most appropriate business model(s) necessary to achieve corporate objectives.

E-business

Businesses around the world are on the verge of a revolution, as the web shifts the power from the firm to the customer. Products and services are now being purchased by consumers who are able to obtain more information, and thereby becoming more discerning.

The electronic communication revolution will mean that distance will no longer determine the price of communicating electronically. Adept use of e-commerce will become arguably the most important form of competitive advantage for businesses. It has the potential to create new business models and to find new ways of doing things. The benefits of e-commerce come not only from speeding up and automating a firm's internal processes but also from its ability to spread the benefits to other members of its supply chain.

E-business will eventually be deployed throughout an entire industry's supply chain, linking manufacturers, assemblers, distributors, marketers and customers. A single press of a button will trigger many processes throughout the chain. Table 1 provides a summary of the strategic implications of e-business. The provision of services will increasingly become more important than mere products. Web pages will deliver bespoke services, such as help for consumers in making their choices or stock management for business partners. Fixed prices will give way to reflect true market worth, and firms will join together to make convenient packages for the customer.

Table 1 Strategic implications for e-business

	E-commerce	Strategic implications
Communication	The falling costs and increases in capacity of communications	Death of distance. Virtual firms can become a reality.
Business model	The traditional business model is inappropriate for e-business.	Virtual organisations will be used to capture cost savings and overthrow established practices.
IT	Existing IT systems have not adequately dealt with the customer.	Traditional IT systems will have to complement the Internet.
E-revolution	Commoditisation will make it extremely difficult for firms to differentiate their products.	Need to refine and implement new e-business strategies.
Value	The finance function does not currently provide much added value in the current e-business environment.	Redesign traditional financial planning, control and evaluation techniques.

King and Clift assert that most businesses will migrate to e-business in four stages.

- *Website:* Organisations make their presence in e-business. Attempts will be made to integrate their site's buying and selling processes into the organisation's back office, customer and marketing systems.

- *Connect website to supply chain:* Involves connecting the web site's capabilities to supply chains. For example, it is anticipated that the reduction in paperwork will reduce costs.

- *Form alliances:* Alliances will be formed to operationalise the new business model. Electronic share dealing on the internet is an example of this.

- *Industrial convergence:* E-business makes it possible for industries to combine expertise and produce package solutions.

Part C: Using information competitively

The massive scale changes taking place in global markets now make it imperative that organisations (private and public sector) fully understand the business applications of e-commerce and are able to formulate, implement and evaluate corporate, business and operational strategies. We speculate whether accountants are well positing to influence strategic direction in these e-business times.

The e-business accountant: fact or fiction?

It is interesting to note that, despite budgetary control being the genesis of strategic management, accountants still focus on budgets for strategic planning.

This has been highlighted by Gluek *et al*, who observed four phases of strategic management. This has been echoed by Phillips and Moutinho, who, applying Gluek *et al*'s model to the service sector, see the evolution of strategic management consisting of our phases: first, budgetary control, where the main focus is the setting and achievement of budgets; second, long-range planning, which focuses on medium-term forecasting; third, strategic planning, where the main emphasis is to think strategically; and then, strategic management, where there is an attempt to alter and create the future for the organisation. Moreover, in the age of one-to-one relationship marketing, e-business has now arguably helped to create a fifth phase, which involves understanding customer needs and customer values.

Table 2 Evolution of strategic management

Phase I	Phase II	Phase III	Phase IV
Budgetary control	Long-range planning	Strategic planning	Strategic management
Operational control	Planning for growth	Strategic control at HQ	Strategic control at SBU
Annual budget	Extrapolation of budgets	Strategic plans	Implementation barrier
Internal focus	External focus	Systematic external audit	Suitable planning framework
Attain budget	Forward planning	Strategic vision	Competitive advantage

For many accountants, e-business requires new skills and a fresh mindset. A single push of a button means that e-commerce can operate in real time. We speculate that the challenge for accountants is to provide timely and meaningful information through strategic financial analysis which support their firm's decision to invest in e-business.

Pitturro highlights three critical areas that impact the effectiveness of the e-business accountant:

- The cost of the investment in e-commerce can be hard to evaluate, and costs can escalate as the technology is implemented.

- Accountants should weigh the costs, risks and benefits of e-commerce investments.

- Accountants should integrate e-commerce financial planning with IT and other functional processes.

According to Ray Lane, president and chief operating officer of Oracle, the economic structure of companies is changing. Existing financial statements can cope with physical assets. However, they cannot cope with intellectual capital or knowledge, which is the difference between real tangible value and market value. Lane asserts that the real value of a company in the future will be how fast information can be gathered throughout the world, analysed, have value added to it, and then be redistributed back into the value chain. The faster the cycle, the more value that is added to the company.

Many organisations still believe that e-business can be ignored until it is more fully developed. However, according to recent research, e-business will become commonplace, in years, rather than decades, which may be too late for the current non-adopters or those companies that are unable to design and implement the business models adopted by companies like Cisco.

Adapted from *Management Accounting*, February 2000

5 GLOBALISATION

5.1 The Internet is one of a range of factors that have encouraged organisations to think and act globally.

> **KEY TERM**
>
> **Globalisation** is a term that is used to describe the trend towards standardised products, services, tastes and organisational policies worldwide.
>
> The term also encapsulates the way organisations that operate in more than one country design their marketing policies and control systems to meet the expectations of global consumers.
>
> In the context of information systems, globalisation is the process of transforming a business and its information system from a national context to a global context.

5.2 Some would say that **global organisations** are rare. Industry structures change, foreign markets are culturally diverse, and the transformations brought about by developments in information technology mean that the world market is in a state of **turbulence**.

5.3 Changes that have happened in the world market-place over the past decade include:

(a) **Globalisation of business** - increased competition and global customers.

(b) **Science and technology** developments.

(c) Increased mergers, acquisitions and **strategic alliances.**

(d) Changing **customer values** and behaviour.

(e) Increased **scrutiny** of business decisions by government and the public.

(f) Increased **deregulation** and co-operation between business and government.

(g) Changes in **business practices** - downsizing, outsourcing and re-engineering.

(h) Changes in the **social and business** relationships between companies and their employees, customers and other stakeholders.

(i) The World Wide Web has enabled even very small organisations to establish a global presence.

5.4 Factors encouraging the globalisation of world trade include the following.

(a) **Financial factors** eg Third world debt. Often the lenders require the initiation of economic reforms as a condition of the loan.

(b) **Country/continent** alliances which foster trade and tourism.

(c) **Legal factors** such as patents and trade marks, which encourage the development of technology and design.

(d) **Stock markets** trading in international commodities.

(e) The level of **protectionist** measures.

(f) The **Internet**.

5.5 The effect of globalisation on a firm could include:
- Lower barriers to entry, hence incoming competition
- Opportunities to compete abroad via exports
- Opportunities to invest abroad
- Opportunities to raise finance from overseas sources of capital

5.6 Some argue there is an increasing number of 'stateless corporations', whose activities transcend national boundaries, and whose personnel come from any country.

(a) **Multinationals** have strong links to the home country. For example strategic decision-making, head office functions and R&D are usually based in the home country.

(b) **Global**

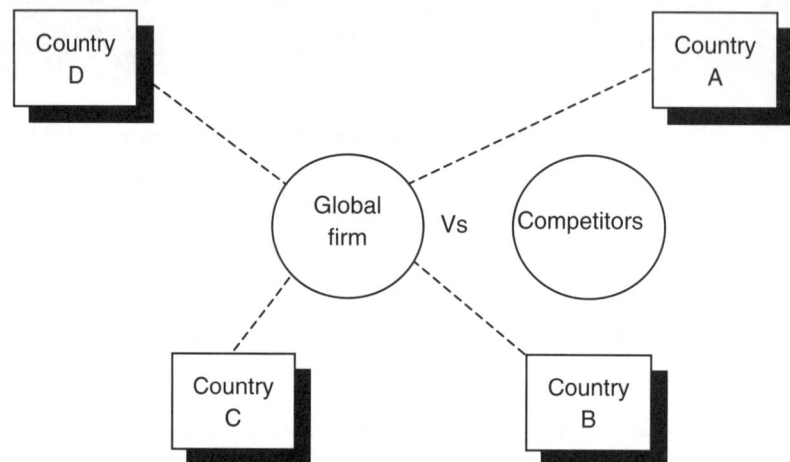

5.7 Many firms are setting up global alliances and firms such as BT see their ambitions as being worldwide.

5.8 Do these stateless corporations really exist?

(a) **Workforce.** Most multinationals have less than half of their employees based abroad.

(b) **Ownership and control of multinationals remain restricted.** Few so-called global companies are currently quoted on more than two stock markets, but more and more are seeking a listing in a number of financial markets.

(c) **Top management is rarely as multinational in composition** as the firm's activities.

(d) National residence and status is important for **tax reasons**.

(e) **R&D.** The bulk of a typical multinational's research and development is generally done in the home country, where strategic decisions are made. But this is changing, especially as R & D is sometimes subcontracted.

(f) Where **capital is limited**, 'global' companies stick to the home market rather than developing overseas ones.

(g) Finally, profits from a global company must be **remitted somewhere.**

5.9 Do multinationals have to be big?

(a) Open markets and common standards now make it easier for small firms to sell products worldwide, as these barriers are lower.

(b) A website is relatively cheap to set up and can be accessed from anywhere in the world. Global courier companies such as FedEx provide efficient and relatively cheap delivery worldwide.

(c) Capital markets are now open to smaller companies.

5.10 International business conditions affect:

(a) The nature of the industry.

(b) The various positions of different countries, the size and wealth of their markets and the prosperity and efficiency of their productive bases.

(c) The management, by governments or international institutions, of the framework in which business is done.

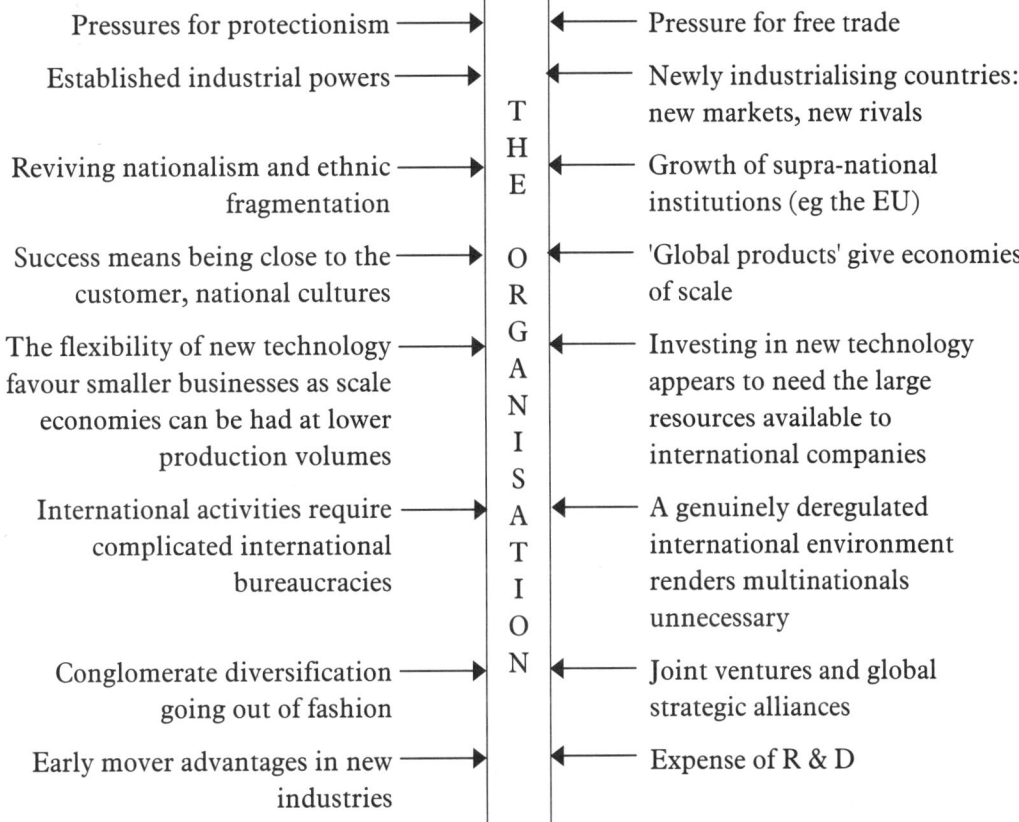

5.11 Before getting carried away by notions that the world is splitting into trading blocks, remember that:

(a) There is increasingly free movement of capital.

(b) Global trade is becoming liberalised.

(c) Some of the world's markets offering the greatest potential for growth (eg India and China) are not part of a 'trading block'.

(d) New technology, such as the Internet, makes it harder to enforce trade barriers.

5.12 Many countries have limited or controlled their trading activities, with varying success. **Protectionist measures to restrict competition** from overseas include:

(a) **Quotas** on the number of items that can be imported.
(b) Import **bans**.
(c) Restrictions on **foreign ownership** of certain industries.
(d) **Tariffs**.

Part C: Using information competitively

5.13 Business people and politicians have had an ambivalent attitude in the past towards this issue. Free trade s favoured by imported or multinationals, but protectionism give businesses the benefit of a cosy domestic market. Their inefficiencies are not penalised and customers pay higher prices.

5.14 Also bear in mind that 'protectionist' measures are not the only barrier to entry. Differences still exist in:

- Tax regimes
- Wage levels
- Infrastructure
- Language and culture
- Skills levels
- Prosperity

Developing a global business strategy

5.15 Businesses that wish to pursue some form of global strategy have several options:

(a) **Domestic exporter.** Most activities are based in the organisation's home country. Offices in other countries are controlled from the central office in the home country.

(b) **Franchiser or licensing.** The product or service is designed to strict specifications at a centralised location, but countries have their own production and distribution facilities. Breweries often allow production under licence in 'foreign' countries. The major international burger chains are franchisers.

(c) **Multinational.** Some activities are centralised, but others are managed within individual countries. Most multinationals set administrative and control procedures centrally, and allow local offices to decide production and marketing strategies. Many motor vehicle manufacturers operate as multinationals.

(d) **Transnational entity.** Activities are viewed and managed on a global basis. There may be an office that is recognised as 'Head Office' but the location is not a significant factor. Some degree of localised differentiation and control may be established but the organisation is viewed and managed as a global concern. Global Internet portals such as Yahoo! are probably closest to this definition.

5.16 In order to make the choice between these types of strategy, a company must assess its 'global logic' - the compelling strategic factors in its industry. A global logic may involve customers' demands, purchasing factors, competitiveness, industry specifications or size, and governmental or local regulations.

5.17 Just having a global presence does not guarantee that a company will enjoy global competitive success. It has to exploit the opportunities for value creation that its global presence offers. Global firms can create value by:

- Adapting to local market demands
- Achieving economies of global scale
- Finding the optimal locations for different activities
- Ensuring swift transfer of knowledge between business units

Developing a global information strategy

5.18 An organisation's global information management strategy defines how the organisation develops and organises its Global Information Systems (GIS). A global information system is any system that processes information, or assists decision-making, in a global context.

7: The Internet as a strategic business tool

5.19 The global information management strategy addresses issues such as centralised versus decentralised communications architectures, standards, and data management. It must also ensure its alignment with the global strategy of the organisation.

5.20 A global IS strategy should match the corporate structure and strategy. It needs to support global business drivers, provide for national differences, and include an IS architecture suitable for globalisation.

5.21 Establishing the necessary alignment requires the involvement and co-operation of both the senior business planner and senior IS technology manager. Both should learn from each other's field of expertise and plan a global strategy pro-actively together.

5.22 There are four main strategies for global information systems.

   (a) **Centralised**. All systems development and operation is performed in one place.

   (b) **Decentralised**. Each country develops and operates its own systems.

   (c) **Duplicated**. All systems development is performed in one place, but each country implements and maintains its own systems.

   (d) **Networked**. Systems development and operation is performed in many locations. Some, or all, systems may then be implemented worldwide.

5.23 These four global business strategies can be **matched** to the strategies for global information systems.

   (a) A **domestic exporter** will usually be suited to a centralised system as activities are based in the home country. Some local systems may be required to comply with local regulations, eg Data Protection legislation.

   (b) **Franchiser** or licensing organisations operating schemes are suited to a duplicated IS approach. This approach best matches the business strategy.

   (c) A **multinational** strategy is suited to a decentralised IS approach. This approach best matches the business strategy.

   (d) A **transnational entity** is suited to a networked IS approach.

5.24 The relationships described above appear straightforward. In real business situations things are unlikely to be so clear-cut. Use the information above as a framework for considering the **best fit** between global business strategy and global information systems.

Globalisation - other issues

Global Business Drivers (GBDs)

5.25 GBDs are a means for assessing high-level global information requirements. These drivers concentrate on areas of the business organisation (resources, operations, and risk) and their consistency with the business entity throughout the global organisation. Business drivers should shape IS plans.

5.26 Senior management has a better view of the regional differences and perspective variations and must be involved in the GBD analysis. Identifying global business drivers may require market research. An analysis of global business drivers could help the company better prioritise their global systems requirements.

Part C: Using information competitively

Organisation structure

5.27 The transnational organisation structure is well-suited to achieve global integration, local differentiation, and worldwide innovation. This form of organisation encourages the formation of partnerships and alliances to meet the general goals.

5.28 Organisations may form an **alliance** to combine their strengths and eliminate their weaknesses. **Competition** and **collaboration** are both important. A business needs strategies for competition while promoting strategic alliances with leading international companies.

5.29 Many modern multinational companies are formed by buying foreign subsidiaries. The subsidiaries often develop their own information infrastructure, which slowly become nearly impossible to integrate.

5.30 When organisations adopt a global business strategy the IS may need to be changed to reflect this global view. This is particularly difficult if designers of the local system become the designers of the global system without fully understanding the global strategy. A **global team** is necessary.

Global projects and global workgroups

5.31 Global projects are **risky** because of their size, scope, and commitment. Project risks are partially caused by rapid change in business conditions and unforeseen differences among local requirements.

5.32 Workgroups that have members based in many countries need a common communication and work **collaboration system**. Groupware and international communication systems should allow access to documents and scheduling tools. E-conferencing facilitates discussion.

5.33 Technology is not the limiting factor in many globalisation projects. Backgrounds, cultures, and beliefs are more limiting than technology.

Global market

5.34 The Internet is a global information system that empowers the consumer with more **choice** and new markets. A customer anywhere in the world can participate in any market. Only companies who can anticipate customer expectations and act quickly will survive.

5.35 There needs to be a **legal framework** in place to support the transactions on the global marketplace.

5.36 Global competition has made quality a required attribute of products sold in the world markets. In many industries, advances in information technology permit a defective product to be **traced** back to a particular worker, machine or supplier

5.37 Companies must deal with customers in other countries whose tastes vary from that of local customers. To adapt to such changes, companies need to establish and maintain a database of **customer information**.

5.38 Operating in a global market necessitates a **global delivery system**. A global delivery system is able to track the status, and in the case of a physical product the location, of a resource or order anywhere in the world.

5.39 A transnational system enables the identification of resource surpluses and shortages in different areas, so resources can be moved to where they are most needed.

5.40 The global economy is a knowledge economy, in which knowledge is the prime source of competitive advantage. To generate the knowledge needed to succeed in this environment, managers must develop organisational networks in which knowledge can be shared. But they must be sensitive in their dealings with participants; problems will arise if people are treated as assets that can churn out knowledge on demand.

Case example

The Elements of Globalisation (twelve general elements and twelve Internet related elements)

Twelve Elements of Globalisation

1. Increased Exposure to Political Risk. Companies that expand across national boundaries increase the uncertainties they face.

2. Increased Exposure to Natural Disasters. The major, global tectonic plates lie, to a substantial extent, under the emerging markets. It is largely in the emerging markets that the great earthquakes and volcanic eruptions occur. But worse, it is also in the emerging markets that governments have built the least dependable infrastructures.

3. Increased merger and acquisition activity. Given the greater commonality in standards and in business across national borders, enhanced profits and market share can be achieved through mergers and acquisitions more quickly than through building operations in different countries. Massive, new horizontal mergers that combine firms with similar core competencies are especially likely to occur.

4. New Forms of Competition and Co-operation. Firms that enter foreign markets will be subject to new forms of competition. Other companies operating in those markets may be unknown and may pose serious challenges. But companies will also co-operate with other companies in new ways, becoming mutually interdependent even though they may simultaneously compete.

5. New Cultural Sensibilities. Going global means enhancing efficiency and profitability by taking advantage of the best available talent drawn from everywhere in the world. Companies now appoint senior management regardless of the countries from which they come. To do that most effectively, however, means that companies have to drop the biases and cultural sensibilities that arise naturally from their countries of origin. A new global culture arises within the firm itself, a culture that executives from the original host countries often find difficult to adopt.

6. 'Virtual' Hierarchies. As companies spread their operations geographically, managers increasingly have responsibility for staff in different countries. The managers are challenged to establish meaningful interpersonal relationship with their staff, who often come from an entirely different culture. Worse, the managers need to establish such relationships with people with whom they are not in day-to-day, face-to-face contact. The telephone, email, teleconferencing, and, of course, increased air travel, are the new bases for establishing meaningful interpersonal relationships. This is a massive challenge to the parties in the relationship - staff as well as management.

7. Best Practices. By acting as a single firm with a global, supranational culture, the excuses that justified preserving national practices disappear. Globalisation means operating everywhere as a single firm and instituting similar best practices everywhere. That puts pressure on firms to learn of global best practices either through consulting firms oriented toward generating competitive intelligence or to firms, themselves, striving to learn what best practices are by studying their competitors.

8. Alliances. Globalisation allows for many new types of alliances. Shell, for example, has established alliances by working out exchange programmes with chemical companies in Asia. In exchange for their supplying Shell's Asian customers with output from their Asian plants, Shell supplies their North American customers from its plants in the US.

9. Finance. Globalisation reduces the primacy of any particular company location or its country of origin. As a result, capital in a global firm is allocated on the basis of expected risk-adjusted returns. Competition for the firm's global budget is intensified, and better risk-return calculations must be performed in order to warrant a capital allocation. Established operations and headquarters location in a truly global firm offer no advantages in the intensified competition for capital.

Part C: Using information competitively

10. Speeding the Globalisation of Suppliers. A firm's decision to globalise will reverberate throughout its supply chain and affect all the firms that supply it with services. Global firms often look to suppliers and to service firms that can provide it with goods or services on a global basis.

11. Winners and Loser from Globalisation. While globalisation will provide immense aggregate benefits to producers and consumers alike, it will not provide those benefits equally. Globalisation will produce very big winners; but it will also produce big losers.

12. Backlash to Globalisation. The transition to globalisation for countries will not be easy or smooth. Inevitably, a backlash against globalisation will be generated that will organise and pressure the state to resist, if not reject, globalisation. States that succumb will be the long-term losers. They may succeed in preserving the structure of their economies. They may become ever more quaint in the process and ever more desirable, as a result, as a place to visit. But you wouldn't want to live there. Those countries will be poorer as a result.

Twelve Elements of the Internet and Globalisation

1. Instantaneous Communications. The Internet is the greatest distance killer of them all. It offers virtually-free, virtually-instantaneous global communications, allowing coordination and management to occur anywhere, everywhere, all the time.

2. Multi-shift Operations. For goods that can be digitally transformed, the Internet allows two- or three-shift operations per day.

3. Supply Chain Management. The recent spate of online buying portals, organised vertically by industry, suggests the possible efficiencies to be gained from global supply-chain management. New suppliers can enter the competition to supply raw material, parts, equipment, and services- whatever global firms buy - through the Internet. The consequence will be to drive prices down, eroding supplier margins. Less-efficient suppliers will be driven out of business and suppliers across national boundaries will be stimulated to consolidate.

4. The Flattened Hierarchy. The Internet and the global distribution of the corporation will combine to flatten organisational hierarchies. Power in firms will be diffused to local operations. Firms will be held together by common culture and brands and by people who have moved through various global operations and, in the process, established bonds of association.

5. The Unbounded Corporation. Just as corporations become borderless, so will they become unbounded. The distinct boundaries of the past - where it was simple distinguishing who was in the corporation and who was not - will become blurred. More and more professional workers will relate to firms as consultants rather than employees. More workers will be part-time.

6. The Disappearance of the Middle. Globalisation generates firms of ever-larger geographic scale and ever-larger financial strength, a process facilitated by the Internet. Simultaneously, the Internet facilitates the entry of new players, especially new niche players. In the future, the global economy will be dominated by relatively few giant firms and a vast number of niche players and small, new entrants.

7. Information Rules. Increasingly, the value of a firm will be seen as the value of its historical and contemporary human capital. Its accumulated knowledge from its history as embodied in its products and processes, as well as the knowledge of its current workforce and their capacity to generate and accumulate new human capital, as well as its knowledge of its suppliers and especially its customers are the bases for competitive advantage. Companies that understand that the value of their products and services is the value of the information they embody will be relatively successful and relatively major users of the Internet.

8. Non-Governmental Organisations (NGOs) as Countervailing Powers. As businesses globalise, a major countervailing power has arisen - global NGOs. Powerful, global NGOs have arisen through the sophisticated use of the Internet. NGOs will bring massive pressure to bear on companies to 'protect' the environment, adopt 'fair' practices with their local labour forces, and to the people in the areas in which they operate. If reputation and brand are everything in global business, NGOs have become powerful challengers to the global reputations of business.

9. The 'Digital Divide'. A great deal of energy has been spent on the challenge of the 'digital divide.' Conventionally the term refers to the consequences of the unequal distribution of access to the Internet. The poorest sectors of any population are likely to be least able to gain such access. If being connected and being Internet savvy is the hallmark of the involved citizen in the twenty-first century, and if being connected is a path to economic well-being, then the digital divide will reinforce existing inequalities. The term has less often been applied to countries. But the same phenomenon applies. Countries whose citizens do not use the Internet will invariably suffer lower rates of growth and be less a part of the accelerating globalisation than connected countries and companies.

10. New Entrants. But as surely as the 'digital divide' threatens the well-being of whole countries, the Internet also offers solutions to the backwardness of many states. Countries not yet wired can skip the technological stages through which the more-developed countries passed. They now can skip copper entirely and move directly to wireless communication, at far less expense than laying copper cables would cost. But it is also the case that the Internet allows firms in developing countries to participate in commerce in a way simply impossible in the past. The Internet (and globalisation) means that in a network there is no centre and there is no periphery. As India has shown, if it can be put on a screen, it can be produced in a developing country.

11. Service: Not Just Production. As margins continue to be driven down, manufacturers will bundle their products with services. That will provide extra values to consumers, higher margins for producers, and especially provide manufacturers of what will essentially become commodities with enhanced competitiveness.

12. The 'Clash of Connectivity'. As the Internet and businesses continue to tie ever-larger portions of the world's peoples into networks of communications and economic interdependence and a new, global culture spreads, the chances for conflict between those peoples and between their states will diminish. The conflicts in the future will occur among the not connected and between the connected and the not connected.

From the *International Political Economy, IPE,* Volume 7, Number 6, March 2000

Exam focus point

A question in June 2003 required candidates to describe the four business strategies (domestic exporter, multinational, franchiser and transnational) and to describe the information technology strategy that best compliments each of these (centralised, decentralised, duplicated or networked).

Part C: Using information competitively

Chapter roundup

- The **Internet** is a global network linking millions of computers. The World Wide Web (**WWW**) is a system of Internet servers that support specially formatted documents. A group of documents accessed from the same base web address is known as a **website**.

- Most organisations now have a **website**, and some conduct **transactions** over the Internet.

- The major growth of **e-commerce** so far has been in the Business to Business (B2B) sector.

- The Internet provides opportunities to **automate tasks** which would previously have required human intervention.

- Establishing links to the Internet brings **security risks**. Suitable systems, policies and procedures should be implemented to minimise these risks.

- **Hacking** involves attempting to gain unauthorised access to a computer system, usually through telecommunications links. A **virus** is a piece of software which infects programs and data and possibly damages them, and which replicates itself. Viruses often use e-mail links to spread.

- **Encryption** aims to ensure the security of data during transmission. Encryption involves scrambling the data at one end of the line, transmitting the scrambled data, and unscrambling it at the receiver's end of the line.

- **Firewalls** are used to prevent Internet users from accessing private networks connected to the Internet, especially intranets. All communications entering or leaving the intranet pass through the firewall, which blocks those that do not meet the specified security criteria.

- **Electronic commerce** means conducting business electronically via a communications link. An older technology that is covered under the electronic commerce umbrella is **Electronic Data Interchange** (EDI).

- The Internet and e-commerce **challenges traditional business models**.

- Ensuring '**back-office**' **operations complement web-based operations** is vital.

- When developing **a strategy for e-commerce** consider:
    - Organisation and culture
    - Systems and infrastructure
    - Training
    - Customers

- **Globalisation** describes the trend towards standardised products, tastes, pricing and organisational policies worldwide.

- The global economy is a **knowledge economy**, in which knowledge is an important source of competitive advantage.

- **Global Business Drivers** (GDBs) may be used to assess high-level global information requirements.

- An organisation's **global information system** should complement the organisation's global business strategy.

7: The Internet as a strategic business tool

Quick quiz

1. List five current uses of the Internet.
2. What tasks are typically automated by a website?
3. How do ISDN and ADSL technologies improve Internet efficiency?
4. Distinguish between encryption and authentication.
5. What is a virus?
6. List five ways in which the Internet and e-commerce differ from normal business practices.
7. What is required to set up an e-business?
8. List four global business strategies.
9. List four strategies for global information systems.

Answers to quick quiz

1. [Five of]
   Dissemination of information
   Product/service development (test marketing)
   Transaction processing (B2B and B2C)
   Relationship enhancement
   Recruitment and job search
   Entertainment

2. Frequently-Asked-Questions, order status checking, keyword search, interview style information gathering, e-mail, bulletin boards and requests for personal contact.

3. Through allowing faster transfer of data.

4. Encryption involves scrambling and unscrambling data to prevent unauthorised 'eavesdroppers' obtaining useful data. Authentication ensures a message has come from an authorised sender.

5. A small program that infects systems and possibly damages them.

6. It challenges traditional business models.
   Benefits are available to organisations of all sizes.
   It challenges the need to pay for some information.
   It encourages speed of product/service delivery.
   It creates new communication networks and business alliances.

7. Telecommunications infrastructure, hardware, software (including 'shopping cart'), an SSL certificate, payment processing mechanism, delivery system, customer information gathering tool, feedback mechanism, promotional effort and a maintenance capability to keep the site running and up-to-date.

8. Domestic exporter; Franchiser; Multinational; Transnational.

9. Centralised; Decentralised; Duplicated; Networked.

Now try the questions below from the Exam Question Bank.
Question 15 includes detailed guidance with the question and answer.

Number	Level	Marks	Time
8	Exam	10	18 mins
15(a)	Exam	8	14 mins

Part D
The impact of information technology

Chapter 8

IMPLEMENTING CHANGE

Topic list	Syllabus reference
1　Planning and implementing change	8(a), 8(b), 8(c)
2　Causes of information systems failure	8(a), 8(b), 8(c)
3　The development and implementation process: what can go wrong	8(a), 8(b), 8(c)
4　System building tools and techniques	8(a), 8(b), 8(c)
5　System changeover and evaluation	8(a), 8(b), 8(c)

Introduction

The modern business environment requires organisations to adapt to ever-changing environmental conditions. In this chapter we explain the importance of having a process to manage organisational change. We examine in detail the issues surrounding a common type of change – the implementation of a new information system.

Study guide

24 – Success and failure

- Identify major problem areas when implementing information systems
- Apply organisational impact analysis
- Identify criteria needed to assess whether a system is successful
- Describe the principal causes of information system failure and how to overcome them
- Discuss problems of implementation: people-oriented theory, system oriented theory, and interaction theory
- Describe the relationship between the implementation process and the system outcome

25 – Managing change

- Discuss the appropriate strategies to manage the implementation process
- Discuss formal planning control framework and tools
- Evaluate the impact of alternative system building techniques and tools
- Explain how to manage risk
- Understand the importance of having a process to manage change in an organisation

Exam guide

The wider issues surrounding management of change are very topical and therefore highly examinable.

Project management tools and techniques may be of some relevance to your answer, but questions at this level are likely to require you to understand the 'big picture'. (Project management is covered in detail in Paper 2.1.)

Part D: The impact of Information Technology

1 PLANNING AND IMPLEMENTING CHANGE

1.1 **Change**, in the context of organisation and management, can occur in many areas.

- The **environment**
- The **products** the organisation makes or the **services** it provides
- **How** products are made, or who makes them
- Management and **working relationships**
- Organisation **structure or size**

1.2 Change can affect individuals in a variety of ways.

(a) **Physiologically**, both as the natural product of ageing and as the result of external factors (eg a change in work patterns).

(b) **Circumstantial changes** such as living in a new house, establishing new relationships or working to new routines. This involves letting go of things and learning new ways of functioning.

(c) Change affects individuals **psychologically.**

  (i) **Disorientation** before new circumstances have been assimilated.

  (ii) **Uncertainty** may lead to **insecurity**, especially acute in changes involving work and/or fast acclimatisation (a steep learning curve may lead to feelings of incapacity).

  (iii) New expectations, challenges and pressures may generate **role stress** in which an individual feels discomfort in the role he or she plays.

  (iv) **Powerlessness.** Change can be particularly threatening if it is perceived as an outside force or agent against which the individual is powerless.

Resistance to change

1.3 Resisting change means attempting to preserve the existing state of affairs against pressure to alter it.

1.4 General **sources of resistance** to change include:

(a) **Attitudes or beliefs,** perhaps arising from cultural, religious or social influences.

(b) **Loyalty** to a group and its norms.

(c) **Habit**.

(d) **Politics** - in the sense of resisting changes that might weaken the power base of the individual or group or strengthen a rival's position.

(e) The way in which any change is put forward and **implemented**.

(f) **Personality**.

1.5 **Immediate causes** of resistance in any particular situation could include:

(a) **Self-interest** - if the status quo is perceived to be preferable.

(b) **Misunderstanding and distrust** - if the reasons for, or the nature and consequences of, the change have not been made clear.

(c) **Contradictory assessments** - disagreement over the likely costs and benefits of the change.

(d) **Low tolerance of change itself** - differences in tolerance of uncertainty.

1.6 Possible **reactions** to proposed change are outlined below:

(a) **Acceptance:** whether enthusiastic espousal, co-operation, grudging co-operation or resignation.

(b) **Indifference:** usually where the change does not directly affect the individual evidence is apathy, lack of interest, inaction.

(c) **Passive resistance:** refusal to learn, working to rule; pleas of ignorance or defensiveness; procrastination.

(d) **Active resistance:** deliberate 'spoiling', go-slows, deliberate errors, sabotage, absenteeism or strikes.

Planning and implementing change

1.7 A systematic approach should be established, for planning and implementing changes.

Step

1. Determine need or desire for change in a particular area.

2. Prepare a tentative plan.
   - Brainstorming sessions a good idea, since alternatives for change should be considered

3. Analyse probable reactions to the change

4. Make a final decision from the choice of alternative options
   - Decision taken either by group problem-solving (participative) or by manager alone (coercive)

5. Establish a timetable for change
   - 'Coerced' changes can probably be implemented faster, without time for discussions.
   - Speed of implementation that is achievable will depend on the likely reactions of the people affected (all in favour, half in favour, all against etc).
   - Identify those in favour of the change, and perhaps set up a pilot programme involving them. Talk with the others who resist the change.

6. Communicate the plan for change
   - This is really a continuous process, beginning at Step 1 and going through to Step 7.

7. Implement the change. Review the change.
   - Continuous evaluation and modifications

The change process

1.8 In the words of John Hunt (*Managing People at Work*): 'Learning also involves re-learning - not merely learning something new but trying to unlearn what is already known.' This is the thinking behind the three-stage approach to changing human behaviour, which may be depicted as follows.

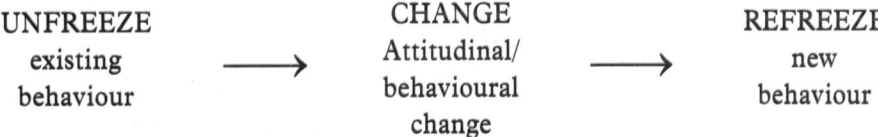

Step 1. **Unfreeze** is the most difficult stage of the process, concerned mainly with 'selling' the change, with giving individuals or groups a **motive** for changing their attitudes, values, behaviour, systems or structures.

(a) If the need for change is immediate, clear and necessary for the survival of the individual or group, the unfreeze stage will be greatly accelerated.

(b) Routine changes may be harder to sell if they are perceived to be unimportant and not survival-based.

(c) Unfreezing processes need four things

- A trigger (eg a crisis).
- Someone to challenge and expose the existing behaviour pattern.
- The involvement of outsiders.
- Alterations to power structure.

Step 2. **Change** is mainly concerned with identifying what the new, desirable behaviour should be, communicating it and encouraging individuals and groups to adopt it. The new ideas must be shown to work.

Step 3. **Refreeze** is the final stage, implying consolidation or reinforcement of the new behaviour. Positive reinforcement (praise, reward) or negative reinforcement (sanctions applied to those who deviate from the new behaviour) may be used.

Strategies for change management

1.9 Each of the causes of change identified below can be dealt with in a different way.

Cause	How to deal with it
Parochial self-interest	**Negotiation** (eg offer incentives to those resisting on grounds of self-interest).
Misunderstanding	This is best dealt with by **educating and reassuring** people. Trust has to be earned.
Different viewpoints of the situation	Change can be promoted through participation and by **involving potential resisters**.
Low tolerance of change	Force the change through and then **support** the new behaviours it requires. In short, people have to be encouraged (by carrot and stick methods) to adopt the new methods.

Champion of change model: the role of the change agent

1.10 New information systems developments need management support. The **champion of change model** recognises the importance of change being led by a **change agent**, who may be an individual or occasionally a group.

Step 1. **Senior management** decide in broad terms what is to be done.

Step 2. They appoint a **change agent** to drive it through. Senior management has three roles.

- Supporting the change agent, if the change provokes conflict between the agent and interest groups in the organisation
- Reviewing and monitoring the progress of the change
- Endorsing and approving the changes, and ensuring that they are publicised

Step 3. The change agent has to **win the support of functional and operational managers,** who have to introduce and enforce the changes in their own

8: Implementing change

departments. The champion of change has to provide advice and information, as well as evidence that the old ways are no longer acceptable.

Step 4. The change agent **galvanises managers into action** and gives them any necessary support. The managers ensure that the changes are implemented operationally, in the field. Where changes involve a new information system it is ultimately the users who are responsible for operating the new system.

Case example

Change Management, a pragmatic approach in Abbey National plc.

There have been many internal changes in Abbey National since becoming plc.

- Change from 49 to 5 mortgage administration centres.
- Set up of 3 Teleservice Centres.
- Introduction of postal accounts.
- Reduction in the number of branches.
- Combine administrations of Scottish Mutual and Abbey National Life under same customer service structure and systems.

People do not resist change - they resist what they perceive that they will lose. Perception = reality.

Communication is critical and should be planned and managed by those who are communicating change. **The effects of good communication**:-

- Reduces uncertainty
- Builds commitment
- Shapes assumptions
- Involve the people in the process

COMMUNICATE TO GAIN COMMITMENT - DON'T GET THE COMMUNICATION WRONG!

The communication process

Step 1. Project team 'sell' concept to managers and supervisors

Step 2. Supervisors present to their team with support from project team

Step 3. Two day briefing/training for supervisors

Step 4. On-ground support for supervisors throughout implementation

Step 5. Remove support gradually

Step 6. Continuous improvement course

Step 7. Formal handover to managers

Change issues encountered at Abbey National plc

- Supervisor's confidence destroyed (security blanket removed)
- No PC experience to operate spreadsheets
- Task of planning day takes too long, no time to do other work
- This would not work in our area because we are different
- Frightened of raising issues
- Focus on backlogs - no time to do process management

Summary

- Involve the people who are impacted al all stages
- Caveat on initial stages or market sensitive projects
- Communicate, communicate, communicate - tailored, early, often - if you have nothing to say people may believe you have a hidden agenda
- Consider the cultural differences

Part D: The impact of Information Technology

- Do not forget managers

What if you do not have the time to go through all the stages and give the level of support people require?

- Anticipate as many issues as possible
- Mobilise maximum power
- Expect/prepare for resistance

Source: *CIMA articles database*

2 CAUSES OF INFORMATION SYSTEMS FAILURE

2.1 Most research seems to indicate that the major cause of information systems failure is **inadequate user involvement**. Users need to be involved in the development process at all stages – including system design.

2.2 Other common causes of dissatisfaction with information systems include those outlined below.

(a) IS project managers were often **technicians**, not managers. Technical ability for IS staff is no guarantee of management skill - an individual might be a highly proficient analyst or programmer, but **not a good manager**.

(b) The project manager may accept **an unrealistic deadline** - the timescale is fixed early in the planning process. User demands may be accepted as deadlines before sufficient consideration is given to the realism of this.

(c) **Poor or non-existent planning** is a recipe for disaster. Unrealistic deadlines would be identified much earlier if a proper planning process was undertaken.

(d) A lack of **monitoring** and **control**.

(e) Users **change their requirements**, resulting in costly changes to the system as it is being developed.

(f) **Poor timetabling and resourcing**. It is no use being presented on day 1 with a team of programmers, when there is still systems analysis and design work to do. The development and implementation of a computer project may take a considerable length of time (perhaps 18 months from initial decision to operational running for a medium-sized installation); a proper plan and time schedule for the various activities must be drawn up.

2.3 The project manager has a number of **conflicting requirements**.

(a) The **systems manager**, usually the project manager's boss, wants the project **delivered on time**, to specification and within budget.

(b) **User** expectations may be misunderstood, ignored or unrealistic.

(c) The project manager has to plan and supervise the work of **analysts** and **programmers** and these are rather different roles.

2.4 The project manager needs to develop an **appropriate management style**. What he or she should realise is the extent to which the project will fail if users are not consulted, or if the project team is unhappy. As the project manager needs to encourage participation from users, an excessively authoritarian style is not suitable.

2.5 A project is affected by a number of factors, often in **conflict** with each other.

(a) **Quality** of the system required, in terms of basic system requirements.

(b) **Time**, both to complete the project, and in terms of the opportunity cost of time spent on this project which could be spent on others.

(c) **Costs** and resources allocated to the project.

2.6 The balance between the constraints of time, cost and quality will be different for each project.

(a) If a system aims to provide competitive advantage then time will tend to be the dominant factor.

(b) If safety is paramount (eg an auto-pilot system) then quality will be most important.

(c) If the sole aim of a project is to meet administrative needs that are not time dependent, then cost may be the dominant factor.

2.7 The relationship can be shown as a triangle.

The Time/Cost/Quality Triangle

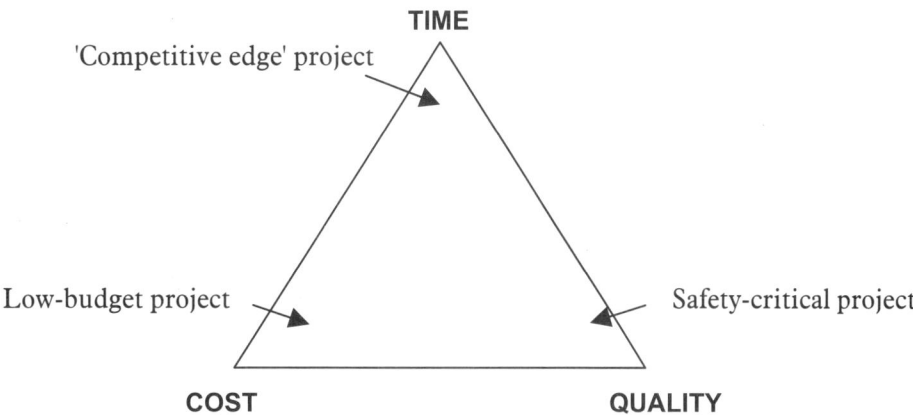

2.8 The balance of time, cost and quality will influence decision making throughout the project – for example whether to spend an extra £5,000 to fix a problem completely or only spend £1,000 on a quick fix and implement a user work-around?

Dealing with slippage

2.9 When a project has slipped behind schedule there are a range of options open to the project manager. Some of these options are summarised in the following table.

Action	Comment
Do nothing	After considering all options it may be decided that things should be allowed to continue as they are.
Add resources	If capable staff are available and it is practicable to add more people to certain tasks it may be possible to recover some lost ground. Could some work be subcontracted?
Work smarter	Consider whether the methods currently being used are the most suitable – for example could prototyping be used.
Replan	If the assumptions the original plan was based on have been proved invalid a more realistic plan should be devised.

Action	Comment
Reschedule	A complete replan may not be necessary – it may be possible to recover some time by changing the phasing of certain deliverables.
Introduce incentives	If the main problem is team performance, incentives such as bonus payments could be linked to work deadlines and quality.
Change the specification	If the original objectives of the project are unrealistic given the time and money available it may be necessary to negotiate a change in the specification.

2.10 Some of the reactions to slippage discussed above would involve changes that would significantly affect the overall project. Other possible causes of changes to the original project plan include:

- The availability of new technology
- Changes in personnel
- A realisation that user requirements were misunderstood
- Changes in the business environment
- New legislation eg Data protection

2.11 The **earlier** a change is made the **less expensive** it should prove. However, changes will cost time and money and should not be undertaken lightly.

2.12 When considering a change **an investigation** should be conducted to discover:

(a) The consequences of **not** implementing the proposed change.
(b) The impact of the change on **time, cost** and quality.
(c) The expected costs and benefits of the change.
(d) The risks associated with the change, and with the status-quo.

Case example

WHY CAN'T WE BUILD SOFTWARE LIKE WE BUILD BUILDINGS?

Introduction

The software development industry has a reputation for poor project performance. This makes many organisations reluctant to undertake large development projects.

The Project Manager's Responsibility

The project manager plays the same role within a software development as they would in a construction project: their aim is to finish the job within time and cost to the quality required.

Get the Right Person for the Job

Just imagine that you have built a garden shed and a passer-by compliments you on your achievement. The passer-by then asks since you've made such a good job of the shed would you build a new three-bedroom house. After all, it will utilise the same materials, just more of them. It's not very likely is it?

Yet many people learned how to use a PC-based database development application such as Microsoft Access, Dbase, or Paradox, and then went on to build 'commercial' systems. In many cases these were not designed to be commercial systems, they just started as a useful place to store information, then grew until they became a vital source of information.

Appropriate Methodology

Every size of building project requires its own set of processes to most cost effectively complete. Software is no different. Applying skyscraper standards to a house will be expensive and result in over-engineering. When setting up a software development project the same rules apply. Select the right methodology and ensure that your developer is experienced with this methodology.

Reusable Components

When building, there is little point in designing non-standard sizes into a building then trying to fit standard components into the design. These components are often as simple as the garage or interior doors, but could well include items which cannot easily be built on site, such as sealed unit double-glazing.

In the software industry, the reuse of code or objects is a relatively recent development. As with buildings, if you are going to use existing components, the design must be created in such a way as to accommodate them. In the early years of software development these components would be simple subroutines which could be copied into the code to perform simple tasks such as date verification. More recently the advent of commercially successful component infrastructures such as CORBA, the Internet, ActiveX or Java Beans, has triggered a whole industry of off-the-shelf components for various domains, allowing you to buy and integrate components rather than developing them all in-house. Reusability shifts software development from programming software (a line at time) to composing software (by assembling components) just as a modern builder does not fabricate their own material but assembles the delivered components.

Responsibility of the Project Manager

The project manager is key to the success of any project and must be able to manage both people and other resources. The key role of the manager is not simply in monitoring progress but is in fixing things when they go wrong. This is the case in both industries.

Create the Environment

The project manager can create a little bit of 'project magic' by establishing a project environment which allows project participants to operate effectively and co-operatively. This type of project environment is significantly more effective than an aggressive environment.

Issue Resolution

In the building industry, the issues that arise are more likely to be physical in nature. If a team is gathered around a hole in the ground or a piece of building which doesn't quite fit, they can start to suggest solutions by measuring, drawing or simply explaining what they think will fix it.

In the software industry, the issues that arise are more likely to be abstract. However, the need for the sponsor to understand the problem is just as important. Any explanation that can be given in terms which mere mortals can understand is worth far more than the exact technical definition, especially if the Sponsor is required to make a decision on how to resolve the issue.

Conclusion

The use of modern methodologies and modelling techniques allows much of the risk of software development to be reduced. The rigorous use of CASE tools applies standards which are as close to regulations the software industry has at present. The development environments, frameworks and object libraries of software developers are gaining in sophistication to a point where many of the risks are already written out of a new development.

It may take a few years to come to terms with the international implications of electronic commerce over the Internet. The changes in taxable revenue of having a business process independent of location will have far-reaching effects. This is likely to be the next challenge of the technology industry.

Adapted from a paper prepared by Synergy International 1999

---

3 THE DEVELOPMENT AND IMPLEMENTATION PROCESS: WHAT CAN GO WRONG

3.1 Problems that occur when implementing a new information system can usually be traced to deficiencies in the development process. The table in paragraph 3.2 outlines some common mistakes that adversely affect the implementation process - and the systems development

Part D: The impact of Information Technology

stage or activity they relate to. (You may wish to refresh your knowledge of the Systems Development Lifecycle by attempting Question 1 below.)

Question 1
Outline the main phases of a 'typical' systems development lifecycle model.

Answer
The SDLC models a disciplined approach to system development. There are six stages, although in practice some stages may overlap. (The stages or activities relevant to paragraph 3.2 are in bold.)

SYSTEMS DEVELOPMENT LIFE CYCLE	
Feasibility study	Briefly review the existing system
	Identify possible alternative solutions
Systems investigation	Obtain details of current requirements and user needs such as data volumes, processing cycles and timescales
	Identify current problems and restrictions
*Systems **analysis***	Consider why current methods are used and identify better alternatives
*Systems **design***	Determine what inputs, processing and storage facilities are necessary to produce the outputs required
	Consider matters such as program design, file design and security
	Prepare a detailed specification of the new system.
*Systems **implementation***	Write (**programming**) or acquire software, **test** it, **convert** files, install hardware and start running the new system
*Review and **maintenance***	Ensure that the new system meets current objectives, and that it continues to do so

The cycle begins again when a review suggests that it is becoming difficult for an installed system to continue to meet current objectives through routine maintenance.

3.2

Stage/activity	Problems
Analysis	The problem the system is intended to solve is not fully understood.
	Investigation of the situation is hindered by insufficient resources.
	User input is inadequate through either lack of consultation or lack of user interest.
	The project team is unable to dedicate the time required.
	Insufficient time spent planning the project.
Design	Insufficient user input.
	Lack of flexibility. The organisation's future needs are neglected.
	The system requires unforeseen changes in working patterns.
	Failure to perform organisation impact analysis. An organisational impact analysis studies the way a proposed system will affect organisation structure, attitudes, decision making and operations. The analysis aims to ensure the system is designed to best ensure integration with the organisation.

Stage/activity	Problems
	Organisational factors sometimes overlooked include: • Ergonomics (including equipment, work environment and user interfaces) • Health and safety • Compliance with legislation • Job design • Employee involvement
Programming	Insufficient time and money allocated to programming. Programmers supplied with incomplete or inaccurate specifications. The logic of the program is misunderstood. Poor programming technique results in programs that are hard to modify. Programs are not adequately documented.
Testing	Insufficient time and money allocated to testing. Failure to develop an organised testing plan. Insufficient user involvement. User management do not review and sign-off the results of testing.
Conversion	Insufficient time and money allocated to data conversion. Insufficient checking between old and new files. The process is rushed to compensate for time overruns elsewhere.
Implementation	Insufficient time, money and/or appropriate staff mean the process has to be rushed. Lack of user training increases the risk of system under-utilisation and rejection. Poor system and user documentation. Lack of performance standards to assess system performance against. System maintenance provisions are inadequate.

Overcoming user resistance

3.3 A recurring theme when examining the reasons for information system failure is user resistance. We will look at specific system building tools and techniques designed to ensure user involvement in the development process, and therefore reduce user resistance, later in this chapter. We will now examine the findings of MIS researchers into the causes of user resistance.

3.4 The three types of theories to explain user resistance are explained in the following table.

Part D: The impact of Information Technology

Theory	Description	Overcoming the resistance
People-oriented	User-resistance is caused by factors internal to users as individuals or as a group. For example, users may not wish to disrupt their current work practices and social groupings.	User training. Organisation policies. Persuasion. User involvement in system development.
System-oriented	User-resistance is caused by factors inherent in the new system design relating to ease of use and functionality. For example, a poorly designed user-interface will generate user-resistance.	User training and education. Improve user-interface. Ensure users contribute to the system design process. Ensure the system 'fits' with the organisation.
Interaction	User-resistance is caused by the interaction of people and the system. For example, the system may be well-designed but its implementation will cause organisational changes that users resist eg reduced chance of bonuses, redundancies, monotonous work.	Re-organise the organisation before implementing the system. Redesign any affected incentive schemes to incorporate the new system. Promote user participation and encourage organisation-wide teamwork. Emphasise the benefits the system brings.

Overcoming implementation risks

3.5 In addition to securing management and user support of the implementation effort, implementation risks can be reduced by anticipating potential implementation problems and developing strategies to avoid or overcome these problems.

3.6 Each project will carry a different level of risk. The way in which a project is managed should be geared to its level of risk. The four techniques that may be used to control the risks inherent within a project are described in the following table.

Technique/ definition	Comment
External integration tools link the world of the implementation team to that of users.	Applicable where projects are relatively unstructured and therefore require user involvement at all stages. Used to obtain user input and commitment to the system design decided on. Examples include: • User involvement on the project team • User steering committees • Formal user review and approval of specifications • User involvement in training and installation

8: Implementing change

Technique/ definition	Comment
Internal integration tools ensure the implementation team operates as a cohesive unit.	Applicable in projects with high levels of technology. Tools should ensure efficient working relationships are established among the (predominantly technical) project team. Examples of formal planning and control tools include: • Selecting a project manager with technical, administrative and people skills • Selecting experienced, technically strong team members • Consultation on key design decisions • Regular team meetings • Using staff with a track record of working well together • Participative management • If a required skill is not available internally purchase it from outside the organisation
Formal planning tools structure and sequence tasks, enabling estimates of resource requirements to be established. **Formal control tools** monitor project progress towards task completion and the fulfilment of goals.	Formal planning and control tools are applicable where projects are structured and have a low reliance on technology. The system design is fixed and relatively simple. These projects are the least risky and therefore most likely to be able to be controlled using formal techniques. Examples include: • Critical path analysis • Gantt charts • Project Evaluation and Review Techniques (PERT) (The formal techniques of project management are covered in detail in Paper 2.1.)

3.7 The three key dimensions that influence project risk are project size, project structure and the level or complexity of the technology involved. The project management tools applicable at various risk levels are shown in the following table (from *Laudon and Laudon*).

Project structure	Technology level	Project size	Degree of risk	Project Management tools
High	Low	Large	Low	High use of formal planning High use of formal control
High	Low	Small	Very low	Medium use of formal planning High use of formal control
High	High	Large	Medium	Medium use of formal planning Medium use of formal control
High	High	Small	Medium-low	High use of internal integration
Low	Low	Large	Low	High use of formal planning High use of formal control High use of external integration
Low	Low	Small	Very low	High use of formal control High use of external integration
Low	High	Large	Very high	High use of internal integration High use of external integration
Low	High	Small	High	High use of internal integration High use of external integration

Part D: The impact of Information Technology

4 SYSTEM BUILDING TOOLS AND TECHNIQUES

The spiral model

4.1 When developing systems where requirements are difficult to specify it is unrealistic to follow a sequential process (such as the SDLC) which relies on getting things correct at each stage of development before starting subsequent activities. In these more complex situations the spiral approach is appropriate.

4.2 The spiral model represents an **evolutionary approach** to systems development. It involves carrying out the same activities over a number of cycles in order to clarify requirements and solutions.

4.3 The first spiral model was developed by *Boehm*. The model is shown below.

Boehm's spiral model

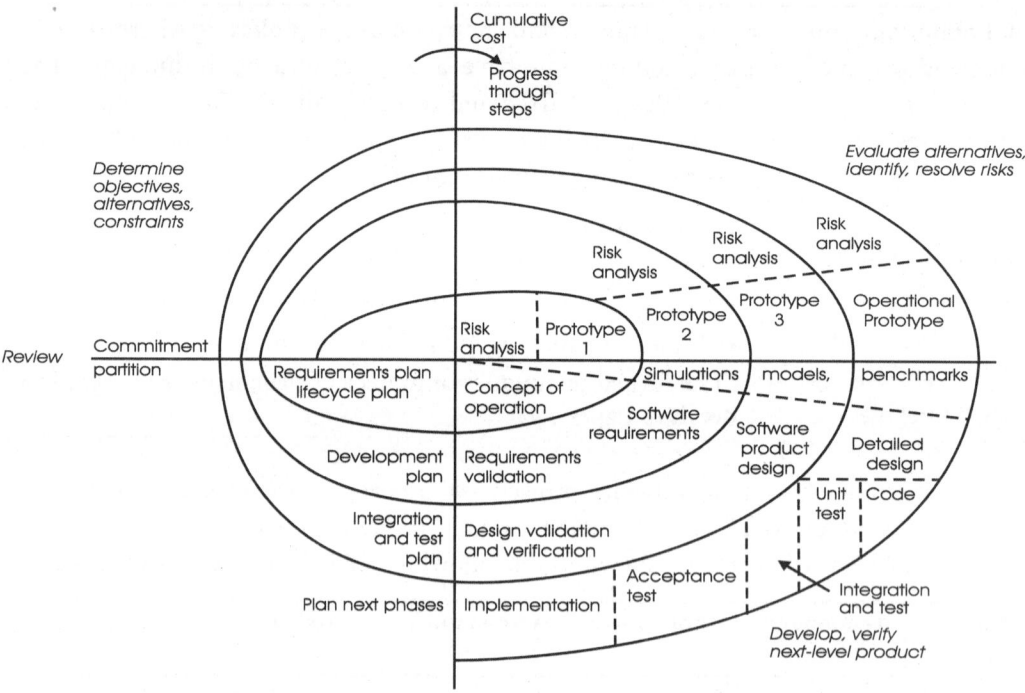

4.4 The development process starts at the centre of the spiral. At the centre requirements are not well-defined. System requirements are refined with each rotation around the spiral. The longer the spiral, the more complex the system and the greater the cost.

4.5 The model is divided into four quadrants.

(a) Top left

- Objectives determined
- Alternatives and constraints identified

(b) Top right

- Alternatives evaluated
- Risks identified and resolved

(c) Bottom right

- System development
- Covers the activities described in the waterfall model (including implementation)

(d) Bottom left

- The next phase in the development process is planned

4.6 The spiral approach aims to avoid the problems of the lifecycle model (lack of user involvement, long delays). It is usually used in conjunction with prototyping which we look at later in this chapter.

Methodologies

4.7 Another way to facilitate systems development is to use a systems development methodology.

> **KEY TERM**
>
> A systems development '**methodology**' is a collection of procedures, techniques, tools and documentation aids which will help systems developers in their efforts to implement a new information system.

Characteristics of methodologies

Characteristic	Comment
Separation of logical and physical	The initial focus is on business benefits – on what the system will achieve (the logical design).
User involvement	User's information requirements determine the type of data collected or captured by the system.
	Users are involved throughout the development process.
Diagrammatic documentation	Diagrams rather than text-based documentation are used as much as possible to ensure the focus is on what the system is trying to achieve – and to aid user understanding of the process.
Data driven	Most structured methods focus on data items regardless of the processes they are related to.
	The type of data within an organisation is less likely to change than either the processes which operate on it or the output information required of it.
Defined structure	Most methodologies prescribe a consistent structure to ensure a consistent and complete approach to the work. For example, the Structured Systems Analysis and Design Method (**SSADM**) suggests five modules: Feasibility, Requirements Analysis, Requirements Specification, Logical Systems Specification and Physical Design.

4.8 *Jayaratna (Understanding and Evaluating Methodologies,* 1994) estimates that there are over 1,000 branded methodologies in use. A popular systems development methodology is the Structured Systems Analysis and Design Method (**SSADM**). This was originally designed for use by the UK Government – but is now widely used in many areas of business.

Part D: The impact of Information Technology

4.9 All methodologies seek to facilitate the '**best**' solution. But 'best' may be interpreted in a number of ways, such as **most rapid** or **least cost**. Some methodologies are highly **prescriptive** and require rigid adherence to stages whilst others are highly **adaptive** allowing for creative use of their components.

4.10 In choosing the **most appropriate methodology**, an organisation must consider the following questions.

- To what extent does the methodology facilitate **participation**?
- Does it generate **alternative solutions**?
- Is it well documented, **tried and tested**?
- Can component tools be selected and used as required?
- Will it facilitate the use of computer-aided tools and prototyping?

Advantages and disadvantages of methodologies

4.11 The **advantages** of using a methodology are as follows.

(a) Detailed **documentation** is produced.

(b) **Standard methods** allow less qualified staff to carry out some of the analysis work, thus **cutting the cost** of the exercise.

(c) Using a standard development process leads to **improved system specifications**.

(d) Systems developed in this way are **easier to maintain and improve**.

(e) **Users are involved** with development work from an early stage and are required to sign off each stage.

(f) The emphasis on **diagramming** makes it easier for relevant parties, including users, to **understand** the system than if purely narrative descriptions were used.

(g) The structured framework of a methodology **helps with planning**. It defines the tasks to be performed, sets out when they should be done and identifies an end product. This allows control by reference to actual achievements rather than to estimates of progress.

(h) A logical design is produced that is **independent of hardware and software**.

(i) Techniques such as data flow diagrams, logical data structures and entity life histories **allow information to be cross-checked** between diagrams and ensure that the system delivered does what is required.

4.12 The use of a methodology in systems development also has **disadvantages**.

(a) It has been argued that methodologies are ideal for analysing and documenting processes and data items at an operational level, but are perhaps **inappropriate for information of a strategic nature** that is collected on an ad hoc basis.

(b) Some are a little **too limited in scope**, being too concerned with systems design, and not with their impact on actual work processes or social context of the system.

(c) Arguably, methodologies encourage excessive documentation and **bureaucracy** and are just as suitable for documenting bad design as good.

Computer Aided Software Engineering (CASE)

4.13 Computer Aided Software Engineering tools are used in systems development to automate some development tasks, such as the production of documentation, and to provide an efficient tool to control developmental activities.

8: Implementing change

> **KEY TERM**
>
> **CASE tools** are software tools used to automate some tasks in the development of information systems eg generating documentation and diagrams. The more sophisticated tools facilitate software prototyping and code generation.

4.14 There are a range of CASE tools available. Some focus on certain phases of development such as analysis and design, others may be used throughout the complete development lifecycle.

4.15 The range of facilities offered by CASE tools are shown in the following table.

Stage of system development project	Possible use of CASE tools
Project initiation	• Generate project schedules in various formats
Analysis and design	• Produce diagrams eg flowcharts, DFDs, ERMs, ELHs • Generate data dictionary
Design (logical and physical)	• Produce system model diagrams • Data structures • Automate screen and report design
Implementation	• Installation schedule • Program code generator
Maintenance	• Version control • Change specification and tracking

4.16 CASE tools can be grouped into Upper CASE tools (sometimes referred to as analysts' workbenches) and Lower CASE tools (sometimes referred to as programmers' workbenches).

Upper CASE tools (analysts' workbenches)

4.17 Upper CASE tools are geared towards automating tasks associated with systems analysis. They include:

(a) **Diagramming tools** that automate the production of diagrams using a range of modelling techniques.

(b) **Analysis tools** that check the logic, consistency and completeness of system diagrams, forms and reports.

(c) A **CASE repository** that holds all data and information relating to the system. The **Data dictionary** records all data items held in the system and controls access to the repository. The dictionary will list all data entities, data flows, data stores, processes, external entities and individual data items.

Lower CASE tools (programmers workbenches)

4.18 Lower CASE tools are geared towards automating tasks later in the development process (after analysis and design). They include:

Part D: The impact of Information Technology

(a) **Document generators** that automate the production of diagrams using a range of modelling techniques.

(b) **Screen and report layout generators** that allow prototyping of the user-interface to be produced and amended quickly.

(c) **Code generators** that automate the production of code based on the processing logic input to the generator.

Advantages of using CASE tools

4.19 Advantages of CASE include the following.

(a) **Document/diagram preparation** and amendment is quicker and more efficient.

(b) **Accuracy of diagrams** is improved. Diagram drawers can ensure consistency of terminology and maintain certain standards of documentation.

(c) **Prototyping** (see later in this section) is made easier, as re-design can be effected very quickly.

(d) **Blocks of code can be re-used**. Many applications incorporate similar functions and processes; blocks of software can be retained in a library and used (or modified) as appropriate.

Examples of CASE tools

4.20 Examples of CASE tools include Select's **SSADM Professional**, Rational's **ClearCase** and **AxiomSys** from STG.

Example 1: Automated diagram production

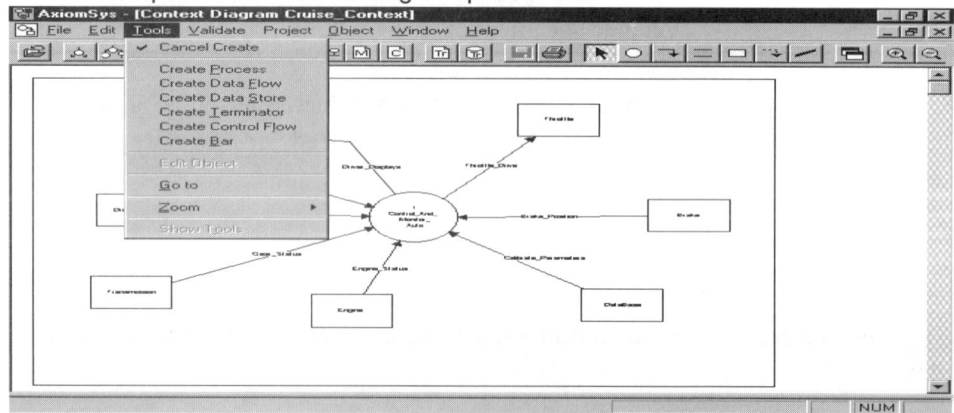

Example 2: Code generating and checking

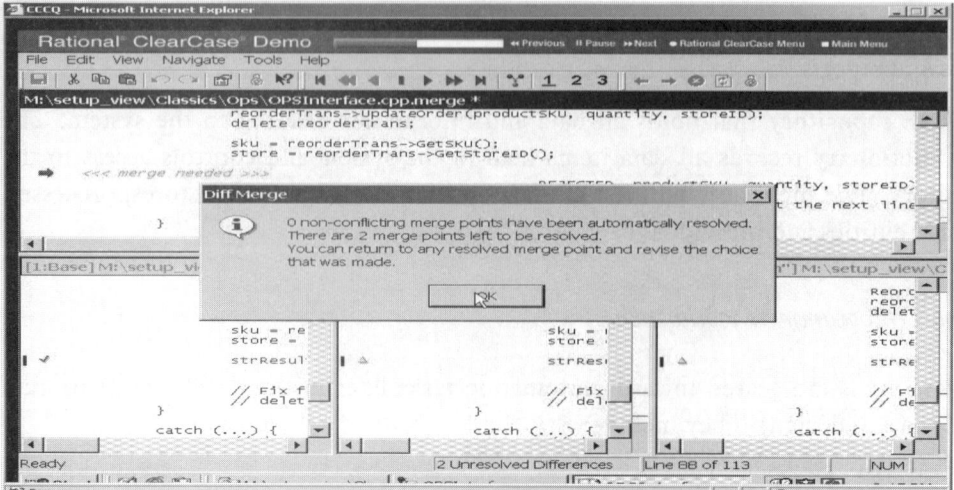

8: Implementing change

Example 3: Version/change control

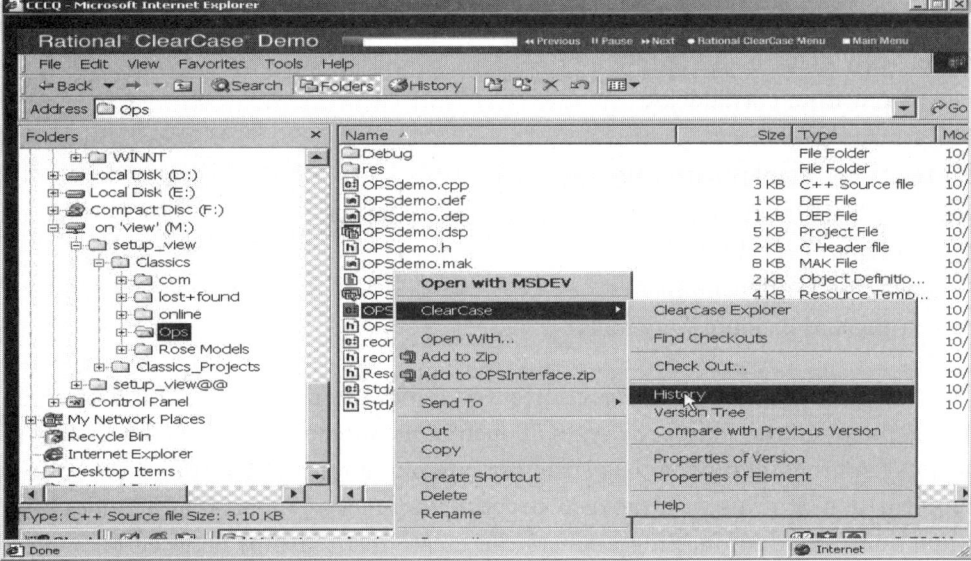

Fourth generation languages (4GLs)

4.21 As computer languages have developed over time, certain types of computer languages have become identified with a generation of languages. The four generations are explained in the following table.

Generation	Comment
First	Machine code. Program instructions were written for individual machines in binary form (a series of 1s and 0s).
Second	Assembly languages. Still machine specific, programs were written using symbolic code which made them easier to understand and maintain.
Third	High-level languages such as COBOL, BASIC and FORTRAN. These languages have a wider vocabulary of words, enabling commands to be closer to everyday language. Programs produced are able to be moved between similar computers.
Fourth	There is no formal definition of a Fourth Generation Language (4GL). Fourth-generation languages are programming languages closer to human languages than typical high-level or third generation languages. Most 4GLs use simple query language such as 'FIND ALL RECORDS WHERE NAME IS 'JONES'

4.22 A fourth generation language is a programming language that is easier to use than languages like COBOL, PASCAL and C++. Well known examples include **Informix** and **Powerhouse**.

> **KEY TERM**
>
> A **Fourth Generation Language (4GL)** is a high-level computer language that uses commands that are closer to everyday speech than previous languages. 4GLs usually also include a range of features intended to automate software production.

4.23 Most fourth generation languages use a graphical user interface. Icons, objects, help facilities, pull down menus and templates present programmers with the options for building the software. Sections of code are often treated as components, which may be used

Part D: The impact of Information Technology

(maybe with slight modifications) in a variety of applications. A 4GL will often include the following features (many of these features could also be provided by a CASE tool).

- Relatively easy to learn and use
- Often centred around a database
- Includes a data dictionary
- Uses a relatively simple query language
- Includes facilities for screen design and dialogue box design
- Includes a report generator
- Code generation is often automated
- Documenting and diagramming tools

4.24 4GLs are often used to facilitate **object-oriented programming**. With object-oriented programming, programmers define the types of operations (functions) that can be applied to data structures (in programming, a data structure refers to a scheme for organising related pieces of information). In this way, the data structure becomes an object that includes both data and functions. In addition, programmers can create relationships between one object and another. For example, objects can inherit characteristics from other objects.

4.25 One of the principal advantages of object-oriented programming techniques over procedural programming techniques is that they enable programmers to create modules that do not need to be changed when a new type of object is added. A programmer can simply create a new object that inherits many of its features from existing objects. This makes object-oriented programs easier to modify (a group of objects with some common properties may be referred to as a **class**).

4.26 4GLs enable a more flexible approach to be taken to software production than under the traditional Systems Development Lifecycle. Using a 4GL, changes to the program design and to the code itself can be made relatively easily and quickly. This allows development to follow a pattern like the Spiral model, with users able to make amendments based on prototypes.

Examples taken from 4GLs

4.27 The following screenshots are taken from the Metamill 4GL.

Example 1: Automated diagram production

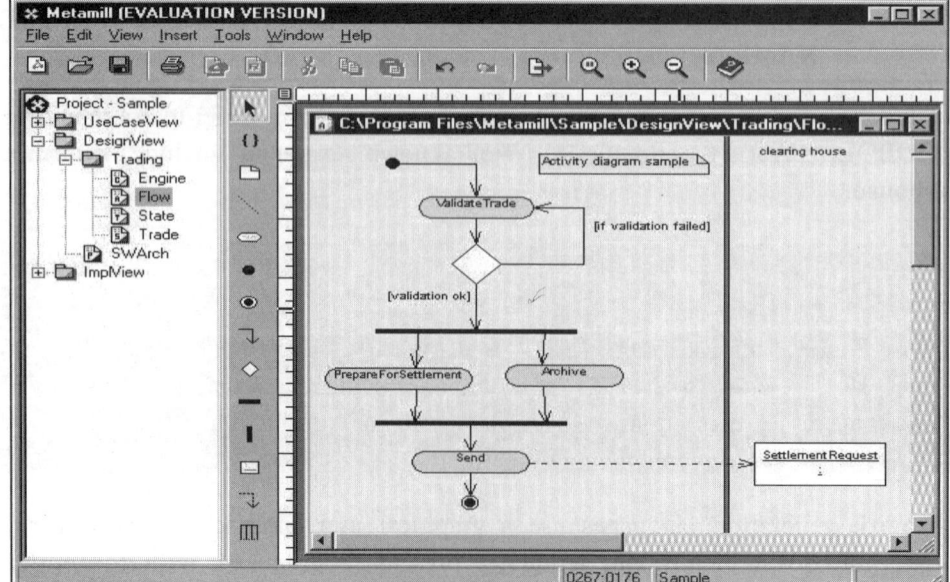

Example 2: Class properties window

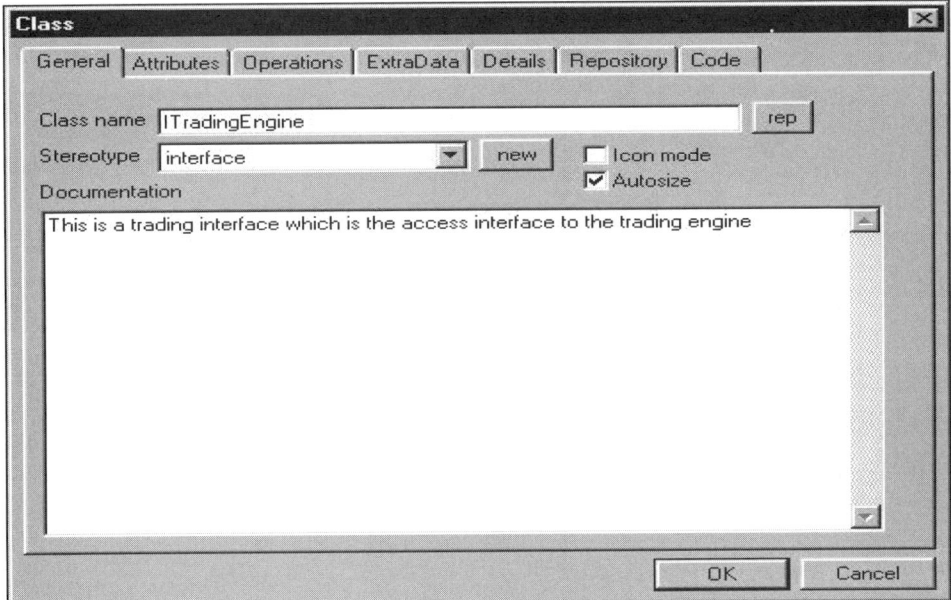

Prototyping

4.28 The use of 4GLs, together with the realisation that users need to see how a system will look and feel to assess its suitability, have contributed to the increased use of **prototyping**.

> **KEY TERM**
>
> A **prototype** is a model of all or part of a system, built to show users early in the design process how it will appear.

4.29 As a simple example, a prototype of a formatted screen output from a system could be prepared using a graphics package, or even a spreadsheet model. This would describe how the screen output would appear to the user. The user could make suggested amendments, which would be incorporated into the next model.

4.30 Using prototyping software, the programmer can develop **a working model of application program quickly**. He or she can then **check with the data user** whether the prototype program that has been designed appears to **meet the user's needs**, and if it doesn't it can be amended. The process is shown in the following flowchart.

The prototyping process

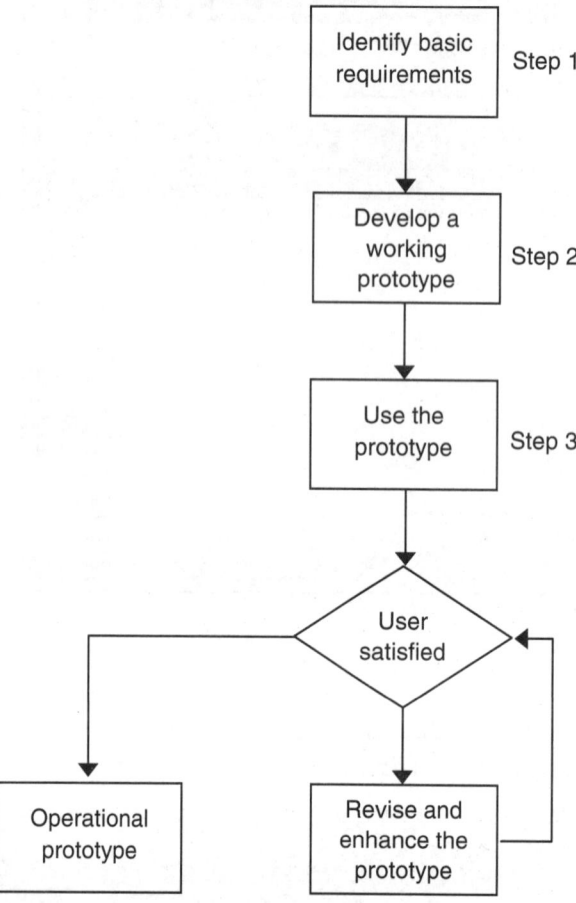

Advantages and disadvantages of prototyping

4.31 The **advantages** of prototyping.

(a) It makes it possible for programmers to present a 'mock-up' version of a proposed system to users **before a substantial amount of time and money** have been committed. The user can judge the prototype before things have gone too far to be changed.

(b) The process facilitates the production of **'custom built'** (bespoke) software rather than off-the-shelf packages which may or may not suit user needs.

(c) It makes **efficient use of programmer time** by helping programmers to develop programs more quickly.

4.32 **Disadvantages** of prototyping.

(a) Some prototyping tools are **tied** to a particular make of **hardware**, or a particular **database system**.

(b) It is sometimes argued that prototyping tools are **inefficient** in the program codes they produce, so that programs are bigger and require more memory than a more efficiently coded program.

(c) Prototyping may help users to steer the development of a new system towards an **existing system**.

(d) As prototyping encourages the attitude that changes and amendments are likely, some believe prototyping tools encourage programmers to produce programs quickly, but to neglect program quality.

Structured walkthroughs

4.33 Structured walkthroughs are a technique used by those responsible for the design of some aspect of a system (particularly analysts and programmers) to present their design to **user representatives** – in other words to 'walk' them through the design. Structured walkthroughs are **formal meetings**, in which the **documentation** produced during development is **reviewed and checked**.

4.34 These presentations are used both to **explain** the new systems to users and also to offer the users the opportunity of **making constructive criticism** of the proposed system and suggestions for further amendments/improvements.

Question 2

What, besides identification of mistakes (errors, omission, inconsistencies etc), would you expect the benefits of a walkthrough to be?

Answer

(a) Users become involved in the systems analysis process. Since this process is a critical appraisal of their work, they should have the opportunity to provide feedback on the appraisal itself.

(b) The output from the development is shown to people who are not systems development personnel. This encourages its originators to prepare it to a higher quality and in user-friendly form.

(c) Because the onus is on users to approve design, they are more likely to become committed to the new system and less likely to 'rubbish' it.

(d) The process focuses on quality of, and good practice in, operations generally.

(e) It avoids disputes about who is responsible for what.

Joint applications development

4.35 Joint Applications Development (JAD) describes the partnership between users and system developers.

4.36 JAD was originally developed by *IBM* to promote a more participative approach to systems development. The potential value to an organisation may be as follows.

(a) It creates a **pool of expertise** comprised of interested parties from all relevant functions.

(b) Reduced risk of systems being **imposed** by systems personnel.

(c) This **increases user ownership** and responsibility for systems solutions.

(d) Emphasises the **information needs of users** and their relationship to business needs and decision making.

4.37 There are a number of possible **risks** affecting the potential value of JAD.

(a) The relative **inexperience of many users** may lead to misunderstandings and possibly unreasonable expectations/demands on the system performance.

(b) The danger of **lack of co-ordination** leading to fragmented, individual, possibly esoteric information systems.

4.38 The shift of emphasis to applications development by end-users must be well managed and controlled. An organisation may wish to set up an **information centre** to provide the necessary support and co-ordination.

4.39 Achieving change requires a **commitment** to change by the people affected by the change. Getting commitment is **expensive**, and calls for an investment of time, effort and money.

Rapid applications development

4.40 **Rapid Applications Development (RAD)** can be described as a quick way of building software. It combines a managed approach to systems development with the use of modern software tools such as **prototyping**. RAD also involves the **end-user** heavily in the development process.

4.41 RAD has become increasingly popular as the pace of change in business has increased. To develop systems that provide competitive advantage it is often necessary to build and implement the system quickly.

4.42 RAD can create difficulties for the project manager as RAD relies to a certain extent on a lack of structure and control.

5 SYSTEM CHANGEOVER AND EVALUATION

System changeover

5.1 Once the new system has been fully and satisfactorily tested the changeover can be made. This may be according to one of four approaches.
- Direct changeover
- Parallel running
- Pilot operation
- Phased or 'staged' changeover

Direct changeover

5.2 The old system is **completely replaced** by the new system **in one move**.

5.3 This may be unavoidable where the two systems are substantially different, or where the costs of parallel running are too great.

5.4 While this method is comparatively **cheap** it is **risky** (system or program corrections are difficult while the system has to remain operational).

5.5 The new system should be introduced during **a quiet period**, for example over a bank holiday weekend or during an office closure.

Parallel running

5.6 The **old and new** systems are **run in parallel** for a period of time, both processing current data and enabling cross checking to be made.

8: Implementing change

5.7 This method provides a **degree of safety** should there be problems with the new system. However, if there are differences between the two systems cross-checking may be difficult or impossible.

5.8 There is a **delay** in the actual implementation of the new system, a possible indication of **lack of confidence,** and a need for **more staff** to cope with both systems running in parallel.

5.9 This cautious approach, if adopted, should be properly planned, and the plan should include.

(a) A firm **time limit** on parallel running.

(b) Details of **which data** should be **cross-checked**.

(c) Instructions on how **errors** are to be dealt with eg previously undiscovered errors in the old system.

(d) Instructions on how to report and act on any **major problems** in the new system.

Pilot operation

5.10 Pilot operation involves selecting part or parts of an organisation (eg a department or branch) to operate running the new system in parallel with the existing system. When the branch or department piloting the system is satisfied with the new system, they cease to use the old system. The new system is then piloted in another area of the organisation.

5.11 Pilot operation is **cheaper** and **easier to control** than running the whole system in parallel, and provides a **greater degree of safety** than does a direct changeover. There are two types of pilot operation.

Phased changeover

5.12 Phased changeover involves selecting a complete section of the system for a direct changeover, eg in an accounting system the purchase ledger. When this part is running satisfactorily, another part is switched – until eventually the whole system has been changed.

5.13 A phased series of direct changeovers is less risky than a single direct changeover, as any problems and disruption experienced should be isolated in an area of operations.

5.14 The relative advantages and disadvantages of the various changeover methods are outlined in the following table.

Method	Advantages	Disadvantages
Direct changeover	Quick	Risky
	Minimal cost	Could disrupt operations
	Minimises workload	If fails, will be costly
Parallel running	Safe, built-in safety	Costly-two systems need to be operated
	Provides way of verifying results of new system	Time-consuming
		Additional workload
Pilot operation	Less risky than direct changeover	Can take a long time to achieve total changeover
	Less costly than complete parallel running	Not as safe as complete parallel running

247

Part D: The impact of Information Technology

Method	Advantages	Disadvantages
Phased changeover	Less risky than a single direct changeover	Can take a long time to achieve total changeover
	Any problems should be in one area – other operations unaffected	Interfaces between parts of the system may make this impractical

Evaluation

5.15 In most systems there is a constant need to maintain and improve applications and to keep up-to-date with technological advances and changing user requirements. A system should therefore be **reviewed** after implementation, and periodically, so that any unforeseen problems may be solved and to confirm that it is achieving the desired results.

5.16 The system should have been designed with clear, specified **objectives**, and justification in terms of **cost-benefit analysis** or other **performance criteria**.

5.17 Just as the feasibility of a project is assessed by reference to **technical, operational, social and economic factors,** so the same criteria can be used for evaluation. We need not repeat material that you have covered earlier, but here are a few pointers.

Cost-benefit review

5.18 A cost-benefit review is similar to a cost-benefit analysis, except that **actual** data can be used.

5.19 For instance when a large project is completed, techniques such as **DCF appraisal** can be performed **again,** with actual figures being available for much of the expenditure.

Question 3

A cost-benefit review might categorise items under the five headings of direct benefits, indirect benefits, development costs, implementation costs and running costs.

Give two examples of items which could fall to be evaluated under each heading.

Answer

Direct benefits might include reduced operating costs, for example lower overtime payments.

Indirect benefits might include better decision-making and the freeing of human 'brainpower' from routine tasks so that it can be used for more creative work.

Development costs include systems analysts' costs and the cost of time spent by users in assisting with fact-finding.

Implementation costs would include costs of site preparation and costs of training.

Running costs include maintenance costs, software leasing costs and on-going user support.

Efficiency and effectiveness

5.20 In any evaluation of a system, two terms recur. Two key reasons for the introduction of information systems into an organisation are to improve the **efficiency** or the **effectiveness** of the organisation.

> **KEY TERM**
>
> **Efficiency** can be measured by considering the resource **inputs** into, and the **outputs** from, a process or an activity.

5.21 An activity uses **resources** such as staff, money and materials. If the same activity can be performed using **fewer resources**, for example fewer staff or less money, or if it can be completed **more quickly**, the efficiency of the activity is improved. An improvement in efficiency represents an improvement in **productivity**.

5.22 Automation of an organisation's activities is usually expected to lead to greater efficiency in a number of areas.

(a) The **cost** of a computer system is lower than that of the manual system it replaces, principally because jobs previously performed by human operators are now carried out by computer.

(b) The **accuracy** of data information and processing is improved, because a computer does not make mistakes.

(c) The **speed** of processing is improved. Response times, for example in satisfying customer orders, are improved.

> **KEY TERM**
>
> **Effectiveness** is a measurement of how well the organisation is achieving its **objectives**.

5.23 Effectiveness is a **more subjective** concept than efficiency, as it is concerned with factors which are less easy to measure. It focuses primarily on the relationship of the organisation with its environment. For example, automation might be pursued because it is expected that the company will be more effective at **increasing market share** or at satisfying **customer needs**.

5.24 Computing was originally concerned with the automation of '**back office**' functions, usually aspects of data processing. Development was concerned with improving **efficiency**.

5.25 Recent trends are more towards the development of '**front office**' systems, for example to improve an organisation's decision-making capability or to seek competitive advantage. This approach seeks to improve the **effectiveness** of the organisation.

Metrics

> **KEY TERM**
>
> **Metrics** are quantified measurements used to measure system performance.

5.26 The use of **metrics** enables **system quality** to be **measured** and the early identification of problems.

5.27 **Examples** of metrics include system response time, the number of transactions that can be processed per minute, the number of bugs per hundred lines of code and the number of system crashes per week.

5.28 Metrics should be devised that **suit the system in question** – those given above are simply typical examples.

5.29 Many facets of system quality are **not easy to measure** statistically (eg user-friendliness). Indirect measurements such as the number of calls to the help-desk per month can be used as an indication of overall quality/performance.

5.30 Metrics should be carefully thought out, objective and stated **clearly**. They must measure **significant aspects** of the system, be used consistently and **agreed with users**.

Performance measurement

5.31 It is not possible to identify and isolate every consequence of a project and the impact of each on organisational effectiveness. To achieve some approximation to a complete evaluation, therefore, certain **indirect measures** must be used.

(a) **Significant task relevance** attempts to observe the results of system use.

For example, document turnround times might have improved following the acquisition of a document image processing system, or minutes of meetings might be made available and distributed faster following the addition of a company secretarial function to a local area network.

(b) The **willingness** of users **to pay** might give an indication of value.

Charge-out mechanisms may provide an indication of how much users would be prepared to pay in order to gain the benefit of a certain upgrade, for example the availability of a particular report.

(c) **Systems logs** may give an indication of the value of the system if it is a 'voluntary use' system, such as an external database.

(d) **User information satisfaction** is a concept which attempts to find out, by asking users, how they rate their satisfaction with a system. They may be asked for their views on timeliness, quality of output, response times, processing and their overall confidence in the system.

(e) The adequacy of system **documentation** may be measurable in terms of how often manuals are actually used and the number of errors found or amendments made. However, low usage of a user manual, for instance, may mean either that the manual is unclear or that the system is easy to operate.

Question 4

Operational evaluation should consider, among other issues, whether input data is properly provided and output is useful. Output documents are often produced simply because 'we always print it'.

How might you identify whether a report is being used?

Answer

You could simply ask recipients if they would object to the report being withdrawn.

A questionnaire could be circulated asking what each recipient of the report does with it and assess its importance.

A charge-out system could be implemented - this would be a strong incentive to cancel requests for unnecessary output.

5.32 **Performance reviews** will vary in content from organisation to organisation, but the matters which will probably be looked at are as follows.

(a) The **growth** rates in file sizes and the number of transactions processed by the system. Trends should be analysed and projected to assess whether there are likely to be problems with lengthy processing time or an inefficient file structure due to the volume of processing.

(b) The clerical **manpower** needs for the system, and deciding whether they are more or less than estimated.

(c) The identification of any **delays** in processing and an assessment of the consequences of any such delays.

(d) An assessment of the efficiency of **security** procedures, in terms of number of breaches, number of viruses encountered.

(e) A check of the **error rates** for input data. High error rates may indicate inefficient preparation of input documents, an inappropriate method of data capture or poor design of input media.

(f) An examination of whether **output** from the computer is being used to good purpose. (Is it used? Is it timely? Does it go to the right people?)

(g) Operational **running costs**, examined to discover any inefficient programs or processes. This examination may reveal excessive costs for certain items although in total, costs may be acceptable.

Improving performance

5.33 **Computer systems efficiency audits** are concerned with improving **outputs** from the system and their use and/or reducing the costs of system **inputs**. With falling costs of computer hardware and software, and continual technological advances, there should often be **scope for improvements** in computer systems.

Outputs from a computer system

5.34 With regard to outputs, the efficiency of a computer system would be enhanced in any of the following ways.

(a) **More outputs** of some value could be produced by the **same input** resources.

For example:

(i) If the system could process **more transactions** per minute.

(ii) If the system could produce **better quality management information** (eg sensitivity analysis).

(iii) If the system could make information **available to more people**.

(b) **Outputs of little value** could be **eliminated** from the system, thus making savings in the cost of inputs, processing and handling.

For example:

(i) If reports are produced **too frequently**, should they be produced less often?
(ii) If reports are **distributed too widely**, should the distribution list be shortened?
(iii) If reports are **too bulky**, can they be reduced in size?

(c) The **timing** of outputs could be better.

Information should be available in good time for the information-user to be able to make good use of it. Reports that are issued late might lose their value. Computer systems could give managers **immediate** access to the information they require, by means of file enquiry or special software (such as databases or spreadsheet modelling packages).

(d) It might be found that outputs are not as satisfactory as they should be, perhaps because:

(i) **Access** to information from the system is limited, and could be improved by the use of a **database** and a **network** system.
(ii) Available outputs are **restricted** because of the **method of data processing** used (eg batch processing instead of real-time processing) or the **type of equipment** used (eg stand-alone PCs compared with client/server systems).

Inputs to a computer system

5.35 The efficiency of a computer system could be improved if the same volume (and frequency) of output could be achieved with **fewer input** resources, and at **less cost**.

5.36 Some of the ways in which this could be done include the following.

(a) **Multi-user** or **network** systems might be more efficient than stand-alone systems.

Multi-user systems allow several input operators to work on the same files at the same time, so that if one person has a heavy workload and another is currently short of work, the person who has some free time can help his or her busy colleague - thus improving operator efficiency.

(b) **Real-time** systems might be more efficient than batch processing.

(c) Using computers and external storage media with **bigger storage** capacity.

A frequent complaint is that 'waiting time' for the operator can be very long and tedious. Computer systems with better backing storage facilities can reduce this operator waiting time, and so be more efficient.

(d) Using more **up-to-date software**.

5.37 Management might also wish to consider whether time spent **checking and correcting** input data can be eliminated. An **alternative method of input** might be chosen. For example bar codes and scanners should eliminate the need to check for input errors.

8: Implementing change

Chapter roundup

- A **systematic approach** should be established, for planning and implementing **changes**.

- Causes of dissatisfaction with information systems include:
    - Poor project management
    - Unrealistic deadline
    - Inadequate planning, monitoring and control
    - Insufficient user involvement
    - Insufficient resources
    - Conflicting requirements (Time, Cost, Quality)

- There are three types of theories to explain **user resistance**. **People-oriented** theory attributes user-resistance to factors internal to users as individuals or as a group. **System-oriented** theory attributes user-resistance to factors inherent in the new system design relating to ease of use and functionality. **Interaction theory** attributes user-resistance to factors related to the interaction of people and the system.

- The four techniques that may be used to control the **risks** inherent within a project are:
    - **External integration tools** link the world of the implementation team to that of users
    - **Internal integration tools** ensure the implementation team operates as a cohesive unit
    - **Formal planning tools** structure and sequence tasks, enabling estimates of resource requirements to be established
    - **Formal control tools** monitor project progress towards task completion and the fulfilment of goals

- **System building tools and techniques** include:
    - The SDLC (sequential)
    - The spiral model (evolutionary)
    - Methodologies (consistent, structured)
    - CASE tools (automate design and documentation)
    - 4GLs (enable quicker programming)
    - Prototyping (enables system to be 'seen' earlier, facilitates user involvement)
    - Structured walkthroughs (involves users)
    - JAD (user-developer partnership)
    - RAD (combines JAD and tools such as prototyping)

- There are four main approaches to system **changeover**.
    - Direct changeover
    - Parallel running
    - Pilot tests
    - Phased or 'staged' implementation

- Ways in which a system can be **evaluated** include:
    - Cost-benefit review
    - Efficiency and effectiveness
    - Metrics
    - System logs
    - User-satisfaction surveys

Part D: The impact of Information Technology

Quick quiz

1   List five general sources of resistance to change.
2   How may people-oriented user resistance be overcome?
3   List three formal project planning and control tools.
4   List five system building tools and techniques.
5   Direct changeover is the most risky system changeover method. TRUE or FALSE?.

Answers to quick quiz

1   [Five of]
    Attitudes or beliefs eg religious, cultural, social influences.
    Loyalty to a group and its norms.
    Habit.
    Politics (in the wider sense).
    The method of change.
    Personalities.
    (*You may have thought of others*)

2   User training, organisation policies, persuasion and user involvement in the development process.

3   Three are: Critical path analysis, Gantt charts, Project Evaluation and Review Techniques (PERT).

4   [Some are listed below - we have provided the brief description to jog your memory regarding the key feature of the tool or technique]
    The SDLC (sequential)
    The spiral model (evolutionary)
    Methodologies (consistent, structured)
    CASE tools (automate design and documentation)
    4GLs (enable quicker programming)
    Prototyping (enables system to be 'seen' earlier, facilitates user involvement)
    Structured walkthroughs (involves users)
    JAD (user-developer partnership)
    RAD (combines JAD and tools such as prototyping)

5   TRUE.

Now try the question below from the Exam Question Bank

Number	Level	Marks	Time
13	Exam	15	27 mins

Chapter 9

THE IMPACT OF IT ON WORK PRACTICES

Topic list	Syllabus reference
1 The impact of IT on organisations	9(a), 9(b)
2 IT and the employee/employer relationship	9(b)
3 Individual information requirements	9(a)
4 Social, political and ethical issues	1(a)

Introduction

The impact of technology on organisations over the last ten years has been dramatic. This chapter explores some of the issues arising from this change.

The chapter concludes with a discussion of the wider ethical issues raised by the increasingly significant role of information technology, and the power of information systems, in today's society.

Study guide

5 – Ethical issues

- Analyse the relationship among ethical, social and political issues raised by the impact of information systems
- Identify the major moral dimensions of an information society
- Apply an ethical analysis to scenarios
- Discuss the design of organisational policies for ethical conduct

26 – Individual's information requirements

- Discuss the use of IT to manage individuals' information requirements
- Identify how information systems can support the tasks of the manager *(Also see Chapter 2)*

27 – Employee/employer relations

- Discuss the impact of IS/IT on employee/employer relations in terms of: Shorter chain of command, flatter organisational structures, wider span of control, de-skilling of operatives
- Describe the concept of socio-technical design in respect to employee/employer relations
- Discuss the organisational development issues resulting from the need to develop and implement information systems

Exam guide

The material covered in this chapter could be applicable to many questions that on first reading have 'nothing to do with ethics or the wider role of IT'. Questions that mention issues such as e-mail monitoring or the distribution of personal information may provide scope for a discussion of wider issues. As always though, answer the question rather than writing a general discussion.

Part D: The impact of Information Technology

1 THE IMPACT OF IT ON ORGANISATIONS

Organisation structure

1.1 Information systems and information technology have played a significant role in the development of the modern business environment. For example, modern communications technology makes decentralised organisations possible, allowing decision making to be passed down to 'empowered' workers or outsourced to external companies.

1.2 There is a trend towards smaller, more agile companies. Flexibility and speed are increasingly seen as the key to competitive advantage. Advances in IT have allowed complex operating processes to be accelerated and made feedback information available almost immediately.

Span of control

1.3 Span of control, or 'span of management', refers to the number of subordinates responsible to a superior. If a manager has five subordinates, the span of control is five.

1.4 Business automation and rationalisation, and improved management information systems, have often resulted in reduced staffing levels. In particular, layers of middle management have been removed in many organisations. Managers or staff 'lower down' the hierarchy have been empowered to make decisions previously made by middle managers. Information technology has therefore had the effect of flattening organisation hierarchies and **widening spans of control**.

1.5 There is no universally 'correct' size for the span of control. The appropriate span of control will depend on:

(a) **Ability of the manager**. A good organiser and communicator will be able to control a larger number. The manager's work-load is also relevant.

(b) **Ability of the subordinates**. The more experienced, able, trustworthy and well-trained subordinates are, the easier it is to control larger numbers.

(c) **Nature of the task**. It is easier for a supervisor to control a large number of people if they are all doing routine, repetitive or similar tasks.

(d) The **geographical dispersal** of the subordinates, and the **communication system** of the organisation.

(e) The availability of **good quality information** to assist in decision making.

Tall and flat organisations

1.6 The span of control has implications for the 'shape' of the organisation. An organisation with a narrow span of control will have more levels in its management hierarchy – the organisation will be narrow and **tall**. A tall organisation reflects tighter supervision and control, and lengthy chains of command and communication.

1.7 An organisation of the same size with a wide span of control will be will be wide and **flat**. The flat organisation reflects a greater degree of delegation - the more a manager delegates, the wider the span of control can be.

9: The impact of IT

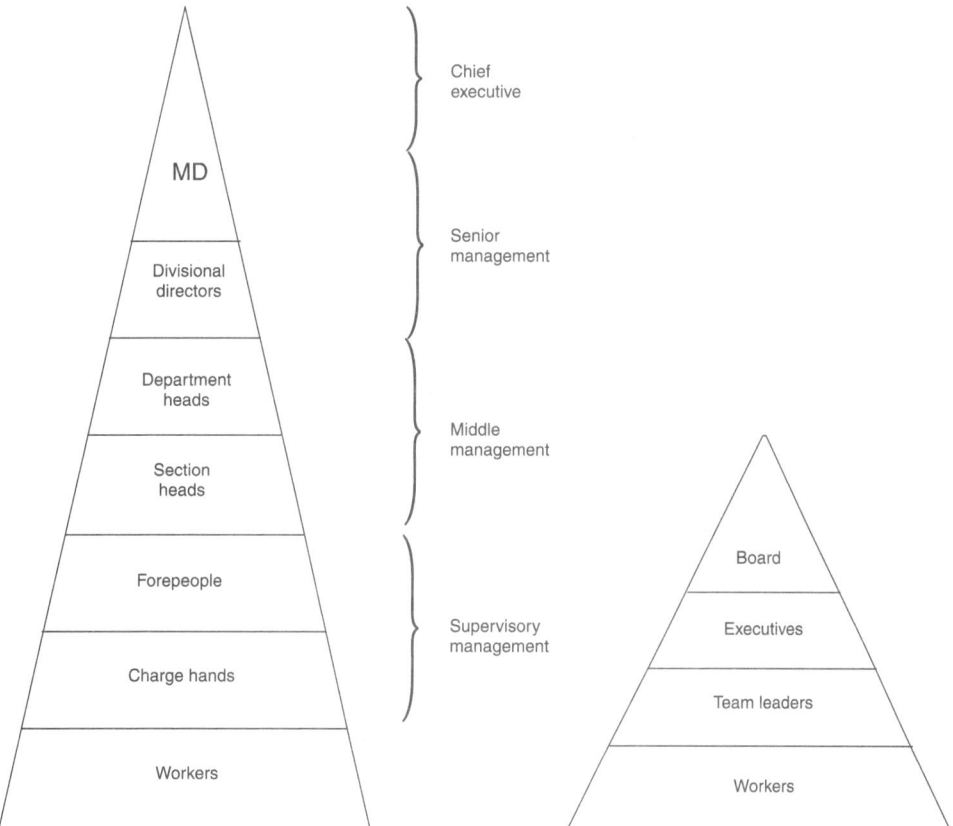

1.8 Some writers argue that tall organisation structures are too **inflexible** for the modern business environment. Disadvantages of tall structures are:

(a) The extra management levels increase costs eg salaries, office accommodation.

(b) They create a longer chain of communication. Management is more remote from operations - information may be distorted or blocked.

(c) Management responsibilities overlap and become confused as the size of the management structure gets larger.

(d) The same work passes through too many hands.

(e) Planning is more difficult because it must be organised at more levels.

(f) The rigid structure can stifle initiative and damage the motivation of subordinates.

(g) There are more 'rungs' available on the promotional ladder, but there are unlikely to be real increases in responsibility between levels.

1.9 The advantages of flat structures are the opposite of the statements above. The disadvantages of flat structures are the loss of management **control** and possible lack of organisation **coherency**. Tall structures may be better suited to situations where rigid supervision and control is required.

1.10 An **information system**, such as an intranet, can help provide organisation unity and coherency in flat, decentralised organisations.

1.11 The trend towards flatter structures is evidenced by talk of an 'e-lance economy', characterised by shifting **coalitions** of small firms collaborating on particular **projects**.

Organisation structure and information systems

1.12 The structure of an organisation and the way in which the organisation's information system is arranged are **related** issues.

Part D: The impact of Information Technology

1.13 **Centralised** systems means holding and processing data in a central place, such as a computer centre at head office. Data will be collected at 'remote' (ie geographically separate) offices and other locations and sent in to the central location.

1.14 **Decentralised** systems have the data/information processing carried out at several different locations, away from the 'centre' or 'head office'.

1.15 As we have emphasised elsewhere in this Text, Information systems strategy **should support the overall business strategy**.

Other effects of IT on organisations

Routine processing

1.16 The processing of data can be done in bigger volumes, at greater speed and with greater accuracy.

Digital information and record keeping

1.17 Information storage and transmission is now largely digital rather than paper-based. However, many people like 'hard copies' and print out information as required. Far from reducing the use of paper, computer systems seem to have encouraged greater use of paper.

1.18 The nature and quality of management information has also changed.

   (a) Managers have access to more information - for example from an ESS. Information is also likely to be more timely, accurate, reliable and up-to-date.

   (b) More detailed planning is possible through the use of models (eg spreadsheets).

   (c) Information for control should be more readily available.

   (d) Decision making should improve as a consequence of better quality information.

Employment issues

1.19 The infiltration of IT into almost every area of business means that the vast majority of employees are now expected to utilise information technology. IT skills are required and new ways of working have emerged.

Technological change

1.20 A reliance on information technology commits an organisation to **continual change**. Systems are likely to be superseded after a few years.

Customer service

1.21 Information technology has enabled organisations to provide better customer service. Customer databases, EDI, extranets, websites, datamining and other systems discussed throughout this book can all be applied to improving service levels.

Interoperability and open systems

1.22 Interoperability means that any party can **share** and **exchange** information and facilities with other parties without having to use the same service provider or technology platform. Interoperability facilitates the formation of strategic alliances and encourages collaboration across organisation boundaries.

9: The impact of IT

1.23 The term 'open systems' is a similar concept to interoperability although it is usually (but not always) used in the context of different systems within the same organisation. An open systems infrastructure supports **organisation-wide functions** and allows for the transfer of information between networks and systems.

Backward compatibility

1.24 Technology is said to be backward compatible if it can use files and data created with an older similar technology. Backward compatibility makes the adaptation of new technologies less risky and less time-consuming - it eliminates the need to start afresh.

Legacy system

1.25 A legacy system is a computer system or application program which continues to be used because of the prohibitive cost of replacing or redesigning it. The implication is that the system is large, monolithic and difficult to modify.

1.26 Legacy software may only run on antiquated hardware, and the cost of maintaining this may eventually outweigh the cost of replacing both the software and hardware. Recent developments in software have been towards systems that can interact with legacy systems - often through an ability to import data from such a system.

Information markets

1.27 The term '**information market**' reflects the growing view that information is a **commodity** which can be bought, sold or exchanged.

1.28 There has been a growing realisation that information is a resource and that it has many of the characteristics of any other resource. A key theme of this syllabus is the benefits which information, properly managed and used, can bring to an organisation.

Developments in communications

1.29 Communications technology is probably having a greater impact on organisational life than computers are at present. **E-mail** provides a quick and **efficient** means of communicating worldwide.

1.30 **Voice mail** systems allow **flexibility** in communication time and location. Computer Telephony Integration (CTI) systems can **route** incoming calls (they can be frustrating, particularly for callers with non-standard enquiries). CTI also enables information about callers to be gathered and stored allowing **personalised** communication.

1.31 Computer conferencing systems and organisation-wide **bulletin boards** encourage **communication** – both formal and **informal**.

1.32 **Video-conferencing** allows face-to-face contact between people who are spread widely across the world. If a video-conference is deemed sufficient, **travel costs** can be reduced.

2 IT AND THE EMPLOYEE/EMPLOYER RELATIONSHIP

2.1 The widespread use of information technology in the workplace has affected the relationship between employers and employees. Some of the effects are explained in the following table.

Effect of IT	Comment
Reduced need to follow the chain-of-command	Information technology allows quick and easy communication between staff at all levels. For example, an employee may be willing to e-mail the managing director, but would be unwilling or unable to telephone him or her.
	Efficient channels of communication that operate independently of the organisation hierarchy reduce the need to pass communications up the chain of command.
Information overload	Computing and communications developments have led to the capture, analysis and transmission of ever-increasing amounts of information. However, only relevant information is useful. An excess of irrelevant information is harmful - a person is more likely to miss or mis-interpret vital information if they are swamped with irrelevant material. We cover approaches to avoiding information overload later in this chapter.
	Some would argue that information overload has caused significant employee **stress**.
Nature of work	Technology has enabled the automation of many unskilled and semi-skilled tasks. This has resulted in the degrading of old skills and the requirement for employees to learn new skills.
	Some employees have found the change to well-established working patterns extremely stressful. Others have preferred to take redundancy or early retirement.
	Employers may need to provide training and re-training programs for staff.
	As technology becomes more user-friendly there could be opportunities for greater flexibility and job rotation.
Close business relationships regardless of geographical location	Information technology enables people located all over the world to enjoy close working relationships.
	Technology enables operations to be sited anywhere in the world. For example, many 'UK' call centres are based in India. To enable staff to make 'small talk' with UK-based clients, staff keep up-to-date with UK news, weather, sport and even soap operas via the Internet.
More flexible working arrangements	Advances in technology mean many tasks are able to be performed off-site. The need for flexibility in employee and employer attitudes has resulted in trends away from 'a job for life', towards shorter terms of service, freelance workers and contracting. Part-time positions are increasing.
	We look at homeworking later in this chapter.
Greater monitoring and control	Improved information systems should help managers to plan and control work more effectively.
	Technology also enables untrusting employers to monitor employee behaviour. <ul><li>Closed-circuit cameras are now relatively cheap and easy to operate</li><li>Personal e-mail sent using the organisation's server can be monitored</li><li>Computer Telephony Integration (CTI) systems record phone numbers called and the call length</li></ul>
	Privacy laws regarding such activities differ from country to country. In many countries relevant law is still developing.

Remote working or homeworking

2.2 Some employers have encouraged **remote working** or **home working**, sometimes in conjunction with a move towards a pool of **freelance workers**. Developments in information technology (eg e-mail) allow these workers to be based off-site, often at home. Homeworking is sometimes known as **telecommuting**.

2.3 The **advantages to the employer** of homeworking include:

- Cost savings on office accommodation
- A larger potential pool of employees eg those with young children
- Flexibility - if homeworkers are freelance who work only when required

2.4 The **advantages to the employee** include:

- No time is wasted commuting
- Work can be organised around other commitments
- In some situations there may be less distractions out of the office

2.5 The **disadvantages for employers** are chiefly problems of **control**. Managers who like to practise close supervision and who lack trust in their employees may view homeworking as an opportunity for laziness.

2.6 The problems of control depend to a large extent on the individual involved. Other issues for the organisation might be as follows.

- Co-ordination of the work of different homeworkers
- Training – where and when will training be performed?
- Culture – homeworkers are relatively isolated from organisation cultural influences

2.7 Problems for homeworkers include:

- Isolation
- Domestic intrusions
- Adequate space
- If contracting or freelance, fewer employment rights

Case example

Flexibility (and trust) is required for homeworking arrangements to succeed.

For example, BPP authors are able to work from home two days per week. The arrangement works well as the work performed by authors is relatively self-contained. However, when a book is nearing completion, final corrections pass fairly regularly between writers and the typesetting studio.

At this stage of the process homeworking is not practical as it would slow down production.

Sociotechnical design

2.8 The way in which information systems are designed can impact on the employer-employee relationship. While modern system building approaches attempt to ensure end-user input into system design this input tends to focus on operational aspects of the system.

2.9 Sociotechnical design looks at the wider picture. It recognises that an organisation is a **sociotechnical** system, consisting of three sub-systems.

(a) A formal **structure**.

(b) A **technological system** consisting of the work to be done, and the machines, tools and other facilities available to do it.

(c) A **social system** consisting of the people within the organisation, the ways they think and the ways they interact with each other.

> **KEY TERM**
>
> **Sociotechnical design** attempts to produce information systems that are technically efficient but also take into account organisational and staff needs.

2.10 Sociotechnical design gives users a say in the design of the information system and a say in the **role of information systems** in their workplace. A sociotechnical design plan would include human factors such as work group structures and job satisfaction. Technical and social factors are considered together and the alternative that best meets technical **and social** objectives is selected..

2.11 By ensuring organisational and social objectives are considered, employers are **reducing the risk** of a new system causing unforeseen disruption. In particular, employee acceptance of the system should be increased.

2.12 Before adopting a sociotechnical approach employers must be sure that they do wish to take employees' views into account. To solicit employee views, and then **ignore** them, is likely to cause **resentment** and increase the risk of employee rejection of the system.

2.13 'Human issues' a sociotechnical approach could consider include:

- The skills required to operate the system and the skills of employees
- Task variety - ensuring monotonous tasks are spread around
- Autonomy - ensuring supervision and monitoring levels are not oppressive
- Ergonomics and employee health and safety issues (eg breaks from VDU work)
- User interface design

3 INDIVIDUAL INFORMATION REQUIREMENTS

Critical success factors

> **KEY TERM**
>
> **Critical success factors** are a small number of key operational goals vital to the success of an organisation.

3.1 We discussed critical success factors (CSFs) in Chapter 2 in the context of determining the information requirements of an organisation. We will now look at how CSFs can be used to establish the information needs of individual managers.

3.2 The organisational CSFs that an individual manager is responsible for should be the driving force behind the manager's information needs. The process is summarised as follows.

Step 1. Interview managers to obtain their Critical Success Factors.

Step 2. Aggregate individual CSFs to establish organisational CSFs.

Step 3. Determine the performance indicators used to monitor each CSF (explained in Chapter 2).

Step 4. Determine what information is required to track each performance indicator.

Step 5. Review information and information systems to establish if this information is available.

Step 6. Take action to provide any missing information (eg system amendments, new systems).

Step 7. Provide each individual manger with a summary of the information that will be provided to support the CSFs they are responsible for.

Information overload and intelligent agents

3.3 Many managers complain that they receive too much irrelevant information. There are two main approaches to avoiding information overload. Firstly, the **characteristics of the information** need to be considered (remember the ACCURATE mnemonic from Chapter 1). Secondly the **number of information sources** feeding an individual can be managed.

Limiting the number of information sources

3.4 The approach taken to limiting the sources of information will depend on the situation. In some instances it may be sufficient to implement temporary measures to **delay** non-urgent information reaching a person at a particularly busy time. Other situations may require a **permanent change** to information flows. Some examples are shown in the following table.

3.5

Limiting tool	Comment
Delegate to colleagues	Communications regarding certain issues may be dealt with by others within the organisation. For example, routine client contact could be delegated to junior staff, and only strategic issues referred 'up the chain'.
Review reports received for duplication	Regular reviews of information received should be made. If information is duplicated one source should be deleted. The review should also consider what information would best be received together to aid interpretation.
Re-route incoming telephone calls	A secretary could be allocated to take telephone messages, putting through only calls of significance that require immediate attention. To be effective, the instructions concerning calls that should be put through, and how messages should be relayed must be specific.
Voice-mail	While voice-mail can be frustrating when trying to reach someone, it may be useful to temporarily divert calls to voice-mail when work pressures require no interruptions - and no other staff are available to divert calls to.

Part D: The impact of Information Technology

Limiting tool	Comment
Filter incoming e-mail	E-mail programs have the ability to review and re-direct messages based on the message content, priority, sender and/or intended recipients. Non-selected messages may be copied to a selected person, or redirected to a non-urgent inbox to be dealt with later.
Use an Internet news-clipping service	A person may face a constant stream of industry-related journals. These should be reviewed for relevant information - a time-consuming process. However, a news-clipping service could review relevant journals and newspapers on the Internet, and forward via e-mail copies of articles that meet user-defined criteria.
Use intelligent agents	These are discussed below.

KEY TERM

Intelligent agents are programs that perform tasks such as retrieving and delivering information and automating repetitive tasks.

3.6 **Intelligent agent** software can be applied to monitor an individual's use of a computerised system and 'learn' what the user wants, and does not want, to know from what he does day-by-day.

3.7 Although the theory behind agents has been around for some time, agents have become more prominent with the growth of the Internet. Many companies now sell software that enables you to **configure an agent to search the Internet** for certain types of information.

3.8 The term **intelligent agent** is used to denote a computer system that has the following properties.

(a) **Autonomy**: agents operate without direct intervention.

(b) **Social ability**: agents interact with other agents and people.

(c) **Reactivity**: Agents perceive their environment and respond to changes that occur in it.

(d) **Pro-activeness**: agents do not only act in response to their environment, they are able to exhibit goal-directed behaviour by **taking the initiative**.

3.9 **Interface agents** are computer programs that employ artificial intelligence techniques in order to provide assistance to a user dealing with a particular application. A fairly crude example is the Office Assistant within Microsoft Office.

3.10 An **information agent** is able to collate and manipulate information obtained from various sources to meet parameters set by users and other agents. The information sources may include traditional databases or Internet searches.

Case example

Intelligent software agents – an attempt at classification

The following are examples of developed, ready-to-run, agent software that may be used on a company intranet to enhance information retrieval and knowledge management. Agents may be categorised as:

9: The impact of IT

Interface agents

Interface agents are used to decrease the complexity of the increasingly sophisticated and overloaded information systems available. They may add speech and natural language understanding to otherwise dumb interfaces, or add presentation ability to systems.

System agents

System agents run as integrated parts of operating systems or network protocol devices. They help managing complex distributed computing environments by doing hardware inventory, interpreting network events, managing backup and storage devices, and performing virus detection. These agents do not primarily work with end-user information.

Advisory agents

Advisory agents are used in (complex) help or diagnostics systems.

Filtering agents

Filtering agents are used to reduce information overload by removing unwanted data, ie data that does not match the user's profile, from the input stream. Simple versions are built-in to many e-mail clients and Agentware and InfoMagnet provide a more general kind of server-based filtering capabilities.

Retrieval agents

Retrieval agents search and retrieve information and serves as information brokers or documents managers. Many products claim to be retrieval agents, including the client-based AT1, BullsEye, Go-Get-It, Got-It, Surfbot, and WebCompass, and the server-based Agentware and InfoMagnet.

Navigation agents

Navigation agents are used to navigate through external and internal networks, remembering short-cuts, pre-load caching information, automatically bookmarking interesting sites. IBM's Web Browser Intelligence (WBI - pronounced Webby) is an example.

Monitoring agents

Monitoring agents provide the user with information when particular events occur, such as information being updated, moved, or erased. Enterprise Minder does this but is no agent. WBI from IBM has this as a feature, as do BullsEye and SmartBookmarks.

Recommender agents

Recommender agents are usually collaborative; they need many profiles to be available before an accurate recommendation can be made. Examples are Agentware, Firefly, and GroupLens, which are all server-based. Learn Sesame is an exception that is user-oriented and bases its conclusion on the user's previous behaviour.

Profiling agents

Profiling agents are used to build dynamic sites with information and recommendations tailored to match each visitor's individual taste and need. The main purpose is to build customer loyalty and profitable one-to-one relationships. Available examples are Agentware, Firefly, and GroupLens on the server side. Learn Sesame and IBM's Knowledge Utility also do this but on a user-oriented level.

3.11 Agents are an example of **'push' technology.** Instead of searching through large quantities of information to find what is relevant, selected information is 'pushed' to the user. Newsclipping services, that search selected publications for articles that meet user-defined criteria, work on similar principles.

4 SOCIAL, POLITICAL AND ETHICAL ISSUES

4.1 In this section we look at the social, political and ethical issues raised by the impact of information systems.

Part D: The impact of Information Technology

Social issues

4.2 The growing influence of information systems is part of a larger trend towards an accelerated **pace of change** in modern society.

4.3 To put this in perspective, consider the following.

The first wave

4.4 When the world changed from a **hunting and gathering culture** to an **agricultural age**, lifestyles changed and the speed of life accelerated. Old definitions and institutions collapsed and new ones took their place.

4.5 The agricultural age defined wealth as **land and property**. Little changed from generation to generation. You looked to the past as a guide to the future. The family farm was the focal point of everyday life. Values revolved around the church and the family.

The second wave

4.6 A **second wave** occurred when the world changed due to the **industrial revolution**. Again, the speed of life changed, human attitudes and patterns of interaction changed, and old power structures were replaced by the new.

4.7 **Wealth** in the industrial age was based on **capital goods made from raw materials**. Those who owned and manipulated the raw materials and their products gained power and affluence. The future was defined by the present. The influence of the extended family was reduced; the nuclear family becoming dominant.

4.8 The concept of the **'job'** was also invented by the industrial age. It pulled the children off the farms to the cities. A job required an employee to be at a certain place for a set amount of time, to do repetitive tasks, and to 'work' at producing things that were not immediately relevant to the individual's life in exchange for wages.

4.9 The industrial age saw the creation of vacations, health insurance, and sick days. Some found this change traumatic and resisted. Respect for the wisdom of the elders of the society declined as their power was bypassed; they no longer controlled the source of wealth, and their knowledge was irrelevant to the new age.

The third wave

4.10 The **third wave** is the present change from the industrial age to the **communications** age or **information society**. As this shift occurs, we can expect life to speed up even more and we can anticipate new patterns of human interaction.

4.11 We can see evidence of the new age. The average life cycle of a business is now only seven years. Technologies are being superseded before they have been fully implemented eg WAP.

4.12 The communications age looks to the future to decide what needs to be done. The world is changing so fast that businesses must attempt to predict the future.

4.13 **Wealth** in the information society is linked to **knowledge**. The rich and powerful of our era will be those who find ways to turn raw data into usable knowledge. This generation needs creative, inventive, imaginative people. Technology is not just a collection of fun toys, a playground for nerds, it is livelihood, wealth, and well-being. Just as the concept of the 'job'

was an industrial age concept, there is evolving a new entity. The structure of '**jobs**' is reducing as the industrial age fades.

Social changes

4.14 The increased pace of change requires visions of the future to be rapidly adaptable, that long-range plans be flexible, and that we build in mechanisms for adjusting to change. The society of the future will need people who are open-minded, tolerant and **flexible**.

4.15 People are becoming exposed to much greater volumes of information. It is estimated the amount of information in the world is doubling every seven years. It is no longer adequate to learn something once. Skills and knowledge must be **continually updated** to keep up with new developments.

4.16 New communication tools are destroying old power structures. As knowledge flows it empowers consumers. Consumers can scan the world for the best deals.

4.17 The Internet allows people to self-educate. The individual is empowered, particularly the individual who is flexible, self-motivated, and who has strong data-gathering and organisational skills.

4.18 Some commentators believe the information age will allow for greater individual choice, decentralisation of power (less centralised planning), a reduced urban population, a change from top-down leadership to lateral leadership, and a faster rate of adopting and dropping identities as jobs change frequently.

4.19 The following social phenomena are made possible by developments in information technology.

   (a) **Reduced urban congestion**

   People can obtain what they want without leaving their desk. This should make shops and roads less crowded. In the long-term it may affect where people choose to live.

   (b) **Consumer choice**

   A computer search for an item or service can be done in seconds, whereas it could take hours, days or weeks to find exactly what was wanted by more conventional means. Consumers are also not restricted to local providers: they can do business with any company in the world that has a website. On the one hand this increases choice for consumers, but on the other it may make the purchase decision more difficult, because there are more options.

   (c) **The 'size' of society**

   Following on from point (b), society itself becomes global. People do business in places and with organisations that they would never have considered or even known about before.

   (d) **Time management and quality of life**

   Rather than being restricted to business hours, people can obtain what they want 24 hours a day. This helps people to manage their time and do what they want to do at their own convenience.

   (e) **Interaction**

   Instead of dealing face-to-face or voice-to-voice with others, people interact with their computer. If human contact is valued, this makes the experience a poorer one. On the

Part D: The impact of Information Technology

other hand it removes some possible sources of conflict.

(f) **Work opportunities**

There will be fewer opportunities for people who are not IT literate. Automated tools may decrease the number of sales roles that involve direct contact with others. There may be greater opportunities to work in call centres and distribution related roles.

Privacy

4.20 Within industry and commerce there are two important categories of privacy; consumer privacy and employee privacy.

4.21 **Consumer privacy** considers the information compiled by data collectors such as marketing firms, insurance companies and retailers, the use of credit information collected by credit agencies and the rights of the consumers to control information about themselves and their commercial transactions.

4.22 The extensive sharing of personal data is an erosion of privacy that reduces the capacity of individuals to retain control of factors which may affect their lives. Organisations involved in such activities have a responsibility to ensure privacy rights are upheld. The problems involved in the transfer of consumer data include:

- The potential for combining data to create detailed profiles of individuals
- The potential for data to be sold to unscrupulous vendors
- Problems correcting inaccurate information

4.23 **Employee privacy** deals primarily with the growing reliance on electronic monitoring and other mechanisms to analyse work habits and measure employee productivity. An important employee right is the right to control or limit access to personal information provided to an employer.

4.24 In the modern workplace there are increasing opportunities to monitor activity. Potential problem areas include:

- Programs that allow user files and directories to be monitored
- Systems that enable interception and scrutiny of communications
- Monitoring programs that track worker productivity and work habits
- Computer controlled close circuit television (CCTV) surveillance systems

Political issues

4.25 One of the main political issues of the information age is the extent to which governments should 'interfere' or legislate in the new environment. Some relevant political issues are outlined in the following table.

9: The impact of IT

Issue	Comment
Privacy	Privacy is not just a social issue – it also has political consequences. The power of computer systems makes them a threat to the privacy of the individual. Increasingly, decisions are made about individuals on the basis of information held on computerised systems.
	As a result, most countries have introduced legislation designed to protect the individual. In the UK the current legislation is the Data Protection Act 1998. (Data Protection legislation is covered in detail in Paper 2.1).
	Key points of the UK Act are:
	Data users have to register with the Data Protection Registrar.
	Individuals (data subjects) are awarded certain legal rights.
	Data holders must adhere to the data protection principles.
Prosperity	For a modern economy to prosper the information systems operating in that country need to be of good quality.
	Governments therefore have a vested interest in the standard of systems operating and being developed.
	It is not uncommon for governments to sponsor schemes encouraging higher standards in software development, and to encourage the adoption of best practices such as those recommended by the International Standards Organisation (ISO).
Property rights	Software, knowledge and other intellectual property is often reasonably easy to duplicate.
	Copyright (protection from copying a particular product) and patent (the right to develop an underlying idea) laws apply to software.
	There is difficulty enforcing laws to protect software. Copyright is usually asserted within the software licence agreement. However, 'Corporate Over-Use' - the installation of software packages on more machines than there are licences for - is common. The length of time it takes to patent an idea is too slow to be of use to software developers.
	The Internet means property stored in digital format can be transferred anywhere in the world in seconds. Any possible action against abusers of property rights is then complicated by differing international laws.
	Software suppliers are now trying to protect themselves and change attitudes towards software piracy. Organisations such as the Federation Against Software Theft (FAST) have encouraged the reporting of illegal software use within the business community. However, prosecutions are still reasonably rare compared to the extent of the problem. The software industry also believes penalties are inadequate.

Part D: The impact of Information Technology

Issue	Comment
Equality	To prosper in the information society people need access to information, knowledge and information technology.
	This phenomena has the potential to disenfranchise those who are unable or unwilling to learn how to use the new technologies. The potential of lower income groups being bypassed by technological developments has led to fears of the development of a permanent underclass.
	Government initiatives may be required to ensure all sectors of society are given the opportunity to develop the skills required in the information age.

4.26 The UK government's paper *Our Information Age* highlights the importance of capitalising on the opportunities of the information age to improve people's quality of life, their education and the UK's wider industrial competitiveness. It takes the view that information technology is central to these aims and undertakes that new developments in communications and computing will be reflected in proposals to help modernise government. The Government's approach is based around five central themes: transforming education, widening access, ensuring competition and competitiveness, fostering quality and modernising Government.

Case example

Technology Breeds (and Solves?) Uncertainty

Economists are struggling to cram the value of new technologies and services into the models they rely upon for forecasting. That the man responsible for monetary policy is fretting about the limits of his tools is worrisome at a moment when the US economy is on the threshold of recession.

Technology products have extremely short life cycles and often are more valuable when they are combined to provide services (such as high-speed corporate networks) than they are as stand-alone products.

Economists used to be more confident in their forecasting skills. For a while in the 1960s we were increasingly mesmerised by the possibilities of econometric models as a crystal ball, However, we soon learned that the economic structure did not hold still long enough to capture its key relationships.

Ironically, technology can help dig economists out of the hole that technology has put them in. For example, technology might let economists gather data on transactions in near real time. Sampling electronic point-of-sale systems in stores could yield amazingly fast retail sales figures.

As the Nasdaq bubble has shown, people have been very confused by technology's impact. But now that we understand that we have been in a cloud, we can better harness technology to help us find a way out. When we emerge, what lies ahead could be an era of clarity where technology finally enhances our knowledge more than it promotes and then confounds our speculation.

Business 2 daily insight March 28 2001

Ethical issues

KEY TERM

Ethics is concerned with judgements about whether human behaviour is morally right or wrong.

4.27 The ability that information systems have to change the way in which businesses and society operates mean that they are a powerful cause of change. The power and potential of information systems, and the general tend towards businesses being expected to act ethically, has led to discussion regarding the ethical use of information systems.

Ethical analysis

4.28 The ethical factors relevant to a business situation or scenario depend on the particular circumstances involved. There are however five concepts relating to ethical questions:

Ethical concept	**Comment**
Accountability	Individuals and organisations are accountable for their actions (including their actions regarding the information they hold).
Responsibility	Individuals and organisations are accountable for their actions. Those who make a decision should consider and take responsibility for the consequences of that decision. The wider effects of the decision should be given due consideration.
Liability	Those who breach ethical norms should be liable to punishment, and those who have suffered as a result of a breach should be compensated.
Legal process	There should be a mechanism to ensure laws are applied and enforced fairly and correctly.

4.29 The concepts described above may be relevant to ethical situations in business (or in examinations). When faced with a scenario that has ethical implications, the following approach may help you identify and explore the relevant issues.

Step 1. Separate facts from judgements.

Step 2. Identify the ethical issues requiring judgement.

Step 3. Identify the key stakeholders and their vested interests.

Step 4. Identify the options available.

Step 5. Evaluate these options and their consequences, including the wider, ethical consequences.

Step 6. Is a compromise required/available?

Step 7. Decide, communicate and implement the most appropriate course of action.

4.30 Ethical judgements will vary, depending on who is making the judgement. We will look at **three examples** relating to the use of information systems.

(a) Suppose a university's computer is used for sending an e-mail message to a friend or for conducting a full-blown private business (billing, payroll, inventory, etc.). An observer could say that both activities are unethical (while recognising a difference in the amount of wrong being done). Another might say that the latter activities were wrong because they tied up too much memory and slowed down the machine, but the e-mail message wasn't wrong because it had no significant effect on operations.

(b) A university lecturer uses her account to acquire the current grade average of a student from a class which she instructs. She obtained the password for this restricted information from someone in the Records Office who erroneously thought that she was the student. An observer could say that the instructor acted wrongly, since the only person who is entitled to this information is the student. Another may ask why the instructor wanted the information. If she replied that she wanted it to be sure that her grading of the student was consistent with the student's overall academic performance record, some may agree that such use was acceptable.

(c) At a particular university, if a professor wants an e-mail account, all she or he need do is request one but a student must obtain faculty sponsorship in order to receive an account. Some observers may think this policy perfectly acceptable. Someone else may, on the other hand, question what makes the two situations essentially different (e.g. are professors assumed to have more need for e-mail than students? Are students more likely to cause problems?

There are no right or wrong answers to such questions, as in 'grey areas' moral and ethical judgements depend on who is making them.

Question 1

Here are questions covering a variety of issues that may arise in connection with the use of IT.

- Is personal e-mail private?
- Is it necessary to encrypt e-mail files?
- Is it appropriate to read someone else's computer files without permission?
- Is it acceptable to copy computer programs or data files?
- Is material on the Internet free?

Think about the relevant issues from the points of view of: the organisation that owns the system; the individual accessing the system or information; and (where applicable) the individual whose privacy could be invaded.

Exam focus point

A question in December 2002 required candidates to identify the social and ethical issues arising from implementing a home-based telesales system.

Chapter roundup

- Information systems and information technology have played a significant role in the development of the modern business environment including encouraging the **flattening** of **organisation hierarchies** and widening **spans of control**.

- Other **effects of IT on organisations** include:
    - Routine processing (bigger volumes, greater speed, greater accuracy)
    - Digital information and record keeping
    - New skills required and new ways of working
    - Reliance on IT
    - New methods of communication and of providing customer service
    - Interoperability (encourages collaboration across organisation boundaries) and open systems
    - The view of information as a valuable resource
    - The view of information as a commodity which can be bought, sold or exchanged ('information market')

- The widespread use of information technology in the workplace has affected the relationship between **employers and employees**:
    - Reduced need to follow the chain-of-command
    - Information overload
    - Nature of work
    - Close business relationships regardless of geographical location
    - More flexible working arrangements
    - Greater monitoring and control

- **Sociotechnical design** attempts to produce information systems that are technically efficient but also take into account organisational and staff needs.

- **Critical success factors** (CSFs) can be used to establish the **information needs** of individual managers.

- To avoid **information overload**, only good quality information should be communicated (ACCURATE mnemonic). The number of information sources feeding an individual can be managed.
    - Delegate to colleagues
    - Review reports received for duplication
    - Re-route incoming telephone calls
    - Voice-mail
    - Filter incoming e-mail
    - Use an Internet news-clipping service
    - Use intelligent agents

- **Ethics** is concerned with judgements about whether human behaviour is morally right or wrong.

- Information systems are a powerful cause of **change**. The power and potential of information systems, and the general tend towards businesses being expected to act ethically, has led to discussion regarding the **ethical use of information systems**. Relevant issues include:
    - Responsibility
    - Liability
    - Fairness
    - Equality
    - Intellectual property
    - Accountability
    - Legal process
    - Privacy
    - Prosperity

Part D: The impact of Information Technology

Quick quiz

1. List five factors that should be considered when considering an appropriate span of control.
2. Define interoperability.
3. 'Information overload is not a serious problem More information is better than less.' Do you agree? Briefly justify your answer.
4. A sociotechnical system consists of three sub- systems. Name them.
5. Distinguish between consumer privacy and employee privacy.

Answers to quick quiz

1. Ability of the manager.
   Ability of the subordinates.
   Nature of the task.
   The geographical dispersal of the subordinates.
   The availability of good quality information.
2. Interoperability refers to the ability of entities to share and exchange information and facilities with other parties without having to use the same service provider or technology platform. Interoperability facilitates the formation of strategic alliances and encourages collaboration across organisation boundaries.
3. An excess of irrelevant information is harmful - a person is more likely to miss or miss-interpret vital information if they are swamped with irrelevant material.
4. A formal structure.
   A technological system consisting of the work to be done, and the machines, tools and other facilities available to do it.
   A social system consisting of the people within the organisation, the ways they think and the ways they interact with each other.
5. Consumer privacy considers the information complied by data collectors such as marketing firms, insurance companies and retailers, the use of credit information collected by credit agencies and the rights of the consumers to control information about themselves and their commercial transactions.
   Employee privacy deals with the use of electronic monitoring and other mechanisms to analyse work habits and measure employee productivity.

Now try the questions below from the Exam Question Bank. Question 16 includes detailed guidance with the question and answer.

Number	Level	Marks	Time
5	Exam	15	27 mins
10	Exam	13	23 mins
16(a)	Exam	10	18 mins

Exam question bank

Questions 1 - 3 and 13 - 15 of this Exam question bank are from the **Pilot Paper**.

Questions 15 and 16 include **detailed guidance** within the question and answer.

Exam question bank

1 SOFT SYSTEMS METHODOLOGY *36 mins*

Consultants have recently been employed by ACCA to analyse the requirements for a revised education programme. The consultants used Checkland's Soft System Methodology in their initial investigation and proposed the following root definition.

Root definition:

'An ACCA owned system which is operated by ACCA staff and students, employers and sponsors; to transform a collection of differently rated professional modules into a highly rated professional programme which offers increased student choice and provides greater practical relevance and cogency within each named module, with students, employers and sponsors having a major say in its structure, content and style of delivery.'

Required:

(a) List an appropriate set of CATWOE criteria for the Root Definition. **(6 marks)**

(b) **Draw a conceptual model based on the Root Definition and the CATWOE criteria.**
 (10 marks)

(c) Explain the role that conceptual models play in Checkland's Soft Systems Methodology.
 (4 marks)

 (20 marks)

2 THE VALUE CHAIN *36 mins*

Porter contends that competitive advantage cannot be understood by looking at a firm as a whole. It does, however, stem from the many discrete activities a firm performs in designing, producing, marketing, delivering and supporting its products. A generic value chain is shown below.

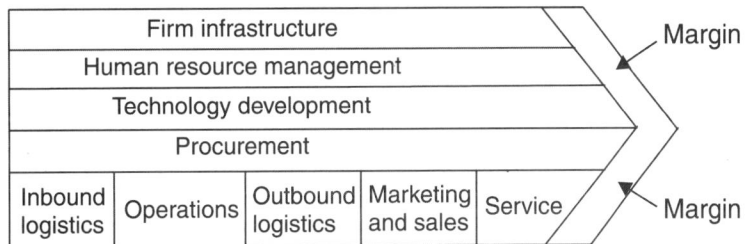

Figure 1: The Value Chain (from Porter, M. Competitive Advantage)

Required:

(a) Define what is meant by a 'value activity'. **(2 marks)**

(b) Briefly explain the difference between primary and support activities. **(3 marks)**

(c) Briefly describe each of the activities named in the value chain. **(5 marks)**

(d) Explain why the value chain technique is important when developing an information system and an information technology strategy. **(10 marks)**

 (20 marks)

3 BESPOKE SOFTWARE OR AN OFF-THE-SHELF PACKAGE *36 mins*

The choice to develop a purpose written application software system or to purchase a ready-written package is one that faces all company executives with responsibility for IS/IT strategy.

Required:

Discuss the strategic issues involved. **(20 marks)**

Exam question bank

QUESTIONS 4 - 7 ARE BASED ON THE FOLLOWING SCENARIO

Q.NET

Q.NET sells books on the Internet. It has a turnover of £50 million with gross profits of £5 million. Operating costs are relatively low because most transactions are carried out electronically by the computer system with little or no manual intervention. Q NET's main expense is interest on bank loans which were used to purchase initial hardware and software and provide some working capital for new business. Over £20 million was invested in computer hardware, software, stocks of books and warehousing space when the organisation commenced business last year. Interest repayments alone mean the Q.NET is unlikely to see any profit being made in the next three years.

Business strategy and vision

The overall vision of Q.NET is to obtain 10 per cent of the retail book market within three years with a positive net profit. The underlying business strategy of Q.NET supports this vision by providing:

- Appropriate information to, and ordering facilities for, customers
- Basic financial information for management
- Suppliers with appropriate information on book sales

Information systems - ordering and sales

Expenditure on hardware and software for transaction processing included mainframes linked to the Internet to receive orders from customers, maintenance of a large database of books in print and sophisticated encryption technology to ensure that payments on the Internet are secure. Some sections of the hardware configuration were below the recommended specification when they were implemented.

Q.NET, along with the other major bookshops on the Internet, offers information on up to four million books in print. Books are ordered over the Internet using a secure landline and credit card facility. Despatch of popular titles is normally within 48 hours; rarer books in four to five weeks. All Internet booksellers offer a similar lead-time for orders. Payment is made with the customer's authorisation for a credit card transaction on despatch of the order. Payments are made to suppliers within the standard credit period of 30 days.

Customers purchase books after identifying their book requirements by author or book title from the database of books maintained by Q.NET. Information provided about each book includes price and shipping time; popular books also have a scanned image of the cover. Additional information on each book is available on Q.NET's database, although the lack of bandwidth from the database to the Internet server means that this information cannot be displayed to the customer.

Details of customer orders are maintained on the system for six weeks, or until the order is fulfilled. This information is then removed from the hard disk to save space.

Information system for sales and support staff

Sales and support staff work from their homes using Virtual Private Network (VPN) to access the main computer systems at Q.NET's head office. Sales and support staff are required to:

- Answer customer queries via e-mail
- Check stock movements and order additional copies of popular books, which would normally be in excess of normal forecast sales
- Review new books from publishers so that Q.NET's website can be updated with details of each book prior to publication
- Write amendments to the website to add new books and remove discontinued books

Each member of staff focuses on one of the main activities outlined above. Staff work from home, partly as a result of the security of the VPN, but mainly to minimise the use of expensive office space. Q.NET provided all the hardware and software required and had no difficulty in recruiting the 25 staff required. However, six months after initial recruitment, more than half of the staff have resigned and Q.NET is facing increasing charges from having to reallocate computer hardware to new support staff as well as, in some situations, providing appropriate ISDN telephone connections to the VPN.

Future activities

The board of Q.NET is concerned that the organisation is not using technology effectively to gain any competitive advantage over its rivals.

One proposition is to have additional EDI links to major book publishers to order books that Q.NET currently does not have in stock. However, the publishers are unwilling to be locked into this type of agreement in case they are seen to be favouring one bookshop over another.

4 Q.NET: IT STRATEGY AND COMPETITIVE ADVANTAGE *36 mins*

Required:

Evaluate how Q.NET can use IT to gain competitive advantage using Porter's Five Forces model as a framework for your answer. **(20 marks)**

5 Q.NET: STAFF RETENTION *27 mins*

Required:

Discuss the reasons why sales and support staff turnover is so high. Explain methods for improving the retention of these staff. **(15 marks)**

6 Q.NET: INFORMATION STRATEGY *12 mins*

Required:

Evaluate the purpose of an information strategy in a commercial organisation. **(7 marks)**

7 Q.NET: IT AND BUSINESS STRATEGY *14 mins*

Required:

Evaluate how effective the IT system at Q.NET is in supporting the business strategy. **(8 marks)**

8 THE INTERNET: THREATS AND OPPORTUNITIES *36 mins*

The Internet provides opportunities for business but also carries a threat.

Required:

Identify the current threats and opportunities Internet developments bring to Internet businesses (eg an Internet Service Provider), and to non-Internet related businesses.
(20 marks)

QUESTIONS 9 - 12 ARE BASED ON THE FOLLOWING SCENARIO

LT plc

LT plc provides telecommunication services ranging from residential telephones to large corporate Intranets. The organisation has 20 million customers and a turnover of several billion pounds. Most customers are satisfied with the level of service received. The main area of concern for customers has been that pricing structures are not always clear and appear to favour individual corporate customer needs rather than residential markets.

Over the past few years, LT plc has built up an unparalleled analogue telephone communication network which it owns and maintains itself. Most other telecommunication companies, including new entrants into the market, lease or rent at least part of their communication network. LT plc has been able to offer more reliable services and fault-fixing times than any other company.

In recent years, LT plc has also been the dominant market leader with over 90% market share in all of its business sectors. However, deregulation of the telecommunications market from 1 January 1999 has meant that its monopolistic power has been significantly weakened in many areas. The Board of LT plc has tended to see this as a threat rather than an opportunity. The view arose partly from a fear of losing market share and partly because information systems were internally focused and so could not provide the necessary competitor information.

One way the Board of LT plc sought to maintain market share has been by forming strategic alliances with similar telecommunications companies in other countries. This strategy has been largely successful, with profits being maintained from these international ventures. However, as a result of IT strategy and information

Exam question bank

systems being focused on overseas markets, very little attention was paid to the domestic competition or investment during 2001 or the earlier part of 2002.

Other competitive challenges

LT plc is now facing intense competition in its home market from a small number of new companies which will be able to offer new services including:

- Digital television
- Internet on TV
- Films on demand

All these services are being provided over new fibre-optic telephone lines which LT plc has not invested in significantly. However, no one organisation currently offers all services as a comprehensive package and LT plc currently is considering providing this service.

LT plc is also finding it difficult to obtain information on the home market. The development of its Executive Support Systems (ESS) has followed the strategy of the company, providing summary and detailed information about overseas competitors. This has had the effect of losing focus on the home market.

LT plc is facing competitive challenges not only from additional services that are being offered, but also from a significant amount of cross-selling of services. For example a competing company recently offered a telephone service including access to the five main satellite television channels for the price of LT plc's domestic telephone service. LT plc's market share is now being eroded in all areas partly because the company cannot match the offers on price terms and partly because of the time taken to make strategic decisions to offer competing services.

Integrated digital service

Some telecommunications companies are now able to provide a fully integrated service of traditional telephone, digital cable TV, Internet access and home shopping. LT plc should be able to provide this service by 2003. The system effectively means that consumers, in the domestic and overseas markets, could order their shopping, browse the Internet, view films on demand and make telephone calls, possibly with integrated video, from their living room.

LT plc's response to the competitive challenge

In an attempt to provide more timely decisions and meet the expected demand for new services, in June 2002 the Board of LT plc set up four autonomous business units within the organisation. Each unit was to focus on a specific market such as large corporate organisations, domestic users etc. Each unit was to report back to the Board by December 2002 with an indication of the problems faced by that unit and recommendations for resolving those problems. Early indications are that there are common problems facing all units. These problems include:

- A lack of information on how to set prices for new services.
- Lack of understanding on how to set the existing IT system to stop the fall in market share.
- Lack of available capacity in the existing IT infrastructure (bandwidth) to provide enhanced services to domestic customers.
- Lack of key critical success factors for each business unit.
- Lack of understanding of the social and economic impact of the enhanced services on society.

The Board of LT plc is starting to consider these issues and has requested more information.

---

9   INFORMATION SOURCES   *27 mins*

Required:

Explain the sources of information that can be used to assist in the setting of prices for the future integrated digital service. Show why each source of information is required by LT plc.

15 Marks

---

10   IMPACT ON SOCIETY   *23 mins*

Required:

Discuss the possible effects that an Integrated Digital Service, as outlined in the scenario, could have on employment and society.

13 Marks

Exam question bank

11 INFORMATION/BUSINESS STRATEGY *21 mins*

Required:

Discuss the problems that LT plc is facing because its systems are not sufficiently supporting the business strategy of re-focusing onto the home market. Describe the actions that can be taken to overcome these problems. **12 Marks**

12 EXECUTIVE SUPPORT SYSTEM (ESS) *18 mins*

Required:

Explain what type of information an ESS could provide and show how this would improve decision making for the Board of LT plc. **10 Marks**

QUESTIONS 13 - 15 ARE BASED ON THE FOLLOWING SCENARIO

Pattersons Electrical Suppliers

Pattersons Electrical Suppliers own a chain of retail outlets throughout the city and surrounding area. In recent years they have expanded these outlets from their one original store to the current seven stores. The head office is based on the original site. The business originated as a cash and carry company supplying the public with all types of electrical appliances, varying from light bulbs to fridge freezers. Electrical goods supply is a very competitive business; Pattersons have to compete with all the national suppliers that tend to dominate the market. In order to compete successfully they have adopted a business strategy of fast turnover and low profit margins coupled with a high customer service level.

Each store holds approximately nine thousand item lines; the majority of the smaller items are on display in the sales area, a selection of the larger appliances are also on display, this is complemented by a variety of brochures that carry information about the whole range of products. Experienced sales personnel are available to assist customers in their selection of appropriate goods. Following selection and payment of goods, customers tend to 'carry' the smaller items from the store; larger items are delivered within forty-eight hours. Each store has its own warehouse that is replenished when necessary from the company's main storage depot; the main storage depot's inventory control system is managed by head office.

Every store has its own computer system to control the day-to-day business; all of these are linked to the head office system. Information technology and information systems (IT/IS) development strategy has gone hand in hand with the business strategy that has enabled the dramatic expansion of the business. The IT centre is based in the head office and offers support to all of the satellite stores.

The Chairman and the Board of Directors recently employed the services of a business management consultant; the major aim of the exercise was to aid the development of a business strategy for the medium-to-long term. At a recent meeting of the board, the directors discussed the consultant's report. One of the recommendations stated 'Pattersons have previously been successful in automation and rationalisation of its business processes, maybe it's time for the business to consider reengineering in its future long-term business strategy'. This statement resulted in a heated discussion and disagreement, so much so that it was eventually decided to commission an internal study that would report back to the board at a later date.

A further recommendation involved the development of an integrated inventory distribution system. Currently when goods reach their re-order level in the individual stores and the main storage depot cannot supply the goods, they are purchased from suppliers even though other stores have more than adequate levels of the goods. It was decided to conduct a feasibility study, including a cost-benefit analysis before the proposed project would be given support.

Overall the consultant's report was encouraging, generally indicating a healthy business position from a management perspective. One point of concern was the recent implementation of a company-wide computerised shift scheduling system, for the shop workers, warehouse personnel and support staff. This system basically involves the scheduling of shift patterns and hours worked by the individuals. Previously individuals negotiated their working shifts with middle management within the bounds of certain parameters, number of shifts per week, maximum number of hours etc. There is resistance to the imposition of the system, thus the system is not fully utilised. To work successfully the system requires a great deal of manual intervention and updating. Generally the system is viewed as a failure by both middle management and the staff affected.

Exam question bank

13 PATTERSONS ELECTRICAL SUPPLIES: INFORMATION SYSTEM FAILURE *27 mins*

In the scenario it was stated that the implementation of the computerised shift scheduling system had 'failed'. Recent research suggests that IT investment has emerged as a high-risk, hidden-cost process. At least 20% of such spend is wasted, and between 30-40% of IS projects realise no benefits whatsoever, however measured, failures and rejections are commonplace.

Required:

Discuss the reasons for the apparent high levels of failure in the implementation of information systems. Make reference to the computerised shift scheduling system recently installed into Pattersons. **(15 marks)**

14 PATTERSONS ELECTRICAL SUPPLIES: IT/IS STRATEGY AND BUSINESS STRATEGY *36 mins*

A statement in the scenario 'Information technology and information systems (IT/IS) development strategy, has gone hand in hand with the business strategy this has enabled the dramatic expansion of the business.'

Required:

(a) Discuss the implications and importance of this statement in respect of Pattersons and possibly the majority of all businesses, if they wish to survive and succeed in the twenty-first century market place. **(10 marks)**

Mr Smith the business consultant claimed, 'Pattersons have previously been successful in automation and rationalisation of its business processes, maybe it's time for the business to consider reengineering in its future long term business strategy'.

Required:

(b) Explain in terms of business processes what he meant by the terms: automation, rationalisation and reengineering. (Give examples where appropriate in relation to the case study.) **(10 marks)**

(20 marks)

15 QUESTION 15 ALSO REFERS TO PATTERSONS, AND INCLUDES DETAILED GUIDANCE - SEE THE FOLLOWING PAGE.

Exam question bank

15 PATTERSONS ELECTRICAL SUPPLIES: INTERNET, EXTRANET, INTRANET   *45 mins*

Currently Pattersons computer based systems applications portfolio predominantly consists of in-house business systems. They are considering expanding this portfolio to include the 'new' web-based technologies and systems.

'There is one major change in information technology on whose importance business executives, academics and technologists all agree. It is the explosive growth of the Internet and related technologies and applications and their impact on business, society and information technology. The Internet is changing the way businesses are operated and people work and how information technology supports business operation and end-user work activities' O'Brien (1999).

Required:

Describe and discuss the impact of the above quote with reference to the case study where appropriate in terms of:

(a) Business-to-Consumer commerce (Internet).

   Include in your answer customer requirements.   **(10 marks)**

(b) Business-to-Business applications (extranet).

   Include in your answer how major business functions can be supported by electronic commerce.   **(8 marks)**

(c) Internal business processes (intranet).   **(7 marks)**

   (25 marks)

Approaching the answer

You should read through the requirement, and then re-read and annotate the question, highlighting points to include in your answer. An example is shown below.

Pattersons Electrical Suppliers own a chain of retail outlets throughout the ==city and surrounding area==. In recent years they have expanded these outlets from their one original store to the current seven stores. The head office is based on the original site. The business originated as a cash and carry company ==supplying the public== with all types of electrical appliances, varying from light bulbs to fridge freezers. Electrical goods supply is a very ==competitive business==. Pattersons have to ==compete with all the national suppliers== that tend to dominate the market. In order to compete successfully they have adopted a business strategy of ==fast turnover and low profit margins== coupled with a ==high customer service level==.

> [city and surrounding area] → Use website to extend reach?
> [competitive business] → Competitors web-based activities
> [fast turnover and low profit margins] → Efficient internal processes essential
> [high customer service level] → Website must match this level

Each store holds approximately ==nine thousand item lines==; the majority of the smaller items are on display in the sales area, a selection of the larger appliances are also on display, this is complemented by a ==variety of brochures== that carry information about the whole range of products. Experienced ==sales personnel are available to assist== customers in their selection of appropriate goods. Following selection and payment of goods, customers tend ==to 'carry' the==

> [nine thousand item lines] → Easy access to large number of product details
> [sales personnel are available to assist] → Can such assistance be automated?

283

[Annotation: Consider delivery and back-office procedures]

smaller items from the store; larger items are delivered within forty-eight hours. Each store has its own warehouse that is replenished when necessary from the company's main storage depot; the main storage depot's inventory control system is managed by head office.

[Annotation: Intranet could improve co-ordination]

[Annotation: Strategies must remain aligned]

Every store has its own computer system to control the day-to-day business; all of these are linked to the head office system. Information technology and information systems (IT/IS) development strategy has gone hand in hand with the business strategy that has enabled the dramatic expansion of the business. The IT centre is based in the head office and offers support to all of the satellite stores.

[Annotation: Do staff have the skills required for web/intranet/extranet?]

[Annotation: IT/IS considered?]

The Chairman and the Board of Directors recently employed the services of a business management consultant; the major aim of the exercise was to aid the development of a business strategy for the medium-to-long term. At a recent meeting of the board, the directors discussed the consultant's report. One of the recommendations stated 'Pattersons have previously been successful in automation and rationalisation of its business processes, maybe it's time for the business to consider reengineering in its future long-term business strategy'. This statement resulted in a heated discussion and disagreement, so much so that it was eventually decided to commission an internal study that would report back to the board at a later date.

[Annotation: Role of new technologies]

[Annotation: Integrate with intranet/extranet/Internet]

A further recommendation involved the development of an integrated inventory distribution system. Currently when goods reach their re-order level in the individual stores, and the main storage depot cannot supply the goods, they are purchased from suppliers - even though other stores have more than adequate levels of the goods. It was decided to conduct a feasibility study, including a cost-benefit analysis before the proposed project would be given support.

[Annotation: An improved stock system is essential]

Overall the consultant's report was encouraging, generally indicating a healthy business position from a management perspective. One point of concern was the recent implementation of a company-wide computerised shift scheduling system, for the shop workers, warehouse personnel and support staff. This system basically involves the scheduling of shift patterns and hours worked by the individuals. Previously, individuals negotiated their working shifts with middle management within the bounds of certain parameters; number of shifts per week, maximum number of hours etc. There is resistance to the imposition of the system, thus the system is not fully utilised. To work successfully the system requires a great deal of manual intervention and updating. Generally the system is viewed as a failure by both middle management and the staff affected.

[Annotation: Could be available to all on the intranet]

[Annotation: System not working correctly, avoid these mistakes in future implementations]

Currently Pattersons' computer based systems applications portfolio predominantly consists of in-house business systems. They are considering expanding this portfolio to include the 'new' web-based technologies and systems.

> Availability of expertise? Outsource?

'There is one major change in information technology on whose importance business executives, academics and technologists all agree. It is the explosive growth of the Internet and related technologies and applications and their impact on business, society and information technology. The Internet is changing the way businesses are operated and people work and how information technology supports business operation and end-user work activities' O'Brien (1999).

> Re-read the quote, identify relevant points from scenario

Required — Ensure you do both

Describe and discuss the impact of the above quote with reference to the case study where appropriate in terms of:

(a) Business-to-Consumer commerce (Internet).

Include in your answer customer requirements. (10 marks)

> Importance of actual service matching website promises

(b) Business-to-Business applications (extranet).

Include in your answer how major business functions can be supported by electronic commerce. (8 marks)

> Purchasing/stock control? Other functions not included in (a) or (c)

(c) Internal business processes (intranet). (7 marks)

> Communication, product specs, HR issues including shifts

Answer plan

Then organise the things you have noticed and your points arising into a coherent answer plan. Not all the points you have noticed will have to go into your answer – you should spend a few minutes thinking them through and prioritising them.

(a) **B2C (Internet)**

Intro

- Access to all consumers with Internet access - expanding market
- Competitors in electrical goods offering on-line option

User requirements

- Website must provide product info
- User-friendly, easy to use
- Returns/support policy and procedures
- How products delivered?
- On-line transaction processing?

Customer retention/website promotions

- Loyalty schemes?
- How can website attract NEW customers

Other points

- Use of information collected from website visitors/customers
- Cross-selling

(b) **B2B (extranet)**

Intro

- Define and explain extranet

Stock

- Automated re-ordering via links to supplier
- Order history available to suppliers - indication future requirements?

Suppliers

- Improved communication links
- Access to marketing info that could influence future stock requirements
- Use extranet to facilitate EDI?
- Closer relationship

Payments

- Supplier payment via EFT?
- Automated discounting for prompt payment

Other points

- Links to banking organisations - financial management

(c) **Internal (intranet)**

Intro

- Define and explain intranet

E-mail, bulletin boards

- General use of e-mail
- Bulletin-board style discussions
- Product query database

General info sharing

- Information held in one location available to all
- Should reduce stock-outs
- Detailed product specs available
- Info more easily maintained and updated
- General competitive info can be shared with all staff

You should flesh out the points contained in your plan and link them to form a coherent answer. Structured answers, with short paragraphs, should help ensure your answer remains focussed.

16 INFORMATION OVERLOAD
36 mins

The HK Consultancy Company specialises in helping organisations to benefit from the implementation of IT systems. On a typical client project, staff from HK Consultancy will review the use of IT within an organisation, identify how staff should be using the IT systems, obtain information about the proposed IT systems and then ensure that the revised IT system meet the requirements of the users.

As the newly-appointed, experienced management accountant, your responsibilities include ensuring that the information systems of the company support its strategic direction, and advising the board of any changes that could be made to the overall company strategy. Prior to your appointment, the board recognised that growth in its existing market was limited, and required some diversification to meet the consultancy's objectives of sales and profit growth.

An intranet has been established utilising a package which provides databases for technical information, bulletin boards, electronic mail and customer contact information. The intranet is used by the management accountant frequently throughout the day, mainly to answer e-mails, but also to check information on the technical databases and bulletin boards. You also receive information from:

- Professional staff who visit client organisations, in the form of verbal queries and written reports
- Various journals specialising in IT systems
- Administration staff who produce client proposals for review prior to sending out consultants to potential clients
- Telephone queries directly from clients regarding the status of different projects
- The Internet, where different client and competitor websites are reviewed on a daily basis by the management accountant

Your first project is to provide a report to the board summarising the company's current strategic situation compared to its major competitors and suggesting alternative strategies for diversification.

Required

(a) As the management accountant, it is important that you are able to focus on this project. Briefly explain the concept of information overload, then explain how you would refine or amend the information system in the HK Consultancy to limit the amount of information being delivered to you. **12 Marks**

(b) Evaluate the characteristics that should apply to the information being given to the management accountant to ensure that the information is quickly and accurately understood. **8 Marks**

(Total 20 marks)

Approaching the answer

You should read through the requirement, and then re-read and annotate the question, highlighting points to include in your answer. An example is shown below.

The HK Consultancy Company specialises in <mark>helping organisations to benefit from the implementation of IT systems</mark>. On a typical client project, staff from HK Consultancy will review the use of IT within an organisation, identify how staff should be using the IT systems, obtain information about the proposed IT systems and then ensure that the revised IT system meet the requirements of the users.

— HK has much in-house expertise relating to IS

287

Exam question bank

[Annotation: Information required to support high level decisions]

As the newly-appointed, experienced management accountant, your responsibilities include ensuring that the information systems of the company support its strategic direction, and advising the board of any changes that could be made to the overall company strategy. Prior to your appointment, the board recognised that growth in its existing market was limited, and required some diversification to meet the consultancy's objectives of sales and profit growth.

[Annotation: Information systems strategy will require adjusting if overall company strategy changes]

[Annotation: Could be expanded - extranet?]

An intranet has been established, utilising a package which provides databases for technical information, bulletin boards, electronic mail and customer contact information. The intranet is used by the management accountant frequently throughout the day, mainly to answer e-mails, but also to check information on the technical databases and bulletin boards. You also receive information from:

- Professional staff who visit client organisations, in the form of verbal queries and written reports [Annotation: Potential for frequent interruptions]

[Annotation: Could be e-mailed or posted on intranet]

- Various journals specialising in IT systems

- Administration staff, who produce client proposals for review prior to sending out consultants to potential clients

[Annotation: Delegate? Use extranet?]

- Telephone queries directly from clients regarding the status of different projects

- The Internet, where different client and competitor websites are reviewed on a daily basis by the management accountant

[Annotation: Intelligent agents? IT journal review too?]

Your first project is to provide a report to the board summarising the company's current strategic situation compared to its major competitors and suggesting alternative strategies for diversification.

[Annotations: High-level, comprehensive; External info required; 'Forward looking' info required]

Required

(a) As the management accountant, it is important you that you are able to focus on this project. Briefly explain the concept of 'information overload', then explain how you would refine or amend the information system in the HK Consultancy to limit the amount of information being delivered to you. (12 marks)

[Annotations: Use broad definition, not just 'computers'; Procedures, IT screening tools, delegation]

(b) Evaluate the characteristics that should apply to the information being given to the management accountant to ensure that the information is quickly and accurately understood. (8 marks)

[Annotations: Consider 'ACCURATE' mnemonic; Remember that scenario tells us accountant focussing on strategic issues]

Answer plan

Then organise the things you have noticed and your points arising into a coherent answer plan. Not all the points you have noticed will have to go into your answer – you should spend a few minutes thinking them through and prioritising them.

(a) **Information overload and information system amendments**

   Intro
   - Explain information overload
   - Include role of advances in IT/IS in increasing amount of info available

   Steps to limit information reaching management accountant
   - Telephone queries to go through secretary
   - Delegation of some tasks
   - Use Internet newsclipping service to send targeted information
   - Intelligent agents to monitor websites

(b) **Information characteristics**

   Intro
   - Accountant's current tasks require info to support strategic decisions

   Information characteristics (use ACCURATE mnemonic to jog memory)
   - Needs to see big picture - summarised
   - Presentation should aid understanding
   - Complete
   - Timely
   - Relevant
   - Some outward-looking info

You should flesh out the points contained in your plan and link them to form a coherent answer. Structured answers, with short paragraphs, should help ensure your answer remains focussed.

Exam answer bank

Exam answer bank

1 SOFT SYSTEMS METHODOLOGY

> **Tutorial note.** Soft Systems Methodology (SSM) is included in the syllabus for the first time in a final level ACCA examination. The examiner has stated that SSM is highly examinable, so ensure you are familiar with the theory and related techniques. The information in the question provides almost all of the answer to part (a), allowing some easy marks to be obtained. Part (b) is more difficult, although again most of the events are provided within the question. For part (c), some basic comments about SSM are required – there are only four marks available in this section so detailed comment is not necessary.

(a) The CATWOE criteria for the root definition can be listed as follows.

Client	Future ACCA students
Actor	ACCA staff, Students, Employers and Sponsors
Transformation	A highly rated professional programme offering increased practical relevance and cogency
Weltanschauung	Students, Employers and Sponsors should have a major say in the structure, style and delivery of the programme
Owner	ACCA
Environment	Professional business and commerce

Exam answer bank

(b)

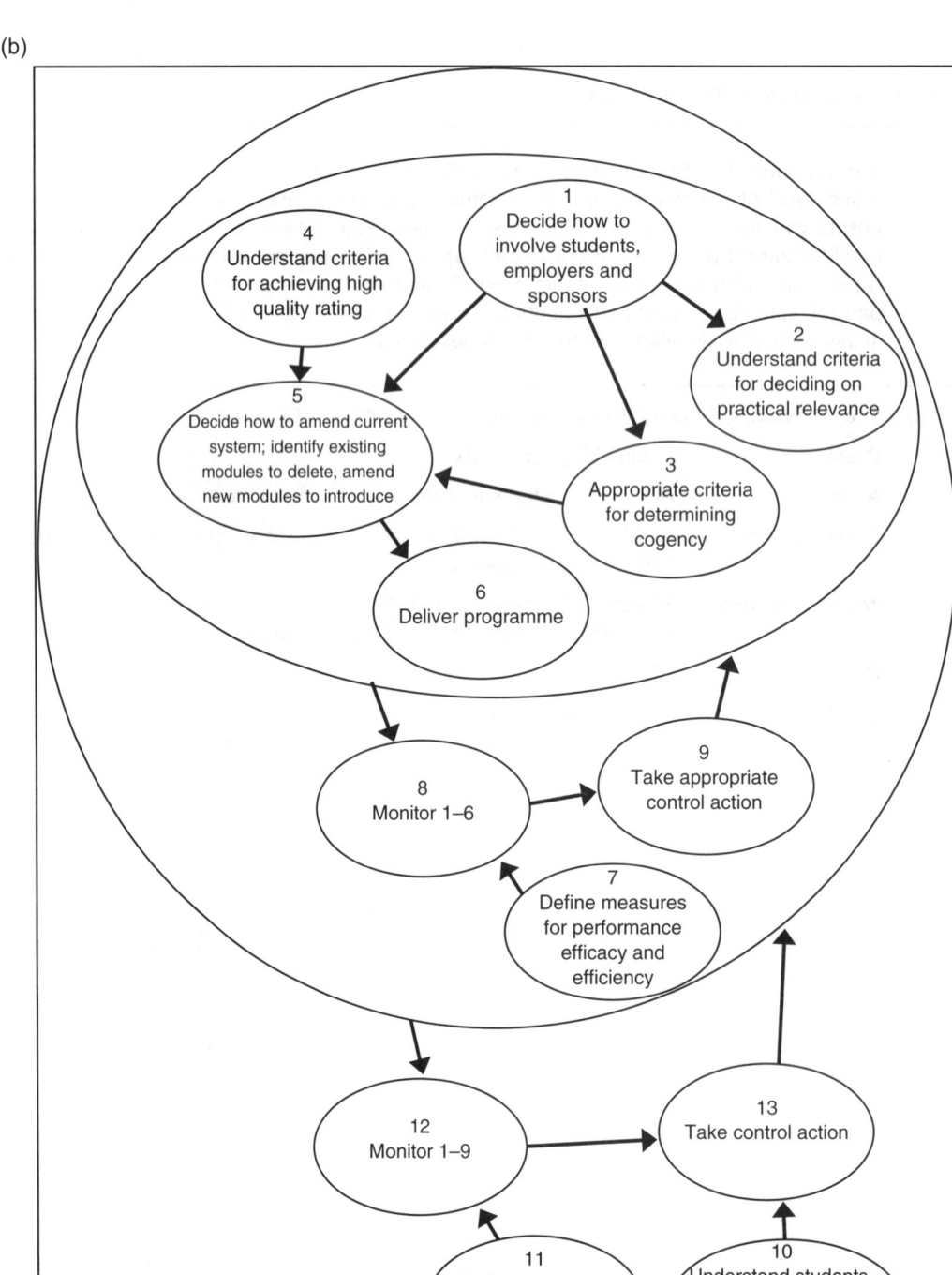

(c) In Checklands Soft Systems Methodology, conceptual models are activity models focusing on what needs to be done in a system. The model therefore shows key activities such as 'deliver program' or 'take control action' rather than explaining how these activities will take place.

The model provides the actions necessary to satisfy the root definition, based on the worldview in the CATWOE criteria. How the activities will actually be carried out in the 'real world' is unclear, and discussion will be needed to clarify the situation. The model does provide a basis for this discussion by ordering the activities or events that must take place and noting some of the feedback that is required within the system.

2 THE VALUE CHAIN

> **Tutorial note.** The first three sections of this question rely on knowledge of the value chain. If you have studied the Value Chain (you should have – it is a key topic in Paper 3.4!) parts (a) to (c) offer a rare chance to pick up good marks for simply reproducing book knowledge. Explaining the nine sections of the value chain in part (c) is only worth 5 marks so be concise.
>
> Part (d) requires a little more thought. Start by considering how the value chain breaks an organisation up into different activities, then move on and explain how IT can link those activities.

(a) A value activity is an activity which adds value to the product or service being produced by an organisation. The activity contains two parts:

1   A physical component includes all the physical tasks required to complete that activity.

2   The information processing component encompasses all the steps required to capture, manipulate, and channel the data necessary to perform the activity.

(b) A primary activity is an activity which involves the making of a product or service, including the distribution, sale and after-care service for that product or service.

A support activity is an activity which supports the primary activities or other support activities. Support activities include procurement, product and technology development, human resource management and administration and infrastructure services.

(c) **Activities in the value chain**

(i) **Inbound logistics**

Activities to receive, store and distribute the inputs required to produce goods and services, such as stock control and contacts with suppliers.

(ii) **Operations**

Activities involved with producing the product or service including manufacture, packaging and testing.

(iii) **Outbound logistics**

Activities to send the product to the consumer including warehousing and distribution.

(iv) **Marketing and sales**

Activities to receive orders from customers to purchase products and services and other activities involved in inducing potential customers to purchase the product or service such as advertising and promotion.

(v) **Service**

Activities to help retain product value including after-sales service, provision of parts and training of installers and repairers.

(vi) **Procurement**

Purchasing any necessary inputs.

(vii) **Technology development**

Development of machines, computers, processes and systems and expertise of staff.

(viii) **Human resource management**

Activities to train, develop and provide remuneration to staff.

(ix) **Infrastructure**

Maintenance of the general infrastructure of the organisation including management, finance and planning.

(d) The value chain is important when developing an IS or IT strategy because it allows the organisation to be split into the distinct activities outlined in the value chain. This model can then be used to assess the effectiveness and efficiency of resource use within each activity in the chain.

Efficiency is a measure of how well resources are being used, with measures including profitability, capacity use and the yield obtained from that capacity. Effectiveness relates to how well resources are allocated to those activities which are most competitively significant within the value chain. The assessment will involve monitoring the activities in terms of people, capital technology use and possibly R&D.

Having identified areas which could be more efficient or effective from the value chain analysis, the IS / IT strategy can be used to try and determine how those activities, and in particular the competitively significant activities, can be improved. Specific areas that may be investigated include:

(i) Can **linkages** between the different activities be improved by the use of IT? For example, information from support activities may be made available to primary activities on a timelier basis.

(ii) Can the **information flow** through primary activities be improved? For example, linking sales and marketing with operations or outbound logistics using a central database to provide sales and marketing with on-line details of products being produced.

(iii) Can more effective links be formed with **external entities**? For example, can inbound logistics be improved by using EDI or allowing suppliers access to Intranet databases concerning stock availability (in other words setting up an Extranet).

(iv) Can using IT **decrease the cost** of any activity? For example, is there room for more automation or transformation of activities, or even re-engineering using currently available IT tools and techniques?

In conclusion, the value chain provides a valuable method of looking at the organisation, helping managers to focus on the linkages between activities, allowing consideration of where IT can improve effectiveness and efficiency of those links or individual activities.

3 BESPOKE SOFTWARE V AN OFF THE SHELF PACKAGE

> **Tutorial note.** Be careful, the focus of this question is not the advantages and disadvantages of purchasing third party software! However, some of the points made can be obtained from thinking about third party purchase. Try and think from the strategic view downwards; this should help you think of these 'bigger picture' issues.
>
> Keep your answer moving. Try and discuss a range of points, rather than focussing on two or three points only.

The strategic issues regarding choice of software development are explained below.

(i) **Company IT strategy**

The strategy concerning previous application development can be considered. If applications have been written in-house or always purchased externally, then the organisation is more likely to continue. Changing strategy will need a careful review, especially as integration of software may be more difficult.

(ii) **Business requirements**

The choice of software must match the requirements specification for the particular application. Commercially available software may not meet all the specific requirements of the organisation because the software is written for general use. A strategic decision must be made whether to accept the limitations of the commercially available product or write the application in-house. Taking the latter option may involve higher risk of software failure because module and program testing will also be required; commercially available software will already have passed these tests.

(iii) **Business risk**

Purchasing ready written packages means placing reliance on the third party supplier to maintain and upgrade the software. If the software is business critical then this reliance may be unacceptable so in-house development is necessary.

(iv) **Competitive advantage**

The organisation may have seen an area of competitive advantage in the use of software. In house writing may be required because commercially available software does not support this requirement or because the idea needs to be kept secret as long as possible. Involving third parties in user acceptance testing of ready written software may mean that the competitive advantage from using the software becomes public knowledge sooner than expected.

(v) **Timescale**

The amount of time before the software has to be implemented may affect choice of development. Ready written software is available straightaway but in-house development will take months, and in some cases years. If the software is required immediately, then purchase is likely to be the only alternative.

(vi) **Skills available**

If the organisation has an experienced in-house software development team, then in-house writing is feasible. The lack of in-house experience raises the strategic decision of whether or not to establish this team, or purchase ready written software. Establishing a new development team also involves risk because the team will not have worked together before and they will have to understand the interfaces with other software in the organisation to ensure that the new software is compatible.

(vii) **Software licensing agreements**

One alternative to simply purchasing ready written software is to amend that software to meet the specific business requirements of the organisation. This may provide a relatively cost-effective method of meeting specific requirements without full software development in-house.

However, the licensing implications of this decision must also be investigated. The option may become too expensive where significant licensing costs have to be paid. The issue of whether the software writer will release the source code of the software, or whether amendments have to be made by the writer must also be considered. Amending the software at a third party involves strategic risks of loss of control of development and placing reliance on the third party for software maintenance. These risks may not be acceptable so in-house development will be required.

(viii) **Availability of software language**

Some ready written software is developed in specific software languages that are not generally available for purchase. If that language cannot be purchased, then this limits the development decision to purchasing the ready written software or possibly writing the software in a different, and possibly less effective, language.

4 Q.NET: IT STRATEGY AND COMPETITIVE ADVANTAGE

> **Tutorial note.** The requirement instructs you to use Porter's Five Forces model as a framework for your answer – ensure that you do this by using each force as a separate heading.
>
> However, don't fall into the trap of simply explaining Porter's Five Forces. You must relate each force to the situation described, and most importantly, focus on how Q.NET could use IT for competitive advantage.
>
> Ensure your answer is reasonably balanced across each of the Five Forces, although if you feel one area to be more relevant than the others do make the points you believe are relevant.
>
> Try to be concise; there are a wide range of issues to include within the 36 minutes available.

How Q.NET could use each of Porter's Five Forces to gain a competitive advantage is explained below.

Rivalry between competitors

Q.NETs competitors are all organisations that sell books. Ways in which Q.NET could achieve an increase in sales compared to competitors include:

Improved customer service.

Additional investment in the IT infrastructure, and closer links with book suppliers, will facilitate more efficient operations in ordering, stock and dispatch. The end result will be a reduction in the time between a customer placing an order and delivery of that order.

Exam answer bank

Improved marketing.

Book, customer and transaction data will be able to be stored in a database, and used for competitive purposes. For example, tailored information can be presented to a customer whenever they access Q.NET's website. The type of marketing information presented would be influenced by past purchases, and the customer profile. This will encourage the development of a long-term relationship with the customer, and will further differentiate Q.NET from traditional booksellers.

Threat of substitutes. The publishing industry is undergoing rapid change with the growth of the Internet. Books (paper based products in general) are under threat from the new digital communication forms.

Alternatives to books include buying the material on CD-ROM, to be viewed on screen and a hard copy printed off if required. Alternately, printed material could be accessed and read on a website, or downloaded from a website. A hybrid product, combining a paper book, a CD or DVD and website links is likely to become the norm in some areas of publishing.

Q.NET should monitor developments in this area and consider moving into the 'e-books' industry.

Threat of new entrants. New book re-sellers entering the market could attract customers away from Q.NET. The high capital costs required to set up as an Internet based re-seller form some protection against this (ie entry-barrier), although this barrier is unlikely to be effective against a large organisation. The establishment of a strong Q.NET brand and reputation, combined with competitive pricing policies will form the most effective long-term barrier.

The establishment of a close relationship with suppliers, cemented through the use of mutually beneficial systems (eg EDI links) should discourage new entrants. To compete effectively any new entrant would need a similar relationship.

The power of buyers. A customer can buy the same book from a number of sources. As the product is identical, the deciding factor for the customer will be a combination of price and service. Books are a relatively low value, non-essential product. Collective action by buyers is therefore unlikely.

The main power of buyers in this market is the ease by which they can change supplier. Buyers can switch to other websites within seconds to compare book prices and delivery times. Search engines are also available which will check the various Internet suppliers and provide a summary of prices on those sites. A person may also pass a number bookshops several times a day without making a special trip (eg on the way home from work).

So, as well as price and service, further incentives such as 'book miles' or 'loyalty discounts' for repeat purchasers may be justified.

The power of suppliers. An individual title is usually only produced by one publisher. The supplier therefore holds a monopoly position for that individual book. Q.NET cannot therefore threaten to switch suppliers to obtain a better price. On the surface it would appear the supplier is in a very powerful position. However, the price of books is consistent within the market. Consumers know that a paper-back novel costs £X and a hard-back reference book costs £Y. The supplier would realise that any price increase would result in a higher retail price and meet consumer resistance.

By establishing closer IT links with a supplier Q.NET may be able to facilitate the operation of Just in Time systems – reducing supplier stock-holding costs. This partnership approach should benefit the competitive position of both Q.NET and the supplier.

5 Q.NET: STAFF RETENTION

> **Tutorial note.** After reading the requirement, quickly re-read the case study searching for points that could be relevant to staff retention. Wider issues such as organisational culture may be relevant, as well as factors more directly related to working conditions.
>
> The second part of your answer should suggest ways the problems you have identified could be addressed – although you could also bring in other points relevant to sales and support staff retention.

Sales and support staff turnover could be high for any of the following reasons.

Exam answer bank

There is no sense of belonging.

For most employees Q.NET is simply the organisation that pays their wages. There is little employee consultation regarding the direction of the company, resulting in low levels of employee commitment.

Lack of job variety.

Using a computer for most of the day to either answer e-mails or make changes to the website book database would become monotonous. Concentration levels and motivation would be hard to maintain. Employees are likely to become bored and may seek other jobs that appear more interesting. A related issue is that constant computer use can cause eye strain and Repetitive Strain Injury – anyone developing these problems is likely to leave.

No 'in-person' customer contact.

Employees will receive e-mail messages concerning problems customers have encountered using Q.NET, and will be subject to the 'stress' complaint brings, but will not experience the satisfaction of hearing a satisfied customer say 'thank-you'. This lack of personal contact is likely to be demotivating. Demotivated employees are likely to leave either of their own accord or because their performance is not deemed acceptable.

Homeworking issues.

Many employees may find homeworking difficult. The **distractions** caused by working at home, such as family members and neighbourhood noise, can make concentration difficult. Employees working at home may also miss the **social interaction** of colleagues.

Methods that Q.NET could use to improve staff retention are outlined in the following paragraphs.

Encouraging interaction with other employees.

This interaction could take the form of organised meetings, on maybe a bi-monthly basis. The geographic spread and cost of the meetings would have to be considered. Providing e-mail and telephone connections now so that employees can share problems and simply talk socially may provide a partial solution to the problem.

Introducing work rotation.

Periodically changing the tasks performed by staff may help to alleviate boredom. Employees could answer e-mails and provide input to the web pages on alternate days.

Re-structure the sales and support team.

This would be a more radical approach. Constant re-recruitment costs will eliminate any savings homeworking has brought. Q.NET may wish to look into the feasibility of locating all staff in an expanded office.

6   Q.NET: INFORMATION STRATEGY

> **Tutorial note.** This question is slightly unusual, as it does not require you to refer directly to the situation described in the scenario. However, as the question is part of the Q.NET case study, you should consider the Q.NET situation when deciding what to include in your answer.
>
> You can collect the seven marks on offer by providing a brief definition of an information strategy, and then explaining what you consider to be the most important elements of the overall purpose of an information strategy.
>
> Our answer shows one way of answering this question – a wide range of points could have been made.

The purpose of an information strategy in a commercial organisation is to ensure information is best used to support operations, support the business strategy and facilitate customer service.

Supporting operations.

Operational level information will be required by individual user departments. The information should enable the department or unit to meet its responsibilities under the business strategy. For example, if the business strategy includes limiting the time between customer orders and delivery, accurate order-status and stock information must be available.

Exam answer bank

Supporting the overall business strategy.

The overall aims of an organisation should be reflected in the stated overall business strategy, which will outline what that organisation wants to do and how it will be achieved. The information strategy should support the business strategy by providing appropriate information to those who require it. The information provided should be geared towards specific goals and strategies of the organisation.

Facilitating customer service.

In the 'consumer age' customers are increasingly requesting information about a product or service, so they can make an informed purchase. The amount of information required will vary depending on the nature of the product or service. For example customers may only want to check the ingredients of a food item, but would require extensive information if purchasing a new car. Part of the organisation's information system should therefore be externally focused to ensure that appropriate information is available for customers. The information may be made available to customers on websites, included in targeted brochure mail-outs or provided as part of an advertising campaign.

7 Q.NET: IT AND BUSINESS STRATEGY

> **Tutorial note.** This question can be answered by relating the issues you raised in the previous question to Q.NET.
>
> There are a number of weaknesses in the IT system used at Q.NET – re-read the case study to identify these, and then comment on how these impact on Q.NET's ability to fulfil its business strategy.

The effectiveness of the IT system at Q.NET can be evaluated in terms of how well it provides the information to meet the objectives of the information strategy.

Supporting operations.

The system does not provide supplies with customer purchase information. If this information was available, suppliers could calculate more accurately the ongoing demand for books. Book production and delivery could then be modified to meet Q.NET's specific sales requirements. This would ultimately support the core function of getting books to customers as quickly as possible.

Supporting the overall business strategy.

The information system can only provide detailed customer history for six weeks. This is a major limitation preventing the best use of information. The non-availability of this information will hand a competitive advantage to booksellers able to build detailed purchase histories and target customers appropriately. Seasonal patterns in purchasing will not be apparent, meaning incorrect buying decisions may be made.

Facilitating customer service.

All of the information on an individual title is not available to customers. This is a weakness, as people are more likely to purchase a product that they can not physically touch if they have sufficient information to reassure them.

8 THE INTERNET: THREATS AND OPPORTUNITIES

> **Tutorial note.** The requirement includes four elements, which provide headings for each part of your answer: Internet businesses threats; Internet businesses opportunities; non-Internet businesses threats; non-Internet businesses opportunities.
>
> Identify threats and opportunities Internet developments bring, and allocate them to the relevant heading. A detailed discussion of each threat or opportunity is not required, but you must provide enough information to make it clear what it is you are referring to.
>
> Our answer is set out in table format – this is not necessary. If in an examination you find it easier to use standard layout then do so, but use clear headings and short paragraphs that make it clear that you are making a number of separate points.

Exam answer bank

Opportunities and threats for Internet businesses

	Opportunities	Threats
Communications	• New service opportunities, such as Internet access and content hosting. • Demand for higher-bandwidth connectivity and backbones.	Disintermediation of circuit-switched voice telephony by packet-switched Internet. Retail to wholesale traffic migration. Central office port/ architecture imbalances.
Computers	• New product opportunities, such as high-speed connectivity devices and Internet software. • New electronic distribution channels.	Shifting importance of computers versus networks. Likelihood of commoditisation. New electronic distribution channels.
Consumer electronics	• New product opportunities, such as portable web browsers and Internet-savvy set-top boxes. • New electronic distribution channels.	Increased competition from high-tech firms and products. Potential decline of existing product categories. New electronic distribution channels.
Website content developers	• Niche content growth opportunities. • Emerging genres of interactive content. • Opportunities for capturing greater share of content distribution business.	Devaluation of some content, given low entry barriers and perfect competition. Need to adapt existing content to interactive environment.

Opportunities and threats for non-Internet related businesses

	Opportunities	Threats
Banking	• On-line account information. • Electronic payment via the Internet. • Withdrawal and deposit of electronic cash onto stored value cards and smart cards.	The need for branch offices will diminish. Managing electronic information will become more important for individuals. Disintermediation to 'interface' providers.
Health care	• Globally accessible medical records. • Telemedicine and remote diagnoses. • Searchable databases of medical research.	Patient confidentiality may be threatened as records are made available electronically. Disintermediation of inefficient insurers and claims processors.
Retailing	• Electronic storefronts reaching global markets. • Intelligent agents who search out the lowest price for specific products. • Electronic Data Interchange (EDI) over the Internet.	Thousands of niche retailers will emerge. The service aspect of retailing will assume increasing importance. Disintermediation of inefficient retailers.

General issues

- **Security**

There is an exposure to thieves and vandals who are using the net, for instance hackers attempting to 'crack' passwords. The Internet is still not yet entirely safe for large business transactions.

- **Technology**

  Lack of uniform standards; transfer of graphics and video can be costly.

Exam answer bank

- **Legal issues**

    Need more laws governing electronic commerce; are email contracts and electronic signatures legal?

9 INFORMATION SOURCES

> **Tutorial note.** To ensure you make a good number of points, it is useful to use a series of headings. Our answer splits information sources between internal and external sources – this is not strictly necessary, but it does help ensure a wide range of sources are considered. An answer plan, in which you note your initial thoughts, should provide likely headings. There are numerous possibilities that could have scored well for this question – the answer we provide is only an example.

To assist in the setting of prices for the future Integrated Digital Service LT plc should gather and analyse information from both **internal** and **external** sources.

Internal sources

(i) **Executive support system (ESS)**

It is stated in the scenario that LT plc's ESS contains 'summary and detailed information about overseas competitors'. It is probable that at least one overseas competitor is either already providing or has plans to provide a similar integrated digital service.

Although differences in local market conditions would have to be taken into account, the overseas competitor information would help LT plc establish a competitive price. For example it may be possible to establish the estimated cost of providing the service to each subscriber - vital pricing information.

(ii) **Other accounting information**

Other information systems have been internally focused. It is likely therefore that, even though LT plc is new to digital communications, costing data is available on at least some of the individual services that will make up the integrated service. This information should help establish the cost of providing the integrated service. When cross-referenced with other information (such as the number of subscribers expected over the next ten years) a 'break-even' price may be established.

(iii) **LT plc's strategic plan**

Any price setting exercise will need to consider the overall strategy of LT plc. What type of 'image' does LT plc wish to portray – and would this fit best with a high quality service at a premium price, or with a lower level of service and budget pricing.

The internal information gathered will help ensure LT plc sets a price that is sustainable given expected cost levels, is consistent with overall organisation strategy and maximises returns.

External sources

External sources of information that would assist in the setting of prices for the integrated service would include:

(i) **Economic information**

Sources of economic predictions include the government, newspapers and specialist economic agencies and publications. The economic outlook in LT's country would influence the number of customers that would subscribe to the service and the price potential customers would be prepared to pay. Key indicators would include predicted interest rate, inflation and unemployment levels.

(ii) **Market research**

Some market research should be carried out to establish an expected take-up rate of the new service. The number of customers expected will impact significantly on price setting and profitability. The research should include questions that establish consumer pricing expectations for such a service.

(iii) **Competitors**

LT plc is facing intense competition from companies offering very similar services. Price will therefore be a major consideration of consumers when choosing (or changing) supplier. LT plc will be unable to attract a significant number of subscribers to its service if prices are set significantly higher than those of competitors.

As the integrated service will include a range of services, prices of other integrated service providers as well as telephone companies, Internet Service Providers and pay television companies will all need to be considered.

The **external information** gathered will help ensure LT plc does not set a price significantly higher than competitors. Economic conditions will also give an indication of what price the market could be expected to bear, while interest rates and inflation expectations will influence the cost of investing in new equipment – which would in turn affect pricing decisions.

10 IMPACT ON SOCIETY

> **Tutorial note**. This question requires you to think outside the information provided in the scenario. As with many questions at Level 3, there are a wide variety of points that could be included – two completely different answers could both score well. Ensure you make approximately the same number of points relating to employment and society. This is easiest if you split your answer into two parts. You should be aware of some relevant issues from your studies – for example from Chapter 9 of this book. You should also be able to think of some relevant points 'on the spot', for example our answer manages to relate the concept of information overload to the question.

An integrated telephone, digital cable television, Internet and home shopping service has the potential to impact on employment and society. The extent of any impact will depend on the popularity of the service.

The **effects on employment** would include those discussed below.

Redundancies at traditional telephone companies. Companies that provide solely telephone services are likely to experience a reduction in demand as consumers are attracted to integrated services. This would cause a fall in profitability, which may lead to redundancies. These companies are likely to either diversify or go out of business.

Reduction in 'high street' retail staff. The number of website and home shopping transactions will increase, causing a reduction in demand in traditional shopping outlets, and a reduction in the number of staff required. However, this is likely to be at least partially offset by an **increased need for distribution staff** - processing orders received through digital channels.

Increased opportunities in all areas of television. As cable television expands, the number of 'small' cable television companies increase. These stations will require staff.

Increased **demand for IT literate staff.** For example, marketing staff are likely to need some knowledge of websites, as the importance of web-based information and transactions increases.

More opportunity for **homeworking/teleworking.** As the number of people with access to the Internet increases, organisations may consider employees working from home - particularly for 'screen-based' tasks.

'**Society**' describes the habits and customs of a group of people and the way they organise what they do. The integrated service could have the following **effects on society**.

Reduction in shopping journeys undertaken. If more people obtain the goods and services they require without leaving their home, this should reduce the number of shopping trips. This should benefit society as a whole as pressure on public transport and total car exhaust emissions should both be reduced.

Increased consumer choice. Consumers with Internet and/or digital home shopping access are able to source goods and services from all over the world. This leads to a truly **global society** in which people make purchases, send e-mails and have phone conversations with people and organisations from all around the globe.

Exam answer bank

The growth of a 24 hour society. People will be able to place orders and enjoy on-line leisure pursuits 24 hours a day. This helps people to manage their time and do what they want to do at their own convenience.

Reduced human contact. Instead of dealing face-to-face with others, people will increasingly interact with their PC or television screen and keypad.

The amount of information available to a large percentage of the population will increase significantly. People may experience **information overload** when making a previously simple decision such as 'what shall I watch on television tonight.' At the same time the **value placed on information and knowledge** will increase.

11 INFORMATION/BUSINESS STRATEGY ALIGNMENT

> **Tutorial note.** You may wish to re-read the scenario with the aim of identifying problems LT plc is facing because systems are not focussed on the home market. Some problems may not be obviously due to information deficiencies – for each problem you identify decide whether better quality information could reduce the problem and you may find it is in fact a relevant point for your answer.

The systems at LT plc have not been adapted in line with the re-focus on the home market, resulting in a mismatch between current strategy and the systems used. This has led to a number of problems.

Information required to make informed decisions about the domestic market is not readily available. Time and effort has to be spent gathering and analysing this information in an ad-hoc manner. The end result is that decisions are taking too long to be made. Not only is decision making slow, but the ad-hoc nature of the information they are based on increases the risk of making a bad decision. This could erode market share and profitability, and damage consumer perceptions of LT plc.

There is confusion on how to set prices for the new service. Price is likely to be key in the fight for market share, and in profitability. Information regarding the cost to LT plc of providing the service, and about competitors' pricing polices is vital to the development of a realistic pricing strategy.

LT plc it is taking too long to react to competitor initiatives. This is causing an erosion of market share because of the time it is taking to react to competitor initiatives. There is a lack of understanding on how to stop this fall. This problem must be addressed immediately. The customers leaving LT plc are unlikely to return in the short to medium term. New customers will also be hard to attract, as unsatisfied customers will harm LT plc's reputation.

There is insufficient bandwidth available to domestic customers. This is a major factor in the loss of market share and a major barrier to the growth of the integrated service. Customers will not tolerate 'slow' data transmission or being unable to access the services they want because of overloading.

To address these problems LT plc should take the following actions.

Key targets need to be identified that must be achieved if the re-focus on the domestic market is to prove successful (ie **critical success factors**.) Systems need to be developed that monitor and report the status of these factors, and staff need to be trained so they are able to perform tasks to the required standard.

LT plc therefore needs to implement **an ESS that provides information that supports decision-making in the domestic market**. This ESS should include competitor intelligence showing how IT is being exploited in the home market. Results of market research relating to domestic market consumer perceptions and expectations should also be available within the ESS.

To **stop the fall in market share**, either **significant investment** in hardware or the **purchase of additional bandwidth** from an outside source, will be required to improve the service available to current and future customers. An **aggressive pricing policy** may also be needed to re-establish LT plc in the domestic market.

The detailed data that is held on overseas competitors should be analysed to see if any have faced **similar situations**. If they have, lessons may be able to be learnt from their experience. **Data mining** tools may be useful in analysing the data to reveal previously hidden relationships.

Exam answer bank

12 EXECUTIVE SUPPORT SYSTEM (ESS)

> **Tutorial note.** Start your answer with a single sentence description of the type of information an ESS should provide. This will earn you an easy mark, and provides a reference point for the material you include in your answer. You should then explain the type of information ESS provide – citing examples from LT plc. It is essential that you then explain how this information would improve decision-making. Only answers that included the link between the ESS information and how the information would improve decision-making would have scored well.

An Executive Support System (ESS) should provide senior executives and the Board of LT plc with **easy access to high-level summarised data**, obtained from internal and external sources.

At the heart of LT plc's ESS will be a **corporate model** containing information such as the LT plc corporate structure, critical success factors etc. The model will also contain rules (developed in consultation with the Board and senior executives) as to how the information should be **presented and aggregated**.

The ESS will **summarise and analyse information** from LT plc's transaction systems, with the ability to 'drill-down' to view underlying data in greater detail. The Board will therefore be able to select and view information relating to a single business unit such as telephone services, a combination of units, information for geographic regions or for the organisation as a whole.

Whenever possible, **competitor data** should be gathered and incorporated into the ESS. For example the Board of LT plc should be able to compare the (estimated) profitability of a competitor's integrated service against services provided individually. When analysed against competitors' pricing information, LT should be able to make **more informed** pricing decisions.

Data manipulation facilities should enable comparison with budget, prior year data, other business units, competitors and trend analysis. These features should give the Board a clearer picture of the environment, allowing more informed decision-making.

For example, the ESS could include market share data for LT plc and competitors, and show when LT plc's market share falls or rises above predetermined limits. The board could then use the data manipulation facilities to cross-reference this information with pricing and marketing expenditure data. Over time a greater understanding will be gained of the relationship between different variables affecting the market, reducing uncertainty in decision making.

By highlighting results outside pre-determined limits the ESS focuses management attention where it is most required. The ESS information is initially screen-based, with printouts only for matters requiring further investigation. This will **prevent information overload** and **improve decision-making**.

13 PATTERSONS ELECTRICAL SUPPLIES: INFORMATION SYSTEM FAILURE

> **Tutorial note.** The requirement allows you to discuss all reasons that contribute to the failure of information systems. These reasons should be reasonably well-known to you from your studies. Use these general reasons as headings – then explain how this reason contributes to the failure of implementation systems in general. Then, for each reason, comment on the situation at Pattersons.

There are four main reasons for systems failure during implementation.

(i) **Lack of user involvement**

One of the key success criteria for system implementation is to have user input with effective communication between the users and designers of the system. User involvement means that

(1) Users have opportunities to ensure that the new system meets their requirements.

(2) Users are more likely to feel that they own the finished product, and so are more likely to use the final system.

(3) It will be more difficult to reject the final system.

In Pattersons, it is unclear how much involvement users have actually had in system development or implementation. The fact that users see the system as a failure indicates that user involvement

305

Exam answer bank

was severely limited. Any lack of involvement, or breakdown of communication will increase the risk of system failure.

(ii) **Level of management support**

Management support is normally essential to ensure the success of any project. Managers will normally be involved with a project to:

(1) Show commitment to that project
(2) Understand the issues and problems involved so these can be addressed quickly
(3) Ensure all other interested parties are also involved with the project.

The fact that management also views the shift system as a failure indicates lack of management support for the project. The change in work practices also appears to be cumbersome, which may be one of the reasons for lack of support and potential rejection of the project now. If management were not involved, then this is another reason why users will also not been involved with implementation.

(iii) **Level of complexity and risk**

There are three factors, which affect the level of complexity and risk in a project.

Firstly, a large project is more likely to fail at implementation than a small project. Size can be stated in terms of expenditure, duration of the project, number of staff involved and number of business units affected.

In Pattersons, the shift project appeared to affect the whole organisation; this gave a high risk because many business units were affected and many staff. The duration and expenditure are unclear, but given the size of the project, it is likely to have been expensive and lasted a reasonable amount of time. The risk of failure based simply on project size, is high.

Secondly, the type of project structure also affects the risk of failure. Well-structured projects are less likely to fail at implementation than poorly-structured projects. Structure provides a framework for the project, decreasing the risk of failure.

In Pattersons, it is not clear how structured the project actually was. However, the high level of user intervention now indicates that the initial analysis was not carried out very effectively. Similarly, the resistance to the system indicates lack of involvement and appropriate user sign-off of the different project stages. It is therefore likely that the project suffered from poor planning and structure and this has increased the risk of failure.

Thirdly, the experience available in respect of the technology being used. The user of newer technology and relative inexperience of IT staff will also increase the risk of failure. Newer technology may not be fully understood, while lack of experience will increase risks, as staff may not understand how the software works.

In Pattersons, it is not clear why the IT system requires manual amendments. This situation may have arisen because the technology is new and it has not been implemented correctly, so this has increased the risk of failure.

(iv) **Management of the implementation process**

Poor management of the implementation process in terms of

- Poor estimation of the time to complete the project
- Not allocating sufficient resources to the project, and
- Poor communication between members of the project team

will all increase the risk of project failure.

In the case of Pattersons, it is not clear how far these factors actually affected the project. However, not meeting user requirements does indicate some poor management, possibly in terms of communication, and this may have attributed to the failure of the project.

Exam answer bank

14 PATTERSONS ELECTRICAL SUPPLIES: IT/IS STRATEGY AND BUSINESS STRATEGY

> **Tutorial note.** For part (a), think about the integration of IT/IS and business strategy, and how one supports the other, then important areas such as information provision and the benefits of IT may start to become apparent. You could use the different levels of information required by an organisation to provide structure to your answer – but remember to answer the question, not simply describe different types of information and strategy.
>
> In part (b), structure your answer around the three terms mentioned in the question. The requirements of this part are specific – so do exactly what is expected. Start by explaining automation in general terms, then relate this definition to the situation at Pattersons. Do this for each of the three terms, and you will score well.

(a) Business strategy and IS/IT strategy are normally developed together in an organisation, because the IS/IT provides essential support to the overall business strategy. For example, information systems will be required to provide appropriate information for each level of management to enable the business to be run efficiently.

The information that can be provided by the IS/IT systems is outlined below.

(i) **Strategic level information.** This is for the use of senior managers and will relate to long term planning. For example, in Pattersons, information may be provided to assist in decisions regarding the location of new stores.

(ii) **Management level information.** Information to support the activities of monitoring, controlling and decision making carried out by middle managers. In the case of Pattersons, information may be provided on total sales by product line and current stock levels to help in planning promotions or special offers within certain stores.

(iii) **Knowledge level information.** This is information to support the knowledge workers in an organisation. Pattersons may provide customer databases for workers to try and identify trends in customer data in order to improve advertising and overall sales.

(iv) **Operational level information.** Within Pattersons, as in any retail organisation, this will relate to current stock levels, re-order details, information about individual sales invoices etc. The information will be summarised and input to the MIS for additional analysis.

Almost any organisation can provide these information systems for their managers and workers. To remain competitive, Pattersons will need to ensure that the appropriate systems are in place to provide the necessary management information.

If the business and IS/IT strategies are not congruent with each other, then there is a danger that either appropriate information will not be provided, or that the IT infrastructure will be built up without reference to the information requirements of the organisation. Careful planning is therefore needed, with control from the Board level, to ensure that these errors do not occur.

Appropriate IS/IT strategy planning will be facilitated by the appointment of a Chief Information Officer to the Board of directors. This individual will be responsible for:

(i) Developing the information systems in-house to meet business needs. For example, there may be the opportunity to re-structure the whole ordering and sales processes within Pattersons by using Internet related technology. However, any change must be carried out in accordance with the business aims of Pattersons.

(ii) Looking for opportunities to use IT to create business advantage. Within Pattersons, this will involve the use of the proposed Internet site.

(iii) Ensuring that the IT systems support the overall business strategy. The proposed Internet site must fit in with the overall strategy at Pattersons. Establishing the site without appropriate planning may cause significant problems, such as rejection of the site by store managers because they feel that their store income is threatened.

(iv) Ensuring that sufficient IT resources are available to maintain and develop systems. For example, the directors may require additional information about actions of competitors including Internet links to their sites and information services such as Reuters. The CIO will need to ensure that appropriate IT infrastructure is available to support this business requirement.

Exam answer bank

The important point is to ensure that the IT / IS strategy is congruent with the business strategy. Pattersons appears to have achieved this, although changes in the future will need to be planned and monitored closely to ensure that this remains the case.

(b) **Automation** refers to the computerisation of existing tasks and procedures. IT is used to make those existing tasks more efficient and effective, rather than to amend or change the tasks to provide additional benefits.

This use of IT is a fairly low risk strategy, as the business processes are essentially unchanged. Within Pattersons, automation will have occurred in the sales systems, probably by installing electronic point of sale equipment and in stock control and monitoring by maintaining the stock balances on a database. However, the underlying process of the customer paying for goods at a checkout, and stock balances being available from some form of stock recording system, are essentially unchanged.

Rationalisation involves some changes to the business, normally to make existing processes more effective or efficient in some way by linking them together.

The need for rationalisation can occur from two main areas:

(i) Business reviews indicate that existing IT systems would be more efficient if they were linked. For example, stock control information is available on a computer system, and details of stock items sold are also recorded electronically. However, the stock database is only updated with sales information at the end of each working day. Linking these two systems on-line provides the benefit of sales being recorded immediately in the stock system. Real-time stock information is now available rather than the balances being up to one day out of date.

(ii) The process of automation may start to cause inefficiencies in other areas. For example, when a sale is made, customer details are entered into a computer system. However, those details are printed out to provide a list of goods to obtain from a warehouse, with the list being sent in the post to arrive at the warehouse next day for delivery in say, one week. Previously, when customer details were recorded manually, there was no expectation that goods would be available within say 48 hours, but now that information is captured electronically, a seven day delivery seems a very long time. Automation is also needed to link the sales systems with warehouse stocks to provide quicker response times.

The Pattersons business appears to have rationalised the IT systems already as an integrated accounting system and 48 hour delivery of goods from a warehouse are already available.

Re-engineering involves the re-design of business processes to try and maximise the benefits from IT. Savings are normally obtained in terms of reduced cost, elimination of duplicated activities, or improved speed of response from the processes.

The process of re-engineering will involve a review of the entire business processes, with the expectation that IT will provide different, and significantly more efficient work methods. Change in this respect will be much more significant than either automation or rationalisation. Because change is significant, re-engineering is a high-risk strategy for any organisation.

Before re-engineering can take place, the organisation will need to consider what the objective of each business process is, and how IT can best support that process. This means re-designing the process, rather than simply making it more efficient by automation. In the context of Pattersons, setting up the Internet site is a form of re-engineering because this is a different method of carrying out business compared to cash and carry; the latter could not be adopted to provide Internet trading so new processes are required.

15 PATTERSONS ELECTRICAL SUPPLIES: INTERNET, EXTRANET, INTRANET

> **Tutorial note.** If you have used the Internet to buy something, think what attracted you to a specific organisation's website. Remember also that some contact may best be conducted using other means – such as the telephone – but that the website could facilitate this through features such as 'call back requests'. It is vital the back-office procedures are in place to meet any requests made via the website.
>
> In part (b) our answer, and the suggested outline from the ACCA, explains methods of sharing information electronically. The extranet could be used as the platform that facilitates a whole range of data and information exchange.
>
> For part (c), think of the intranet as an internal Internet that facilitates the sharing of information with internal customers.

(a) The Internet provides businesses with access to a rapidly expanding market of customers as the number of people with access to the Internet increases. Most businesses have established their own website in an attempt to take advantage of this growth. A business that does not provide some form of web purchasing option, or at least viewing of products on-line, risks losing customers to competitors who do provide these options.

Start with a brief explanation of the Internet

(i) **User requirements**

Potential customers require information when visiting a store or a website. Key data that must be available includes product, price, availability, features of the product and any additional charges such as delivery or insurance contracts to guard against product failure. The website must provide this information in an easy-to-use format.

Pattersons could establish a website providing this information (the site can be linked to the integrated stock system). However, the concept of cash-and-carry would be lost as all purchases would have to be delivered to the customer, unless a 'pick up from store' option was made available. Also, Pattersons would not be able to offer the services of their trained sales representatives, as the Internet simply displays text and pictures, and not interactive customer service. An alternative would be to provide a telephone call back system (similar to Dell computers) where customers can click on a web-link and receive a call from a Patterson sales representative to discuss their purchase.

Vital that web-based operations are integrated with back-office systems

(ii) **Retaining the customer**

Customers are likely to visit a number of websites to compare prices and product details. Providing some form of personalisation of the website for repeat visits, such as welcoming the customer by name or displaying a list of products already reviewed, would help make the site more customer friendly. Software is available to provide this type of service on the Internet.

Again Pattersons could establish a website to provide these features. Any other features that will add value to the site, such as offering a list of related products or spare parts for the product being purchased could also help to make the site more attractive to customers.

Could mention 'cookies', but don't become bogged down with technical aspects

(iii) **Incentives to use the web site**

Using the Internet for purchasing does provide a risk that sales will fall in the individual shops maintained by Pattersons. However, new customers may also be reached, especially those who are not located within travelling distance of a Pattersons store, or who do not like shopping for large electrical items. In this situation, providing some incentive to use the web site such as coupons or a loyalty points scheme may help to attract additional purchasers.

Want new customers rather than cannibalising existing sales

(iv) **Other value added activities**

When a purchase is made on a website, customer information will be stored by the supplier's computer system. This information can be used to help provide repeat business for the organisation.

Databases, datawarehousing, datamining and CRM could all be relevant

For example, if a vacuum cleaner is purchased from Pattersons, then an e-mail can be sent to that customer in a few weeks with information about replacement bags for that cleaner. Similarly, data can be mined to identify relationships in purchases, for example, Pattersons may find that customers purchasing a washing machine often purchase a tumble dryer a few months later. Offers can be sent via e-mail direct to the customer including coupons for tumble dryer purchase.

(b) An extranet is an extension of an internal intranet. The intranet provides information about an organisation such as stock levels, customer details, product information etc. to employees within that organisation. An extranet means making this information available to specific third parties. For example, the Dell database of technical information about computers is made available to some customers to help diagnose faults with those computers.

> Start with a brief explanation of an extranet

Pattersons may be able to use direct electronic links with customers and suppliers to provide business benefits, particularly in managing the supply chain.

Stock levels. Suppliers can be given access to stock levels at Pattersons. Where stocks fall below a re-order level, either at head office or a store, the supplier will automatically send replacement stocks. This will benefit Pattersons because less employee time is spent reviewing stock levels and replacement stocks will be sent immediately they are required.

> Focus on business processes

Supplier communications. E-mail can be used to inform suppliers about new stock requirements or changes to trading conditions. This communication method provides significant time and cost savings over other forms of communication. For example, Pattersons can inform suppliers about upcoming promotions on specific products so that more of those items can be produced ready for re-sale.

Stock purchasing. Information concerning stock deliveries and receipts can be sent by Electronic Data Interchange. This will again provide time and cost savings in terms of staff as well as providing up-to-date information on stock movements. Pattersons already has an integrated order system, so linking this to an external EDI system is possible.

> The extranet could facilitate the sharing and exchanging of information with other businesses

Payment. Payments can be made electronically using Electronic Funds Transfer. This will speed up the payment process, if Pattersons want to do this. Similarly, payments can be made automatically based on the receipt of goods. For example, Pattersons may want to reward quicker delivery of goods by paying those suppliers in a few days rather than a few weeks.

Other applications, such as financial management of funds are available, although these may have limited use for Pattersons at the moment.

(c) An intranet is an internal Internet-like network for use within an organisation. The intranet uses the same technology as the Internet, namely a web-browser to view web pages. However, those pages are only available to employees in the organisation and so they will normally contain information specific for use by those employees.

> Start with a brief explanation of an intranet

An intranet may be able to assist staff at Pattersons in various ways.

(i) **Provision of internal e-mail and discussion forums**

E-mail can be used as a basic communication tool within the company. However, discussion forums can be set up to provide a forum on various matters such as product queries. A sales representative in one store may not know the answer to a question concerning a product. This query can be placed on a discussion database, and a representative in a different store may be able to provide the answer. This system will help to improve the knowledge of different products being sold.

> Choose internal processes related to Pattersons' situation

(ii) **Remote sharing of information**

Intranets allow information on central databases to be viewed from any location. In this situation, stock levels at head office and all stores could be viewed enabling sales representatives to confirm stock availability across all stores, and hopefully increase overall sales. This system will provide a significant advantage over the current system of centralising information at head office only.

> Use the information contained in the scenario

(iii) **Sharing of reference material**

Any reference material, such as detailed information about products or even the organisation's telephone list, can be placed on the intranet. As well as making it more accessible to all members of staff, this also allows for efficient and timely update. The information can be updated frequently in one location rather than having out-of-date paper-based copies of the information in each store. Having better information on products will also help provide enhanced customer service.

Other information such as competitor prices and promotional activities can also be shared via the intranet, making all staff more aware of the competitive environment.

16 INFORMATION OVERLOAD

> **Tutorial note.** The requirement states that you should 'briefly' explain the concept of information overload – this implies that the majority of the marks for this question will be awarded for the other parts of the requirement.
>
> When discussing amendments to the HK consulting information system, think of 'information system' in its broadest sense. Any process, procedure or tool used to collect, process, store, analyse or communicate information could be brought into your answer.

(a) Developments in information technology and information systems have enabled organisations to collect, store and analyse large quantities of information. This should lead to better decision making. However, as the quantity of information available has increased, it has become more important to ensure that individuals only receive the information that they require to do their job. Otherwise, the danger is that an individual will be swamped by so much information that they will overlook the information that is most important.

[Start with a brief explanation of information overload]

Action that could be taken to limit information being received include:

Route incoming telephone calls via a secretary.

The accountant should not face regular telephone interruptions. A secretary should be allocated to take telephone messages, putting through only calls of significance that require immediate attention. To be effective, the instructions concerning calls that should be put through, and how messages should be relayed must be specific.

[Don't ignore 'obvious' or simple solutions if they are relevant]

Using intelligent agents.

Agents could be set up to obtain information from the Internet or an internal intranet. The criteria set down as to what should be retrieved should be specific to reduce the likelihood of irrelevant information being selected. The use of agents would reduce the amount of time the accountant would need to spend reviewing websites.

[Provide enough explanation to show you understand what you are saying]

Delegate some client contact.

Some decisions the accountant is taking may not require the consideration of such a senior person. Ongoing routine contact with clients could be delegated to one of the more junior managers. This should considerably limit the information received by the accountant.

[People are an important part of information systems]

Subscribing to a newsclipping service.

The reviewing of journals for relevant information is time-consuming. A news clipping service could review relevant journals and newspapers and forward via e-mail copies of those articles that meet specific criteria.

Filtering e-mail.

Up-to-date e-mail programs have the ability to review and re-direct messages based on the message content, priority, sender and/or intended recipients. The accountant may decide only to review messages that are sent as urgent or which contain specific text,

[Ensure you apply 'book knowledge' to the scenario]

311

Exam answer bank

such as a client name. The non-selected messages could be copied to a selected person, or just redirected to a non-urgent inbox for review later.

(b) The accountant has a strategic decision-making role within the organisation. Strategic decision-making requires information with the following characteristics:

> *The type of information required depends on what it will be used for.*

The information should be **summarised**. An overview of how a given situation could affect the organisation as a whole will be of more use to the accountant than the detail. Detail may be available in the form of appendices should this be required.

Information should be **presented appropriately**. The method of presentation should help understanding. It may be appropriate to present information in an electronic document, which can be amended quickly, rather than in a paper-based report. If information is presented in the form of a lengthy report, a table of contents and summary of the report's findings should be provided at the beginning. The report should also have appropriate paragraphs and headings and use clear language. If appropriate, the information may be posted on the company's intranet (if the contents are not confidential and the intranet is used efficiently by those who need to view the information).

> *Again, don't be afraid to 'state the obvious' if it is relevant.*

The information needs to be **complete**. All the information that can affect a decision should be received and reviewed. Strategic decisions based on incomplete information could result in an inappropriate strategy being followed.

The information must be **timely**. In many situations, circumstances may change quickly, meaning information goes out of date rapidly. Strategic decisions often depend on 'first mover' advantage.

The information should be **relevant**. Information should be filtered to remove material not relevant to the recipient. Irrelevant information contributes to information overload.

> *You may have chosen other characteristics. At this level there are usually a range of answers that would score well*

Information for strategic decision-making should also include **external** information – such as competitor and industry related information.

Index

Index

Note: **Key Terms** and their references are given in **bold**

Acceptance, 225
Accounting rate of return (ARR), 125
Accounting records, 19
Action, 104
Active resistance, 225
ADSL, 184
Advantages of database systems, 85
Alliances, 215
Amazon.com, 193
Analysis, 232
Analysis tools, 239
Analysts' workbenches, 239
Application Service Providers (ASP), 164
Artificial intelligence (AI), 77
Asymmetric Digital Subscriber Line (ADSL), 184
Audit trail, 32
Authentication, 188
Automate, informate, transformate, 118

B2B world, 204
Back-up, 31
Backward compatibility, 259
Balanced approach, 13
Bargaining power of customers, 153
Bargaining power of suppliers, 152
Barriers to entry, 152
Batch processing, 26
Bespoke development risks, 169
Bespoke software, 168, 169
Beta versions, 186
Boehm's spiral model, 236
Boot sector viruses, 188
Bottom up, 50
'Brick or click', 183
Browsers, 180
Bulletin boards, 183
Business analysis, 129
Business automation, 112, 113
Business case, 124
Business case development, 124
Business case justification, 125
Business case report, 129
Business led, 50
Business Process Engineering, 115
Business Process Re-engineering (BPR), 112, **113**, 114, 115, 116
Business rationalisation, 112, 113
Business Re-engineering, 112, 113

Business strategy, 38
Business system, 110
Business to Business (B2B) sector, 182
Business-to-business 'infomediaries', 182

C++, 241
CAD, 73
Call-back buttons, 183
Capability, 39
Capital costs, 126
CASE repository, 239
CASE tool, 239
Centralised, 213
Centralised processing, 258
Chain-of-command, 260
Change, 224, 226
Changeover, 246
Check digits, 31
Checkland's SSM, 104, 105
Child segment, 83
Class, 242
Clickstreams, 192
Cobra report, 116
Code generators, 240
Competitive advantage, 43, 46, **155**
Competitive rivalry, 154
Competitive strategies, 43
Complex, 39
Computer aided manufacturing, 158
Computer Aided Software Engineering (CASE), 238
Computer automated design (CAD), 159
Computer conferencing, 259
Computer integrated manufacturing, 158
Computer Telephony Integration (CTI), 259
Conceptual model, 107
Consultancies, 20, 163
Consumer privacy, 268
Contagion, 148
Contingency, 32
Continuous gap, 133
Control, 148
Control totals, 31
Controlling, 4
Cookies, 191
Copyright, 172
Copyright, Designs and Patents Act 1998, 172
Corporate over-use, 171

Index

Corporate strategy, **38**, 45
Corporate systems, 111
Cost categories, 126
Cost control, 229
Cost leadership, 156
Critical success factors (CSF), **51**, 52, 53, 54, 147, **262**
Cryptography, 195
Culture, 60
Current Situation Analysis (CSA), 130
Customer databases, 158
Customer needs, 61
Customer relationship management (CRM), 89, 159, 202
Customer service, 196, 258
Customers, 61, 88, 153, 196, 258

Data, 4
Data administration, 149
Data capture, 18
Data dictionary, 239
Data independence, 81
Data integrity, 30
Data mart, 87
Data redundancy, 81
Data warehouse, 86
Data workers, 70
Database, 81, 115
Database management system (DBMS), 81
Database structures, 82
Database system, 81, 82
Datamining, 90
Decentralised, 213
Decentralised processing, 258
Decision making, 5
Decision Support System (DSS), **25**
Decision support tools, 115
Delphi model, 61
Departmental level systems, 111
Depersonalisation, 102
Design, 232
Development costs, 126
Developments in communications, 259
Diagramming tools, 239
Dial-back security, 188
Differentiation, 156
Digital divide, 216
Digital television, 181
Direct changeover, 246
Direction, 39
Disaster recovery plan, 32, 33
Disruptive power, 115

Distribution, 190
Divisional level systems, 111
Document generators, 240
Document image processing, 75
Document imaging systems, 73
Document reading methods, 20
Domain name, 181
Domestic exporter, 212, 213
Dropper, 187
Duplicated, 213
Dynamic pricing, 194

Earl, 49, 50, 130, 151
Earl's grid, 130
Earl's three leg analysis, 49, 50
E-business, 207
E-business strategic implications, 207
E-commerce, 47, **189**, 190, 193, 194, 195, 198, 206
E-commerce benefits, 195
E-commerce dangers, 195
E-commerce disadvantages, 194
E-commerce investment case, 206
E-commerce strategy, 198
Effectiveness, 248, 249
Efficiency, 248, 249
EFTPOS, 21
Electronic business, 207
Electronic commerce, 47, **189**, 190, 193, 194, 195, 198, 206
Electronic Data Interchange (EDI), 20, 153, 159, 190
Electronic marketing, 191
Electronic Point of Sale (EPOS), 21
E-mail, 183, 201
E-mail tracking systems, 183
Employee privacy, 268
Employee/employer relationship, 259
Empowerment, 256
Enabling technology, 144
Encryption, 186, **187**
End-user development, 172, 173
Enterprise analysis, 51
Enterprise Resource Planning (ERP), 89, 158
Environment, 18, 39, 111, 224
Environmental scanning, **20**, 142
EPOS systems, 21, 158
Equality, 270
ERP, 89, 158
ESS, 23
Ethical analysis, 271
Ethical issues, 270, 271

Index

Ethics, 270, 271
Exchange rate, 59
Executive Support System (ESS), **23**
Expert systems, 73, 78, 115
Explicit knowledge, 70
Extended experience, 203
External information, 19
External integration tools, 234
Extranet, 76
Extrapolation, 132

Facilities Management (FM), 162
Factory quadrant, 131
FAQs, 200
Feasibility study, 101
File creation, 246
File viruses, 187
Financial services, 194
Firewalls, 186, 188
First wave, 266
Flat organisation, 256, 257
Flattened hierarchy, 216
Focus, 156
Formal control tools, 235
Formflow, 75
Fourth generation language (4GL), **241**
Franchiser, 212, 213
Freelancers, 257
Frequently-Asked Questions (FAQs), 183
Fuzzy logic, 73
Fuzzy logic, 81

Gap analysis, 130, **132**, 133
General environment, 56
Generic strategies, 43
Globaisation, 209, 213
Global Business Drivers (GBDs), 213
Global business strategy, 212
Global delivery system, 214
Global information strategy, 212
Global Information Systems (GIS), 212
Global market, 214
Global organisations, 209
Global workgroups, 214
Globalisation, 215
Groupware, 73

Hackers, 186
Hacking, 186
Hammer and Champy, 113

Hard properties, 100
Hard systems approach, 100, 101
Hardware cost, 126
Hash totals, 31
Heuristics, 78
Hierarchical model, 82
Hierarchy of systems, 111
High potential applications, 132
Hoaxes, 189
Homeworking, 261
HTML (HyperText Markup Language), 180
Hyperlinks, 74
HyperText Transfer Protocol (http), 180

Implementation, 233
Implementation process, 231
Inbound logistics, 158
Incentives, 182
Incremental approach, 164
Indifference, 225
Inflation, 59
Informate, 118
Information, 4
Information analysis, 130
Information as a commodity, 11
Information audit, 129
Information benefits, 14
Information bureaux, 20
Information centre (IC), 246
Information director, 17
Information infrastructure, 17
Information management, 15
information management (IM) strategy, 15
Information market, 259
Information needs assessment, 130
Information overload, 260, 263
Information services, 20
Information society, 11, 29
Information system, 4
Information system benefits, 128
information system security, 29
Information systems manager, 17
Information systems planning, 61
Information systems strategy, 17, 18, 39, 45, 48
Information technology strategy, 49
Informix-4GL, 107
Infrastructure led, 50
Initiation, 147
Inputs, 252
Inside out, 50
Insourcing, 167

317

Index

Installation costs, 126, 128
Institutional strategies, 43
Intangible costs, 126
Integrated Services Digital Network (ISDN), 184
Integration, 81, 149
Integration, 27
Integrators, 192
Integrity, 82
Intellectual property rights, 269
Intelligent agents, 73, **264**
Intention, 104
Interaction theory, 234
Interactive websites, 116
Interest rates, 59
Internal data sources, 18
Internal integration tools, 235
Internal rate of return (IRR), 125
International business conditions, 211
International Standards Organisation (ISO), 269
Internet, 20, 46, 153, 173, 180, 183, 186
Internet distribution, 190
Internet growth, 181
Internet kiosks, 181
Internet problems, 184
Internet sales and marketing, 191, 199
Internet security issues, 186
Internet uses, 181
Interoperability, 258
Intranets, 73, 75
Investment workstation, 76
Investment workstations, 73
IS gap, 134
IS/IT Strategy, 44
ISDN, 184
IT impact on organisations, 256

Java, 241
Join, 85
Joint Applications Development (JAD), 245
Joint venture sourcing, 164

Key encapsulation, 195
Key operational applications, 132
Key performance indicators, 52
Key recovery agent (KRA), 195
Keys, 195
Keyword search, 183
Knowledge, 70
Knowledge creation, 71

Knowledge management, 70
Knowledge Work Systems (KWS), 25, 70, 76
Knowledge Workers, 25, 70
KPIs, 52

Learning and action, 105
Legacy system, 259
Legal framework, 57
Liaison, 17
Libraries, 20
Licences, 171
Lifecycle approach, 101
Limit checks, 31
Logic bomb, 188
Logical design, 237
Logical structure, 81
Lotus Notes, 74
Lower CASE tools, 239

Machine tool control, 158
Macro viruses, 188
Magnetic Ink Character Recognition (MICR), 21
Magnetic stripe cards, 21
Management, 45
Management information, 45
Management Information Systems (MIS), 23, 24
Manufacturing requirements planning (MRPII), 158
Many-to-many relationships, 83
Maturity, 149
McFarlan, 131
McFarlan's applications portfolio, 132
McKenney, 131
Meaning, 104
Megatrends, 199
Membership functions, 81
Methodology, 237
Metrics, 249
Mixed approach, 50
Multinationals, 210, 212, 213
Multiple sourcing, 164
Mutidimensinal data analysis, 87

Natural language, 77
Network model, 82, 83
Networked, 213
Neural networks, 73, 80
New entrants, 152

Index

Nolan's Six Stage Growth Model, 147
Nolan's stage hypothesis, 147
Non-Governmental Organisations (NGOs), 216

OAS, 25, 73
Objectives, 147
Object-oriented Programming, 242
OCR, 21
Office Automation System (OAS), 25
Office automation system, 25, 73
Off-the shelf package, 168, 169
One-to-many relationship, 83
On-line analytical processing (OLAP), 87, 88
On-line processing, 26
Open systems, 259
Operating costs, 126
Operational information, 6
Operational level systems, 111
Operations, 39
Operations planning, 44
Optical Character Recognition (OCR), 21
Optical Mark Reading (OMR), 21
Organisation impact analysis, 232
Organisation structure, 44, 224, 256
Organisational information requirements, 49
Organisational learning, 71
Outbound logistics, 158
Outputs, 251
Outsourcing, 162
Overwriting viruses, 187

Parallel running, 246
Parsons generic strategies for IS, 55
Passive resistance, 225
Payback period, 125
People- oriented theory, 234, 235
Perceptive systems, 77
Performance indicators, 52
Performance measurement, 5
Performance review, 251
Personal Digital Assistant (PDA), 181
Personnel costs, 126
PEST analysis, 56, 61
PEST factors, 56
Phased changeover, 247
Physical design, 237
Physical security, 30
Physical structure, 81
Pilot operation, 247
Planning, 4

Pointers, 84
Political and legal environment, 57
Political issues, 268
Porter's five forces, 152
Porter's value chain, 156
Portfolio analysis, 134
Privacy, 268, 269
Process, 113
Process control, 158
Producers, 192
Product-market strategies, 43
Programmers' workbenches, 239
Programming, 233
Programming tools, 170
Project, 85
Projection, 132
Property rights, 269
Proprietary software, 153
Prosperity, 269
Prototype, 243
Push technology, 265

Range checks, 31
Rapid applications development (RAD), 246
Rational model, 40
Ratios, 52
Real world, 105
Reference works, 20
Refreeze, 226
Relational data structure, 84
Relational model, 82, 84
Remote working, 261
Report generator, 240
Resistance to change, 224
Resource analysis, 130
Resource planning, 44
Resources, 39
Return on investment (ROI), 125
Revenue costs, 126
Rich picture, 109
Rivalry, 154
Robotics, 77
Robots, 158
Rockart, 51
Root definition, 106
Root segment, 83

Scanners, 21
Scenarios, 128
Scoring model, 135
Screen layout generator, 240

Index

Search engine, 180
Second wave, 266
Security, 29
Security and the Internet, 186
Select, 85
Sensitivity analysis, 128
Service bureaux, 162
Service Level Agreement (SLA), 165
Service Level Contract (SLC), 165
Share registrar companies, 145
Short-termism, 59
Signatures, 195
Simple gap, 133
Smart cards, 22
Social change, 59, 102, 267
Social issues, 266
Sociotechnical design, 261, **262**
Socio-technical systems, 112
Soft systems approach, 102
Soft Systems Methodology (SSM), 104, 105
Software houses, 163
Software licences, 171
Span of control, 256
Spiral model, 236
SSDAM, 237
Stakeholders, 45, 144
Status checking, 183
Steering committee, 45
Strategic analysis approach, 41, 51, 52
Strategic applications, 132
Strategic business objectives, 40
Strategic choice, 43
Strategic grid, 131
Strategic information, 5
Strategic information systems, 48
Strategic level information system, 23
Strategic planning, 38
Strategic quadrant, 131
Strategic-level systems, 48
Strategy, 38
Strategy for e-commerce, 198
Strategy implementation, 44
Strategy selection, 43
Structured Systems Analysis and Design Method SSADM, 237
Structured walkthroughs, 245
Substitute products, 153
Subsystems, 111
Suppliers, 152
Supply chain, 192, 216
Support activities, 159
Support applications, 132

Support quadrant, 131
Switching costs, 153, 182
SWOT analysis, 142
System, 110
System hierarchy, 111
System- oriented theory, 234
Systems analysis, 129
Systems development lifecycle (SDLC), 101, 232
Systems evaluation, 248
Systems integration, 162, 165
Systems integrity, 30
Systems methodology, 100
Systems practice, 100

Tacit knowledge, 70
Tactical information, 5
Tall organisation, 256
Task environment, 56
Technical issues, 61
Technological change, 258
Telecommunications networks, 115
Telecommuting, 261
Telephone banking, 152
Testing, 233
Third wave, 266
Three leg analysis, 50
Three legs of IS strategy development, 49
Time bomb, 188
Time share, 162
Time/Cost/Quality Triangle, 229
Top down, 50
Touch screens, 22
Tracking technology, 116
Transaction costs, 182
Transaction Processing Systems (TPS), 26
Transactions, 4
Transformate, 118
Transnational, 212, 213
Transparent pricing, 193
Trojans, 188
Turnaround quadrant, 131
Types of information system, 23
Types of strategy, 43

Uncertainty, 56
Unfreeze, 225
Universal Resource Locator, 180
Upper CASE tools, 239
URL, 180
User groups, 173

Index

User resistance, 233, 234
Users of information, 16

Value, 39
Value chain, 156
Value chain analysis, 157
Videoconferencing, 259
Virtual company, 192
Virtual hierarchies, 215
Virtual reality systems, 73, 77
Virtual Supply Chain (VSC), 192
Virtual warehouses, 158
Viruses, 187
Voice mail, 259
Voice recognition, 22

W^{2}R, 124
W^{3}2B, 125
WAP phones, 181
Website, 116, 180
Website essentials, 196
Website integration with back office, 196
Wizards (interview style interface), 183
Workflow, 75
World Wide Web (www), 180
Worms, 188
www, 180

Zero based budgeting, 113
Zuboff, 118

See overleaf for information on other
BPP products and how to order

ACCA Order

To BPP Professional Education, Aldine Place, London W12 8AW
Tel: 020 8740 2211　　　　　　　　　　　　　　Fax: 020 8740 1184
email: publishing@bpp.com　　　　　　　　　online: www.bpp.com

Mr/Mrs/Ms (Full name) _____

Daytime delivery address _____

Postcode _____ Scots law variant Y / N

Daytime Tel _____ Date of exam (month/year) _____

POSTAGE & PACKING

Study Texts

	First	Each extra	Online
UK	£5.00	£2.00	£2.00
Europe*	£6.00	£4.00	£4.00
Rest of world	£20.00	£10.00	£10.00

£ ____　£ ____　£ ____

Kits

	First	Each extra	Online
UK	£5.00	£2.00	£2.00
Europe*	£6.00	£4.00	£4.00
Rest of world	£20.00	£10.00	£10.00

£ ____　£ ____　£ ____

Passcards/Success Tapes/MCQ Cards/CDs

	First	Each extra	Online
UK	£2.00	£1.00	£1.00
Europe*	£3.00	£2.00	£2.00
Rest of world	£8.00	£8.00	£8.00

£ ____　£ ____　£ ____

Grand Total (incl. Postage)　£ _____

I enclose a cheque for
(Cheques to *BPP Professional Education*)

Or charge to Visa/Mastercard/Switch

Card Number _____

Expiry date _____　Start Date _____

Issue Number (Switch Only) _____

Signature _____

Order Table

	6/03 Texts	1/03 Kits	1/03 Passcards	MCQ Cards	Tapes	8/03 i-Learn	8/03 i-Pass	Virtual Campus
PART 1								
1.1 Preparing Financial Statements	£20.95	£10.95	£6.95		£12.95	£34.95	£24.95	£90.00
1.2 Financial Information for Management †	£20.95	£10.95	£6.95	£5.95		£34.95	£24.95	£90.00
1.3 Managing People	£20.95	£10.95	£6.95	£5.95	£12.95	£34.95	£24.95	£90.00
PART 2								
2.1 Information Systems	£20.95	£10.95	£6.95			£34.95	£24.95	£90.00
2.2 Corporate and Business Law**	£20.95	£10.95	£6.95		£12.95	£34.95	£24.95	£90.00
2.3 Business Taxation FA 2002 (for 12/03 exams)	£20.95	£10.95	£6.95		£12.95	£34.95	£24.95	£90.00
2.4 Financial Management and Control †	£20.95	£10.95	£6.95		£12.95	£34.95	£24.95	£90.00
2.5 Financial Reporting	£20.95	£10.95	£6.95		£12.95	£34.95	£24.95	£90.00
2.6 Audit and Internal Review	£20.95	£10.95	£6.95		£12.95	£34.95	£24.95	£90.00
PART 3								
3.1 Audit and Assurance Services	£20.95	£10.95	£6.95		£12.95		£24.95	
3.2 Advanced Taxation FA 2002 (for 12/03 exams)	£20.95	£10.95	£6.95		£12.95		£24.95	
3.3 Performance Management †	£20.95	£10.95	£6.95		£12.95		£24.95	
3.4 Business Information Management	£20.95	£10.95	£6.95		£12.95		£24.95	
3.5 Strategic Business Planning and Development	£20.95	£10.95	£6.95		£12.95		£24.95	
3.6 Advanced Corporate Reporting	£20.95	£10.95	£6.95		£12.95		£24.95	
3.7 Strategic Financial Management	£20.95	£10.95	£6.95		£12.95		£24.95	
INTERNATIONAL STREAM								
1.1 Preparing Financial Statements	£20.95	£10.95	£6.95	£5.95				
2.2 Corporate and Business Law (International Variant-9/03)	£20.95							
2.5 Financial Reporting	£20.95	£10.95	£6.95					
2.6 Audit and Internal Review	£20.95	£10.95	£6.95					
3.1 Audit and Assurance Services	£20.95	£10.95	£6.95					
3.6 Advanced Corporate Reporting	£20.95	£10.95	£6.95					
Success in your Research and Analysis Project – Tutorial Text (8/03)	£19.95							
Learning to Learn (7/02)	£9.95							

Subtotal £ _____

We aim to deliver to all UK addresses inside 5 working days; a signature will be required. Orders to all EU addresses should be delivered within 6 working days. All other orders to overseas addresses should be delivered within 8 working days.
* Europe includes the Republic of Ireland and the Channel Islands. † 6/02 for 12/03 exam. **The new edition published in 8/03 is for the 6/04 exam only.** ** For Scots law variant students, a free *Scots Law Supplement* is available with the 2.2 Text. Please indicate in the name and address section if this applies to you.

ACCA – Paper 3.4 Business Information Management (6/03)

REVIEW FORM & FREE PRIZE DRAW

All original review forms from the entire BPP range, completed with genuine comments, will be entered into a draw on 31 January 2004 and 31 July 2004. The names on the first four forms picked out will be sent a cheque for £50.

Name: _____ Address: _____

How have you used this Text?
(Tick one box only)
☐ Home study (book only)
☐ On a course: college _____
☐ With 'correspondence' package
☐ Other _____

Why did you decide to purchase this Text?
(Tick one box only)
☐ Have used complementary Kit
☐ Have used BPP Texts in the past
☐ Recommendation by friend/colleague
☐ Recommendation by a lecturer at college
☐ Saw advertising
☐ Other _____

During the past six months do you recall seeing/receiving any of the following?
(Tick as many boxes as are relevant)
☐ Our advertisement in *ACCA Student Accountant*
☐ Our advertisement in *Pass*
☐ Our advertisement in *PQ*
☐ Our brochure with a letter through the post

Which (if any) aspects of our advertising do you find useful?
(Tick as many boxes as are relevant)
☐ Prices and publication dates of new editions
☐ Information on Text content
☐ Facility to order books off-the-page
☐ None of the above

Which BPP products have you used?

Text	☑	MCQ cards	☐	i-Learn	☐
Kit	☐	Tape	☐	i-Pass	☐
Passcard	☐	Video	☐	Virtual Campus	☐

Your ratings, comments and suggestions would be appreciated on the following areas.

	Very useful	Useful	Not useful
Introductory section (Key study steps, personal study)	☐	☐	☐
Chapter introductions	☐	☐	☐
Key terms	☐	☐	☐
Quality of explanations	☐	☐	☐
Case examples and other examples	☐	☐	☐
Questions and answers in each chapter	☐	☐	☐
Chapter roundups	☐	☐	☐
Quick quizzes	☐	☐	☐
Exam focus points	☐	☐	☐
Question bank	☐	☐	☐
Answer bank	☐	☐	☐
List of key terms and index	☐	☐	☐
Icons	☐	☐	☐

	Excellent	Good	Adequate	Poor
Overall opinion of this Text	☐	☐	☐	☐

Do you intend to continue using BPP Products? ☐ Yes ☐ No

Please note any further comments and suggestions/errors on the reverse of this page. The BPP author of this edition can be e-mailed at: barrywalsh@bpp.com

Please return to: Katy Hibbert, ACCA Range Manager, BPP Professional Education, FREEPOST, London, W12 8BR

ACCA – Paper 3.4 Business Information Management (6/03)

REVIEW FORM & FREE PRIZE DRAW (continued)

TELL US WHAT YOU THINK

Please note any further comments and suggestions/errors below.

FREE PRIZE DRAW RULES

1. Closing date for 31 January 2004 draw is 31 December 2003. Closing date for 31 July 2004 draw is 30 June 2004.
2. No purchase necessary. Entry forms are available upon request from BPP Professional Education. No more than one entry per title, per person. Draw restricted to persons aged 16 and over.
3. Winners will be notified by post and receive their cheques not later than 6 weeks after the draw date.
4. The decision of the promoter in all matters is final and binding. No correspondence will be entered into.